ROUTLEDGE LIBRARY EDITIONS: JAPANESE LINGUISTICS

Volume 1

LANGUAGE AND THE MODERN STATE

LANGUAGE AND THE MODERN STATE
The Reform of Written Japanese

NANETTE GOTTLIEB

LONDON AND NEW YORK

First published in 1991 by Routledge.

This edition first published in 2019
by Routledge
2 Park Square, Milton Park, Abingdon, Oxon OX14 4RN

and by Routledge
52 Vanderbilt Avenue, New York, NY 10017

Routledge is an imprint of the Taylor & Francis Group, an informa business

© 1991 Nanette Twine (Gottlieb)

All rights reserved. No part of this book may be reprinted or reproduced or utilised in any form or by any electronic, mechanical, or other means, now known or hereafter invented, including photocopying and recording, or in any information storage or retrieval system, without permission in writing from the publishers.

Trademark notice: Product or corporate names may be trademarks or registered trademarks, and are used only for identification and explanation without intent to infringe.

British Library Cataloguing in Publication Data
A catalogue record for this book is available from the British Library

ISBN: 978-1-138-36949-8 (Set)
ISBN: 978-0-429-40043-8 (Set) (ebk)
ISBN: 978-1-138-39434-6 (Volume 1) (hbk)
ISBN: 978-0-367-00172-8 (Volume 1) (pbk)
ISBN: 978-0-429-40108-4 (Volume 1) (ebk)

Publisher's Note
The publisher has gone to great lengths to ensure the quality of this reprint but points out that some imperfections in the original copies may be apparent.

Disclaimer
The publisher has made every effort to trace copyright holders and would welcome correspondence from those they have been unable to trace.

Language and the Modern State
The reform of written Japanese

Nanette Twine

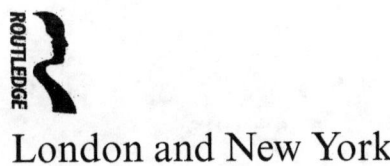

London and New York

First published 1991
by Routledge
11 New Fetter Lane, London EC4P 4EE

Simultaneously published in the USA and Canada
by Routledge
a division of Routledge, Chapman and Hall, Inc
29 West 35th street, New York, NY 10001

© 1991 Nanette Twine

Typeset in 10/12pt Times Autologic, by Times Graphics, Singapore

Printed in England by T.J. Press, Padstow, Cornwall

All rights reserved. No part of this book may be reprinted or reproduced or utilized in any form or by any electronic, mechanical, or other means, now known or hereafter invented, including photocopying and recording, or in any information storage or retrieval system, without permission in writing from the publishers.

British Library Cataloguing in Publication Data
Twine, Nanette
   Language and the modern state: the reform of written Japanese (The Nissan Institute/Routledge Japanese Studies series).
   1. Japanese language. Sociological aspects
   I. Title
   495.6
   ISBN 0-415-00990-1

Library of Congress Cataloging in Publication Data
Twine, Nanette
   Language and the modern state: the reform of written Japanese/ Nanette Twine
   p.   cm.—(The Nissan Institute/Routledge Japanese Studies series).
   Includes bibliographical references
   ISBN 0-415-00990-1
   1. Japanese language—20th century. 2. Japanese language—Reform. 3. Language policy—Japan.
   I. Title II. Series.
   PL525.6.T95 1991
   306.4'4952'0904—dc20

To Hans, Susan, and Gregory

Contents

List of figures	ix
Acknowledgements	xi
Introduction	1
1 Language and modernization: The Japanese experience	6
2 Pre-modern styles	33
3 Early stirrings: Education and the press	74
4 Language and politics	108
5 The role of literature	132
6 The final stages	163
7 The opposition	184
8 The standardization debate	207
9 The problem of orthography	224
Conclusion	257
Appendix	261
Glossary	286
Notes	290
Bibliography	303
Index	327

List of figures

Figure 2.1	Okototen	37
Figure 2.2	Varieties of *kambun*	42
Figure 2.3	*Sōrōbun* in Maejima's petition 'Kanji Gohaishi no Gi' ('Proposal for the Abolition of Chinese Characters')	51
Figure 2.4	*Sōrōbun* in an official government notice, *Chūgai Shimbun*, 3 April 1868	
Figure 2.5	*Sōrōbun* in a letter published in the Chūgai Shimbun, 6 April 1868	53
Figure 2.6	Two versions of a *sōrōbun* letter by Fukuzawa Yukichi	55
Figure 2.7	*Wabun* written in the early Meiji Period	58
Figure 2.8	A passage from Ihara Saikaku	65
Figure 2.9	A passage from Jippensha Ikku	66
Figure 2.10	*Gazoku setchūbun* of the early Meiji Period	69
Figure 3.1	Colloquial style in a recorded sermon of Shibata Kyūō	76
Figure 3.2	A section of the original text of Hirata Atsutane's *Kodō Tai-i* (*Outline of the Ancient Way*) and its modern rendering	77
Figure 5.1	Colloquial style and Western punctuation in Futabatei's *Ukigumo* (*The Drifting Cloud*)	140
Figure 5.2	Colloquial style in Bimyō's *Musashino* (*The Plain of Musashi*)	146
Figure 5.3	Colloquial style in Sōseki's *Wagahai wa Neko de aru* (*I am a Cat*)	157
Figure 5.4	Colloquial style in Tōson's *Hakai* (*The Broken Commandment*)	158

Figure 5.5	Colloquial style in Mushakōji's *Yūjō* (*Friendship*)	160
Figure 9.1	Modern punctuation in Shimizu Usaburō's 'Kishūsan Sekitan Kantei no Setsu' ('Expert Opinion on Coal from Kishū')	252

Acknowledgements

Some sections of this book have appeared previously in the journals *Monumenta Nipponica* (Chapter 8 and the script reform segment of Chapter 9) and *Visible Language* (the punctuation segment of Chapter 9). They are reprinted here, with slight alterations, by kind permission of the editors.

Many people have assisted in the preparation of this book. Thanks are due to Professor Emerita Joyce Ackroyd, who supervised the PhD dissertation in which it originated, albeit in a somewhat different form; to my colleagues at Griffith University, in particular Mr Eiji Katō and Mrs Naoko Kikkawa, for their patient and invaluable help with difficult Japanese readings; to Professor Alan Rix of the University of Queensland and Professor Jiri Neustupný of Monash University, who provided thoughtful feedback on Chapters 1, 4 and 8; and finally, to my husband and children for their support and forbearance.

Introduction

This book examines a comparatively recent event in the history of written Japanese, namely the process whereby a modern colloquial style was developed in the context of the overall modernization of Japan. So striking is the difference wrought by this change in the last hundred years that a government statute of 1868 would now be virtually incomprehensible to a modern reader not specially trained to read the Sino-Japanese then in use. What happened, in effect, was that the nation changed the way in which it wrote its language in response to various social imperatives which emerged during the period of rapid social change which followed the overthrow of the feudal government in 1868, not least of which was the importance of involving the entire nation in the push to modernize. While debate on modernization theory is wide-ranging and sometimes controversial, it may safely be argued that in any country it is essential to gain the co-operation of the masses in order to expedite the transformation from feudal to industrial society. The linguistic situation in Japan in 1868 made this aim difficult to achieve; the written language of public life clung to the archaic literary conventions of bygone ages which, by virtue of their difficulty and the lack of a national education system, remained almost exclusively the province of the upper classes. The replacement of diverse classical traditions with a uniform style of writing based on the grammar and vocabulary of a standard form of the spoken language, and therefore comprehended by any literate Japanese, was needed to put an end to the traditional upper-class monopoly of access to information and to offer the opportunity for full involvement in public life to the nation as a whole.

As the Meiji Period (1868–1912) advanced, the demands of a changing society made it clear that some sort of change in the written language of public life was both essential and inevitable. The spread of education, the establishment of a communications network, the emergence of the modern novel of psychological realism, the growth of the press, the attempts at educating the masses in western political theories – these factors and more combined to underline the inadequacies of the existing situation. What was needed was the application of Karl Deutsch's 'strategic simplification', whereby a language is reshaped to better perform its modern tasks as a crucial cog in the mechanism of a growing state by ridding itself of those older features which slow down the transmission of messages.

This book will examine the process whereby this strategic simplification took place in Japan, beginning with a discussion in the first chapter of the background to the problem and the reasons why change was indicated. It should be noted that the focus of the book, and of the term 'language reform' as used in its pages, is the written language of public life, except in so far as reference to the spoken language in the area of standardization and as the basis of colloquial style is necessary. Further, when literature is discussed, only prose is examined as the major thrust for modernizing the written language came in that area, although stylistic changes did also occur in poetry with the development of what was known as 'new-style poetry'. The second chapter explores the history, characteristics, and spheres of use of the four major styles found in documents and literature at the beginning of the modern period. Chapters 3 and 4 examine respectively initial moves towards language reform in the fields of education and the printed media, and the awareness of some intellectuals active in the civil rights debate of 1874–84 of the value of colloquial style as a tool in political education. Chapter 5 discusses the pivotal role of the modern novel in ensuring acceptance of colloquial style by both modelling it for an intellectual readership and polishing it into a medium acceptable to that readership. Chapter 6 recounts and examines later developments including initial steps in official co-ordinated language planning at bureaucratic level in the wake of Japan's victory in the 1894–95 Sino-Japanese war which revived flagging interest in the reform of the national language, now to be used outside the country for the first time. This chapter will cover the period from approximately 1895 to 1946, placing most emphasis on the years 1895–1902 but also following the later progress of conversion to colloquial style in various fields as a result

Introduction 3

of initiatives set in motion during that period. Chapter 7 considers the main arguments against colloquial style put forward by its detractors, and examines alternative proposals, including the Classical Standard. Chapters 8 and 9 explore the issues of standardization and orthographic reform, necessary adjuncts to stylistic simplification in modernizing the written language. The final section is a bibliography of texts which researchers in recent Japanese language history should find useful.

Inevitably, in a book whose readership is likely to consist of both those who can read Japanese and those who cannot but who are interested in the subject as a case study of language modernization, the problem arises of how much Japanese should be used by way of illustration, and in what form. I have provided separate illustrations in Japanese script to give an idea of the changing visual complexity of texts; in-text references, however, are romanized except where the use of characters is essential. Wherever possible, English sources are cited in addition to Japanese; where published translations are available, these are cited in order to enable non-speakers of Japanese to follow up references if they so desire.

Another problem has been that of avoiding the use of too many Japanese terms in the text and ending up with an annoyingly italicized page which is of little help to those who do not know Japanese and is visually irritating to those who do. I have replaced Japanese terms with English as much as possible but in some sections, particularly in the examination of archaic styles in Chapter 2, the discussion has called for the use of Japanese words either to illustrate or to specify and describe more precisely than is possible using English. This may at times become obtrusive, but seems preferable to the alternative of clumsy circumlocutions.

A short explanation of Japanese orthography is necessary if those unfamiliar with it are to understand the significance of comments on script reform. Modern Japanese is written using a combination of three scripts: *kanji* (Chinese characters) and the two phonetic scripts *hiragana* and *katakana*. As is described in more detail in Chapter 2, *kanji* were imported early on from China in the absence of any native script, but were not in themselves sufficient to represent the Japanese language in writing because of the widely differing features of the two languages. In Chinese, each character represents a separate morpheme; in Japanese, the presence of verbal and adjectival inflexions and postpositions not found in Chinese made the development of a supplementary script imperative.

4 Language and the Modern State

Hiragana and *katakana* were evolved to meet this need. Both scripts represent the same forty-six basic sounds, more when voice marks are added to some symbols. Although Sino-Japanese texts were written in a combination of Chinese characters with *katakana* well into this century, the rounded, flowing *hiragana* have today replaced *katakana* in writing those sections of a text where characters cannot represent Japanese grammatical features. *Katakana*, more angular in appearance, are now reserved for foreign loanwords and names (other than words and names of Chinese origin) and domestic telegrams. The following example illustrates how the three scripts are used together. The sentence 'I learned Japanese in Australia' is written in Japanese as *Watashi wa ōsutoraria de nihongo o naraimashita*

（私はオーストラリアで日本語を習いました）

Chinese characters are used for the pronoun 'I' (*watashi*), the noun 'Japanese' (*nihongo*) and *nara*, the stem of the verb 'to learn' (*narau*). *Hiragana* are used for the case-markers *wa* (topic) and *o* (direct object), the postposition *de* ('in'), and the past-tense verbal inflexion *-imashita*. The foreign place name 'Australia' is represented phonetically in *katakana*. Both the number of Chinese characters in use and the complexity of their shapes were much greater in the Meiji Period than now.

It should also be noted for the non-specialist reader that the historical 'periods' referred to throughout the text are the era names of traditional Japanese chronology. Since the overthrow of the Tokugawa shogunate and restoration of the Emperor in 1868, era names have corresponded to the reigns of successive emperors. The major developments traced in this book took place in the Meiji Period (1868–1912), Taishō Period (1912–26), and Shōwa Period (1926–89). Chapter 2 also deals with earlier developments in the Tokugawa or Edo Period (1600–1867). Other dates are given as they occur in the text.

Japanese names are given surname first, in the Japanese manner, except when citing books published in English by Japanese authors where the authors themselves have adopted the western order. Certain novelists are referred to by their literary names rather than their surnames where that is the usual practice.

The ramifications of the modernizing of written Japanese are far-ranging and diverse. I do not pretend to have covered all of them here; there are obvious gaps, such as the effects of colloquial style in poetry and drama. Although my discussion of the process covers the period from 1866 to 1946, the bulk of the material deals with the Meiji and early Taishō periods when the most significant progress was made. What I have tried to do is present the salient points of the issue in condensed form, to give the background and subsequent developments in the hope of facilitating further research into various aspects not fully covered here.

1 Language and modernization
The Japanese experience

All languages are at any given moment in a state of change and will continue to be so as long as their speakers continue to inhabit a constantly changing social milieu. New words are coined for the lexicon, and the widespread acceptance in speech or writing of usage formerly considered 'wrong' provokes outraged reaction from purists of a prescriptive bent from time to time in letters to editors of major newspapers and journals. Language *must* change, as long as people and their social mores continue to do so. Natural linguistic change is always under way, whatever the language, albeit at a relatively slow rate.

It sometimes happens, however, that some aspect of a particular language, usually its written representation, ceases for some reason to keep pace with natural evolution and becomes, as it were, ossified at a particular stage of its development. Even then, its lexicon at least remains susceptible to increase; but in general, the traditions of the past exert a stronger influence on its manner of expression than those of the present. Often, as was partly true in the case of Japan, and of Europe before vernacular languages supplanted Latin, the written language thus preserved is not the language of that society at all but a foreign language imported at some much earlier date and enshrined as the literary language because its cachet as the language of a dominant power meant it was accorded greater prestige than the native language.

In most cases where this has happened, there has come a time in the history of that society where consciously engineered language change is seen as desirable in response to certain specific stimuli, notably the need to modernize. The resulting push to modernize the language in line with the new needs of the society says much about the urgency with which that society regards its priorities of the moment and its approach to them, to the extent that its leaders are even prepared to attempt to modify one of its most basic features in an effort to speed up the social transformation.

The term 'language modernization' implies that some aspect of a particular language requires modification before it can meet the requirements of the society it serves. Where the society in question is undergoing that transformation of its social, political and economic institutions necessary before it can take its place on an equal footing with other nations in the modern world, its language must have the flexibility to accommodate and grow with the changes. This is seldom a problem with the spoken language, except in so far as lack of standardization may constitute a barrier to communication between speakers of disparate dialects across the nation; it is the written language which changes more slowly, and upon which opposition to change is most likely to focus. Elements inimical to the smooth dissemination of information throughout the society constitute a hindrance to the process of social change by slowing down the effective functioning of instrumental aspects such as education and mass communication. To modernize the language is to change it in such a way that it becomes capable of acting as a facilitator for the involvement of the populace as a whole in the social transformation being undertaken. Certain perceived inadequacies must be remedied or at least minimized in order to enable it to function more effectively as a tool of communication on the national level under the changed circumstances of the society it serves. The lexicon must grow to reflect the multiplicity of new concepts, institutions, and objects abroad in society; this may occur either through an influx of foreign loanwords, or the coining of neologisms, or a combination of both. Syntactic changes may also occur under the influence of foreign languages or in response to changes in patterns of thought and logic as a result of new value orientations. And where there is a written language which clings to traditional forms prized for their cultural significance but inappropriate for modern use, it must be pruned and reshaped to a form more suited to the current needs of its users. This break with the literary forms of the past is likely to engender bitter opposition from upholders of the old traditions, who endow these with cultural values of prestige and erudition and fear that to depart from them will result in cutting off the people from their cultural heritage.

A basic assumption underlying modernization is the notion of perfectibility, that change in a certain direction indicates progress towards a 'better' state of affairs, or a state more in harmony with the realities of the situation. While it seems reasonable to apply this same concept of perfectibility to reshaping the written language the better to serve the needs of the modern community, in Japan in the Meiji Period the idea was at first vigorously resisted, despite the frequent calls for reform in other fields. The notion struck at the roots of the contemporary intellectual view of writing not primarily as a servant of man but as an artistic and intellectual show-case, and as the province of the upper class, an idea carried over from the feudal era when only peers and samurai received government sponsored instruction in the archaic styles then in use. To suggest that the written language be modernized to serve the requirements of society as a whole by being based on the contemporary spoken language threatened not only these attitudes but also to a certain extent the dominance of the élite. They were loath to relinquish attitudes ingrained by Confucianism as controllers of information and education which had been reinforced through the perpetuation of classical literary conventions too difficult and time-consuming for ordinary people to master to any significant degree. The statement that writing is a cultural phenomenon which reflects social stratifications is well and truly borne out by the example of early Meiji Japan, where the written language of the élites was incomprehensible to most commoners and exemplified the gulf dividing the classes.

The leaders of a modernizing nation must ideally evolve an agenda in which elements deemed necessary to the process are ordered in smooth progression, those required for the achievement of a greater goal being assigned a higher priority than those not regarded as stepping stones to something else. It is clear that language modernization ought to be one of the very first tasks tackled, since upon its successful implementation depends the greater efficiency of such other vital adjuncts of social transformation as education and communications.

The immediate political task facing the Meiji leadership after the downfall of the Tokugawa regime was to establish the authority of the state through the creation of a powerful centralized bureaucracy, a condition necessary for achieving that sovereignty which is one of the principal attributes of the modern nation-state. Rejai and Enloe, differentiating the concepts of nation and state, define a nation as 'a relatively large group of people who *feel* that they belong together by virtue of sharing one or more such traits as common language, religion or race, common history or tradition, common set of customs, and common destiny', while a state is 'an independent autonomous political structure over a specific territory with a comprehensive legal system and a sufficient concentration of power to maintain law and order.'[1] It is clear that Japan was and had been for some time a nation-state, a socially cohesive and politically autonomous territory, faced now with the urgent necessity for modernization to secure and fortify its position in the modern world into which it had been propelled. In order to reshape the written Japanese language into a vehicle capable of assisting rather than hindering this task, several things were required: the replacement of archaic élite-bound literary styles with a modern colloquial style employing the grammar and vocabulary of the spoken language in writing, the choice of one variant of spoken Japanese to act as the standard upon which this new written language should be based, and orthographic reform in the shape of the rationalization of the large number of Chinese characters then in use as well as the adoption of punctuation.

Linguistic developments often reflect other non-linguistic social factors operating in a given society, and this is particularly noticeable in the area of the relationship between language and nationalism. If we accept that social change may require concomitant language reform, and that, as Deutsch demonstrates, a period of active social mobilization usually acts as a catalyst for the beginning of nationalistic fervour,[2] then it is clear that the modernization of language may become a factor in the growth of a sense of national unity and identity, just as national pride may have a role to play in motivating language planning. The basis for national sentiment derived from linguistic homogeneity was already present to a certain degree in Japan, where the same language in one form or another was spoken throughout the territory. Leaders gradually came to recognize that what was needed in the wake of the tremendous social upheavals following the Meiji Restoration was the fashioning and refining of that language into an instrument which would serve the nation both as a means of achieving its various planned reforms and as a focus of national pride, an element in a sense of nationalism – defined by Fishman as 'the organizationally heightened and elaborated beliefs, attitudes and behaviours of societies acting on behalf of their avowed ethnocultural self-interest'.[3]

Kelman, in his discussion of language as a unifying force at both the sentimental and instrumental levels, expands on the benefits of a common national language in facilitating the planning of national development by central authorities on the one hand and enabling social mobility and equality of participation in the system by individuals on the other, and argues that language policies should be based on purely functional considerations, leaving aside the elements of nationalism.[4] In the Japanese case, both elements contributed to early language planning. Unlike other developing nations where territorial limits may have been defined with little reference to socio-cultural identity, or where several regional or local languages coexist, none with any particular claim to a literary tradition, or where the official language of politics and higher education is that of another country as in former colonies, Japan brought to her modern era a long-standing, well-defined literary tradition and a comparatively high rate of literacy among her population. Fishman categorizes such a nation as a cluster B nation, or old developing nation, one which has for a long time embodied the attributes of both nation and socio-cultural identity.[5] Such a nation in its approach to language planning faces not the problem of national language selection but rather that of modification of an existing asset, which in Japan took the form of a classical written tradition heavily dependent on Chinese for its source, with even those varieties which attempted to avoid the foreign element still adhering to centuries-old literary conventions. As we have seen, it became clear as the Meiji Period progressed that in order to develop the written Japanese language into a useful resource at both instrumental and sentimental levels it would be necessary to rid it as far as possible of classical forms and to find some compromise with the long-standing and deeply entrenched influence of Chinese, in order to enable the development of a style of writing much closer to a standardized form of contemporary speech.

What does language modernization involve? It involves first the identification and then the reshaping of those areas of the language which are seen as hindering other aspects of social change in some way. Such issues most commonly include standardization, development of a colloquial style, orthographic change, and augmentation of the lexicon. The first of these, standardization, is particularly important where several discrete languages coexist within the borders of a nation, or where extreme dialectal variation within the one language places difficulties in the way of communication between speakers.

Language planning and modernization, the relationship between language and nationalism, and the process of standardization have for some time been the focus of sustained scrutiny by a number of socio-linguists, notably Ferguson, Fishman, Neustupný, Garvin, and Haugen.[6] One may find in the growing body of literature on language planning several theoretical discussions of points in the process of language modernization which are reflected in the Japanese experience of standardization of the written language, among them the relationship between standardization and colloquialization, the primacy of the written language in standardization, the role of literature in modelling the desired norm, and the intrinsic reciprocal connection between nationalism and language reform.

A survey of the literature of both nationalism and modernization, and in particular of their socio-linguistic aspects, indicates that a standard language has an important function both in expediting the flow of information necessary to social change and in providing a focus for national pride in the language of the country. Ferguson defines language standardization as 'the process of one variety of a language becoming widely accepted throughout the speech community as a supradialectal norm', and adds that the concept of standardization also includes the notions of increasing uniformity of the norm itself and explicit codification of the norm.[7] Garvin and Mathiot concur, in their definition of a standard language as 'a codified form of a language, accepted by and serving as a model to, a larger speech community'.[8] Standardization is often an aspect of language planning, a conscious attempt to shape the language in a manner consistent with the objectives of the policy makers in response to a perceived problem of inadequacy in respect of some part of those objectives. As Haugen asserts, language planning attempts primarily to shape the formal written manifestation of language.[9] In Japan as everywhere else when standardization is at issue, it was the written language which became initially the major target of scrutiny in the standardization debate, both for its own properties and as a stepping stone ultimately to a standard form of spoken Japanese.

Stylistic reform by the development of a modern colloquial style is essential in situations where there is a wide disparity between the spoken language of a society and the manner in which its members write. When the writing used as the medium of public life is so different from speech as to require considerable thought and ingenuity in its execution and comprehension, whether it is a foreign language which has been adopted through historical happenstance as that society's mode of written expression or a classical form of the native language which has been made sacrosanct through centuries of veneration of its form, content often suffers at the expense of form and writing becomes an exercise in scholarship rather than an automatic instrument of daily business. As a considerable amount of education is required to master literary conventions of this sort, they then become almost exclusively the province of those with the leisure to devote to such learning. In a feudal society this means the upper class, those not burdened with the necessity of day-long toil to keep themselves alive, so that the written language then becomes a kind of invisible class barrier, by its difficulty and its dissimilarity to the spoken language denying the non-leisured classes access to printed debate on matters which concern them. If the co-operation of the populace as a whole is then sought to work towards achieving some sort of major transformation, the society is faced with two choices: either to educate the entire population in the intricacies of the existing written tradition, or to replace that tradition with a form of writing which can be understood by any member of that society able to read because it is based on the spoken language of daily life. The former alternative is time-consuming and does nothing to challenge the view that good writing is and should remain a thing apart from daily life; the latter likewise cannot be achieved overnight, and is likely to arouse the ire of conservatives who fear both the undermining of traditional literary values as to what constitutes acceptable educated usage and also the loss of their society's cultural heritage.

Where the written language is character based, stylistic reform alone is not sufficient for language modernization unless the issue of whether orthographic reform is likewise warranted is further examined. If the number of characters is limited to a reasonable quota based on those in daily use, and if the spatial organization of the text is such that the reader is enabled to follow the flow of the passage without undue difficulty, then standardization and the development of a colloquial style will effectively dispel most of the problems. If, however, the number of characters deemed necessary is greatly in excess of actual requirements, if the forms of those characters are complex and difficult to master, and if lack of basic punctuation impedes comprehension, then no matter how the syntax and lexicon of writing are simplified the reader and writer will still encounter difficulties as form continues to obscure content. The reverse is also true, of course: script reform alone is not sufficient to produce a workable modern written language. In a situation such as that which prevailed in Japan, where archaic styles were further complicated by a visually complex orthography, both style reform and script reform must be undertaken together or success in one will founder because of lack of progress in the other. This was a lesson not easily learned by Meiji Period advocates of script reform, who neglected style reform to the eventual confounding of their efforts. Their work was not in vain, however; it served as a warning, so that when the first government body was set up to look into language reform its charter included both the dissemination of colloquial style and an examination of the orthographic situation.

Perhaps the least difficult aspect of language modernization is that of lexical change. Even in societies where classical modes of writing prevail, the lexicon is flexible and capable of extension. In a situation of rapid social change involving industrialization and institutional transformation, the lexicon must expand to admit words for objects and concepts not previously known in that society. This is done by adopting loanwords from other languages or by coining neologisms from existing lexical material. In Japan, as we shall see, when the introduction of both the physical trappings of western nations and their underlying intellectual concepts placed a strain on the lexicon, large numbers of loanwords from European languages were adopted which remain part of the language today; in addition, many new words were devised by combining descriptive Chinese characters into new compounds.

Major elements of language modernization, then, include where appropriate stylistic reform, orthographic reform, lexical expansion, and standardization. These changes are effected through a series of steps as follows. First comes the increasing awareness that the existing language system is in some way not appropriate to the new goals being pursued by a society in transition. Lack of a standard language, for example, may hinder the national education process, or prevent social mobility perceived as desirable. Where the written language is based on classical or foreign traditions, or where orthographic conventions need revising, the spread of information through both education and the printed media may be slower than desired. Attempts to fashion modern forms of literature such as naturalistic novels, poetry or drama will prove futile as long as there is no written language based on the contemporary spoken language with which to describe their subject matter. In response to these pressures, there then arises a conviction among certain intellectuals responsive to change that action is necessary, indeed crucial to the successful transformation of the society as a whole. Wilfrid Smith argues that it is the attitudes held by the intellectuals of a traditional society which are the determining factor of the speed of that society's modernization, 'for what gets done depends in the first instance on what is believed to be possible and to be worth doing.'[10] Before any programme of reform can be implemented, it must first be conceptualized and validated in the minds of those in a position to effect the change. The printed media provide a powerful forum for debate of the issue in this phase. In the Japanese case, as we shall see, certain intellectuals played key roles in setting the process of language reform in motion – bitterly opposed at every step, of course, by other scholars equally dedicated to preserving the status quo. The third step in the process takes the form of government intervention to achieve the desired end once those in power have been convinced of its necessity. Ministries of Education, in particular, have a key role to play in assisting with language reform by virtue of their capacity to disseminate the desired norm, whatever the nature of the change, through the classrooms of the nation, whether it be by ensuring that the standard language is used as the medium of instruction or by overseeing the kind of written language used in textbooks.

Let us now move on from the above brief outline of the major steps in language modernization to consider the situation in Japan prior to moves for language reform.

JAPAN

Bun wa hito nari runs the proverb – 'the style is the man', an epigram which encapsulated the attitude of educated Japanese towards the written word at the beginning of, and indeed well into, their nation's modern period. The decades following the Meiji restoration in 1868 were a period of turmoil in Japan, as political, economic and social structures underwent rigorous examination, some being retained, others discarded in the struggle to fashion a nation capable of withstanding western imperialism on its own terms. Hand in hand with large-scale upheavals in public life went sweeping changes in the lives of individuals as legislation abolished the traditional four-tier class structure and offered the ordinary citizen hitherto undreamed-of freedom of choice in occupation, domicile, and social mobility. Officially sponsored education, formerly the privilege of the upper echelon, opened new possibilities for personal advancement; the ethic of *risshin shusse*,[11] of getting ahead in the world through one's own efforts, inspired ambitious people in their thousands to leave their villages and seek upward mobility through education. Nor were the changes restricted to the larger concerns of life; on a more mundane level, western clothing, foods, customs, and habits began to encroach upon Japanese daily life, affecting such fundamental concerns as how people wore their hair or what they ate for dinner.

These developments were mirrored by concomitant linguistic change in both written and spoken Japanese, in particular in the Tokyo dialect which was widely understood throughout the country and was later to be designated the standard language. Certain features characteristic of the modernization period developed in the first two decades of Meiji as the result of exposure to foreign influences and in the wake of internal demographic and social change. The need for a vast number of new lexical items was met by borrowing foreign loanwords (*gairaigo*) and coining numerous neologisms, derived from translations of foreign words. Such measures applied not merely to the description of the physical trappings of western technology (e.g. *kisha*, 'steam train', *denki* 'electricity', *dempō*, 'telegram') but also to that of new abstract ethical and political concepts, such as human rights. Striking features brought about by domestic change included the rising proportion of expressions in Tokyo speech from regional dialects in the wake of the gradual flow of population from the provinces to the capital consequent upon the settling of the political dust, and changes in honorific expressions with the abolition of the feudal class structure. Under the influence of European languages, parts of the written language began to display a number of derivative characteristics, among them the increasingly frequent use of the passive voice and of explicit grammatical subjects, both animate and inanimate.

Despite these changes to the lexicon and to the syntax and register of speech, the written language, or at least that form of it employed by the country's leaders, educators, and intellectuals as the medium of government business and serious literature, remained mired in the classical traditions of both China and Japan, an obstacle to modernization by virtue of its difficulty, relative inflexibility, and aura of élitism. What was needed in order to involve successfully the entire population of the nation in the modernization effort was the initiation of a concerted, planned overhaul of the written language at bureaucratic level. Despite the example of western languages and the exhortations of at first a few and later an increasingly large number of progressive scholars, more than thirty years of the Meiji Period were to elapse before the government took a hand in bringing order and sequence to attempts at language reform, by which time much of the groundwork had been done by individuals working alone or in groups. The reason for the delay in what seems in retrospect to have been such an important and obviously overdue reform lay in the nature of the written language itself, which mirrored the feudal power structure, and in prevailing attitudes to scholarship. The term 'written language', of course, can encompass many things; it is employed in this book in a restricted sense, to mean the forms of written language found in official documents, records, histories, serious literature, criticism, and exposition.

The prose conventions of educated Japanese at the beginning of the Meiji Period were for the most part far from representing the spoken language in writing. Nor was there a defined and uniform spoken language to represent: 250 years of the Tokugawa policy of regional isolation had resulted in a highly segmented society wherein flourished a complicated network of regional dialects, dialectal variations being in some cases so extreme that the story is told of Kyushu samurai having to transact business with their northern counterparts in the language of the Noh drama which employed the speech of Kyoto, then widely understood throughout the country as the dialect of the capital.[12] There was no officially designated standard variant of Japanese, though the dialects of Kyoto and Edo (which replaced Kyoto as the capital in 1868 and was renamed Tokyo) vied for precedence as a language of wider communication among the governing élite and later the merchants and artisans who followed the shifting centre of power from west to east. Dialectal variations aside, the spoken and written languages were markedly dissimilar, the degree of disparity between them ranging from a reasonable correlation in the area of lexicon to a gap in syntax so wide that they might almost have been two different languages. Andō Masatsugu characterizes the Tokugawa Period as a period of dualism in the history of the Japanese language: on the one hand, spoken and written Japanese were very different, while within the spoken language itself there were divisions between the Japanese spoken in Edo and Kyoto, between the various regional dialects, and between various social classes within a dialect.[13]

The written language itself did not conform to a uniform, fixed convention but was divided into several discrete styles determined by the nature of the text, each drawing its vocabulary and syntax from early medieval Chinese or Japanese. There was no single all-purpose style simple enough to be understood by all literate Japanese. The difficulties inherent in employing centuries-old modes of expression were compounded by the vast number of Chinese characters then available for use: more than 10,000 compared to the 1,945 considered necessary today. It was a favourite ploy of scholars wishing to display their erudition to pad out the text of their discourse with unnecessarily complex characters in order to impart a more erudite appearance and tone to their prose. To complicate matters still further, there was an often total lack of punctuation to show phrasing within a sentence or paragraph. No spaces separated words; to extract the sense of the passage, the reader had to be able to recognize sentence finals and other grammatical signals indicating function. It is not uncommon to find in texts of this period page after page either unpunctuated or punctuated only in sketchy fashion by commas and full stops. Where these last *were* in evidence, there does not appear to have been any rigorous convention governing their use. Examination of nineteenth-century government documents, scholarly texts, and novels shows that in some cases the symbols ʼ and ॰ were used to indicate clause and sentence boundaries respectively; in others, the symbol ॰ fulfilled both functions; sometimes commas were used for both, varying the size from that ordinarily used today to others so small as to be barely visible. Paragraphing was often non-existent, or at least rudimentary.

The four major varieties of written Japanese, which will be discussed in detail in Chapter 2, were *kambun, sōrōbun, wabun,* and *wakankonkōbun. Kambun*, or Sino-Japanese, had been the language of Japanese officialdom since the Nara Period (710–84), and its use had been perpetuated during the Tokugawa Period (1600–1867) by the shogunate's emphasis on Confucian studies. Sino-Japanese was in fact the Chinese language as used in Japan, and took a variety of forms, ranging from pure Chinese to a hybrid version incorporating devices to enable a non-Chinese-speaking Japanese to read and write it as his own language. It was valued for its formal and erudite tone (a quality often deliberately fostered by the use of archaic rhetorical devices and stereotyped literary idioms) and was the medium of official business, criticism and exposition, history and other serious literature, and upper-class education, as well as of many of the early Meiji translations of western literature. *Sōrōbun*, so called because of its characteristic use of the verb *sōrō* as the copula, was the epistolary style used in both private and official correspondence and in public notices, reports, archives, laws, and ordinances – in other words, general public service business. It was a direct descendant of a modified form of Sino-Japanese developed in the Middle Ages as the Chinese language in Japan underwent a form of natural linguistic acclimatization with the passage of time. Originally written entirely in Chinese characters, by the beginning of the Meiji Period *sōrōbun* had evolved into a more convenient combination of characters and phonetic script. Unlike *kambun*, its use was not restricted to the upper class; commoner education included classes in *sōrōbun*, although its marked Chinese influence made it difficult to master. Its combination of Chinese features with standard idioms and a fixed vocabulary produced a general effect of stiffness and formality, so that it permitted no real freedom of expression.

Unlike *kambun* and *sōrōbun*, *wabun* (classical Japanese) was predominantly Japanese in tone, but was nevertheless separated by a similar gap of centuries from the contemporary spoken language. It had originated in the novels written in *kana* by ladies of the Heian court, at a period when the development of phonetic scripts made possible for almost the first time the reproduction in writing of the Japanese language. In the early Meiji Period, *wabun* was characterized by a grammar and vocabulary taken from the tenth- and eleventh-century classics. In contrast to the stiff, intellectual tone of Sino-Japanese, classical Japanese was soft and melodious, concerned more with the poetic conveying of atmosphere than with direct statement. It was used in prose by neo-classical scholars, by women as an epistolary style, and in some translations and essays. The fourth style, *wakankonkōbun* (Japanese–Chinese blend), was, as its name suggests, a mixture of Sino-Japanese and classical Japanese, being essentially *kambun* with its usual severity softened by the addition of elements from the gentler *wabun*. Sino-Japanese adhered to Chinese word-order, being written either in Chinese characters alone or in Chinese characters accompanied by phonetic additions to their right to indicate Japanese syntax and word-order. When this was written out using Japanese word-order with all the appropriate additions in phonetic script and an admixture of classical Japanese lexical items, it was called *wakankonkōbun*. While its vocabulary included a fair proportion of contemporary items, it retained many Chinese expressions and occasional idioms using Chinese word-order. The style was used in books and essays composed by literary men (except for those distinctively Sino-Japanese or classical Japanese), in popular literature, and as a general-purpose literary style. It was popular because Sino-Japanese was both too difficult for the lower classes in terms of its remoteness from daily life and the time required to master it, and too formal for describing everyday incidents, while classical Japanese, although simpler, was too flowery and rambling. Literate townsmen found the mixture of Chinese and Japanese easier to understand than its components in isolation. Despite its relative simplicity, however, its narrative grammar remained that of a past era.

ATTITUDES TO WRITING

The fact that educated Japanese saw no need to change the cumbersome situation outlined above reflected a curious attitude on the part of intellectuals towards the nature of writing itself. Rather than viewing the written word as an instrument of communication, its purpose to inform or persuade as effectively as possible, Japanese scholars looked upon it as a kind of show-case for intellectual showmanship, subordinating content to form in the pursuit of ostentatious erudition. They would not countenance the use of the grammar of the spoken language on paper, considering the practice both vulgar and verbose. Long-standing subservience to the prestige of Chinese had resulted in the development of a form of deep-seated literary inferiority complex on the part of the Japanese from which had grown a worship of form for its own sake and a resultant disregard for intelligibility. Enlightenment writer Fukuzawa Yukichi scoffed at the attitude held by scholars of the Chinese and Japanese classics in the late Tokugawa Period, accusing them of regarding clarity as such a stylistic gaucherie that they would often deliberately stud their texts with extraneous, unnecessarily complicated Chinese characters to produce a more 'elevated' tone.[14] Such practices, as well as creating unnecessary difficulty, also effectively ensured that the written language of public life and literature remained the province of the upper class. Sino-Japanese was not to be easily mastered even without such devices, partly because it was either a pure or derivative form of a foreign language and partly because of its adherence to archaic forms of that language. While it was the medium of officially sponsored education, such education was available only to samurai – what education commoners achieved was self-generated.[15] Commoners, occupied with the business of survival, could not afford the years of study required to master the intricacies of *kambun*.

This monopoly of the written language by élites effectively underlined the Confucian exclusion of the lower orders from participation in public life by denying them access to the documents which discussed, recorded, and implemented the functioning of that public life. In other words, ideas about language mirrored ideas about class. It is hardly to be wondered at, then, that the first moves towards replacing fossilized literary conventions with a modern colloquial style, that is, a style of writing based on the spoken language, were met with vituperation from upper-class scholars. Buffeted and deprived of their material privileges by the social changes which followed the end of the feudal period, these men resisted fiercely the idea of further erosion of their dignity and intellectual supremacy in the form of stylistic modernization. To suggest that entrenched attitudes to writing as a class marker should be reversed, that the literary symbols of the upper-class monopoly of education and serious literature should be replaced as the language of public life with the despised colloquial style, hitherto restricted almost exclusively to the dialogue passages of popular literature, was to strike at a fundamental assumption of the élites – that literary vocabulary and syntax were factors in categorizing men as refined or vulgar, powerful or powerless. Language, in this sense, was power. To replace the traditional linguistic manifestations of that power with a democratic literary standard would be to confirm that the old order was indeed past, and to accord the commoner equal status with the aristocrat in this fundamental aspect of daily life.

INDICATORS OF CHANGE

Nevertheless, despite establishment satisfaction with the existing unwieldy system, soon after the Restoration a new set of factors came into play which underlined the need for a simpler form of written Japanese. One of the most immediately obvious was the urgency of disseminating through *education* the new knowledge which came pouring in from abroad. Wilbur Schramm has described education as the chief activity in mobilizing human resources.[16] In times of rapid social change, education acts both as a channel of the knowledge needed to effect the changes and as a means of inculcating in a nation the values perceived by its leaders as conducive to achieving their aims. Anderson sees education in a modernizing society as also shaping the various constituents of a society into a nation and ensuring the suvival of a political state by allowing its officials to co-ordinate administration over large areas.[17] The attainment of these objectives is held back considerably by the necessity to divert a considerable proportion of a student's time to mastering the form of language which is the medium of instruction before being able to digest the information being presented. A national education system was inaugurated in Japan in 1872; but fourteen years later, in 1886, Mozume Takami (1847–1928, Tokyo Imperial University lecturer) commented that his son had been unable to explain to him the content of his Confucian ethics text because of an inability to construe its language.[18]

Wilfrid Smith reminds us that 'every cultural and ideological achievement in human society can be shown to have had an economic aspect'.[19] In 1901, a petition presented to the Diet by the Gembun'itchi Club (a group of advocates of language modernization) seeking the establishment of a national language advisory body, focused on this issue when it lambasted the loss of time and energy wasted on struggling with form in order to master content, citing as a matter of national urgency the removal of this severe economic threat to Japan's competitiveness in the world arena. The establishment of the national education system was one cog in the Japanese response to the discovery of the need to catch up with the technological superiority of the west in order to survive. Traditional Confucian education, which had taken as its principal aim the development of character, proved no longer equal to the requirements of a rapidly evolving industrial society where expedience was paramount. Although the Tokugawa Government had set up centres for the study of certain practical aspects of western learning, among them a college of western medicine and military and naval academies, its efforts were insignificant in the face of the post-1854 demand. Foreign language study was necessary to enable communication with foreign experts. Japanese science and medicine required updating. New technological skills in building railways, telegraph networks, better roads, modern armaments and ships, and all the other appurtenances of a modern society had to be acquired and developed. In addition to the acquisition of these specialized skills, the people at large must be provided with that modicum of education deemed necessary for them to cope with modern life in the age of *risshin shusse*. In all these areas and more, reform of the written language would simplify and shorten the learning process, freeing up valuable time which could be better applied to study.

Just as important as education was the development of a modern *communications* network to expedite the flow of information between individuals and between government and nations. Deutsch, in his search for a conceptual model of the processes of nationalism and nationality, notes that 'processes of communication are the basis of the coherence of societies, cultures and even of the personalities of individuals',[20] while Schramm notes that 'without a sophisticated and efficient development of communication, the base of population, cooperation, industrialization, education, and skills needed in modern industrial society cannot possibly be established'.[21] The convenient and rapid transmission of information is the oil which lubricates a smoothly functioning social machine. In Japan this transmission was assisted by the lifting of restrictions on individual travel and choice of occupation, resulting in a new freedom of social interaction and mobility; the inauguration of a national postal system in 1871; the construction of rail, telegraph, and telephone networks; and the development of mass communication through the mushrooming publication of newspapers and journals after 1870, with its attendant rise of a class of professional communicators.

Of these, the last was particularly significant. Communication between Tokugawa rulers and the people had been by public notice-board. News of fires, earthquakes, and similar calamities was printed on broadsheets until the appearance of the first newspapers after their legalization in 1869, when the new government removed feudal restrictions on political comment by promulgating a set of regulations establishing a framework for the development of a western-style press. From then on, daily and weekly newspapers and magazines were founded in quick succession in Tokyo, Kyoto, Osaka, and other prefectural capitals, the press rapidly becoming an important channel of communication between the ruling élite and the public. The use of Sino-Japanese in the serious press by journalists and contributors, however, severely restricted the range of reader access to the information contained in the contents of its pages, in effect barring those not educated in its intricacies from reading in print intellectual debate on the major issues of the day. What was needed in order to disseminate information was a standard modern colloquial style based on daily speech, a style which could, by its ability to express advanced concepts and nuances of meaning, allow each individual user and reader to participate in the communication process with a freedom not permitted by the élite-monopolized, tradition-bound archaic styles with their rigid conventions and limited lexicon. Ithiel de Sola Pool points out that a growing number of studies have correlated modernization with access to the media of communication, with individuals and villages who have access to the press proving more progressive in attitudes and achievements than those who do not.[22]

The postal service inaugurated in 1871 under Maejima Hisoka (1835–1919) as Postmaster-General provided a further means of communicating information throughout the country by correspondence. No uniform mail service had been possible in feudal times, owing to the individual autonomy of fiefs, the preservation of natural geographical barriers as defence aids, and the lack of a system of rapid transportation.[23] Prior to the Meiji Period, stages had been placed at fixed intervals along the main highways to relay official messages by courier. With the prospering of industry and commerce in the late Tokugawa Period, private couriers began to offer services for business and personal communications. The busiest of these usually made the round trip between Edo, Kyoto, and Osaka three times a month; for a higher fee, express couriers would run day and night, and could cover the distance between Edo and Kyoto in six days. This inadequate and localized courier system continued until finally prohibited as private enterprise in 1873.

After an initial attempt at establishing government control of communication by mail in 1868, the beginnings of the modern mail service came in 1871 with the appointment as Postmaster-General of Maejima, who designed a practical system upon his return from a trip abroad to study European and American postal services. By March the following year, when the Postal Regulations Act was passed, mail was being delivered three times a day in Tokyo. In July, the mail system extended nation-wide, and post offices were established in most port cities and seats of prefectural government. That the post played an important role in breaking down the remnants of feudal isolationism and linking formerly disparate geographical units is illustrated by the following quote from an 1872 article in the *Yūbin Hōchi Shimbun*. The article related to a stretch of treacherous coast road often cut by high seas along the border between Etchū and Echigo.

> Everyone recognized the danger, and at the end of the Tokugawa Period the feudal districts using the road discussed the idea of building a new one. However, some people argued after the fashion of the stoic old militaristic era that treacherous roads made good strongholds, and the water (sic) was dropped. Then the era of progress and enlightenment came, and people realized not only that human life is too sacred to be thrown away so lightly as in the old days, but also that the stoppage of the mails for several days was detrimental to both private and public good.[24]

The establishment of a swift and convenient mail service, at first limited to Tokyo and Osaka but extended in 1872 to the whole of Japan, opened the way to a new freedom in exchanging views with those outside one's immediate area, and contributed to the growing importance of communications as a factor underlining the need for style reform, the existing epistolary style being a variant of Sino-Japanese.

A third factor was the importance of *political education* in the push to reshape the institutions of government along western lines. The first two decades of the Meiji Period were a time of intense political debate as traditional views of society and government were undermined by the introduction of western political theories. Politics preoccupied the major newspapers in this early period of their development, the question generating the most heat being that of an elected assembly. Clashes over the scheduling and electorate of the mooted assembly led to ten years of organized protest by disaffected liberals, commonly called the civil rights movement (*jiyū minken undō*), during which those in favour of the immediate establishment of representative government attempted to spread Rousseau's doctrine of the natural rights of man throughout the country in the face of opposition from supporters of the government's gradualist approach to the matter. Commoners, now no longer excluded legally, could take little part in the printed debate as long as it was conducted in the written language of the upper class which the limitations of their education did not enable them to comprehend with ease. They were in practice effectively excluded from full participation in public life despite the ostensible legal equality of Japanese citizens after the government legislated in 1871 to dissolve feudal class barriers.

It became apparent to certain intellectuals involved in popularizing political theory, both inside and outside the civil rights movement, that it was inappropriate to address the potential future electorate on matters concerning its possible admission to the decision-making process in a language which that electorate could not understand. As the civil rights movement shifted away from its early insistence on an electorate restricted to samurai to a broader view encompassing greater commoner involvement, certain political theorists (among them Ueki Emori) and party newspapers became convinced of the necessity to experiment with using the language of the masses in print in a bid to extend the range of their readership. The deadlock between the dominance of Sino-Japanese and the exigencies of the educatory process had to be broken were their objectives to be realized; the importance of a reader-oriented language of persuasion could not be denied.

Occurring later than the developments just described but underlining just as strongly the urgency of language modernization were the changes wrought in the form, content, and approach of the *Japanese novel*. Under the influence of western literary theories as interpreted by men like Tsubouchi Shōyō (1859–1935) and Futabatei Shimei (1864–1909), the didactic and erotic tales of Tokugawa Period popular literature began to give way to the newly respectable approach of psychological realism in the modern novel. The hitherto lowly status accorded the writer of fiction was rejected by Tsubouchi in *Shōsetsu Shinzui* (*The Essence of the Novel*), an 1886 work of literary criticism which propounded the then radical idea of the novel as an art form worthy of equal respect with poetry and drama.[25] Tsubouchi regarded the novelist's primary function as the faithful, impartial description of man and his environment. Although not going so far as to advocate an across-the-board adoption of colloquial style as the medium for the realistic portrayal of the psyche of the modern individual, preferring instead to restrict its use to dialogue while retaining classical narrative in the *gazoku setchū* tradition, he looked forward to the day when future writers would polish away the faults of the colloquial, remoulding it into a fit means of expression for realistic fiction. Rigid classical styles were no appropriate medium for the sensitive examination of modern dilemmas and psychological intricacies, possessing neither the vocabulary nor fluidity of expression capable of delivering the nuances of nineteenth-century thought and emotion in a time of social upheaval. The profound changes about to occur in the literary world, in addition to according a new dignity and prestige to the novel deemed hitherto ostensibly unworthy of serious consideration let alone production by intellectuals, would suggest a reconsideration of the merits of the despised colloquial style as a language for modern literature.

These were some of the major factors which combined to point out the inadequacies of the existing situation, which may be summed up as follows: the preservation of archaic, élite-monopolized forms in the written language of public life perpetuated Confucian class divisions inappropriate to a now professedly egalitarian society, limiting full participation by all Japanese in the modernization effort by placing restrictions on the accessibility of the information contained in the two most important channels in the transmission of knowledge, the press and the education system. What Japan needed to best equip her people as a whole to absorb the knowledge they required to enable them to adjust to and co-operate in this new national endeavour was a single versatile colloquial style based on a standard form of contemporary speech, such as was found in western countries. In Europe, the medieval dominance of Latin had long since given way to the rise of the vernacular language, enabling literate citizens to comprehend and use the written form of the national language with a minimum of fuss. Several Japanese scholars of the west whose study of European languages enabled them to make comparisons remarked on the convenience of the colloquial style they observed, though few were sensitive to the implications for Japan's future or the lack of any equivalent in their own language.

THE SITUATION ELSEWHERE

In Europe, the supremacy of Latin as the academic, ecclesiastical, and bureaucratic tongue both in speech and writing had become a thing of the past. In earlier centuries, intellectuals writing in the vernaculars spoken by the common people of various countries had helped give shape and definition to their written forms.[26] In Italy, in the early fourteenth century, Dante wrote his *Divine Comedy* for the common reader in the Tuscan dialect, shocking those who held Latin to be the appropriate tongue for poetic expression and setting a precedent for the later work in Italian of Petrarch and Boccacio. In the second half of the fourteenth century, there appeared in the English vernacular Chaucer's *Canterbury Tales*, Langland's *Piers Plowman*, and Wycliff's first English version of the Bible. In 1386, the English parliament passed a statute establishing English as the language of the courts and the parliament. In France, where writing in the national language had begun even earlier in the twelfth and thirteenth centuries with the appearance of Villehardouin's *Conquest of Constantinople* (the first reliable record of the Fourth Crusade to appear in French), Joinville's *Life of Saint Louis*, and others in the twelfth and thirteenth centuries, French replaced Latin as the official administrative language in 1539. By the eighteenth century in western Europe, the former dominance of Latin outside the Church was on the wane. The written forms of national languages had been further entrenched and refined as in, for example, the works of Ronsard (1524–85), Corneille (1606–84), La Fontaine (1621–95), Molière (1622–73), and Racine (1639–99) in France, and in those of Shakespeare, Milton, and the King James Bible in England. In so far as it is possible for written language to approximate spoken, these languages did so, by appearing on the printed page in a form which represented reasonably faithfully the grammar and vocabulary of their spoken counterparts.

The languages with which Japanese scholars of the west came into contact impressed some with their comparative simplicity and immediacy, free of the hegemony of classicism. In *Rangaku Kaitei* (*A Guide to Dutch Studies*, 1783), Ōtsuki Gentaku (1757–1827, Dutch scholar and physician) touched on the matter of the colloquial style he had observed in Dutch books, remarking upon its lucidity and the manner in which it permitted detailed recording of facts. Motoki Masae (1767–1822), in the preface to *Anguria Kōgaku Shōsen* (*First Steps in English*, 1811), commented on the similarity between written and spoken English, while Ōba Sessai, in *Yaku Oranda Bungo* (*Written Dutch: A Translation*, 1855), asserted that the colloquial style in European languages had greatly aided the development of western learning. These initial comments, no more than mere remarks on a foreign custom, prompted the publication in the late Tokugawa Period of a number of dictionaries and grammars for students of Dutch which gave Japanese equivalents in their colloquial rather than literary forms. Japanese intellectuals, therefore, or at least those who had either studied the west directly or read the writings of those who had, were not unaware of the existence of colloquial style in other languages (or indeed in their own) and of its perceived benefits. It was not ignorance which held them back from espousing it, but reluctance to abandon traditional literary conventions.

REQUIREMENTS OF A MODERN STYLE

To facilitate the spread of information, then, Japan needed a modernized written language. To begin with, it must be *standardized*, based on one form of spoken Japanese accepted as the official variant throughout the country. Without standardization of the written language, no attempt to disseminate information nationwide in a coherent manner from a central administration could be expected to proceed smoothly. Then it must be relatively *simple*, not far removed from the comfortable familiarity of everyday speech, so that its users could contemplate the process of writing as an instrument of their daily business rather than as an esoteric exercise in composition. This same simplicity would render it *democratic* in its accessibility to all members of the society, so that no longer would one section of that society maintain a monopoly of information by virtue of the type of language in which it was expressed. It must further be *versatile*, capable of being applied in any field, obviating the necessity of mastering disparate modes of expression depending on whether one were writing, say, a letter or a critical essay. It must be *flexible*, able to express a multiplicity of new concepts as they arose without being restrained by stereotyped idioms and conceits. And it must be *sophisticated*, capable of the refinement and diversity of expression demanded by literature as well as the direct expression appropriate to science and business. Of these requirements, as we shall see, it was the last which provided opponents of reform with their most telling ammunition in their struggle to maintain the status quo. The colloquial style as it existed in Japan, they held, was rendered unsuitable for use in serious writing because of its vulgarity and verbosity, requiring a considerable degree of polishing before it could approach the dignity and refinement of established styles.

The fact that commoners were unable to read Sino-Japanese and other archaic 'aristocratic' styles did not by any means signify that the lower ranks of Japanese were uninterested in reading itself. Literacy rates in the late Tokugawa Period were higher in Japan than in Europe, with Passin estimating even the lowest rate among peasants in isolated areas to have averaged 20 per cent, a figure which rises to 30–40 per cent in the lower peasant levels, 50–60 per cent at the village middle layers, and almost 100 per cent at the top end of the village hierarchy.[27] The degree of literacy varied, of course, from the simple ability to write one's own name to the capacity to read and write complex texts, and some parts of Japan were more active in this area than others. At the end of the Tokugawa Period there existed a wide range of educational institutions varying in scope from small temple schools offering commoners a rudimentary education to government Confucian academies for the higher education of samurai. The government gave official support to schools for the upper class, whose members, as rulers and administrators of the country, required a high degree of education. Commoners with no such goals in view were left to fend for themselves in obtaining basic literacy skills; while schooling was not forbidden them, neither was any official sanction extended until the late Tokugawa Period, and education remained a matter of personal enterprise.

Despite this, the number of private schools for the lower classes in both rural and urban areas multiplied rapidly as the influence of the merchant class increased in the eighteenth and nineteenth centuries. These schools offered basic instruction in the three Rs, supplemented by some kind of moral and occupational training. While some commoners acquired only the bare essentials of literacy, sufficient for the small concerns of everyday life, others developed an advanced ability to read and write. The mushrooming of popular fiction in the Tokugawa Period attests to the degree to which literacy had spread among the commoners for whom these books were written. The Genroku era (1688–1704) saw the growth of a substantial publishing industry, with large publishing houses such as the Hachimonjiya employing professional writers and illustrators. Some editions ran into over 10,000 copies.[28] The many who could not afford their own copies were nevertheless enabled to read them through the agency of lending libraries (*kashihonya*), which began in the early 1700s and reached their maximum growth in the first half of the nineteenth century, being found in remote towns and villages as well as large cities. In 1808, there were 656 such libraries in Edo alone.[29]

The problem lay therefore not in widespread illiteracy, but rather in the nature of the written Japanese used at the official level and the years of arduous study required to master its literary forms and script which placed it out of reach of commoners. The high literacy rate provided fertile ground for future developments. Lerner describes literacy as 'a prime mover in the modernization of every aspect of life ... the basic personal skill that underlies the whole modernizing sequence'.[30] The development of a colloquial style would fuel an already burning fire by giving direction and purpose to existing commoner literacy, signalling a new, more direct relationship between writer and reader by removing the barriers to direct expression and eliminating the need to grapple with the form of the text before grasping its content.

Before it could function effectively, however, the colloquial style as it then existed in Japan, restricted to the tracts of certain popular religious movements and to the dialogue passages of popular fiction, would require a considerable amount of polishing to eradicate its defects and fashion it into a fit medium for educated discourse, serious literature, and government business. There would be several problems to be overcome, the most difficult being that of standardization. The least difficult, at first glance, was the charge of vulgarity. Easy enough to strike out inappropriately worded phrases, one might think, and yet vulgarity was the charge most often and most bitterly leveled by detractors of colloquial style, who saw the use of any part of the spoken language in writing except certain parts of the lexicon as an offence in itself regardless of whether the expressions used were in fact vulgar in the pejorative sense or merely commonplace. A further charge was that of verbosity, of allowing the pen, once freed from the restraints of conventions, to follow the thoughts undisciplined and unchecked. Then there was the question of which of the several versions of the copula should be adopted, the upper class *de gozaru*, the more common *da*, or something in between? These and other problems had to be addressed and solved by advocates of language reform before they could hope to convince their fellow intellectuals, on whose co-operation success would hinge, of the validity of the undertaking.

ROLE OF INTELLECTUALS

To sway intellectuals to the cause of modernization of the written language was crucial to the success of the endeavour. In the

Japanese case, it was the intellectuals, the Confucian-educated former *samurai* turned bureaucrats, who had to be persuaded not only of the unsuitability for modern Japan of the perpetuation of classical literary traditions but also of the advisability of replacing them with a kind of writing which had hitherto been anathema in their eyes. What they would be asked to abandon was an ingrained belief in the desirability of maintaining the concept of *bun*, of writing intended for public scrutiny as an artistic endeavour which ought to remain the object of concentrated effort. For many, the concept of increasing the access to information of the former lower classes was at first too unfamiliar to carry much weight as an argument, after the long years of feudalism when the ban on publication of information or opinion on matters pertaining to government was strictly enforced by censorship. To persuade them to agree to a major shift in attitude on the grounds that stylistic reform would benefit the masses would be an arduous undertaking.

In order to have any chance of being heard, or indeed of possessing the knowledge and background to argue the case, it was essential that advocates of language modernization be intellectuals themselves. What was required was a kind of Trojan horse campaign rather than an assault from without, external attacks upon strongly-defended bastions often resulting in the kind of long-drawn-out, stubborn siege in which neither side emerges victorious except at great cost. Those early scholars who spoke out in favour of change to a man did so *because* they were educated men and had been vouchsafed the opportunity to study the situation in foreign countries. The catalyst in forming their support for what was a radical proposal, given the circumstances, was exposure to the west and discovery of both the different attitude to writing held there and the flourishing state of the vernacular languages in Europe and America. That is not to say, of course, that *all* scholars of the west were struck dumb with admiration of the virtues of colloquial style and hastened to recommend them for the home market; many remained unimpressed. There is no doubt, however, that the western influence profoundly affected the theories of language reformers.

While it is tempting with hindsight to denigrate the tardiness of the majority of Japanese intellectuals in coming to accept the concept of style reform in general and of developing colloquial style in particular, it must be remembered, as Black points out, that the initial push towards modernization was undertaken primarily on defensive grounds, with more thorough modernization not occurring until the late nineteenth century.[31] This ties in with the delay in establishing any form of national body to oversee language planning until after the Japanese victory in the 1894–95 war with China had engendered a feeling of sufficient security and national pride to countenance consideration of matters not perceived as essential to the national interest on a large scale. The changed attitude in the wake of the war led to increased public scrutiny of and interest in the Japanese language, which was now to be used outside Japan for the first time. Only when relieved of the eclipsing urgency of other political moves necessary to ensure the country's survival were its leaders persuaded to listen to the growing clamour in support of modernization of the written language from the by then increasing number of those committed to establishing colloquial style as the normal mode of written expression regardless of the field, and set up an official investigatory body in 1902 to direct and co-ordinate future developments. There were therefore two factors militating against rapid progress in language modernization in the early decades of the Meiji Period, one being the prevailing intellectual attitude to writing, the other the generally perceived inconsequence of the issue in comparison with other matters of greater urgency by those whose natural inclination was to maintain the literary status quo.

These, then, were the tasks which lay ahead for early would-be reformers: the task of convincing the establishment of the desirability of change and of enlisting the aid of those in a position to help, such as newspaper editors and educators; the task of actually converting theory into practice and writing in colloquial style, overcoming problems of standardization and choice of verb forms acceptable to all; the task of addressing the major criticisms directed at colloquial style by its detractors and polishing it into a vehicle just as capable of cultured expression as other styles; and later, the task of eliciting government support to shore up and give official sanction to those very significant initiatives which were made prior to 1900 by individuals or groups working alone rather than under the umbrella of an organization with an official language planning brief. The following chapters will examine how, when, where, and why they were carried out, and, of course, by whom.

2 Pre-modern styles

As a prelude to tracing the process of modernization in written Japanese, we must first consider the nature of the major literary conventions in use at the beginning of the Meiji Period in order to understand the extent to which they hindered the rapidity with which information could be disseminated. It was essential that they be changed, for two reasons: because of their own intrinsic difficulty, given that they bore scant resemblance to the spoken language, and because of the connotations they carried of good writing as a thing apart from daily life, a craft for skilled and inevitably upper-class hands rather than a commonplace accomplishment of ordinary people. The time spent on mass education could be much reduced if students were not first forced to decipher the form of the message before being able to absorb its content. Information of importance to society at large, whether transmitted in the form of official government notices or of intellectual debate in the press, as to the form which the basic institutions of modern Japanese society should take would be lost to all but those with a classical education unless the manner in which it was written was changed to make texts comprehensible to those without such training. It was not enough to attempt to introduce the masses to traditional styles through the education system; to do so merely perpetuated the idea that writing ought to be an artificial construct, not a natural and easy representation of speech on paper. Nor could classical styles do duty in modern forms of literature dependent on psycho-realism – the moral dilemmas of nineteenth-century characters could not be expressed in tenth-century language without at once removing them from their temporal context and restricting the range of lexical items available.

As we have seen in the previous chapter, the various manifestations of formal written Japanese adhered to centuries-old classical traditions and bore only a slight resemblance to the spoken language. As an overall umbrella classification, the term *bungotai* is now used to designate those types of writing based on the lexical and syntactic conventions of a past age, as opposed to *kōgotai*, the modern written colloquial style which, although naturally not identical with the contemporary spoken language, takes from it the majority of its content. Given the prestige accorded by educated men to archaic forms and the low esteem in which they held the colloquial as a means of literary expression, all public documents in the Meiji Period were written in one form or another of *bungotai*.

Within this general grouping, literary language may be categorized in several different ways: by geographical origin of characteristic elements, for instance, as in *wabun, kambun, wakankonkōbun*, and *ōbun* (European style), or by orthography, as in *kanabun* (written in phonetic script) and *kanji-kana-majiribun* (a mixture of Chinese characters and phonetic script), to name just two. The four varieties which will be discussed here are *kambun* (Sino-Japanese), *sōrōbun* (the epistolary style, an offshoot of Sino-Japanese), *wabun* (classical Japanese), and *wakankonkōbun* (a combination of Chinese and Japanese elements), these being the major easily identifiable streams in terms of derivation and, in the case of *sōrōbun*, of application.[1]

KAMBUN

Kambun, or Sino-Japanese, was the oldest and most widely used form of writing. The term *kambun* denotes the Chinese language as used in Japan. In one form or another, it was the medium of official business, of criticism and exposition, of history and critical essays, and of upper-class education, as well as being used in many of the early Meiji translations of western literature. The political debates which enlivened the pages of newspapers and journals in the early years of the Meiji Period were couched in Sino-Japanese, as were petitions, the Five Point Imperial Oath of 1868, and other Imperial edicts.[2]

It should be noted here that the word *kambun* has been used in Japan as a blanket term to refer to several different types of Chinese. *Jun kambun* (pure *kambun*), being either pure Chinese or a Japanese attempt at writing pure Chinese as foreign language, was naturally set out entirely in Chinese characters in accordance with Chinese word-order, which is to say, subject–verb–predicate rather than subject–predicate–verb. The name given to the system of diacritics and glosses evolved over time to help Japanese readers with less than perfect knowledge of Chinese construe the meaning of such a text and manipulate the foreign script in such a way as to enable them to use it to represent their own very different language on paper is *kambun kundoku* (Chinese read in the Japanese manner). The term *kambun kundoku* could refer either to a Chinese text annotated with tiny diacritics on the left to show Japanese word order, *katakana* on the right to show Japanese inflections and particles, and occasional *hiragana* glosses indicating Japanese pronunciation, or to the same text written out in full in Japanese word order, using a combination of Chinese characters and phonetic script, so that it became no longer Chinese but a Japanised rendering of the original. The latter form is also referred to as *kambun chokuyakutai*, *kambun kuzushi*, or *kambun kakikudashi-bun*.

Kambun had been the language of Japanese officialdom since the Nara Period. Its position had been reinforced during the Tokugawa Period by the government's revival of Confucian studies. Thus blessed with official approval, it enjoyed a prestige higher than that of other varieties of writing, and was valued for its conciseness and for its formal and erudite tone, this latter being a quality often deliberately fostered by the use of extraneous archaic rhetorical devices and stereotyped literary idioms.

The influence of the Chinese language upon the Japanese which had resulted in this continuing preference for a foreign language over the native idiom had begun many centuries before when the Japanese people, lacking a script of their own, imported the Chinese writing system during a period of extensive cultural borrowing. The earliest evidence of Chinese characters in Japan is a golden seal unearthed at Hakata Bay in Kyushu in 1784. It is inscribed with the name of a Chinese ruler and was presented to the Japanese ruler in AD 57. The earliest known written records are those of Wang-in (or Wani), who came to Japan in the early part of the fifth century AD and became a secretary at the Court, where his duties included helping to keep the Imperial budget and teaching the Heir Apparent to write Chinese.

The Chinese script was not widely used until after the introduction of Buddhism to Japan. An early historical collection, the

36 *Language and the Modern State*

Nihongi (Chronicles of Japan, 720) relates that in 552 the king of Paekche, a kingdom in south-east Korea known to the Japanese as Kudara, requested assistance from the Emperor Kimmei to repel a threatened attack by Silla, largest of the three Korean kingdoms. With the appeal came a gift of several Buddhist sutras and a holy image, together with an exhortation to the Japanese to adopt Buddhism as the true religion. The gift was followed two years later by a group of Buddhist monks accompanied by scholars well versed in the Chinese classics, music, medicine, and divination. As the original message had indicated that Buddhism had reached Korea via China, it was to China that the Japanese turned for instruction after their adoption of Buddhism as the state religion in 594. There followed a period of extensive borrowing of Chinese thought, customs, and institutions, during which knowledge of Chinese characters spread rapidly in the absence of any indigenous orthography. Early laws and histories were thus all written in Chinese, which was established *ipso facto* as the formal written language, a position it was to maintain in one form or another long after the development of orthographic systems enabling the reproduction in writing of the native Japanese language.

As long as Chinese script was used by Japanese to write Chinese as a foreign language, all was well. Severe difficulties were faced, however, when attempts were made to use the foreign script to write Japanese. While a Chinese character could be pressed into service to represent a word on paper, say 'tree', it was impossible to tell from looking at the character how the Japanese word for 'tree' was pronounced. Furthermore, Chinese was an uninflected language, Japanese was not, posing the problem of how to indicate native grammatical particles and verbal and adjectival inflections. It became necessary to find some means of construing Japanese from Chinese script; the absence of any native orthography meant that this would involve tinkering in some way with the Chinese itself. Various early attempts were made at producing a workable system.

One method tried was the use of *okototen*, a system of diacritics marked on an invisible square around a character to indicate a particular inflection. For example, using the system in Figure 2.1, the word *hikite* would be written

．引

and *hiku koto wa* as

引．

Figure 2.1 Okototen

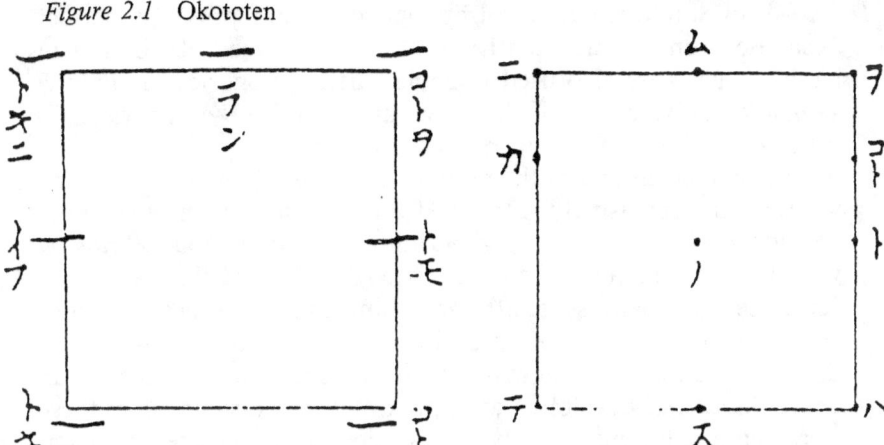

Source: Shimmura Izuru (ed.), *Kōjien* (rev. 3rd. edn), Tokyo: Iwanami Shoten, 1983, p. 322

The process was difficult and cumbersome, and usage varied among different schools of Chinese studies and Buddhist sects. The major drawback of the *okototen* system was that it encoded only grammatical forms and could not be used as a guide to pronunciation. After the end of the Heian period, the development of phonetic *kana* scripts provided an easier means of achieving the same end.[3]

Before the evolution of *hiragana* and *katakana*, however, an earlier attempt at recording Japanese pronunciation had been made using *man'yōgana*, a form of rebus writing whereby Japanese words were painstakingly spelled out with Chinese characters having pronunciations roughly corresponding to each syllable. Any combination of symbols having the right sounds would do; there was no standardization. The name *man'yōgana* was given to symbols used in this way after the eighth century because they were used in the *Man'yōshū* (*Collection of Ten Thousand Leaves*), the first great anthology of Japanese poetry. At first, *man'yōgana* were used to represent Japanese particles and inflections following a Chinese character, as well as to spell out place and personal names. The oldest surviving example is a fifth-century inscription excavated from a burial ground at Edofunayama. During the Nara Period, they were used in Japanese poems – as in the hundred or so in the *Kojiki* (*Records of Ancient Matters*, 712), the oldest extant Japanese book – which were written phonetically to preserve their metre; in records of Shinto rituals and Imperial edicts, to represent the exact Japanese pronunciation used when these were read aloud; and in letters. They were also used in some early dictionaries to give the Japanese equivalents of Chinese words, as in the *Wamyō Ruijushō* (c.934) by Minamoto Shitagō (911–83).

From the beginning of the tenth century, *man'yōgana* came to be written in increasingly cursive forms, from which eventually developed the phonetic *hiragana* and *katakana* scripts. *Hiragana* were Chinese characters so abbreviated as to be intelligible only to Japanese. Originally several hundred in number, reduced in modern times to 46, they were used in poems and letters dealing with daily life, and also in the writings of the noblewomen of the Heian court. *Katakana* developed at approximately the same time; these were representations of only one section of a Chinese character, whereas *hiragana* were concise forms of the whole. They too originally existed in numbers much greater than at present. First developed as an abbreviated form for indicating native pronunciation and grammar in Buddhist texts, they were used mainly by priestly sects in Nara. After 901, however, they came into more general use and their original rather flowing form became more angular.

The eventual appearance of these phonetic scripts meant that it was now possible to write Japanese without resorting to the use of Chinese characters. Why, then, did the Japanese choose instead to retain *kanji* and *kambun*? One reason was the previously discussed love of literary complexity which characterized Japanese scholars right up to the Meiji Period and beyond. The very difficulty of *kambun* rendered it desirable, prestige carrying more weight than practicality; in that sense, its position was analagous to that of Latin in Europe in the Middle Ages. Then there was its conciseness compared to the greater number of symbols needed to represent a work in *kana* – the Chinese sentence

文之起必有由，

requiring only six characters, needed fourteen were it to be written out phonetically in *hiragana* as

ぶんのおこりかならずよしあり

(*Bun no okori kanarazu yoshi ari*, 'There is always a reason for writing'). This characteristic brevity is almost always mentioned in any discussion of *kambun* by Japanese scholars as a strong point in its favour. Miller suggests also, albeit referring to the use of rebus writings, that the idle life of the aristocracy (who were the only ones concerned with reading and writing) caused them to welcome any time-consuming and aesthetically fulfilling intricacy which would fill in the hours of their day.[4] For all these reasons, Chinese in either its pure or hybrid form was perpetuated as the official language, while Japanese written in phonetic script was relegated to private use in poems, diaries, and letters, its public exposure being restricted to women's literature.

Phonetic scripts were also used in conjunction with Chinese characters in the previously mentioned *kundoku* system, where *kun* refers to the Japanese (as opposed to the Chinese) pronunciation of words represented by ideographs. Word-order was indicated by diacritics and numbers, and grammatical information by small *kana* beside the text, so that the *kundoku* system was an imposition of Japanese speech patterns on the alien Chinese language. No evidence has been found of texts doctored in this way until the Heian Peiod, although translation is believed to have been done in the Nara Period without the marks actually being added to the text.[5]

In order to construe a Chinese text into Japanese rather than read it as a foreign language, it was necessary to supply the missing Japanese terminations and particles, and to change the word-order. Whereas a pure *kambun* text would contain no indication as to how this should be done, an annotated *kunten* text would offer some clues. For example, the sentence in Chinese might read:

文之起必有由

With *kunten* added, a kind of cryptic halfway measure, it would become:

文之起必有由

The native pronunciation and grammar thus represented maintained a reasonably close relationship to contemporary speech in the Heian Period, although the influence of the Chinese language meant that *kambun kundoku* texts were clearly differentiated from the *kana* women's literature which flowered during this era by Chinese words and constructions not used in Japanese speech,[6] so that the 'Japanese' produced by doctoring Chinese texts was not really pure Japanese at all but Sino-Japanese, a mixture of predominantly Chinese elements with Japanese addenda and glosses.

As time passed and relations with China lost their former intensity, the corresponding decline in the study of Chinese meant that fewer people were capable of reading and writing Chinese as a foreign language. What passed for it was often an adulterated version, still written in Chinese script but containing elements not found in pure Chinese. The grammar and pronunciations appended to *kundoku* texts remained those of the early Middle Ages despite subsequent changes in the spoken language, and in this may be found the beginnings of the divergence between written and spoken Japanese which increased over the centuries until the dual system of the Meiji Period was reached. During the Muromachi Period (1473–1568), the rise of the warrior class which displaced the nobles as rulers of Japan was mirrored in the spoken language by the growing influence of the type of sturdy, vigorous expressions used by warriors, in marked contrast to the circumlocutory euphemisms favoured by the Court. While literary Japanese clung to already outmoded forms, the spoken language continued to develop and change, absorbing new elements and husking off outdated ones, until by the Tokugawa Period there was a wide gap separating the two.

The traditional *kundoku* style used by such early Tokugawa scholars as Hayashi Razan was often at variance with the original text of the Chinese classics, sometimes even including words with no equivalent in the source material, so that it proved difficult to reconstruct the original from the Japanese gloss.[7] Later scholars, among them Yamasaki Ansai (1618–82), Gotō Shizan (1721–82), and Nonaka Kenzan (1615–53), attempted to bring the *kundoku* version back to the more faithful rendering of the original, producing a kind of 'direct translation' known as *kambun chokuyakutai* which was used well into the Meiji Period. While to a reader accustomed to the modern colloquial style this gives an impression of stiffness and formality, it was welcomed when it first appeared for its freshness and relative simplicity.

Despite this attempt at pruning, however, Sino-Japanese in 1868 remained a mystery to the average lower class Japanese, for whom its esoteric Chinese vocabulary, intricate characters, and archaic syntax divested it of any significance as an everyday reality. Even in *samurai* schools, where it formed the cornerstone of education, the study of *kambun* was often no more than mere rote learning of passages from the Chinese classics without comprehension. In 1866, Maejima Hisoka related a denunciation of this practice by an

Pre-modern styles 41

American missionary, Williams, in Nagasaki. During his earlier service in China, Williams had been puzzled one day by the uproar coming from a house he was passing. Enquiries elicited the information that it was a school, and that the children were merely following the usual practice of committing ancient texts to memory by reciting them aloud, without understanding their meaning. Not even experienced scholars, he discovered, could fathom the exact meaning. Williams lamented the fact that such a deplorable situation, existing even in the homeland of the classics, should be copied in Japan where there existed a perfectly good native language.[8]

Let us look now at a series of simple examples from a modern *kambun* textbook showing the process whereby Chinese is converted into Sino-Japanese. While this is a recent work and thus incorporates some features not characteristic of the early Meiji Period – the orthography of the Japanese version of the Chinese text would have been more likely to be all *kanji-katakana* than mostly *kanji-hiragana*, for example – it will serve as a useful introduction to the techniques involved. Figure 2.2(a) gives a passage from the *Discourses of Mencius* in Chinese, written of course with Chinese characters and word-order, with the addition of the *kunten* clues required to construe it into Japanese. While the word order remains unchanged, tiny reverse symbols on the left, known as *kaeriten*, indicate that the second of the words between which they occur must be read before the first: in sentence 2, for example, the *kaeriten* indicates that the order in Japanese must be 'king-war-likes' rather than the 'king-likes-war' of the original. In sentence 9, the subscript characters for 'one' and 'two' indicate that the two-character word 'hundred steps' must be read before the negative marker 不. Tiny *katakana* at the lower right of the characters show inflections and particles: to the middle character in sentence 2 is added a *katakana mu* to indicate that part of the Japanese verb 'like' (*konomu*) which inflects, while the third character 'war' is followed with both a *hi* to indicate that it is the noun and not the verb 'war' and the postposition *o* which is necessary in Japanese to indicate that 'war' is the object of 'like'. *Hiragana* glosses are used here and there, also to the right of the characters, to show the Japanese pronunciation of the word.

In Figure 2.2(b) the passage no longer preserves Chinese word-order but is written out in the *kambun kuzushi* style, i.e. in a mixture of Chinese characters and phonetic script, in Japanese

Figure 2.2 Varieties of *kambun*

2.2(a)

五十歩百歩 ①孟子對へて曰はく、②「王戰ひを好む。③請ふ戰ひをもって喩へん。④塡然として鼓し、兵刃既に接す。⑤甲を棄て兵を曳きて走る。⑥或いは百歩にして後止まり、或いは五十歩にして後止まる。⑦五十歩をもって百歩を笑はば、則ちいかん」と。⑧惠王曰はく、「⑨不可なり。直だ百歩ならざるのみ。⑩是も亦走るなり」と。

2.2(b)

①孟子對曰、②「王好戰。③請以戰喩。④塡然鼓之、兵刃既接。⑤棄甲曳兵而走。⑥或百歩而後止、或五十歩而後止。⑦以五十歩笑百歩、則何如。」⑧惠王曰、⑨「不可。直不百歩耳。⑩是亦走也。」

（孟子）

2.2(c)

①孟子が（惠王に）お答えして言った。②「王は、戰いがお好きです。③どうぞ戰いのことでもって喩えさせてください。④ドンドンと進擊の太鼓がうち鳴らされ、(兩甲の)武器が交わっているさいちゅうです。⑤(その時ふたりの兵士が)よろいを投げ捨て、武器を引きずって逃げ出しました。⑥ひとりは百歩逃げてから止まり、また

ある人は五十歩逃げてから止まりました。⑦その時、(一方の人が)五十歩しか逃げなかったという理由で、(その人が)百歩逃げてしまった人を笑ったとしたら、どうでしょう。」⑧惠王は言った。⑨「いけない。ただ百歩（逃げたの)でなかっただけだ。⑩この人だって同じように逃げているのだ。」

Source: Tōdō Akiyasu, *Chūto shiki Shirtzu: Kambun Kaishaku*, Tokyo: Sūken Shuppan, 1972, pp. 36–7.
Note: For translation see Appendix.

Pre-modern styles 43

word-order with Japanese inflections and postpositions. Though now Japanese in form, however, the text is unmistakably Sino-Japanese, shot through with Chinese-derived idioms and with the grammatical forms which came to be characteristic of this style. The word *iwaku*, for example, is used before the quotation, to mean 'he said', where a true Japanese rendering would have put the verb after the reported speech; likewise *kofu* (*kou*) appears at the beginning of the sentence rather than at the end to mean 'I would like to . . .' The couplets found in sentence 6 are a distinguishing feature of *kambun* (*aruiwa hyakuhō ni shite nochi todomari, aruiwa gojūho ni shite nochi todomaru*, 'one stopped after a hundred paces, one after fifty'), as is the use of the bracketing *tada–nomi* in sentence nine to mean 'only'. The final section, Figure 2.2(c), is a rendering of the passage into modern Japanese. One difference is the contrast between the paucity of honorifics in the Sino-Japanese and their frequency in colloquial style: the laconic *kofu tatakahi o motte tatohen* ('I beg to illustrate with a military example') of the former, distinguished only by the humility of the *kofu* ('I beg to . . .') flowers into the wordier *dōzo tatakai no koto de motte tatoesasete kudasai* of the latter, as *kotaete* becomes the humble *o kotae shite* and *konomu* becomes *o suki*. The Sino-Japanese grammar has been replaced by its modern equivalents: in sentence 7, for example, the verb form *warawaba*, in which the conjunctive particle *ba* ('if') is added to the *mizenkei*[9] of the verb *warau*, 'to laugh', becomes the modern *waratta to shitara*, while in sentence 9 the negative *narazaru* becomes the modern *de nakatta*. Chinese-derived expressions such as *tenzen toshite* (used to indicate the sound of a drum) and *fuka* ('impossible') have been replaced with the Japanese *dondon to* and *ikenai* respectively. While the *kambun* version is very obviously the more concise of the two, the modern rendering allows much fuller and more detailed expression of the meaning. The former argument was advanced in the Meiji Period in support of Sino-Japanese, the latter by advocates of colloquial style.

The contrast between the foreign-derived Sino-Japanese and classical Japanese literary conventions was naturally not as pronounced in the early Meiji Period as it had been 800 years earlier, the purity of the original Chinese having been eroded to an ever-increasing extent by elements of the Japanese language over the intervening centuries, but Sino-Japanese in the 1870s nevertheless still retained distinct and singular characteristics which set it apart from the indigenous classical tradition. These included the frequent use of rhetorical questions, in particular the structure *iwanya* ... (*ni oite*) *o ya*, and double negatives, such as ... *zaru atowazaru* ('must'); the use of demonstrative pronouns to sum up and emphasize a preceding phrase; inversion of word-order for emphasis, used in all styles but particularly frequent in *kambun*; the causative ... *o shite* ... *shimu*, found only in *kambun*; the construction ... *ba nari* to indicate reason; and expressions such as *subekaraku* ... *beshi* ('it is proper that ...').[10] Its verbs were predominantly formed by the addition of *suru* to *kango* (Chinese words) (e.g. *bemmei suru*, 'to apologize') rather than composite Japanese verbs of the *oyobikaneru* ('to be unable to reach') type made by adding a second verb to the conjunctive form of a first. Its relative conciseness and economy of line in comparison with the prolixity of classical Japanese rendered it more suitable for narrative passages than emotive descriptions; its sentences were generally shorter than the long rambling utterances typical of *wabun*. Examples of its influence found even today in the more formal variety of the modern colloquial style include terms such as *gotoku* ('like'), ... *ni oite* ('in'), *shikaraba* ('if so'), *kedashi* ('perhaps'), *beki* ('should'), ... *ni yotte* ('by'), and *kono toki ni saishite* ('at this time').

Official documents at the beginning of the Meiji Period were written either in Chinese, Sino-Japanese, or *sōrōbun*, with those emanating from the imperial court or temples favouring Chinese. Histories such as the *Dai Nihon Shi* (*Complete History of Japan*), begun in 1657 and not completed until 1906, were written in non-annotated Chinese, as were many other scholarly works. Such was the esteem in which classical Chinese was held that *kangakusha*, scholars of Chinese, at times employed it in such private documents as diaries, travelogues, and occasional essays. Early scholars of the west such as Sugita Genpaku (1733–1817) wrote in *kambun* (*Kaitai Shinsho, A New Treatise on Anatomy*, 1774), as did Nakae Chōmin (1847–1901) much later, in his 1882 *Min'yakuron*, a translation of Rousseau's *Social Contract*. To write for formal purposes, to educated men of the period other than those dedicated to a revival of classical Japanese, meant only one thing: to write in Chinese, pure or adapted.

This occasionally produced less than desirable results, as a Russian expedition led by Admiral Putiatin which arrived about six weeks after Perry discovered:

> The official Japanese reply to the Russian state paper ... had been written in Chinese. Although three members of the expedition had lived and studied in China for years, they were unable to decipher it. When it was returned to the Japanese, their own interpreters could not understand it either. One of the plenipotentiaries, a Confucian scholar, had to translate it into Japanese, before the Japanese interpreters could render it into Dutch to be retranslated into Russian.[11]

Probably most of their difficulties stemmed from the fact that what passed in Japan as pure Chinese was in reality no more than a Japanese approximation.

Kambun had played a major role in the Confucian-oriented education offered in *samurai* schools prior to the Restoration, and it retained its prominence in education well into the Meiji Period. Upon the inauguration of the national education system in 1872, the Ministry of Education designated certain existing works as temporary textbooks until official textbooks could be compiled. These included Fukuzawa Yukichi's *Seiyō Jijō* (*Conditions in the West*), *Moji no Oshie* (*The Teaching of Characters*), and *Gakumon no Susume* (*The Encouragement of Learning*), and sections of Katō Hiroyuki's *Shinsei Tai-i* (*An Outline of True Government*). Fukuzawa and Katō (1836–1916) had both received a traditional education in Chinese studies and normally wrote Sino-Japanese as a matter of course. However, in a bid to facilitate the spread of knowledge about western customs, institutions, and (in Katō's case particularly) political systems among the Japanese, they had made a conscious attempt to simplify the text of these works to some extent, Fukuzawa by using colloquial vocabulary and idioms while still retaining classical grammar and Katō by replacing the classical *nari-keri*[12] literary terminations with the *de gozaru* copula used in speech by *samurai*. While it is true that Fukuzawa's books enjoyed bestseller status, due as much to the unusual clarity of their style as to the information they contained, he was unable to free himself from the influence of his early training, so that the Chinese influence remained, though greatly diminished through his efforts to curtail it. Katō's *An Outline of True Government*, despite its superficial adoption of one of the forms of the copula used in the spoken language, retained a high proportion of bookish Chinese words and phrases and was strongly Sino-Japanese in tone. When the Ministry of Education set up an editorial bureau at the new

Normal School in Tokyo late in 1872 and began producing its own readers, the majority were written in *kambun kundoku*; the material covered ranged from simple words and phrases at the elementary stage to advanced texts at the higher levels.

Haga Yaichi (1867–1927), recalling his early Meiji education in the castle school at Sendai, observed that pupils had no Japanese readers, nor was Japanese grammar taught. Both teachers and students were confused about correct usage of phonetic scripts. Confucius and Mencius were studied in ethics classes, and the *Tsugan Ran'yō*, an abridged version of a longer chronological history of 113 Chinese emperors from 402 BC to AD 960, was set for the combined study of *kambun* and history; Haga recalled that they read it very quickly and had it finished in one school year. *Kambun* was considered the most important subject, and the students themselves regarded it as the most interesting part of the curriculum.[13] The old academies for Chinese studies which had flourished in the Tokugawa Period remained open after the education system began to operate. The children of a certain section of society would put in the required number of hours at a government school and then go off to study, or at least learn by rote, *The Book of Filial Piety*, progressing from there to the four Chinese Classics or to the *Nihon Gaishi* (*Unofficial History of Japan*), a Japanese history written in *kambun*. They did not study the Japanese classics at all, considering them fit only for the amusement of women and children. Guides to writing *kambun* were plentiful, among them Yamamoto Hokuzan's *Sakubun Shikoku* (1780).

Given that the Meiji government was composed of former *samurai* who had received the traditional Confucian education and shared the conviction that proper writing automatically meant Sino-Japanese, it is entirely natural that no real attempt was made to provide students with a more easily understood language filter through which to absorb their other studies for quite some time. Inspired by their studies of the west, a small group of progressive scholars within the Education Ministry, led by the Minister Ōki Takatō (1832–99), did instigate an investigation in 1873 into the possibility of using colloquial Japanese in school textbooks; the plan foundered, however, when the task was entrusted to conservatives committed to maintaining the status quo, who reported inability to develop a feasible method of implementing it.

The serious newspapers which began to circulate early in the Meiji Period were also written in *kambun*, as they were controlled by former *samurai*. They reported current political, economic, and industrial matters, and published topical editorials, petitions, official notices, overseas reports, and contributions on current affairs from readers. Human interest stories and social jottings were considered no part of serious reporting. Government notices were published in either *sōrōbun* or *kambun*, while editorials and items of foreign news were in *kambun kundoku*, usually lacking pronunciation glosses. Even miscellaneous items, though slightly modified by being written in *kanji* and *hiragana* with some pronunciation glosses, held fast to literary syntax. The ordinary citizen who had not been educated to read *kambun* was thus effectively cut off from the main source of news, until, after 1874, popular newspapers appeared to fill this gap, offering social news, human interest stories and serialized novels. Their text was simple and colloquial, even in those few official notices directly affecting the people which they published. Under their influence, a certain amount of colloquial style even began to appear in the miscellaneous columns of the major political newspapers in 1875 and 1876. The trend proved ephemeral, however, and by 1888 both types of newspaper had reverted to a more formal mode of expression.

Kambun was also widely used in several spheres of early Meiji literature. In political novels, which were intended to instruct rather than to entertain, it was the variety of written language most familiar to the readership for which it was intended. In translations of western literature, it was considered more appropriate than classical Japanese, which called up uniquely Japanese associations not applicable to imported fiction. Late Tokugawa Period writers of *gebun*, satires of current fads by scholars and embittered former *samurai*, achieved a ludicrous contrast by using high-sounding Chinese expressions to describe the minutiae of daily life, as in, for example, Terakado Seiken's *Edo Hanjōki* (*A Tale of Success in Edo*, 1832–36). And finally, *kambun* continued as the medium for critical essays, which flourished throughout the Meiji Period. An examination of the *Meiji Bunka Zenshū* (*Collected Works on Meiji Culture*), a 27 volume collection of writings on various facets of life in the Meiji Period, reveals that while written-out *kambun kuzushi* was the most widely used form, pure Chinese prefaces and postscripts were often appended to the body of the texts of dissertations, articles, and translations.[14]

The Sino-Japanese influence lingered on for many years in the colloquial-style novels and translations which began to appear after

1886, as even those authors committed to the use of colloquial style could not easily shake free of their early education. Futabatei Shimei, for instance, first prominent user of the colloquial style in modern Japanese literature, is said to have found it so difficult to eradicate Chinese expressions from his prose when writing *Ukigumo* (*The Drifting Cloud*, 1887–89) that he actually wrote the draft of the second volume in Russian and translated it back into simple Japanese.

SŌRŌBUN

Sōrōbun, so called because of its characteristic use of the verb *sōrō* as the copula, was the epistolary style used by men in both private and official correspondence and in public notices, advertisements, reports, archives, laws and ordinances. While *kambun* remained the exclusive province of the educated male upper class, *sōrōbun* was employed by aristocrat and commoner alike. Commoner education included classes in *sōrōbun*, and the style was employed in commoner records and public official notices as well as in correspondence. It showed a marked Chinese influence, however, due to its origin, and was not easy to master.

Sōrōbun was in fact descended from *hentai kambun* (variant *kambun*), a modified form of classical Chinese developed in Japan in the Middle Ages. The purity of the Chinese written by Japanese had suffered somewhat as the earlier enthusiasm for Chinese studies began to abate after the Heian Period, with a form of natural linguistic acclimatization occurring as indigenous words and expressions began to creep in, along with a certain degree of error in word-order and character usage and the use of honorific expressions. The result became the style normally used in men's correspondence, both private and public, diaries, and records, except on those official occasions when formal Chinese was warranted. It later became also known as *Azuma Kagami* (*Mirror of the Eastland*) style because of its use in that work, a Kamakura Period history of Japan from 1180 to 1266; the fact of its use in a history, when histories had previously been written in Chinese, indicates the growth of its prestige. This style was adopted as the medium of public documents by the Kamakura shogunate so that penal codes (*seibai shiki moku*) and the like were written in *hentai kambun* rather than pure Chinese, as were Tokugawa Period laws and ordinances relating to samurai, court nobles, and Buddhist temples.

Pre-modern styles 49

While *hentai kambun* was still written in Chinese characters, it exhibited a tendency, increasing over time, to interpolate Japanese words, phrases and poems reproduced phonetically by *man'yōgana* or other *kana*. Other characteristics included sporadic departures from Chinese word-order and the use of honorifics not found in Chinese, such as the honorific prefix *go-*, and the verbs *tamau* ('to bestow') and *haberu*. *Haberu* was a verb expressing humility meaning literally 'to wait upon' or 'to serve', used in the Nara Period; it was joined in the Heian Period by *sōrō*, which originally meant 'to wait on' but came to mean 'to be' when used alone. In the twelfth century, *sōrō* began to appear more frequently than *haberu*, at first in private correspondence, and later in official communications, gradually increasing its hold until it became the hallmark of a distinctive epistolary style branching off from *hentai kambun* and known as *sōrōbun*, in which *sōrō* appears both alone as the verb 'to be' and as a polite suffix with other verbs. The spread of this style was facilitated through the use of copybooks known as *ōraimono*, notably the *Teikin Ōrai* (*The Home Letter-Writer*), a correspondence manual written in *sōrōbun* in the early Muromachi Period and used as a model for teaching writing in temple schools.

Although *sōrōbun* was originally written entirely in Chinese characters, by the beginning of the Meiji Period it had evolved into a combination of characters and phonetic script, except for expressions inherited from pure Chinese. Among its distinguishing features was the frequent use of *ateji*, Chinese characters used instead of *kana* in a rebus-like manner to represent inflections. For example, *sōrō majiku* would be

候間敷

instead of

候まじく

sōraeba would be

候得者, not

候えば.

The character 之 often replaced ノ as the possessive marker. This style was further characterized by its many inverted constructions following Chinese word-order. The following are some of the characters which would precede the characters in the text to which they referred while being read after them in Japanese:

被 (passive)
為 (causative)
不 and 無 (negative)
可 (potential)
乍 (*nagara*)
如 (*gotoku*).

For example, *kudasaru beku* ('can do') would occur as

可被下

instead of

下被可

and *zonjinagara* ('though I think') as

乍存

instead of

存乍

Sōrōbun also possessed a distinctive vocabulary of greetings and appellations. There were at least eight words for 'I', including *shosei* and *fushō*, and more than double that number for 'you', depending on the recipient's relationship to the writer. For example, superiors were addressed as *gozensama* or *kiden*, equals as *kika*, *sokka*, or *kenkei*, and subordinates as *omi* or *omae*. The general effect of this combination of Chinese constructions with standard idioms, a high proportion of honorifics, and a fixed vocabulary was one of stiffness and formality, although the degree of course varied with the individual writer.

Figure 2.3 shows part of a petition 'Kanji Gohaishi no Gi' ('Proposal for the Abolition of Chinese Characters') presented to the Shogun Yoshinobu in 1866 by Maejima Hisoka, calling for the abolition of Chinese characters and the use of more colloquial grammar as steps towards simplifying written Japanese. Maejima did not attempt to exemplify his theories in his text, which was couched as the occasion demanded in *sōrōbun*. In the example given, the verb *sōrō* occurs nine times. There are two examples of *ateji* used in place of *kana* to indicate grammatical inflections (*sōraedomo* and *sōraeba*). Inverted word order (underlined) is used nine times, e.g., *zonji tatematsuri* in which the character for

Figure 2.3 Sōrōbun in Maejima's petition 'Kanji Gohaishi no Gi' ('Proposal for the Abolition of Chinese Characters')

敢て奉言上候
学事を簡にし普通教育を施すは国人の知識を開導し、精神を発達し、道理芸術百般に於ける初歩の門にして国家富強を為すの礎地に御座候得ば、成るべく簡易に成るべく広く且成るべく速に行届候様御世話有御座度事に奉存候、

目下御国事御多端にして人々競て救急策を講ずるの際、此の如き議を言上仕候は甚迂遠に似て、御傾聴被下置候程も如何有御座歟と憚入奉存候得共、御国をして他の列強と併立せしめられ候は、是より重且大なるは無之やに奉存候に付不顧恐憚

Source: Maejima Hisoka '*Kanji Gohaishi no Gi*' in *Maejima Hisoka Jijoden*, Hayama: Maejima Hisoka Denki Kankōkai, 1956, pp. 153-4.
Note: For translation see Appendix.

tatematsuri precedes that for *zonji* in the text. Several expressions are peculiar to *sōrōbun*, e.g:

奉存候に付

used for *omoimasu node* ('as I think ...'), and the negative *korenaku*. There are numerous Chinese-derived words and phrases, such as *ni okeru* ('in'), *gotoki* ('like'), and *narubeku* ('as ... as possible'). Most of the script is Chinese characters, with only a few phonetic characters; some expressions which could have incorporated them are written entirely in *kanji*, e.g:

行届候様御世話有御座度事

Figure 2.4 shows the use of *sōrōbun* in an official government notice published in the *Chūgai Shimbun* on 3 April 1868. Note the preponderance of Chinese characters; the distinguishing use of *sōrō*;

Figure 2.4 *Sōrōbun* in an official government notice, *Chūgai Shimbun*, 3 April 1868

○上野山内への布告書

彰義隊忠義奮發并に當御山諸向御警衛に付、赤心の條々宮様御感淺からず、以來恐多くも尊體當局へ御委任被遊候段御沙汰の趣、覺王院より被相達候間此段及廻達候。

Source: Miji Bunka Kenkyūkai (eds) *Meiji Bunka Zenshū* 4, *Shimbun-hen* (3rd edn), Tokyo: Nihon Hyōronsha, 1968, p. 259.
Note: For translation see Appendix.

Pre-modern styles 53

the reverse word order in the *asobasare* and the *aitassare* where the character for *sare* precedes the others but is read last; the ornamental use of the prefix *ai* before the verb in *aitassare*, a feature of this style; and the predominantly Chinese-derived vocabulary. Figure 2.5 is part of a letter from a Japanese national residing temporarily in France which was published in the next issue on 6 April, describing the Paris Exhibition. Although also couched in the epistolary style and sharing many of the features of the official notice – such as the reverse word-order of *kore ari*, and the ornamental use of *ai* before the verb *naru*, a particularly common combination – the letter gives a less stilted impression than the official notice, being a description of things actually seen and incorporating fewer long strings of characters.

Figure 2.5 Sōrōbun in a letter published in the *Chūgai Shimbun*, 6 April 1868

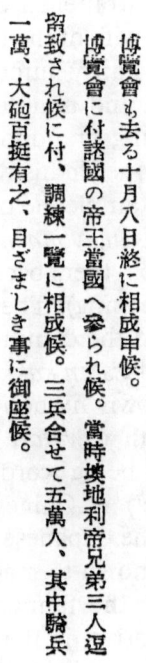

Source: Meiji Bunka Kenkyūkai (eds) *Meiji Bunka Zenshū* 4, *Shimbun-hen* (3rd edn), Tokyo: Nihon Hyōronsha, 1968, p. 261.
Note: For translation see Appendix.

In *The Teaching of Characters* (1873), Fukuzawa Yukichi denounced in scathing terms the high priority placed by scholars of

54 *Language and the Modern State*

Chinese on form to the detriment of content. He illustrated his point by including as a horrible example a *sōrōbun* letter of his own devising in which the script and style were deliberately made so scholarly and abstruse as to contrast ludicrously with the trivial subject matter (Figure 2.6). Fukuzawa deplored the current popularity of this hidebound approach to writing. It involved a practice, he said, which many young people wasted their time trying to emulate, unaware of its pitfalls, and it was for their edification that he had concocted his example. Fukuzawa believed that less is more in every case, be the content important or inconsequential; those who chose difficult characters were poor writers trying to fool their readers by camouflaging the deficiencies of their text with script. In conclusion, he demonstrated how the latter part of his letter could be rewritten, still in *sōrōbun*, but in a simpler fashion. The letter purports to be an appeal for help in finding a new job, however humble, from a person in straitened circumstances vexed by the discourteous attitude of the wife of the friend in whose house he has been a guest for some time. Fairly humdrum subject matter, but the text is replete with difficult and unnecessary characters often used only for the sake of creating grandiloquent compounds where a simpler word would have done. In his rewriting of the first sentence of the section quoted, for example, he omits the word *seisō* ('period of time') from the phrase *san, yonnen no seisō o sugi* ('spending three or four years'), which then becomes the more direct *san, yonnen o sugoshi* (same meaning). The resonant *jikon ni itatte wa* (at present) becomes instead the commonly-used *tadaima to narite wa*, and the Chinese-derived *isshin kakkei no hōhō mo naku* ('I have no means of making my own living') gives way to *dokushin no yowatari ni mo komari*, both *yowatari* ('one's living') and *komaru* ('be in need, hard pressed') being words of Japanese origin. While the word *dokushin* ('single') is Chinese derived, it had become thoroughly absorbed into the Japanese language through constant use and would have been known to readers. And so on to the end, replacing the abstruse with the familiar, the bombastic with the direct, the exotic with the native, in the process reducing the length of the passage by about ten per cent. While to the modern reader the end result still presents difficulties because of its total lack of punctuation and use of the now outdated conventions of *sōrōbun* previously discussed, such as the reverse word order in the final phrase, where the last three characters are read in the order 2–1–3, careful comparison with the original reveals just how many difficult

Figure 2.6 Two versions of a *sōrōbun* letter by Fukuzawa Yukichi, the first abstruse, the second rewritten for clarity

(a) original   (b) rewrite

右の次第にて徒に三、四年をすごし、唯今となりては獨身の世渡りにも困り、春以來友達の家に居候いたし候處、家內にあひそをつかされ、私も心の內には立腹いたし候得共、今更何處へと申し依りすがるべき先きもなく、途方に暮れ候次第、何卒憐れと被思召、よき役人の口へ御取持被下度、實は給金の多き方を望み候得共、差向の處、金の多少を可申場合に無之、門番にても小使にても不苦候間、幾重にも御世話奉願候。

右の次第にて徒に三、四年の星霜を過ぎ、目今に至ては一身活計の方法もなく、春來舊友の家に食客相成居候處、內實は同家の細君、客を待遇するに禮を失し、僕、竊に慣懣に堪へず。されども今去らんと欲して他に依頼す可き處もなく、進退惟谷の場合に陷り當惑の次第に候。何卒右の情實憮然と被思召、可然官途へ御推擧被下度、實は奏任以上を企望致し候得共、差向の處窮鳥枝を撰ぶに違あらざれば、抱關擊柝固より辭する所に非ず、等外出仕にても謹て拜命仕度候間、幾重にも御周旋奉願候也。

Source: Fukuzawa Yukichi '*Moji no Oshie*' (1873) in *Fukuzawa Yukichi Zenshū* 3, Tokyo: Iwanami Shoten, 1959, pp. 610–11.
Note: For translation see Appendix.

characters and abstruse words of Chinese origin have been replaced or omitted in order to render the form more appropriate to the prosaic content in a mode of expression more familiar to contemporary readers, or at least those of a certain standard of education.

Sōrōbun was to remain in widespread use throughout the Meiji Period and beyond, in fact until the end of World War Two, although it soon attracted criticism from early Meiji advocates of colloquial style, who wished to dispense with the practice of using specialized modes of expression in discrete spheres of literary endeavour and saw no virtue in retaining an archaic epistolary convention when what they proposed was an all-purpose idiom sufficiently versatile to perform all functions. Members of the Kana Club, for example, a group formed in 1883 primarily in the hope of replacing Chinese characters entirely with phonetic script but also having as a secondary goal the simplification of other aspects of written Japanese, attempted to employ colloquial style in place of *sōrōbun* in private correspondence, along the lines of a model letter distributed by Ōtsuki Fumihiko in 1887. The issue was not to be settled without a lengthy struggle, however, as part of the overall battle to modernize written Japanese, and the opening stages saw *sōrōbun* in a strong position in both public and private use.

WABUN

Wabun, or classical Japanese, was also known as *gabuntai* or *bibun*. Unlike Sino-Japanese or the epistolary style, it was predominantly Japanese in tone, originating in the Heian Period when the development of the phonetic *kana* scripts first made it easier to write down Japanese in a manner approximating the way in which it was spoken. Had the prestige of Chinese not proved too great, Japanese might then have replaced it as the language of government, histories, exposition, and official business. Chinese characters soon came to be known as men's characters and *kana* as women's writing, however, reflecting the corresponding status ascribed to the sexes in the power structure, so that the late tenth- and early eleventh-century literature of women aristocrats was written almost entirely in phonetic script. As these novels and diaries were phrased in the contemporary idiom of the court, there was no particularly marked disparity between narrative and dialogue; had this practice of writing in the vernacular (the variant of Court Japanese peculiar to one small non-representative section of the community, true, but that section literate and in a position of influence) continued and spread outside women's literature, there might have been no need for a language modernization movement eight centuries later.

Compared to the stiffer, more concise Chinese, *wabun* gave an impression of soft, melodious elegance and grace inherited from *waka* (Japanese poetry), preferring circumlocution and euphemism to bluntness and brevity. Tsubouchi Shōyō, discussing this style in *Shōsetsu Shinzui* (*The Essence of the Novel*, 1885–6) wrote:

> Vague and refined, it is naturally suited to euphemistic, elegant prose, but it lacks a needed air of animation and grandeur. It is like a weak, pliant willow tossed by the wind, or a court lady languishing behind a screen. As well as this seductive charm, *wabun* possesses serene cadences and a natural classical grace, and is therefore not appropriate for descriptions of violent emotions, bizarre behaviour, or debauchery, let alone savagery.[15]

When Murasaki Shikibu wrote *The Tale of Genji* (early eleventh century) in *wabun*, which to her was not classical but contemporary Japanese, these attributes made it well-suited to her descriptions of the leisurely meandering of aristocratic life through the seasons and the years. As time passed, and spoken Japanese began to develop a brisker aspect as a result of the influence of the rise of the warrior class to power, it was this graceful elegant language which was enshrined, in protest, as the matrix of pure written Japanese. Not 100 per cent pure, of course, given the pervasive dominance of Chinese, but nevertheless distinctively Japanese in its mode of expression. Where Chinese preferred shorter sentences, those of classical Japanese were lengthy and meandering. Chinese, of course, was written entirely in Chinese characters, Sino-Japanese predominantly so; in *wabun*, the phonetic *hiragana* script took first place. Honorifics were rare in Sino-Japanese, but abundant in *wabun*, in particular the auxiliary verbs *tamau* and *haberu*, both of which attached to the *ren'yōkei* (conjunctive form) of a verb to indicate humility and respect respectively. Whereas in Sino-Japanese, as we have seen, many verbs were of the type known as *sagyō henkaku dōshi*, a combination of a Chinese noun with the verb *suru*, these were seldom seen in classical Japanese, where many verbs were compounds of the *oyobikaneru* and *uchiwatasu* ('hand over') variety. The main terminations used were the auxiliary verbs *beshi* ('might, can, ought, must'), *tari* (present, past, or perfective), *nari* (copula), and *keri* (past, durative, or affirmative), as well as the final forms (*shūshikei*) of declinable words. Its vocabulary was drawn mainly from the traditional native Japanese lexicon known as *yamato kotoba,* as opposed to Chinese words. In addition, it utilized such characteristic rhetorical devices as *kakekotoba* (pivot words, as in the sentence *sami ni taiko ni ake murasaki no nari katachi* where the pivot word *ake* acts as the verb 'open' in the first half and the noun 'scarlet' in the second) and *makura kotoba* (stock epithets, such as *ashihiki no* prefixing *yama,* 'mountain', or *akanesasu,* 'ruddy' before *hi,* 'sun').

Figure 2.7 is an example of classical Japanese written in the early Meiji Period by Watanabe Yutaka in *Tsūzoku Isoppu Monogatari,* his 1873 translation of *Aesop's Fables.* As is typical of this style, the passage is one long, convoluted, unpunctuated sentence. In orthography, phonetic Japanese symbols outnumber Chinese characters. The four-character phrases common in Sino-Japanese are never

Figure 2.7 Wabun written in the early Meiji Period

むかし或池に群蛙すみて、何事もゆるやかに心まかせなりける
に、互に我慢の振舞まさりて、終に治まりがたくなりければ、ある
日蛙等相集り、天を仰で諸共に、「我輩を統御ゆべきよき主人をた
まはれ」と、願ひ訴へ申したり。天神是を聞き給ひ、盆もなき事な
りと笑つて、只一本の丸柱を天上より投下し給ふ。

Source: Watanabe Yutaka '*Tsūzoku Isoppu Monogatari*' *Meiji Bunka Zenshū V. 22, Honyaku Bungei-hen* (2nd edn), Tokyo: Nihon Hyōronsha, 1967, p. 50.
Note: For translation see Appendix.

found in *wabun*. Its vocabulary, including the Japanese glosses assigned to some Chinese characters, is predominantly made up of native Japanese words of the Heian Period and earlier, such as *morotomo ni* ('together'), *ike* ('pond'), and *nanigoto mo* ('everything'), all of which are also found in the *Tale of Genji* written over 800 years earlier. There are none of the *sagyō henkaku dōshi* found in Sino-Japanese, although the ornamental prefix *ai* before *atsumari* ('gather') is not typical of *wabun*.

Wabun had been originally written primarily by women. After the Heian Period, however, as the power of the court was eroded and Chinese studies began to lose their impetus as political manoeuvrings on the home front absorbed more attention, male aristocrats also began to experiment with writing Japanese modelled on that of Murasaki's former days of glory because of its elegance, a trend reflected not only in original composition but also in the Japanese readings assigned to Chinese characters at this time. This now distilling classical form of Japanese was passed down to later generations as the standard for later literature written in Japanese (as opposed to Chinese) both by women in private writings and by male scholars of the classics. *Wabun* works by Tokugawa Period women writers include *Tsuki no Yukuhe* (*The Home of the Moon*, Arakida Rei, 1732–1806), and *Jōkyō Nikki* (*Diary of a Journey to the Capital*, Nomura Bōtō, 1806–67)). While it was influenced over the years to a certain extent by the spoken language and by elements derived from Chinese, it nevertheless retained enough of an identifiably classical Japanese core to establish it still as a discrete literary convention in the early Meiji Period, when it was used by women in correspondence, men in correspondence to women or near relatives, court ladies in the sort of diaries which had been traditionally kept since Murasaki's day, and in some essays and translations.

A second stream of *wabun* which had appeared in the midTokugawa Period was *gikobun*, or neo-classical Japanese. Ordinary *wabun*, although based on Heian Period Japanese, had been influenced to a certain extent by the changing speech patterns of subsequent eras, so that while it retained classical syntax, its vocabulary was well scattered with contemporary words and phrases. Yano Fumio (1850–1931) noted in *Nihon Moji Buntai Shinron* (*A New Discourse on Japanese Orthography and Style*, 1886) that anyone could read *wabun*, as it was merely ordinary conversation with the postpositions and inflections changed to their classical forms. There were even occasions, he went on, when it was difficult to distinguish *wabun* from *kambun kundoku* written out in full. When this happened, the way to tell the difference was to try omitting all *kana* and reversing the order of some characters; if the passage so treated came out as passable Chinese, then the original must have been *kambun kundoku*. If, on the other hand, merely changing terminations to their modern equivalents resulted in something approximating normal conversation, then it was *wabun*.[16]

It was this divergence from strictly classical vocabulary that exponents of *gikobun* sought to remedy. Neo-classical Japanese was an attempt by adherents of a group of conservative classical scholars to return to pure Heian Period Japanese. Headed by Motoori Norinaga (1730–1801) and Kamo no Mabuchi (1697–1769), these scholars advocated a revival of true *wabun* as part of a protest against what they considered the Tokugawa regime's excessive emphasis on Chinese studies, hoping by reversion to the pure classical style to encourage the study of the Japanese classics among younger men. *Gikobun* writers modelled their style after that of Heian poetry, essays, diaries, and novels, avoiding Chinese words and striving to eradicate all vocabulary except that of the Heian Period; where they did use Chinese words, they assigned to them Japanese readings. They wrote almost entirely in *hiragana*, with as few Chinese characters as possible, as they considered Chinese characters an expression of the Chinese mind and therefore an inappropriate method of representing native Japanese words.

The *Bunshō Hyōgen Jiten* (*Dictionary of Literary Expression*) distinguishes four types of *gikobun*: the elegant, rhetorical prose studded with conventional epithets (*makura kotoba*), word plays (*kakekotoba*), and word associations (*engo*) found in the essays of Kamo no Mabuchi and others; a less highly ornamented version such as that used by Motoori Morinaga in his theoretical essays; descriptive writing somewhere in between the two, exemplified by Fujii Takanao (1764–1840) and Shimizu Hamaomi (1776–1824); and a variant used in correspondence. On the subject of nomenclature, this same dictionary further notes that *gikobun* was known also as *gabun* in the Tokugawa Period, while Hashimoto Shinkichi asserts that it was subsumed under the umbrella term of *wabun* during the Meiji Period.[17]

Exponents of neo-classical Japanese had in common with those of Sino-Japanese a shared disdain for the use in writing of the contemporary spoken language. Their devotion to classicism was not only a recoil from the Chinese influence but also a reaction against the use of the vernacular in the dialogue passages of popular literature. Taguchi Ukichi, in *Nippon Kaika no Seishitsu Yōyaku Aratamezaru Bekarazu* (*We must strive to change the Nature of Japanese Civilization*, 1884), mentioned the practice of *wabun* writers of deliberately selecting classical vocabulary items with the specific intention of distancing their text as far as possible from the colloquial. It was this policy of retrospection which contributed to the gradual disappearance of *gikobun* as the Meiji Period advanced and the search for a workable written language for the new Japan began to gain momentum. Its writers' insistence on classicisms, refusing even those Chinese words which had been thoroughly assimilated into Japanese, placed severe restrictions on its uses. It was not used very much in critical essays in the Meiji Period, but can be seen in literature, for example, in Mori Ōgai's story *Fumizukai* (*The Courier*, 1891) with its copious use of the honorific auxiliaries *mairasu* ('presume to'), *haberu* ('to humbly ...'), *owasu* ('deign to'), and *tamau* ('deign to').

WAKANKONKŌBUN

This style, as its name suggests, was a mixture of Chinese and Japanese elements, being essentially *kambun kundoku* with its severity toned down by an admixture of gentler classical Japanese and also of colloquialisms from the eleventh century on. Described in terms of orthography rather rather than derivation, it is also known as *kanji-kana-majiribun*. Kembō Gōki lists other designations used by Meiji Period scholars, among them *wakan-majiribun, wakanzatsubun, konkōbun,* and *wakankonwabun*; Konakamura Kiyonori coined the term *wakankonkōbun* in 1882, although he intended it to designate only Chinese which included Japanese words written entirely in Chinese characters, the kind of writing found in the eighth-century *Records of Ancient Matters*, rather than the *kanji-kana* mixture the term refers to today.[18]

Katakana-majiribun developed in the Heian Period after the evolution of the phonetic scripts, when Buddhist and Confucian scholars began to annotate texts using *katakana* to interpret Chinese in the *kundoku* method. While this was originally written as

Chinese, with many reverse marks to indicate Japanese word-order and tiny *katakana* diacritics to show syntax, it came with the passage of time to be written out in Japanese word-order with, eventually, full-size *katakana* interspersed among Chinese characters. In appearance it resembled *kambun kundoku*, but whereas that style strove for fidelity to the Chinese original, this offshoot developed a hybrid, more homegrown aspect with native Japanese expressions interwoven among Chinese words and phrases. Later, *hiragana-kanji* combinations were also seen.

The trend to linguistic acclimatization begun in this way in the Heian Period is exemplified by the style of the *Shōmonki*, earliest of the war chronicles, an AD 940 account of the Tenkei rebellion of Taira Masakado said to have been written by a Buddhist priest and described as the most hybrid of hybrid Chinese works. The Chinese bedrock of its text is seamed with small pockets of the spoken language of the times, mainly referring to new social relationships and customs in the east of the country and mirroring the language of the participants rather than that of observers in the distant capital. Gradually, with time, the gap between 'pure' and Japanized Chinese widened. While classical Chinese and Japanese retained their own discrete characteristics, striving for fidelity to their origins, *wakankonkōbun* developed from *hentai kambun* as a composite, always with Chinese as its nucleus but with a significant proportion of native elements, both classical and contemporary colloquial. It became a general-purpose style for men in those private areas which did not require formal Chinese, such as personal correspondence, and was not used by women, who lacked knowledge of its Chinese infrastructure, being restricted to writing only Japanese in phonetic script.[19]

The early twelfth-century *Konjaku Monogatari* (*Tales of Time Past*) offers an example of early *wakankonkōbun*; while its text was relatively rich in native elements, being a collection of fables originally narrated orally, the blending of the diverse elements was at this time still somewhat uneven, not yet having achieved the smoothness of later eras. The style of *Konjaku Monogatari* was somewhere between *hentai kambun* and the later *wakankonkōbun* – its *okurigana* (*kana* added to Chinese characters to show their Japanese inflections) were incomplete, and *kanji* readings were shown only sketchily. It was not until the war chronicles of the Kamakura and Muromachi Periods that the patchiness of earlier attempts was overcome in a successful, polished joining of the strands. Given that it was mainly men who used this style, its masculine tone and male colloquialisms outweighed the softer, more feminine aspect of its classical Japanese component, and made it well suited to the descriptions of battle scenes and military affairs. Japanese scholars uniformly assert its apotheosis to be the *Heike Monogatari* (*Tales of the Heike*), a kind of narrative poem detailing the glories and eventual fall of the Heike clan, authorship and precise date unknown but thought to have been composed somewhere in the mid-thirteenth century. Other war chronicles of this period written in this style include the *Taiheiki* (*Record of the Great Peace*, mid-fourteenth century).

The proportion of classical and colloquial Japanese elements to Chinese varied with the author, some early works such as the *Eiga Monogatari* (*Tales of Splendour*, late eleventh century) displaying a pronounced Japanese influence, later war chronicles more markedly Chinese. Such collections of essays as *Tsurezuregusa* (*Reflections in Idleness*, c.1330), too, have a higher proportion of Japanese elements than the military tales, while there are also variations in the blend between individual war chronicles. Ekoyama Tsuneaki, comparing *Tales of the Heike* with the later *Record of the Great Peace*, points out that Chinese words and expressions occur more frequently in the latter than the former, which contains more Japanese Within the *Tales of the Heike* itself, the scene often determines the mix, with battle scenes strongly Chinese in tone and chapters such as *Kogō* (dealing with doomed love at Court) strongly Japanese Similar internal shifts occur within the *Record of the Great Peace*, but on balance it contains a greater amount of Chinese, incorporating ornate rhetoric in a repetitious manner not found to any great extent in the *Tales of the Heike*.[20]

The elements of contemporary speech found in the war chronicles formed an integral part of the mix rather than remaining peripheral and being used for novelty value as in early works such as the *Shōmonki*, and this was due in large part to the fact that the war chronicles, unlike earlier *monogatari* and *setsuwa* (narratives) which were read privately by aristocrats, were recited to a much wider audience (many of whom were illiterate) of those who had been active in carving out the events of the recent past.[21]

The composite style of the *Tales of the Heike*, which achieved a polished melding and blending of the three elements, became in subsequent eras the major general-purpose literary style outside those spheres already described where the use of formal Chinese and classical Japanese were indicated. It was used in the texts of Buddhist sermons, plays, fairytales, *jōruri* (ballad-dramas), *ukiyozōshi* (a type of Tokugawa Period genre fiction), *haibun* (prose poems), and in Tokugawa Period essays by scholars and literati (except for those which were distinctly *kambun* or *gikobun*). Although its grammar remained that of a past age and its nucleus was Chinese, its more familiar aspect made it popular with literate townsmen, of whom there were many in the Tokugawa Period; many Chinese words had been assimilated into everyday Japanese, and the literate were familiar with the style of the Japanese classics. *Kambun* itself was both too difficult and too formal for describing the commonplace, while *wabun*, though simpler, was too flowery and rambling. The mixture of Chinese, Japanese and colloquial in *wakankonkōbun* was therefore both easier to understand than Chinese or *gikobun* and more appropriate as a general-purpose style.

The appeal of this style for the commoner was further enhanced by its use in the narrative passages of popular literature, supplemented by dialogue written in a style approximating the spoken language. In certain genres, even, narrative was kept to a minimum by substituting illustrations or recounting most of the story in dialogue. When *wakankonkōbun* narrative was combined with colloquial dialogue in this way, the result was known as *gazoku setchūbun*,[22] a blend of elegant narrative with everyday dialogue – in essence *wakankonkōbun* but with a stronger colloquial element.

There are various types of *gazoku setchūbun* to be found in Tokugawa Period genre fiction: the *yomihon* (historical novel) variant, with no particularly striking contrast between dialogue and narrative; the *kusazōshi* (picture book) type, where dialogue was more markedly colloquial; the humorous *kokkeibon* style, with dialogue a faithful reproduction of speech; and the *ninjōbon* (love story) variant, somewhere in between the first two and the third. In all types, the *ga* (elegance) of the narrative passages refers to a blend of classical Japanese and Chinese with a liberal admixture of contemporary vocabulary; the differentiating factor is the proportion of *zoku* (colloquial) in the dialogue

The most polished exponent of *gazoku setchūbun* is generally held to be Ihara Saikaku (1642–93), whose novels of contemporary manners dealt with the twin themes of love and money. Saikaku's dialogue was not by any means unreservedly colloquial; while he adopted some elements of contemporary speech to give a feeling of freshness and vitality, he did not go so far as to attempt full-scale faithful reproduction, with the result that there is often no really noticeable difference between narrative and dialogue and it can sometimes be difficult to tell where one ends and the other begins, given the lack of punctuation of the times. On the other hand, this means that where differences do become obvious, they are not jarring, a criticism sometimes levelled at this manner of writing. Saikaku took an intermediate path between speech and writing in an effort to decrease the gap dividing them and hence avoid displeasing contrasts. At the other end of the spectrum outlined above were works of the *kokkeibon* genre such as Jippensha Ikku's *Tōkaidōchū Hizakurige* (*By Shanks' Pony Along the Tokaido*, 1802–9) which was almost entirely colloquial, with country dialects as well as rough Edo speech incorporated in the dialogue. Figure 2.8 is an example of Saikaku's style, taken from *Kōshoku Ichidai Otoko*

Figure 2.8 A passage from Ihara Saikaku

「今までしらぬ事なり。さもあるべし」と、死人を見れば我が尋ぬる女、「これは」としがみ付き、「かかるうきめにあふ事、いかなる因果のまはりけるぞ。その時連れてのかずばさもなきを、これ皆我がなす業」と、泪にくれて身もだえする。不思議やこの女、両の眼を見ひらき笑ひ顔して、間もなく父本のごとくなりぬ。「二十九までの一期、何おもひ残さじ」と自害をするを、二人の者色々押しとどめて帰る。分別所なり。

Source: Ihara Saikaku '*Kōshoku Ichidai Otoko*' from *Koten Bungaku Zenshū, Ihara Saikakushū* 1, Tokyo: Shōgakukan Inc., 1971, p. 183.
Note: For translation see Appendix.

66 Language and the Modern State

(*The Life of an Amorous Man*, 1682). There is no appreciable difference between the narrative and the dialogue. In the latter the *nari* and *beshi* terminations, the adverb *samo* ('so'), the interrogative pronominal *ikanaru* ('what ...?'), the emphatic final *zo*, and the combination of the negative *zu* with the connective *ba* are all typical of classical Japanese; examples of their use may be found in the *Collection of Ten Thousand Leaves* and in Heian Period court romances. Figure 2.9, on the other hand, is taken from Ikku's *By Shanks' Pony along the Tokaido*, and the homespun character of its

Figure 2.9 A passage from Jippensha Ikku

一軒は片側に茶店軒をならべ、いづれも座敷二階造、欄干つきの廊下桟などわたして、浪うちぎはの景色いたつてよし。茶屋の女 中かどに立て
「おやすみなさいやアせ。あつたかな冷飯もございやアす。煮たての肴のさめたのもございやアす。そばのふといのをあがりやアせ。うどんのおつきなのもございやアす。お休なさいやアせ。

Source: Jippensha Ikku '*Tōkaidōchū Hizakurige*' ('*By Shanks' Pony along the Tokaido*') *Nihon Koten Zensho* 36 (4th edn), Tokyo: Asahi Shimbunsha, 1964, p. 37.
Note: For translation see Appendix.

dialogue is in startling contrast to that of the refined Saikaku piece. The colloquial verb *gozaiyaasu* ('we have') gives a very different tone from Saikaku's elegant *nari* (copula) and *mawarikeru* ('has turned'), while dialectisms such as *attakana* ('warm') also underline the contrast.

Hirata Tomoko, examining the various Meiji styles,[23] analyses Tsubouchi Shōyō's *Shumpū Jōwa* (*The Spring Breeze Love Story*, 1880) and Miyajima Shunshō's *Teremaku Kuwafuku Monogatari* (1879) as examples of *wakankonkōbun*. Her findings are summarized as follows. Sino-Japanese sentences ended in the *shūshikei* (conclusive form) of declinable words and such characteristic auxiliary verbs as *beshi* (supposition), *nari* (report) and *zu* (negative). Classical Japanese terminations included such tense-bearing auxiliary verbs as the perfective *keri* and *tari*, as well as *beshi* and *nari*. *Wakankonkōbun* combined the two. Its vocabulary was a combination of Chinese-derived words with colloquial Japanese; while it contained relatively few classical Japanese words, Japanese glosses were assigned to many Chinese words, a practice which, while it does also occur elsewhere, is particularly characteristic of this style. The Chinese characters for 'prosperity', for example, usually pronounced in Japanese as *eiga*, might be glossed as *tokimeki*, 'castle town' (*tōjō*) as *miyako*. Adverbs were drawn both from classical Japanese (*ge ni* [really], *hitoe ni* [earnestly]) and from Sino-Japanese (*aete* [boldly], *imada* [till now, yet]), with the former outnumbering the latter. Adjectives, on the other hand, show a much higher proportion of *kambun*-type ... *taru* or ... *to* usage than *wabun* expressions. The Sino-Japanese *kakari musubi*[24] *nan*, *zo* and *ya* are used with the classical Japanese sentence-final interjection *kashi* and *kana*. The *kakujoshi* (case indicator) *no* is used, as in *wabun*, to indicate the subject of a modifying clause or of a suppositional clause. Substantives are often omitted. Rhetorical devices included the pivot words and stock epithets of classical Japanese, and the couplets, grandiose chapter headings, and Chinese idioms of Sino-Japanese.

Tsubouchi Shōyō, writing in 1886 on the style of the modern novel, advocated the use of *gazoku setchūbun*, dividing it into two sub-categories: the *yomihon* variant, where classical words account for 70 to 80 per cent of the whole in description and 50 to 60 per cent in dialogue, and the *kusazōshi* type, with a higher proportion of colloquial vocabulary than Chinese. The former he believed to be most appropriate in historical novels, where descriptions of different ranks could be managed by merely adjusting the proportion of classical to colloquial without the danger of a clash between narrative and dialogue. The latter should be reserved for novels dealing with modern life, to which a higher proportion of colloquial was appropriate. Tsubouchi used the analogy of diluting wine with water to warn of the pitfalls in not blending the elements smoothly and skilfully in a manner appropriate to the subject matter:

> Adjusting the proportion of classical to colloquial is like mixing wine with water. It is difficult for a blindfolded person pouring wine to judge the exact amount, because he pours it little by little for fear of overfilling the cup. If he hurries, the wine might overflow and stain the matting. Not to pour enough is gauche, of course; and stains on the matting are unsightly. When water is added to the wine, the quantities are the important thing – they should be adjusted so that the flavour of the wine is not lost. Wine offered to a non-drinker should be well-watered; to a drinking man, much less so. The proportions, however, are entirely up to the author, who needs no instruction from anyone else. He should taste and test it himself, using his own discretion to decide what amounts make the best mix. The wine is classical vocabulary, the water colloquial. Blending them together in one style is exactly like mixing wine and water, an idea which should appeal to devotees of the combination style.[25]

Gazoku setchūbun was perpetuated in the few original novels written during the first ten years of the Meiji Period. Figure 2.10 is an example from *Seiyōdōchū Hizakurige* (*By Shanks' Pony Through the West*, 1870–76), a parody by *gesaku* writer Kanagaki Robun on Ikku's earlier epic of the Tokaido. *Gesaku* serials in this style were also published a few years later in popular newspapers and magazines, the most prominent authors being Robun, Takabatake Ransen, and Somesaki Nobufusa. Several western novels were translated into *gazoku setchūbun* style; *Ōshū Jōfu Gumpō Kiwa*, an 1882 translation of some stories from *The Decameron* by Ōkubo Kanzaburō, and *Rokoku Kibun Kashin Chōshiroku* (1883), a translation by Takasu Jisuke of Pushkin's *Captain's Daughter*, are examples of translations published in *ninjōbon* form, while *The Spring Breeze Love Story* (1880), Tsubouchi Shōyō's translation of Scott's *Bride of Lammermoor*, was rendered in the popular *yomihon* style.

Figure 2.10 *Gazoku setchūbun* of the early Meiji Period

支那の上海シャンハイ共に亦たを出帆して英領なる香港まで舩路四日にて着す
乍麼香港ハ支那の東南の方にある孤嶋なり長サ五里巾三里岩山のみ
にて草木少く平地なし元來支那の領地なりしが近世英吉利領となりしよ
り英人追々住居を移し交易場を開き寺院を建立学問所を設けて人の数も
次第に増し繁昌の港となれり

Source: Kanagaki Robun '*Seiyōdōchū Hizakurige*' *Meiji Bungaku Zenshū V. 1, Meiji Kaikaki Bungakushū* 1, Tokyo: Chikuma Shobō, 1966, p. 25.
Note: For translation see Appendix.

There were other literary styles in use in certain discrete areas in the Meiji Period, such as the *noritobun* of Shinto ritual prayers and the *semmyōbun* of Imperial proclamations, both of which sprang from early offshoots of *kambun*. In general, however, literary styles belonged somewhere within the four varieties described above.

The example in Figure 2.9 from Ikku's work gives some idea of one of the major drawbacks of using the colloquial in writing as perceived by educated men: its often strident vulgarity by comparison with the elegance of classical forms. This loomed large in the minds of those who believed, as many did in the early stages of the language modernization movement, that advocates of colloquial style were in favour of the unexpurgated reproduction of speech rather than a polished representation based on, but naturally not a verbatim transcript of, colloquial grammar and vocabulary. Other criticisms added to this one were that it was much more long-winded than literary styles, a valid criticism when drawing comparisons with the conciseness of Sino-Japanese, but not so easily substantiated in comparison with *wabun*.

Postpositions were different in the spoken language, *de* ('at, in, by') replacing the literary *nite*, for example, and *kara* ('from') the literary *yori*. Adjectival nominatives attached to a following noun with *na* rather than *naru*; sentences often ended with the interjectional particles *sa* ('indeed') and *ne* ('isn't it'). Literary conjunctions such as *shikaru ni* and *saredo* ('however') were replaced by colloquial equivalents, in this case *suru to* and *tokoro ga*. The major difference between the spoken and written languages, however, apart from vocabulary, was in verb forms, particularly in the forms of the copula each used. As a result of pre-Meiji social stratifications there were several different forms of the copula, each identifying its user in terms of class and also indicating varying degrees of respect or humility. Those most commonly used when the colloquial appeared in writing during the Tokugawa Period were *de gozaru*, *de gozarimasu*, *de arimasu*, *desu*, *de aru* and *da*.

De gozaru was used fairly widely in the first half of the Tokugawa Period, by women as well as men, becoming restricted to samurai, doctors and scholars only in the latter half of the period. It originated when the Chinese characters

御座

were adopted as a phonetic representation of the Japanese word *ohashimasu* (respectful form of the verbs 'to be, come, go') after the manner of *man'yōgana*. Later, during the Kamakura Period, they came to be rendered by their Chinese readings as *goza*. To this was added *aru*, resulting in *goza-aru*, which in time was shortened to *gozaru* and used as a polite auxiliary verb. *De gozaru* was the polite form of *de aru*. As we shall see, *de gozaru* was used in the published collections of transcripts of lectures given by the great classical scholar Hirata Atsutane, which appeared in 1811. Given that this termination was that used by the upper class, it was only to be expected that it was the first to appear in Meiji Period attempts at colloquial style by those few educated men bent on language reform. The *de gozaru* style (where the word 'style' here denotes the characteristic form of the copula) was recommended by Maejima Hisoka in his 1866 call for style reform, and was used consistently in enlightenment works in the first decade of Meiji.[26]

Goza(r)imasu and *de goza(r)imasu* were used as polite forms by all classes, high-class merchants using them respectfully to their customers. *Goza(r)imasu* was used in transcripts of Shingaku sermons in the Tokugawa Period. *Gozaru* was the major respect verb of the Muromachi-Tokugawa Periods. At the end of the Muromachi Period, the auxiliary *masu* was added to form *gozarimasu*. Like *gozaru* it was widely used as the polite form of 'to go', 'to come' and 'to be'. *Gozarimasu* was used more widely than *gozaru*, but the shortened form *gozaimasu* did not appear until later in the Tokugawa Period, with *gozaimasu* being generally considered the more polite of the two.

De arimasu appeared often in Tokugawa Period popular literature, in particular in the works of Tamenaga Shunsui. Specifically, it was used by the women of the pleasure quarters – geisha, tea-house women, hairdressers, and courtesans. It was a polite form of *de aru*, although the latter was not restricted in geographical use, being employed widely outside the red light districts by men and women of all ranks. *De arimasu* was confined to this section of the community because *de gozaimasu* was already widespread among the middle and upper classes; when there arose a need for a polite expression midway between *de gozaimasu* and the plain *da* and *de aru*, *de arimasu* appeared among a certain group of those who, while not belonging to the *demi-monde*, had come down in the world to a point not far above it. It did not spread beyond this because it was eclipsed by the rapid development elsewhere of the copula *desu*. There are various theories concerning the origins of *de arimasu*. The *Kōgohō Bekki* (*Supplementary Grammar of the Spoken Language*), published in 1917 by the National Language Research Council, describes it as a new word coined by provincial *samurai* arriving in the capital at the time of the Restoration. It has also been said to be a composite of *de aru* and *masu* created especially for use in Meiji Period lectures. Nakamura Michio, however, convincingly refutes this claim, giving examples from much earlier genre fiction to substantiate his claim that it was used in the pleasure quarters of Edo.[27] When scholars of the west began giving public lectures on topical subjects in the 1870s, *de arimasu* became their characteristic form of the copula, possibly in an attempt to counteract the weakening of effect produced by the lowering of the voice at the end of the sentence.[28]

Desu too, was used by the women of the pleasure quarters, in particular by tea-house women, but was also widespread among ordinary townspeople in the late Tokugawa Period. A study of the dialogue passages of three *ninjōbon* written between 1860 and 1866 shows that it was used in plain speech (as opposed to the respectful *de gozaimasu*) by lower-rank *samurai* and wealthy merchants, among others.[29] Between the late years of the Tokugawa Period and the early years of Meiji, it came to be used as a simple polite termination in conversation between peers.

De aru developed from the Kamakura Period *nite ari*, which gradually became *nite aru* and then *de aru*. It can be seen in medieval *shōmono*. Because it imparted an air of formality, however, it was not widely used until the end of the Tokugawa Period, when it became popular in textbooks on foreign languages. Being a convenient equivalent for the Dutch *zijn* or the English *be*, it was also used in translations of reading primers, science books and histories. Only one of the enlightenment writers of the 1870s chose to adopt it, in the text of a translation of a German science primer, the others preferring *de gozaru*.[30]

Da originated as a contraction of *de aru*. It was not normally used in conversation in Kyoto, the capital, during the Tokugawa Period; its appearance in literature written in Kyoto indicated that the speaker was a provincial from the east. What was used in the Kyoto area was the other contraction of *de aru*, *ja*. *Da* was often found, however, in Buddhist *shōmono* connected with the *Sōtō* school of Zen, where it was used consistently as a copula. Following the shift in geographical focus of popular literature from Kyoto to Edo as the culture of that city developed, the *da* of Edo appeared frequently in dialogue passages of genre novels. *Da* was accepted as the standard plain form of Tokyo speech after the Meiji Restoration.

The written language of public life at the beginning of Japan's modern period, then, was characterized by the four variants described in this chapter. Sino-Japanese and the epistolary style were not only derived from a foreign language, they adhered for the most part to the grammar and lexicon of earlier stages of language development. Classical Japanese, although a written form of the Japanese language itself and thus not burdened with the handicap of exoticism, was likewise divorced from the contemporary spoken language by its emphasis on the literary forms of the past. *Wakankonkōbun*, though an attempt at synthesizing the Japanese and Chinese traditions and probably the least difficult in terms of lexicon, was yet marked as a thing apart from the spoken language by its archaic syntax and idiom. To understand these classical forms required years of training. The difficulties were compounded by a system of orthographic conventions which required rationalization in order to reduce to manageable terms the number and form of characters required for daily life and to simplify the manner in which a text was laid out to facilitate comprehension of its contents. Much was to be gained by a change to a colloquial style based on the contemporary spoken language; but that too involved problems, both the concrete problems of standardization and selection of a copular form and the less easily defined but nevertheless equally substantial stumbing block of entrenched critical attitudes towards what constituted proper writing.

It was against this background of diversity and of both real and perceived advantages and disadvantages which attached to the different varieties of writing that the early stirrings of change made themselves felt. In the following chapter, we shall examine two areas where the need to dispense with this multiplicity of élitist literary conventions and find a way to deal with the inherent defects of the colloquial were about to become particularly important.

3 Early stirrings: Education and the press

In the early stages of the language modernization movement, or *gembun'itchi*[1] movement as it was known in Japan, two of the major areas in which the language issue emerged as important were education and the press. Both formal education on a national scale and newspapers and journals were at that time new to Japan, although as we shall see there had been earlier attempts at certain kinds of popular education. With the coming of the Meiji Period, however, and the emergence of a group known as the Enlightenment scholars, dedicated to the dissemination of the knowledge and ideas they considered essential for Japan's survival, popular education assumed a new importance and was carried out on a much wider scale. It was not long before some of those concerned with education in all its forms and the printed media began to realize the hindrance written Japanese posed to the accelerated spread of information, and by extension, the value of language reform in certain key areas.

The following discussion of early moves towards stylistic reform in the areas of popular education, formal education, and the press is divided into two stages: pre-1877 and post-1877. The break comes approximately then because what early progress had been made in both theory and practice towards the realization of *gembun'itchi* was halted at that point for several years, in part because of repressive government measures against the civil rights movement, which had used colloquial-style prose as a valuable aid in propagandizing the masses.[2]

What use there had been of the grammar of the spoken language in published writing in the late Tokugawa Period had occurred mainly in the areas of popular literature and certain categories of works intended for either religious or secular instruction. We have

Early stirrings: Education and the press 75

already seen in Chapter 2 that popular novelists used the speech of the common man, to a greater or lesser extent depending on the author, in the dialogue passages of their works for reasons in which profit figured equally with verisimilitude.

The use of colloquial style in religious texts dates back to the *shōmono* of the Muromachi Period, verbatim notes of lectures on the Chinese classics and Buddhist scriptures printed using woodblocks by priests of the five great temples of the Rinzai sect in both Kamakura and Kyoto. Later, in the Tokugawa Period, the sermons of the Shingaku movement, a popular religious movement founded by Ishida Baigan (1685–1744) in an attempt to synthesize the precepts of Shinto, Buddhism, and Confucianism and present them to commoners using simple language and familiar allegories, were published in a style that faithfully reproduced the speech of the orator. The sermons of Nakazawa Dōni (1725–1803), for example, were published in a conversational *ja*-copula style as *Dōni Ō Dōwa* (*The Sermons of Dōwa*, 1794–1824), while those of Shibata Kyūō (1783–1837) incorporated both the *ja* and *de gozarimasu* terminations. Figure 3.1 shows a section of one of Kyūō's sermons, recorded by Ko no Takesuke.

In 1811, there was published a series of *kōshakuhon* (lecture books) based on talks given by Hirata Atsutane (1776–1843), Shinto theologian, scholar of the Japanese classics, and leader of the Shinto Restoration movement aimed at purging Shinto of what Hirata regarded as deleterious Buddhist and Confucian influences. Hirata made national lecture tours of Shinto shrines, winning a following among farmers and village officials with his lectures on *kodō*, the ancient way. The lecture books, like the Shingaku readers, were verbatim transcripts of his discourses, recorded by his followers in the *de gozaru* style in which they were delivered. These books, among them *Kodō Tai-i* (*Outline of the Ancient Way*), *Zoku Shintō Tai-i* (*A Further Outline of Shinto*) and *Butsudō Tai-i* (*Outline of Buddhism*), covered a wide variety of topics, from Shinto and Buddhism to the ancient way and Sinology. They opened up for discussion by the public at large, by virtue of their familiar language, areas which had previously been considered the province of scholars; Hirata believed that the ancient learning should be the bedrock of the spiritual life of the entire nation.[3] If one compares the original text of *Outline of the Ancient Way* with a modern rendering (Figure 3.2), one finds very little difference apart from modernized orthography, replacement of the *de gozaru* copula of

Figure 3.1 Colloquial style in a recorded sermon of Shibata Kyūō

人の親の心は闇にあらねども子を思ふ道に迷ひぬるかな
かの親たち夫婦の前に勘當の願書がまはつてくると、母親は大聲を擧げて泣出す。爺親は齒もなきはぐきをくひしばつて、さし俯いてゐらるゝ。やがてくもつた聲で、「おばゝ印形を取つてござれ」母親は返事も出でかね、泣く〲籠笥のひき出から、革財布に入つた印形を、爺親のまへに罝くと、彼のら息子は、雨戸のそとから息をつめて伺うてゐる。其のうちにごて〲と財布の紐をとき、印形をとり出し、肉をつけて、既に制を押うとするとき、母親がその手にすがつて、「先ッ待て下され」といふ。

Source: Shibata Kyūō '*Kyūō Dōwa*', *Yūhōdō Bunko* series 2, 18, Tokyo: Yūhōdō Shoten, 1921, p. 21.
Note: For translation see Appendix.

Hirata's time with *de arimasu*, and other minor grammatical and lexical updating (e.g. *tarikudattaru mono*, 'the dangling thing', becomes *taresagatta mono, – to mo mōshitaru ga*, 'it was said', becomes *to mo iimashita ga, – no gotoku* 'like', becomes *no yō ni*).

Figure 3.2 A section of the original text of Hirata Atsutane's *Kodō Tai-i* (*Outline of the Ancient Way*) and its modern rendering

(a) original　　　　　(b) modern

(a) 抑先日の演説に申したる通り、世の始めかの大虚空の中に漂つたる一つの物より、葦芽の如く萌上つて天と成り、其の天の根と爲つてゐる。一つの物の底にも、又一つの物が垂下り成り、それに國之常立神と、豐斟野神とがおできなされたでござる。其の垂下つたる物を、根國とも、根堅洲國とも申したるが、是れが後に斷離れて、今まのあたり見奉る月と成つたでござる。

(b) さて先日の演説に申したとおり、世の初め、大空に漂う一つの物から、葦の芽のように萌えあがって天ができ、その天の根となっている一つの物の底にもまたもう一つの物がたれさがり、そこに国之常立神と豊斟野神とがお生まれになった。そのたれさがった物を根国とも根堅洲国ともいいましたが、これが後に切り離れて、今、目のあたりに見ている月となったのであります。

Source: (original) Hirata Atsutane 'Kodō Tai-i', Yūhōdō Bunko series 2, 14, Tokyo: Yūhōdō Shoten, p. 433.
(modern version) 'Kodō Tai-i', Nihon no Meichō 24 (ed. Sagara Susumu), Tokyo: Chūō Kōronsha, 1972, p. 119.
Note: For translation see Appendix.

The original reads almost as easily as the modern version, needing none of the exegis required by contemporary Sino-Japanese texts.

These early instances of the use of colloquial style resulted from purely pragmatic motives of profit (in the case of novelists concerned with circulation) and instruction, and were intended to benefit only the common people rather than society at large. Nor was colloquial style used consistently in these fields: as we have already seen, the degree of colloquial grammar even in the dialogue passages of novels varied considerably, with narrative sections written in *wakankonkōbun*, while only the transcripts of Hirata's lectures were published in colloquial style, he himself continuing to write in elegant classical Japanese. While the fact of its presence in these works indicates an awareness of its virtue as a means of communicating ideas and entertainment to those not educated beyond basic literacy, it was at this stage very much regarded by educated men as an expedient, a means to an end, and not as desirable in itself as an all-purpose style.

Several Japanese scholars of the west in the latter half of the Tokugawa Period commented on the similarity between written Dutch and English and the spoken language of these countries, among them Ōtsuki Gentaku, who remarked that the colloquial style he observed in Dutch books possessed the twin virtues of allowing detailed recording of facts and being easy to understand, and Ōba Sessai, who postulated a contributory relationship between the colloquial style of European languages and the development of western learning. While comments such as these were at first no more than observations upon a foreign custom, the notion of applying the same technique to the Japanese language, albeit in the restricted area of foreign language primers, was not long in coming. As interest in western studies increased in the first half of the nineteenth century and a growing number of scholars undertook the study of the Dutch language, there appeared a number of dictionaries and grammars which presented Japanese equivalents in their simple conversational form.

The first Japanese-Dutch dictionary compiled by a Japanese was interpreter Baba Sajūrō's *Rango Yakusen* (1807), which rejected esoteric vocabulary choices in favour of the common and used the grammar of the spoken language in sentence examples. This approach was also adopted by Hendrik Doeff (1777–1835), head of the Dutch trading post on the island of Deshima in Nagasaki Harbour, in *Zūfu Haruma* (pre-1816), a Dutch-Japanese dictionary compiled by Doeff and the Nagasaki interpreters. Its twin prefaces – one by Doeff, one by the Japanese – announced that the colloquial had been deliberately chosen in preference to a more elegant style in order not to obscure the meaning of the Dutch, a revealing aside on the inadequacies of formal written Japanese in this regard. Later, a number of grammar books also appeared using conversational Japanese examples, among them *Yaku Oranda Bungo* (*Dutch Grammar*, Ōba Sessai, 1855–57) and *Oranda Bunten Yakugosen Shohen* (*A Short Dutch Grammar*, Tōda Shōan, 1856).

The English grammars published following the discovery that that language was to prove more useful than Dutch continued the trend, some stating baldly, as did Shioda Kōhachi in his preface to *Wa-ei Shōko Taiwashū* (*Japanese-English Commerical Conversation*, 1857), that they had used the colloquial for simplicity. Foreigners seeking to learn Japanese would naturally seek to learn the spoken language first, so that from that point of view any textbook would use it as a matter of course. For Japanese seeking to learn other languages, however, the departure from the normal canons of written Japanese by adopting colloquial style in order to ensure clarity was a significant admission of the benefits to be gained thereby, at a time when ease and speed of comprehension was important to the national interest.

The grammars were followed by colloquial translations of English readers, among them *Eigaku Hikkei*, an 1872 translation by Yamada Masuyasu of Webster's *Spelling Book*. As the desire for knowledge of western technology spread in the early Meiji Period, these were joined by colloquial translations of English natural science textbooks, such as *Sōyaku Rigaku Shoho*, an 1870 rendering by Nakamura Jun'ichirō of Mary Swift's *First Lesson on Natural Philosophy*. Again, the connection was made by the translators between using the grammar of the spoken language to make the information contained in the books easily available to readers, Gotō Tatsuzō relating in the preface to *Kummō: Kyūri Mondō* (*Beginners' Science: Questions and Answers*, 1872) that he had used the colloquial and avoided classical Japanese or Chinese words wherever possible so that women and children could understand.[4] These translations often attempted a word-for-word correspondence which meant that, given the different structures of the two languages, the Japanese version was sometimes not easy to follow; but the blame here could at least not be laid at the door of the archaic nature of the written Japanese, the difficulty stemming rather from the literal rendering of English constructions not found in Japanese.

These early manifestations of the awareness of the benefits of colloquial style in instruction should not be under-valued for their evident pragmatism. They were recognition on a small scale of the practical problem facing Japan which became one of the bases for the later movement to modernize the written language: the need to educate the nation in a hurry. A simple style would have enormous practical value for education, and it was this realization which prompted the first call for a general reform of the written language by Maejima Hisoka, a government translator at the Institute of Foreign Learning who later became the first Postmaster-General. Maejima presented to the Shogun Yoshinobu in 1866 a petition entitled *Kanji Gohaishi no Gi* (*Proposal for the Abolition of Chinese Characters*), calling for the replacing of Chinese characters with phonetic script and the adoption of simpler grammar in writing.

Maejima's basic premise was that the path to strong nationhood lay in the education of the populace as a whole. His submission began with a declaration to this effect: 'The sum and substance of a nation is the education of its people'.[5] Once the Japanese people were able to learn for themselves about conditions abroad, they would soon realize that they themselves were inferior to no-one, and would develop the national pride and self-esteem so important to Japan's development and prosperity. In Maejima's view, script and style reform were necessary prerequisites for effective teaching. In order to cope with the confusion attendant upon the phasing out of Chinese characters, he suggested, scholars should apply themselves to the task of compiling new grammars and dictionaries, lay down clear rules regarding syntax, and adopt the practice of punctuating texts. As part of the process, he advocated employing the grammar of the spoken language in writing, proposing naturally enough that the copula be the *tsukamatsuru* and *gozaru* of his own *samurai* class rather than forms more widely used among the common people.

That a shogunate employee should present such a petition at a time when the use of Sino-Japanese was actively encouraged by the government indicates the depth of Maejima's concern for his country and his conviction on this issue. He himself, having studied both Dutch and English, had observed first-hand the benefits of a colloquial style in those languages. He made no attempt to illustrate his theory in the text of his petition, which was couched, as was the practice with such documents addressed to the Shogun, in ornate and complicated *sōrōbun*. Two other petitions followed the first: *Kokubun Kyōiku no Gi ni tsuki Kengi* (*Petition concerning a Proposal for Japanese Language Education*) in 1869, presented to the new government with the supplements *Kokubun Kyōiku Shikō no Hōhō* (*How to Implement Japanese Language Education*) and *Haikanji Shikensho* (*A Personal View on the Abolition of Chinese Characters*), and *Gakusei Goshikō ni sakidachi Kokuji Kairyō Ainaritaki Hiken Naishinsho* (*A Report on My Humble Opinion that Reform of our Written Language should Precede the Establishment of an Education System*), presented to Iwakura Tomomi, then vice-president of the Council of State. While the reform of syntax took second place in all three petitions to that of orthography, Maejima stressed in both *Proposal for the Abolition of Chinese Characters* and *How to Implement Japanese Language Education* that writing must henceforth discard its traditional cloak of antiquity and concentrate on the modern colloquial.

Not surprisingly given the circumstances, the petitions evoked no official response, and were not heard of by the general public until they were published much later in 1899 by Maejima and Konishi Nobuhachi. Despite their lack of immediate effect, however, they are significant in the history of the modernization of written Japanese in that they were the first acknowledgement by an educated member of the upper class of the important facilitatory role to be played by a democratic written language in the national effort by its smoothing of the education process. While Maejima's ideas were premature in the social and political context of the time, he nevertheless planted a seed which would germinate some years thence and end in the ultimate coming to fruition of his vision; the establishment in 1899 of the government's Kokugo Chōsakai (National Language Inquiry Board) has been attributed to the then Education Minister Kabayama's endorsement of the ideas expressed in these petitions.[6]

EDUCATION

Education both popular and formal, became a major focus of language reform debate and experimentation during the ensuing twenty years. During this time, the slogan *bummei kaika*, 'civilization and enlightenment', became a catch phrase denoting the goals towards which reform in a variety of fields was oriented. In the area of language reform, too, early advocates from Maejima on cited the difficulty and diversity of written Japanese as a barrier to true civilization, contending that Japan could not count herself the equal of more advanced nations until these defects were remedied. The concept of refashioning the written language thus developed along two lines: it was seen not only as a purely utilitarian and pragmatic means to achieving certain specific practical objectives, but also in a more emotive light as a factor in the development of a sense of national pride and identity.

One novel and extreme method of dealing with the problem was proposed by Mori Arinori (1847–89), politician and Enlightenment scholar who was to become Minister for Education in 1886. During a tour of duty as chargé d'affaires at the Japanese legation in Washington, Mori published a book entitled *Education in Japan* (1873), a collection of letters from various American authorities responding to enquiries by Mori soliciting their views as to the best way of conducting the fledgling education system in his country. Included in a supplement was a letter from William D. Whitney, Professor of Sanskrit Language and Literature at Yale University, to whom Mori had written soliciting his response to the idea of substituting English, or at least a simplified version of English, for Japanese as the national language of Japan. Mori had suggested that given the prevailing disarray in his own language, which did not allow it to be conducive to the attainment of *bummei*, would it not be preferable to replace it altogether with the language of a progressive western country? English possessed the added attraction of being widely understood throughout the world, while Japanese was understood only within Japan.

Whitney's reply was unequivocal: the project was impossible. He knew of no example of such a venture being successfully undertaken, primarily because the customs and culture of an entire nation, so integrally bound up with its language, could not be thus summarily disregarded. Vetoing the idea of wholesale transplantation, Whitney suggested instead a programme for the study of English as a foreign language by Japanese. The only outcome of the proposal was to bring down upon Mori's head an outpouring of ridicule whose echoes were to pursue him for many years.[7]

FUKUZAWA YUKICHI

A few other scholars, meanwhile, had been working on less radical schemes for simplifying the written language. The outstanding early Meiji writer in this regard was Fukuzawa Yukichi, who introduced western civilization to his countrymen with a range of books on various of its facets, among them *Seiyō Jijō* (*Conditions in the West*, 1866), *Seiyō Tabi Annai* (*Guide to Travel in the West*, 1867), *Seiyō*

Ishokujū (*Food, Clothing and Housing in the West*, 1867), and *Sekai Kunizukushi* (*Countries of the West*, 1869), all of which sold widely. *Conditions in the West*, in particular, sold a quarter of a million copies, while one of his later critical works, *Gakumon no Susume* (*The Encouragement of Learning*, 1872–76) recorded even greater sales. The popularity of Fukuzawa's works was due as much to their easy style as to the information and ideas they contained, a style he referred to as *sezoku tsūyō no zokubun* ('familiar, common writing'). In vocabulary, phrasing and script, Fukuzawa's writing was intended for the ordinary person; in syntax, however, it retained classical forms not used in speech, such as the *nari-beshi* terminations, so that the result was a simplified literary style rather than a full colloquial. He trained himself to replace the difficult script and vocabulary which was the hallmark of men of his educational background with easier and more familiar alternatives; one example, recalled in the preface to his collected works, was his substitution in a translation of a Dutch book on castle fortification of the phrase *ōyū no zairyō* ('materials to hand') with the simpler *ariai no shina*. In the same preface, Fukuzawa recalled how, in his early attempts at translation in the late 1850s, he had been much impressed by the easy style of *Ofumisama*, a book written by Muromachi Period priest Rennyō to disseminate the teachings of the Shin sect, which he read through several times until he had memorized it.[8]

Fukuzawa's work and motivation will be examined in the next chapter dealing with his contributions to political education as an aspect of the language modernization process; suffice it to remark here that his efforts to produce a *sezoku tsūyō no zokubun* ('familiar, common writing') were undertaken from a deep desire to impart to as many of his countrymen as possible the knowledge he considered essential to their education. He himself was of *samurai* stock and hence *kambun*-educated.[9] His flouting of the training of his education and denial of the accepted canons of scholarly writing earned him criticism from his peers which strengthened rather than weakened his resolve. After a conversation with one such critic, in which Fukuzawa reiterated his intention of leading the common people towards *bummei* by writing in terms they could comprehend, he had a seal made with the inscription *sanjūichi zokujin*; the strokes of these five characters, condensed into a two-character word, became *sezoku*, the ordinary, the popular in the sense of the common, for which he strove.

The predominant reason for Fukuzawa's insistence on simple writing, so unusual in one of his class, was, as we have seen, his democratic view of education; he viewed such a measure as a natural prerequisite for his scheme to inform the masses, being familiar through his study of Dutch and English and his fact-finding missions to Europe and America with the practice in western languages of approximating speech in writing and the benefits to be gained therefrom. In later years, his efforts at popular instruction went beyond his books to include the publication of two magazines. These were *Katei Sōdan* (*Family Talks*, 1876–78, renamed *Minkan Zasshi, The Folk Journal*, after its first year of publication), containing useful family-oriented articles written by students at Fukuzawa's Keiō Gijuku academy who took care to follow his stylistic precepts; and *Jiji Shimpō* (*The News of Today*), a daily newspaper founded by Fukuzawa in 1882 with the object of disseminating his creed of independence, in which many of his own later works were serialized.

While Fukuzawa did not develop a full colloquial style by using the syntax of the spoken language as well as its vocabulary and phrasing, his work none the less represents a significant advance in the history of language modernization in Japan because of his active and vocal opposition to the intellectual literary tradition of form before clarity. What Maejima preached, Fukuzawa practised, beginning at a time when the shogunate still held power. By exposing large numbers of people to the idea that a scholar could write in a simple and effective manner, he performed important psychological groundwork for later developments. We may assume from the sales figures of his books that the common people needed no persuasion that Fukuzawa's stylistic initiatives were good; the ones who needed convincing, the important ones, those in power whose co-operation would be needed to implement any reforms, were his fellow intellectuals. Many were openly critical of his literary practices. That Fukuzawa himself was still sufficiently under the influence of his own education to continue to distinguish in his own mind between writing for the masses and writing for intellectuals is clear from his preface to Part 5 of *The Encouragement of Learning* in which he apologizes for his use of more learned vocabulary in Parts 4 and 5 on the grounds that they are essays aimed specifically at scholarly readers rather than the general public, and hence required a departure from the common vocabulary used in earlier sections. *Bummeiron no Gairyaku* (*Outline of a*

Theory of Civilization, 1875) was likewise written in a scholarly manner for a learned readership. Nevertheless, Fukuzawa's visibility as a public figure and the example set by his practices are cited by later figures in the *gembun'itchi* movement, among them Ueki Emori, as a contributing factor to their own espousal of the cause of stylistic reform. His style is noteworthy as a halfway point between the old and the new, and as a further, more flamboyant recognition of the value of simple writing in education.

Other scholars concerned with the Enlightenment movement went further than Fukuzawa in the first ten years of Meiji in addressing the masses on important issues in a style which adopted colloquial syntax as well as vocabulary, among them political theorists Katō Hiroyuki and Nishi Amane whose contributions will be discussed in Chapter 4. Shimizu Usaburō (1829–1910, publisher and scholar of western chemistry), who had earlier published the English conversation book *Engirishi Kotoba* (*The English Language*, 1860) using the colloquial *de aru* form of the copula, asserted in his 1874 essay 'Hiragana no Setsu' ('A Theory of Hiragana') that it would be necessary both to evolve a colloquial style and to replace Chinese characters with phonetic script. In his envisaged form of written Japanese, 'there should naturally be no departure from the spoken language. If the written form differs from the spoken language, reading the material will not produce feelings of joy, anger sorrow, and happiness. And education loses its appeal when these emotions are not stimulated'.[10] Despite his exposition of the virtues of the colloquial style, Shimizu did not illustrate his theory in his text, explaining that as he was addressing scholars he had employed the manner of text they were accustomed to reading: 'I am writing here in this style only because men by their nature are habitually inclined to what they have already learned'. Later that year, however, he published *Monowari no Hashigo* (*The Ladder of Physics*), a translation of a science primer for students, in *hiragana* in the *de aru* style. It was the only one of the early colloquial-style Enlightenment works which employed this termination, others preferring the *samurai de gozaru*, among them Ogawa Tameharu's *Usagi no Mondō* (*The Rabbits' Debate*, 1873) and *Kaika Mondō* (*Debate on Civilization*, 1874–75), Yamaguchi Ōko's *Bummei Kaika* (*Civilization and Enlightenment*, 1873–74, notes taken by Yamaguchi from a lecture by Katō Yūichi), and *Meiji no Hikari* (*The Light of Meiji*, 1875, notes from a lecture by Ishii Nankyō). These latter being either arguments couched in the form of a dialogue or verbatim transcripts of a spoken lecture, their presentation of the grammar of speech in writing was of limited impact, Shimizu's primer being the only use of colloquial termination in narrative prose.

By 1875, then, the *concept* of using colloquial style as a vehicle to facilitate popular education was becoming an issue for debate among educated writers and theorists interested in either promulgating pet theories or spreading knowledge for its own sake, with a very small number advocating across-the-board reform of written Japanese. The actual *practice* of writing in colloquial style, however, with the exception of Fukuzawa's intermediate prose, was restricted to a few demonstration pieces, all of which were written with the specific aim of popular education.

In the area of formal education, progress was slow. After the inauguration of the national education system in 1872, translations and general Enlightenment works, including some by Fukuzawa and one by Katō Hiroyuki, were used as makeshift textbooks; although their subject matter was appropriate and their style not too difficult, they had not been written specifically for children and were far from ideal. One which *had* been produced for the young reader was Furukawa Masao's *Chie no Iloguchi* (*First Steps to Learning*, 1871), a reader which began by presenting the two phonetic scripts and then progressed from words to clauses to short sentences. Chapters 23 to 25 gave examples of verbs ending in the polite auxiliaries *-masu* (present), *-mashita* (perfective), *-mashō* (tentative) and other colloquial forms as well as the classical *ari* and *nari*, a practice continued in later lessons. Furukawa was a friend of Fukuzawa Yukichi and was the first head of Fukuzawa's academy, Keiō Gijuku; he, too, had studied Dutch under the same mentor, Ogata Kōan, and had been influenced by that scholar's ideas on clarity and simplicity.[11]

It was not long before the Ministry of Education began compiling its own textbooks, all of which were in Sino-Japanese. A bureau was set up at the new Tokyo Normal School in November 1872 to produce readers for use in the attached primary school; in March, 1873, this combined with the editing section of the Ministry's literature bureau. The first of the readers was *Shōgaku Tokuhon* (*Primary Reader*, ed. Tanaka Yoshikado, 1873), most widely used of the early primers. This was a translation of one of the American series of School and Family readers by Marcius Willson, and was published in a revised version the next year. Another of the same title was *Shōgaku Tokuhon* (eds Sakakibara Yoshino, Naka Michitaka, and Inagaki Chikai, 1873), this one not a translation but an original compilation. All textbooks were to begin with simple phrases and clauses and proceed by grades to more advanced *kambun kuzushi*, in line with the educational background and attitudes of the planners as to what constituted acceptable writing.

This situation did not go entirely unchallenged. The Education Ministry at that time included many progressive scholars of the west, among them Tanaka Yoshikado, Nishigata Takashi, and the Education Minister himself, Ōki Takatō (1832–99). In 1873, when Nishimura Shigeki (1828–1902, educational administrator and scholar of the west) entered the Ministry of Education, he found there a desire to put into practice the *gembun'itchi* principle and he and two or three colleagues were instructed by Ōki to investigate ways and means of introducing colloquial style into the schools. Not surprisingly, as Nishimura himself – a traditionalist in this area – was against the plan, they were unable to suggest any feasible proposal and the project was shelved. That influential men such as Ōki were aware of and willing to seek solutions for the language problem only one year after the establishment of the education system, however, indicates the growing importance attached in the minds of some educated men to the issue.

One small area in which the theories of Ōki and his supporters did materialize was in the teaching of *kotobazukai* (language). The dialectal fragmentation of spoken Japanese meant that people from different regions often had difficulty understanding each other; *kotobazukai* was intended by Assistant Minister for Education Nishigata Takashi as a step towards standardization by instructing school students in a common form of Japanese. In pursuance of this aim, the Education Ministry in 1873 published glossaries and phrase sheets for use in *kotobazukai* classes, in which a certain amount of colloquial grammar was employed in addition to Tokyo vocabulary. Two of the earliest were *Rengohen Ichi* (*Phrasebook: 1*), a series of short questions and answers written for the most part in *de aru* plain style with some *-masu* and *de arimasu* polite semi-formal style, and *Shōgaku Kyōjusho* (*Primary Lesson Book*), which began with a glossary and progressed to short sentences, seven out of eight lessons employing *-masu* and *de arimasu* colloquial style in both dialogue and narrative. The second of these was severly criticized by classical scholar Kurokawa Mayori (1829–1906), who argued that children were already familiar with the spoken language and should be trained instead in the literary grammar they would need as adults.[12]

Colloquial style also appeared briefly in conversation books produced for these classes, all of which were written by men who had studied in the west.[13] Compilation ceased after 1875, however, and textbooks reverted to Sino-Japanese. *Shōgaku Kyōjusho* was revised and republished as *Shōgaku Nyūmon* (*A First Manual of Primary Studies*), with colloquial style replaced altogether by literary style. It was to be 1887 before further initiatives were made toward replacing Sino-Japanese with colloquial style in textbooks.

It is clear from the insistence of educators on the use of Sino-Japanese in textbooks that these men did not regard their manner of writing as something to be jealously preserved for their own use alone, as part of any *deliberate* attempt to restrict the flow of information outside their own milieu. Their emphasis on its preservation as the 'correct' form of writing towards which school students must be guided indicates that they were motivated by a sense of the fitness of things – better the common herd should learn to write 'properly' by being initiated into the mysteries of this formerly aristocratic preserve than that the vulgar colloquial be introduced into writing. Attitudes to the nature of the written word were thus more deeply entrenched than class prejudices in this area, in so far as the two can be separated.

THE PRESS

A second area in which a certain amount of progress was made in the early stages of the language modernization movement was the newly emergent Japanese press. Its contribution was twofold: the serious press provided a forum for intellectual debate on the issue, while the popular press saw the colloquial style pressed into service in the tabloids as a means of boosting circulation among the masses.

The first newspapers to appear in Japan were published in the foreign settlements of Yokohama and Nagasaki after 1861, at a time when the shogunate ban on publication of information or opinion on matters pertaining to government was strictly enforced by censorship.[14] Soon after the Meiji Restoration, in April 1869, the new government removed the restrictions on political comment when it legalized the publication of newspapers with the promulgation of a set of regulations establishing a framework for the development of a western style press. The press rapidly became an important channel of communication between the ruling élite and the public, or at least the intellectual section of the public with the education to comprehend the Sino-Japanese perpetuated in its pages. For villagers not so endowed, newspaper reading-rooms were established where news was read aloud and explained.

In its early stages, the press was sponsored by a combination of private and public interests. By the mid-1870s, however, ownership was totally private and two distinct types of newspaper had emerged. These were the *daishimbun* (major papers, or serious press), the prestige newspapers aimed at an educated readership which discussed political questions; and the *koshimbun* (minor papers, or popular press), written for the entertainment of the masses and featuring reportage of the more sensational run of current events. The *daishimbun*, among them the *Akebono Shimbun*, *Yūbin Hōchi Shimbun*, *Chōya Shimbun*, and *Tōkyō Nichi Nichi Shimbun*, presented discussion by prominent intellectuals of political and social issues in the form of expository essays or editorials, the European-style editorial having been introduced by Fukuchi Gen'ichirō with the 2 December, 1874 issue of the *Tōkyō Nichi Nichi*.

Fukuchi (1841–1906), one of the outstanding journalists of the Meiji Period, was a man of wide-ranging interests and talents.[15] Prior to the Restoration, he had studied Dutch, and had served as a Shogunate interpreter. He had travelled to Europe twice, and to America once. In 1868, he had been imprisoned for attacking the new government in his *Kōko Shimbun*, but had over the intervening years become an influential figure in the Finance Ministry; later, as a journalist, he emerged in the fierce newspaper debate of 1874–75 over the civil rights issue as the chief supporter of the government's gradualist position. As editor of the *Nichi Nichi* from 1874 to 1888, he became well known for his editorials, which he penned under the name Gosō. Fukuchi believed that the serious press should express opinion on all facets of society, whether politics, economics, foreign affairs religion, literature, or education. One of the areas to which he turned his attention was the matter of the written Japanese language

The *Nichi Nichi* of 29 August 1875 carried an editorial entitled 'Bunron' ('On Writing'), wherein Fukuchi noted that government efforts to achieve universal literacy through the fledgling education system were being hampered by the difficulty of written Japanese, so marked that few could achieve real mastery even after a lifetime of effort. What Japan needed, he observed, was a new style, one which would allow people to express their thoughts freely and fully. Dividing the many varieties of writing then current into the two main categories of *kijibun* (forms of classical Japanese) and *ronsetsubun* (forms of Sino-Japanese), Fukuchi paid special attention to the latter. This sort of writing he judged to be much the more difficult of the two, requiring a thorough education in the Chinese classics to comprehend as it was usually simply a collection of Chinese words arranged according to Japanese word-order. Since being employed in translations of western literature, however, it had metamorphosed into a synthesis of English-derived constructions, Chinese vocabulary, and Japanese connective grammar, christened by Fukuchi *nuebun* (fantasy style). Each time Fukuchi read a western book, he avowed the clarity of its prose brought home his own shortcomings as a writer of *nuebun*. Good writing must lap the reader in a sense of familiarity; it must seem real, not strained and contorted. While not advocating total conversion to the grammar of the spoken language, Fukuchi believed the situation could be saved were writers to avoid striving after excessive refinement and return to the familiar. The emotive power of four great works of Tokugawa Period popular fiction he attributed to their use of colloquial vocabulary in the *gazoku setchū* style, a track which modern writers too would do well to follow.

Fukuchi published two other untitled editorials, commenting on the necessity for a simpler style to enable the creation of a truly great Japanese literature but offering no specific suggestions as to how this might be achieved. Like Fukuzawa, he favoured the half-way measure of substituting commonly-used vocabulary items and phrases for the esoteric expressions beloved of *kangakusha* (Chinese scholars). As editor of a prominent newspaper, Fukuchi was in a position to disseminate his ideas widely among his educated readers, and in doing so he performed a significant service in the cause of stylistic reform, for these intellectuals were that section of the community on which would depend the acceptance or rejection of moves towards modernizing the written language. They were the men who controlled education, newspapers, and government, who wrote histories and literary criticism, and who were the repositories of entrenched cultural attitudes towards writing and the form it should take. It was the literary prejudices of these men, heirs through their education to a centuries-old classical tradition, which must first be overcome in order to implement any change in written

Japanese. In addressing his peers on the issue in the language to which they were accustomed, Fukuchi, by virtue of his position, was able to add to the growing debate in a manner calculated to reach a large number of such men.

'On Writing' appeared in the *Nichi Nichi* on 29 August 1875. On the same day, another of the larger newspapers, the *Yūbin Hōchi Shimbun*, published an essay on the style problem by Watanabe Shūjirō (1855–1945). Watanabe had studied English at the Tokyo English Language School. After graduating he became a teacher at the Gakushūin (Peers School) before embarking on a long and distinguished career in the Finance Ministry. In his later years he devoted himself to writing, becoming known mainly as a historian. The essay which appeared in the *Yūbin Hōchi Shimbun* was entitled 'Nihombun o Seitei suru Hōhō no Tai-i' ('Outline of Steps to Regulating Written Japanese'); five days later, on 3 September, it appeared in the *Tōkyō Akebono Shimbun* as 'Nihombun o Seitei suru Hōhō' ('Steps to Regulating Written Japanese'), almost word for word the same, the only difference being orthographical in that the first version appeared in a *hiragana-kanji* combination, the second in a *katakana-kanji* mix. The gist of Watanabe's argument was as follows: writing in the west, being merely the setting down on paper of everyday speech, was simple and convenient, easily understood by the entire literate population. Japan would do well to follow this example, taking as the basis for a new style the words most commonly used in the Tokyo dialect and replacing with phonetic scripts all Chinese characters except numerals. All previous publications, including school textbooks, should be rewritten along these lines; all future publications should conform to these principles. Watanabe recommended a townspeople's *-masu* termination rather than the aristocratic *gozaru*, and illustrated his thesis with examples of the kind of style he had in mind. The body of his text was written in *kambun kuzushi*, for which he apologized in a postscript, justifying it in terms of an expedient to spread his theory by virtue of its wide currency – an interesting reversal of the attitude of earlier scholars who had used colloquial style in order to disseminate *their* particular message.

Watanabe did not confine his activities to writing for the press, but took practical steps towards achieving his aims, petitioning the Education Minister without success in the same month to simplify written Japanese. The significance of his essay lies in the fact that unlike earlier advocates he pushed no particular barrow in calling for style reform, simply arguing in general terms that it would be a good thing for the whole country to have a uniform written language.¹⁶

A third scholar who published an article on language reform in the serious press during this period was Ōtsuki Fumihiko (1847–1928), grandson of Ōtsuki Gentaku, Tokugawa Period scholar of the west. Ōtsuki had studied English as a youth; his interest in the future of written Japanese was keen, particularly in the field of script reform, and he was instrumental in setting up the Kana Club in 1873, devoted to the ideal of replacing Chinese characters with the phonetic Japanese script. Upon entering the Education Ministry in 1872, Ōtsuki had been set to compiling first an English-Japanese dictionary and later a monolingual Japanese dictionary. He was deeply convinced of the need to produce suitable grammars and dictionaries for the new education system, and his essay 'Nihon Bunten Henshū Sōron' ('An Introduction to Compiling Japanese Grammars'), published in the *Chōya Shimbun* on 16 January 1877, dealt mainly with the kind of grammars he felt were needed. The essay concluded with a brief discussion of the reasons why speech and writing were so different in Japan. One particular problem, Ōtsuki felt, was the lack of a standard form of Japanese on which to base a colloquial style. He himself favoured the adoption of the dialect of the capital, Tokyo, as the standard. He saw a role for compilers of grammars like himself in endeavouring to bring writing closer to speech; if their grammars were subsequently to be used in schools throughout the nation, the gap between speech and writing might eventually disappear.

After 1877, no significant essays on the style reform theme were published in the serious press until Fukuchi Gen'ichirō returned to the attack in 'Bunshōron' ('On Writing'), a *Nichi Nichi* editorial published in two parts on 23 and 24 May 1881. Whereas Fukuchi had earlier skirted the question of adopting colloquial grammar as well as vocabulary, reluctant to commit himself fully to it, he now abandoned this conservative approach, opening his editorial with the clear declaration: 'I wish spoken and written Japanese to be as one. They have been so long separate that perhaps this cannot be brought about quickly; but still, I would like to see them brought closer together'.¹⁷ Part 1 contained his criticism of the absurd situation whereby not even the epistolary style could be understood without prior study of Chinese, let alone the style used in official documents. 'And why? Because in Japan, speech and writing are two different things. A style which does not reproduce contemporary speech is not vital; it is dead, like the ancient prose of China, like Greek and Latin in Europe. One might call it a scholar's style, but certainly not an ordinary Japanese style.'[18] The Chinese people, he remarked, despite their great respect for antiquity, certainly did not employ ancient Chinese in their everyday documents. In western countries, even peasants could comprehend the contemporary colloquial style in common use. Writing which only scholars could understand was useless – witness the low circulation of books and newspapers written in such styles, despite their edifying contents. Style reform, Fukuchi believed, was an essential prerequisite to the true enlightenment of the Japanese people.

Part 2 of *On Writing* went on to discuss the problem of orthographic reform, suggesting the eventual adoption of the Roman alphabet but shelving the matter as being too difficult for immediate implementation. Of more immediate concern was the conversion from traditional literary conventions to a modern colloquial style. Scholars might begin by discarding all medieval or ancient vocabulary items not in general use. They should further take steps to abandon literary artifice in favour of clarity, for two reasons. The first: unlike scholars of the Tokugawa Period whose primary tasks were to expound upon the Chinese classics and compose Chinese poetry, modern intellectuals were faced with too much other work to waste time on taffeta phrases. The second: Meiji Period books and newspapers, no longer merely classical expositions and histories, needed to carry information of benefit to modern society in an easily understood style if that information were to reach its target. In short, the tempo of the times had changed completely. If anachronisms were not henceforth weeded out of written Japanese, the gap between speech and writing would widen daily into total separation, when writing would be of no use at all. Writing would be as it should be when it could be read aloud and sound as if someone had just said the same thing in conversation. Modestly or realistically, Fukuchi concluded with the disclaimer that such a goal, despite his commitment to it, was beyond his own power to achieve.

Fukuchi's awareness of the power of the press in facilitating the flow of information needed in the push to modernize the nation is well demonstrated by the second of the reasons advanced above in support of simplifying writing. He was a powerful and influential public figure of these times, and his championing of the cause of language modernization, which will be further discussed in Chapter 4, did much to pave the way for later developments.

While Fukuchi and a few fellow intellectuals were theorizing on style reform in the serious press, a trend towards actually using colloquial style was becoming apparent in the *koshimbun*, or popular press. *Koshimbun*, it will be remembered, dealt in human interest stories and serialized fiction deemed by intellectuals inappropriate to the educatory function of the press but appealing to the lower ranks of readers. In *daishimbun*, reporting the news was secondary to political debate; in *koshimbun*, news was paramount, but a type of news considered not quite respectable. The early *koshimbun* numbered among their Tokyo ranks the *Yomiuri Shimbun* (1874), *Hiragana E-iri Shimbun* (1875, later renamed *Tōkyō E-iri Shimbun*, 1876), and *Kanayomi Shimbun* (1875), while in Osaka there appeared the *Naniwa Shimbun* (1875) and the *Asahi Shimbun* (1879). All aimed to reach a mass readership with the kind of semi-salacious news and gossip items mentioned above, with the exception of the *Yomiuri* which attempted a more serious strain of reporting.

Again with the exception of the *Yomiuri*, these papers were staffed by writers of popular fiction of the type in vogue in the Tokugawa Period. Their main concern was with circulation; accordingly, they pitched the level of difficulty of their text to be within the reach of their readership, in this case the masses who could not read the Sino-Japanese of the serious press and relied on the *koshimbun* for information and entertainment. In pursuance of this objective, the task of actually reading the text was simplified by placing small-print Japanese glosses next to Chinese characters[19] and by using the grammar of the spoken language in place of literary forms. The *Yomiuri* published only those official notices which had a direct bearing on its readers' lives; these were published in the original, but accompanied by a colloquial translation. Social snippets were written from the outset in colloquial style, employing a variety of versions of the copula ranging from the more formal *de gozaimasu* to the plain *da*, as were most articles published in the contributors' columns. The *Hiragana E-iri Shimbun* provided illustrations with its social chit-chat, while the *Kanayomi Shimbun* featured a special column of geisha news, ensuring its popularity in the pleasure quarters. The *Naniwa Shimbun* modelled its approach on the *Yomiuri*, as did the *Asahi*, although the proportion of colloquial style was lower in the latter.

The trend towards using colloquial style in these newspapers continued until the beginning of 1879. New *koshimbun* published after that date, among them the *Iroha Shimbun*, *Azuma Shimbun* and the abovementioned *Asahi Shimbun*, showed a marked increase in the proportion of Sino-Japanese, probably owing to the increased ability of the populace to read that style as a result of the national education system of which it was the main medium of written instruction, so that here the education system in fact acted as a brake on moves towards style reform, however motivated by expediency, in the press. As a result there was a temporary return to the status quo due to the increased dissemination of Sino-Japanese throughout the broader community through textbooks; those formerly excluded were now being initiated into the mysteries, so that the use of the colloquial style in the popular press, motivated as it was by profit concerns rather than by commitment to language reform, could now afford to be discontinued. After 1884, colloquial style was seldom encountered in the popular press.

The temporary adoption of colloquial style in *koshimbun*, expedient though it was, played a twofold role in the language modernization process. First, it reinforced the notion that colloquial style was a viable literary medium which offered benefits in terms of widened readership. Second, it actually brought about a slight unbending in the hitherto uncompromising Sino-Japanese of the larger newspapers. Prior to the appearance of popular newspapers in 1874, the miscellaneous items published in the serious press had all been written in *kambun kuzushi*. After 1875, however, they began to include a small amount of colloquial style, which gradually increased to around 50 per cent. The trend reached its peak in the summer of 1877, when the proportion of colloquial style items of this kind in the *Yokohama Mainichi Shimbun* mounted to 80–90 per cent, but reversed itself a few months later, until by 1878 colloquial style had again disappeared from the pages of the serious press.

In addition to the serious and popular newspapers, a third type of publication in which colloquial style appeared was the enlightenment magazine, intended to spread knowledge and ideas beneficial to the nation. *Minkan Zasshi* (*The Folk Journal*, 1874), for example, was published by Fukuzawa Yukichi's academy at Keiō with the intention of enlightening rural communities. Its articles were mainly written in the simplified literary style practised by

Fukuzawa and his students, but colloquial style appeared in a small scattering.

The most famous publication of this type was *Meiroku Zasshi* (*Meiji Six Journal*, 1874+),[20] the academic journal of the Meirokusha or Meiji Six Society, a group of Enlightenment scholars set up in 1873 (the sixth year of Meiji, hence the name), by Mori Arinori to stimulate scholarship and to provide a forum for intellectual debate on issues pertaining to popular enlightenment. Its ten charter members included Nishimura Shigeki, Fukuzawa Yukichi, Katō Hiroyuki (1836–1916, political theorist and educator), Nishi Amane (1829–97, educator and bureaucrat), and Mitsukuri Rinshō (1846–97, jurist and bureaucrat). The first issue of the society's journal contained a discussion of the language problem in the form of an essay by Nishi advocating the adoption of the western alphabet, which Nishi believed would lead on naturally to the development of a simpler style. As part of his plan, he expressed the hope that:

> 'if there is mutual conciliation between the advocates of the literary style and those favouring the vulgar style, the one refraining from common use of excessively elevated grammatical forms and the other giving full attention to the spoken language, endeavouring to speak as we are able to write, a natural style will become innate, and our language may reach European levels of refinement within a century'.[21]

This essay, like most others published in this journal, was in scholarly Sino-Japanese; occasionally, however, lectures delivered by the society's members at its meetings were published in the idiom in which they were delivered, without first being rewritten into *kambun*. Nishi's own 'Naichi Ryokō' ('Travels in the Interior'),[22] a debate on the issue of travel by foreigners within the country, was one of these, combining the common *da* copula with the more aristocratic *de gozaru*.

Two other journals were *Nanajūichi Zappō* (*Seventy-one News Items*) and *Chie no Kura* (*A Treasury of Wisdom*). The first of these, a Christian magazine published by the Kobe church with intent to evangelize, was launched in 1875, some of its articles being contributed by western missionaries and doctors. In line with the policy statement in the first issue to the effect that a simple style would be employed, colloquial style was used in editorials and to a lesser extent in the contributors' and hygiene columns. One

Early stirrings: Education and the press   97

particularly noteworthy example of its use was *Tenro Rekitei Iyaku*, a translation of Bunyan's *Pilgrim's Progress* published in 66 instalments between 14 April 1876 and 24 August 1877. This was not a direct translation from the English but a retranslation of a Chinese version published in Shanghai in 1869. The first eleven instalments were written entirely in colloquial style, the twelfth in colloquial dialogue and literary narrative, and the remainder with no trace of colloquial style. The translation was republished as a monograph in 1879, its style remaining unchanged with the exception of the first page which had been rewritten from colloquial style into *bungotai*. The use of colloquial style in the opening instalments of *Tenro Rekitei Iyaku* was in accord with the evangelical principles of the magazine. It is not known why the translator discontinued it in later chapters, although Japanese writers have put it down to the fact that the colloquial was merely chosen as a temporary expedient; there was in the choice nothing of the natural connection between expression and the thoughts and ideas behind it.[23] Colloquial style disappeared from the main body of *Seventy-One News Items* itself after 1877.

A Treasury of Wisdom, launched in 1877, was an applied sciences magazine published with the aim of endowing the masses with an elementary knowledge of physics and chemistry as they affected everyday life. Given the enthusiasm for scientific matters in the early Meiji Period, it was very well received. Colloquial style accounted for the bulk of the articles until November 1878, after which time it was seen only occasionally in contributed pieces.

The almost complete disappearance of colloquial style in textbooks, newspapers, and magazines for a period of several years after about 1877 has several possible explanations. One is that its advocates were not yet committed to the notion of language reform across the board as a desirable thing, but used colloquial style as no more than a temporary expedient to help in achieving some particular gain, reverting to what for them was the literary norm when other factors made it appear prudent to do so. One such factor, of course, which constitutes a second explanation in itself, was the growing ability of former commoners to read *kambun* as they were taught to do so in the new education system; colloquial style was thus seen by popular educators and journalists as well as by education planners as no more than a crutch to be discarded once its users were able to stand on their proper literary feet. A third reason may be that the swing away from colloquial style reflected the repressive line taken by the government at this time towards the civil rights movement, some members of which had employed it in a bid to propagandize the masses with their theories. Textbooks were brought completely under the control of the Education Ministry in 1880, after several had been judged injurious to social harmony in the wake of the 1879 Imperial Rescript which attacked the liberal, westernized school system and ordained a return to an education based on Confucian moral principles. As education thus turned away from Europeanization back to traditional lines, away from ideas encouraging the notion of popular rights back to the concept of a submissive people ruled by their betters, the change was reflected in the disappearance of what little colloquial style had previously appeared in textbooks.

THE PRESS REVIVAL

Towards the end of the second decade of Meiji, however, the decline was reversed when the adoption of colloquial style in editorials of newspapers published by the various political parties[24] and the tremendous success of the publication of verbatim transcripts of stories told by the famous raconteur San'yūtei Enchō (1839–1900)[25] led to a revival of interest in the language issue. A second wave of essays advocating style reform began to appear in newspapers and magazines, sparking off a vigorous new debate in the press on the pros and cons of *gembun'itchi* which shaded gradually into acceptance in principle of the idea and a search for the best means of implementation, with ensuing ramifications for education.

One of the earliest to take up the theme again was Taguchi Ukichi, in 'Nippon Kaika no Seishitsu Yōyaku Aratamezaru Bekarazu' ('We Must Strive to Change the Nature of Japanese Civilization', November–December 1884, *Tōkyō Keizai Zasshi*). Taguchi (1855–1905) had studied Dutch and English, with a particular interest in English economics; he became famous as a liberalistic economist and civil rights advocate, and was for a time editor of the Liberal Party's *Jiyū Shimbun*, as well as publishing his own *Tōkyō Keizai Zasshi* (*Tokyo Economic Journal*) as a mouthpiece through which to criticize the government's economic policies. After 1884, he began to preach the necessity of *gembun'itchi* through essays in both the *Tokyo Economic Journal* and the *Rōmaji Zasshi* (*Rōmaji Journal*), the latter being the journal of the Rōmaji Club, committed to the idea of adopting the western alphabet in Japan, of which Taguchi was a member.[26] His interest in and subsequent activities on behalf of language modernization began after a period of direct involvement with the civil rights movement, and were connected with his notions of popular sovereignty, which he viewed as an important reason for style reform. In his essay, Taguchi compared the democratic nature of western culture to the aristocratic nature of Japanese. Post-Restoration Japanese society, he argued, must switch its emphasis away from a small privileged group to the common people. Written Japanese still reflected the hierarchical feudal system, with writers of both Sino-Japanese and classical Japanese striving to make their writing as different as possible from speech. Traditional styles belonged to the upper classes and were unsuitable for continued use; writing in the modern democratic society must be based on speech, to enable any literate person to communicate on paper. In Taguchi's view, Japan should aim for both orthographic and stylistic reform, with the western alphabet replacing both Chinese and Japanese symbols and colloquial style replacing older literary forms. Such reforms would prove of immense benefit to both the arts and the sciences.

The text of the essay itself was written in a mixed *kanji-kana* script, in a comparatively simple *kambun kuzushi* style. To illustrate his theory, Taguchi rewrote it in the Roman alphabet in a *de gozarimasu* colloquial style and published it as 'Nippon Kaika no Seishitsu' ('The Nature of Japanese Civilization') in the *Rōmaji Journal*, in seven parts between June 1885 and June 1886. He continued his argument relating language reform to the changing nature of Japanese culture in a second essay, 'Ishōron' ('On Design'),[27] which dealt with the modernization of the arts. The section on literature stressed the urgency of developing a modern colloquial style, which was essential to the expression of contemporary ideas. Once this style was in hand, Taguchi believed, Japanese literature would have the means to escape the confining mould of *bibun* (elegant prose) and become capable of a true formulation of man's mind. 'Ishōron' was published only two years before the first colloquial-style novels appeared; it is significant as the first positive advocacy of the *gembun'itchi* principle in literature.

In February 1885, a lecture 'Bunshōron o yomu' ('On Reading Bunshōron') presented by Kanda Kōhei at a meeting of the Tokyo Academy was published in the Academy's journal, *Tōkyō Gakushi Kaiin Zasshi* (*Journal of the Tokyo Academy*).[28] It was a discussion and rebuttal of Nishimura Shigeki's 'Bunshōron' ('On Writing') published in the same journal the previous September, which had suggested the creation of a new kind of classical Japanese style which would synthesize elements of east and west. Nishimura had given an overview of the development of the various styles up to the Meiji period, classifying them under the two broad headings of *kambun* and *wabun*; the latter he found too rambling and effeminate for important matters, while the former, though suitably serious in tone, was burdened with characteristics of reverse word-order and difficult characters which resulted from its being essentially a foreign language. He had exhorted scholars to endeavour to improve classical Japanese to the level of *kambun*, which effort would result in a new and better Japanese literature and enhance the image of Japan. In addition to thoroughly familiarizing themselves with classical Japanese grammar, scholars were advised to study the grammar of Chinese and western languages as well, paying particular attention to Greek and Latin; after careful study of the works of famous writers throughout the world, they should then set about creating a new *wabun*.

Kanda (1830–98, bureaucrat and Enlightenment scholar), was far from impressed with Nishimura's proposal, believing it too roundabout and difficult a solution to what he nevertheless agreed was a problem in written Japanese. He himself offered a less elegant but more immediate remedy, taking as his metaphor the provision of food to a starving man: 'Rather than wasting time procuring rare delicacies, one should give him plain food at once. Japan desires grammatical reform today as a starving man desires food; I believe we must adopt a straightforward approach to reform.'[29] He advocated the adoption of the *gembun'itchi* principle: to be a true colloquial style, writing must be understood instantly by a hearer when read aloud, and the only way to achieve this was to base it on the modern spoken language. What few attempts at colloquial style there had already been, he asserted, had been for the most part treated with contempt because they were vulgar in both language and spirit. Could these unattractive qualities be weeded out, however, and the style be refined and polished, it would attract the admiration of society. If speech were tidied up, it would automatically follow that colloquial-style prose would likewise be improved.

Kanda's argument was followed a few months later by the first of three new language-oriented editorials by Fukuchi Gen'ichirō in the *Nichi Nichi: Bunshō no Shinka* (*The Evolution of Writing*, 25-28 July 1885). This was a discussion of the work of the Kana and Rōmaji Clubs which were then working actively towards script reform. Fukuchi gave a potted history of the evolution of written Japanese, emphasizing the strong Chinese influence which still remained its most salient characteristic. The current demarcation between speech and writing he attributed to the fact that writing had developed under the influence of Chinese, a foreign language. While recognizing that this influence could not be eradicated overnight, Fukuchi suggested certain initial changes which would lead on to the eventual emergence of the colloquial style, the most immediately effective and least troublesome being the weeding out of esoteric Chinese words. Script reform he recognized as part of the overall plan for language modernization, but believed that style reform must precede it; without style reform, any change to a phonetic script would merely exacerbate reading difficulties by removing the visual aid of Chinese characters.

Bunshō no Shinka was followed by *Bunshō Kairyō no Mokuteki* (*The Aim of Style Reform*, 16 February 1886) and *Bunshō no Kairyō* (*The Reform of Writing*, 27 January 1887), in which Fukuchi pursued the same line of argument: script reform was pointless without prior style reform. To attempt it given the existing situation would merely make matters worse. If, however, all Chinese words except those which had become part of the everyday language were to be repudiated, writing would naturally become Japanese in tone and come closer to achieving the primary aim of written communication: intelligibility. Despite his earlier disclaimers that his own writing was *nuebun*, Fukuchi did in fact adopt this tactic of vocabulary substitution as editorial policy on the *Nichi Nichi* with the result that the *Nichi Nichi* was mentioned as being the easiest to read of all newspapers.[30]

A fourth scholar to add his voice to the debate was Mozume Takami (1847-1928), then teaching in the literature department of Tokyo Imperial University and an active member of the Kana Club, whose essay 'Gembun'itchi' (March, 1886) is one of the most famous advocacies of stylistic reform of this period. Its ideas were not new, being those currently much under discussion; but it was remarkable as a scholarly discourse which combined theory and practice in one text, whereas earlier exponents such as Kanda, where they had attempted to illustrate, had usually rewritten their original Sino-Japanese text and published it separately.

'Gembun'itchi' was divided into seven sections, the first of which argued that writing should approximate speech. Written Japanese abounded in ancient Chinese words no longer used even in their country of origin which rendered literary Japanese far too difficult as a medium for education – of what use were textbooks if children could not understand the contents unless the style were first construed for them?[31] The adoption of colloquial style, despite its detractors' claims to the contrary, would result in many benefits, not least being a reduction in public taxes in view of the smaller number of teachers which would then be required. Section 2 discussed the ways in which writing diverged from speech: *kambun* was a purely literary medium, never used to reproduce speech, while even those who wrote *wabun* imitated earlier works, reproducing the conventions of earlier centuries rather than the way they themselves now spoke.

The third section dealt with the importance of proper expression. A piece of writing may be assigned a date by a study of its mode of expression. Whereas a person's speech contains no ambiguities or mistakes in tense because speech comes straight from the heart, there are many such errors in written Japanese because writers are merely copying literary conventions, much as a parrot will mimic words it has not heard correctly. If writing were based on speech, such errors would disappear. Section 4 then went on to discuss the inferiority of written Japanese to speech in the same terms: 'What comes from one's own heart is given life by its spontaneity; but an imitation of something else is a lifeless counterfeit'.[32] The Japanese should stop producing mere imitations of archaic styles and adopt their own vigorous, living idiom. The preference for old conventions of those accustomed to using them was dismissed as no more than habit.

Section 5 discussed the abundance of honorifics in spoken Japanese. Mozume recognized that honorifics, having been used for many centuries as a sign of respect and goodwill, had become an integral part of Japanese speech, which gave rise to the fear that speech reproduced in writing would prove impossibly long-winded. He countered with the argument that there was no need to write as if one were conducting a face-to-face conversation; the most appropriate style would be that used in diaries, where honorifics were unnecessary. In the sixth section, he addressed the issue of standardization, claiming that to adopt the *gembun'itchi* principle would result in both increased standardization and greater refinement of the spoken language, as a uniform version of written Japanese was gradually spread throughout the country by the new national mail system and people indulged their natural inclination to take more care over writing than speech.

The conclusion in Section 7 dealt with what Mozume considered the two main differences between speech and writing: tense and conjunctions. Once these were corrected, he believed, the written word would be universally comprehensible. To illustrate his theory, Mozume took examples from twenty-one of the classics, rewriting them with appropriate changes.

Unlike earlier advocates of language reform, who had addressed their fellow intellectuals on the subject in Sino-Japanese, Mozume's entire text was in colloquial style, the first four chapters using the *de aru* termination and the last the polite *-masu* and *de arimasu*. At a time when the issue was coming once more into prominence, his essay was valuable not so much for its ideas, which had been heard before, but for its display of the *gembun'itchi* principle in practice, showing the practical steps whereby traditional conventions could be replaced with the grammar of the spoken language. Hitherto, actual practice of the colloquial style had occurred only in localized areas with purely utilitarian purposes. Now, for the first time, a scholar employed it to instruct his peers.

Many other essays and editorials on the *gembun'itchi* question appeared in the years 1885–87, as enthusiasm grew. Some discussed the problem in general terms; others suggested practical ideas for the implementation of reform; a few, like Mozume's, ventured to give practical displays of the theories expounded. Some, such as *Bunshō no Kairyō* (*The Reform of Writing*, 17, 18, 20 November 1885), an editorial in the *Meiji Nippō*, continued to push the barrow of overt and localized economic gain: its writer asserted that the existing situation hindered the advancement of knowledge and civilization, held down newspaper and magazine circulation, and delayed script reform. Writers and journalists should take the lead in endeavouring to replace *kambun kuzushi* with colloquial style, which step would result in a boost to sales. Others took a more comprehensive view of the overall benefits for the nation of a simpler written language.

By this time, the debate no longer focused upon the desirability or otherwise of the *gembun'itchi* principle, at least among these supporters, but rather upon the question of how best to implement the transition to colloquial style. Not all were convinced, of course; these years and those immediately following were to see bitter controversy between defenders and antagonists.[33] The groundswell of intellectual opinion in favour of the change, however, had observable results in several areas, one of which was education.

EDUCATION: A NEW BEGINNING

The revival of interest in the question of language reform was reflected in education. In 1885, Mori Arinori became Minister of Education in the new cabinet headed by Itō Hirobumi (1841–1909), and proceeded to overhaul the education system with a series of changes which reversed the earlier return to Confucianism and laid the foundation for the system of today. Among these changes was yet another overhaul of the textbook system. Staunch Confucianist Nishimura Shigeki was replaced as head of the Compilation Bureau, and the Confucian ethics primers were abandoned in favour of more impartial textbooks. There now began a revival of interest in the matter of *gembun'itchi* in education. Mori, as we have seen, was aware of the problems inherent in written Japanese, having earlier suggested the substitution of English. In 1879, in his essay 'Shintai no Nōryoku' ('On Physical Fitness'), Mori identified as one of the sources of debility in the Japanese people the study of Chinese literature:

> the writing system of China . . . requires many years of hard and diligent work, from the initial step of learning to copy the characters to the final stage of sophisticated exegesis, before it can be put to any use.

He went on to add:

> if we can put an end to traditional educational practice – the reading of the classics by rote, and attending temple schools – and can bring into use from the very start easy-to-read sentences combining Japanese and Chinese [scripts], and can set up a programme of physical exercises, there is good reason to hope

that young folk in the future will be spared the worst of these debilities.[34]

Despite the urging of a few progressives, the colloquial style had never stood any real chance of being adopted in early textbooks, given the opposition to its use by most intellectuals at a time when loyalty to traditional styles was too strong to allow an unemotional assessment of its potential in education. Fifteen years later, however, in the late 1880s, with more and more voices being raised in support of stylistic reform, public opinion had become more receptive to the idea and the first stirrings of change were being felt in literature. The time was ripe for new initiatives, and against this background there appeared several textbooks which employed the grammar of the spoken language.

The first was *Nihon Tokuhon* (*A Japanese Reader*, 1886), written by publisher Shimpo Iwatsugu and published by the Kinkōdō company, one of the major producers of textbooks in the Meiji Period. This was followed in 1888 by a companion volume, *Kōtō: Nihon Tokuhon* (*Advanced Japanese Reader*), with which Shimpo was assisted by Miyake Yonekichi (1860–1929), educator and advocate of script reform, language standardization, and colloquial style. Shimpo was himself committed to the idea of modernizing the written language. In 1887, he and others began publication of the feminist magazine *Iratsume*, one of its avowed aims being to publish colloquial style novels to assist in the spread of *gembun'itchi*. Two of his colleagues in this enterprise, Nakagawa Kojūrō (1866–1944) and Masaki Naohiko (1862–1940) had won an 1886 essay competition sponsored by Mori on the subject of how to develop one uniform style to replace the many different varieties of writing practised by men and women. Their winning entry had argued that composition and letter-writing should be taught on *gembun'itchi* principles; that teachers, in giving oral instruction, should take care to use proper language; and that textbooks should be written in colloquial style.

A Japanese Reader was therefore an application of the principles of Shimpo and his colleagues vis-à-vis language reform. Its first two volumes were for use in the first year of primary school, as an introduction to 'proper' readers. Twenty of the twenty-two lessons in the second volume were written in colloquial style, in both plain *aru, suru* and polite *masu, de arimasu*; the last two chapters were in literary style as a preparation for readers in higher grades. Despite its stepping-stone nature, however, *A Japanese Reader* was the first significant use of colloquial style in the education system motivated by a desire on the part of the author for wide-reaching language reform rather than by utilitarian considerations.

Two other Education Ministry offerings at this time were *Yomikaki Nyūmon* (*First Steps in Reading and Writing*, September 1886) and *Jinjō Shōgaku Tokuhon* (*Elementary Reader*, May 1887). The former, compiled by Yūmoto Takehiko, was the first textbook published by the Ministry since Mori had overhauled the Compilation Bureau, replacing its head Nishimura Shigeki, a self-confessed opponent of colloquial style, with former deputy-head Izawa Shūji (1851–1917), a man convinced of the need to compile modern textbooks suitable for children and a personal user of colloquial style. The proportion of colloquial style in *First Steps in Reading and Writing* was not large, but is worth noting because it appeared this time in narrative pieces rather than in dialogue. The first volume of *Elementary Reader*, on the other hand, was entirely in colloquial style, most of it in dialogue form rather than narrative.

There followed in quick succession three other textbooks using colloquial grammar: Nishi Tomisada's *Yōgaku Tokuhon* (*A Child's Reader*, May 1887), Shimada Utako's *Kokubun: Shōgaku Tokuhon* (*Japanese Language: A First Reader*, June 1887), and the Tokyo Urban Prefectural Office's *Shōgaku Tokuhon* (*Elementary Reader*, 1888). Nishi was a strong supporter of the *gembun'itchi* principle; not long after the appearance of his textbook, he published an article in a prominent education journal outlining his thoughts on achieving language reform through colloquial style.[35] In the preface to the first volume of *A Child's Reader*, he expressed his eager desire for the day when the idea of *gembun'itchi* would become a reality, adding that in this reader he had based his style upon the kind of speech commonly used by Tokyo gentlemen. The first volume was in colloquial style; the second began with colloquial and progressed to something halfway between that and literary style; while the remaining six volumes were all in a greatly simplified version of literary style. Volumes 1 to 7 of Shimada's reader were also in a simplified literary style, Volume 8 being a collection of excerpts from the Japanese classics. At the end of each volume, however, were appended a few lessons in colloquial style, this being the first time it had appeared in materials for the higher grades. The Tokyo Urban Prefectural Office reader likewise employed colloquial grammar in several lessons per volume, for the higher grades as well as the lower; its author, like Nishi, prefaced the first volume with the explanation that his colloquial was based on refined Tokyo speech and that he, too, looked forward to the day of *gembun'itchi*.

The reappearance of colloquial style in textbooks in the late 1880s was no doubt directly influenced by the revived press debate by intellectuals on the issue of style reform and by the appointment of Mori as Education Minister, a man known to be dissatisfied with the state of written Japanese. A third factor which drew attention to the question at this time was the appearance in 1887 of the first colloquial-style novels by a new crop of young writers influenced by western literary theories. Despite the continued and vehement attacks of critics, by 1887 the movement for language modernization had made significant, if spasmodic, progress since Maejima's proposal in 1886. Whereas Tokugawa Period scholars had almost universally viewed the colloquial with disdain, a growing number of their Meiji counterparts now recognized its unquestionable advantages as a means of spreading knowledge on a national scale. Although it had not gained any noticeable foothold in formal education until the end of the second decade of the Meiji Period, it had become an increasingly common medium for popular education. Many intellectuals had reached the point of accepting in principle the idea of across-the-board language reform in the shape of colloquial style. What was lacking was convincing demonstration of the stated advantages of colloquial style in practice, a gap which was about to be filled as the years following 1887 saw the modern Japanese novel become the proving ground for *gembun'itchi*. Before we examine that process, however, there remains to be investigated one area – political debate – in which attitudes to colloquial style played a significant role.

4 Language and politics

No discussion of the early, utilitarian stages of the language modernization movement would be complete without an examination of the role of its political aspect. The relationship between language and power has been a subject of interest to socio-linguists and educators for many years, in particular the manner in which attitudes to and manipulation of language may be used to control full participation in discussion of issues of national interest by those who do not share the same code as the manipulators. If the élites of a society, whether by accident of tradition or by design, limit access to the information presented in that society's education system and organs of mass communication by perpetuating a mode of expression traditionally the province of the upper class alone, they thereby reserve to themselves control of the flow of knowledge and ideas and the trend of political debate, preventing full involvement in public life by those outside the ruling class.

Just such a situation, as we have seen, existed in Japan during the first twenty years of the Meiji Period, a legacy from the Confucian social order of the feudal period which denied commoners any aspiration to a voice in the running of their society. The use of archaic, difficult Sino-Japanese as the written language of public life during the early modern period in the absence of a simple, versatile, standard colloquial style based on the grammar of the spoken language, and the restriction in practical terms of education in Sino-Japanese to the upper class, in effect reinforced in the written language those feudal class divisions which the new government had officially dissolved. That this was due to deeply entrenched views on what constituted proper writing rather than any active intent to restrict access in no way alleviated the situation.

The most pressing item on the agenda of the Meiji Government was the establishment of a powerful centralized bureaucracy in order to ensure the sovereignty of the new order. Japan had been for some time a nation-state, a socially cohesive and politically autonomous territory. Now she faced the urgent necessity for modernization in order to secure her precarious position in the industrialized world in which she found herself. Central to the modernization process is the nationwide dispersion through improved systems of communication of information deemed by leaders necessary to permit the effective reshaping of political, social, and economic structures. In Japan, as we know, aspects of the national language also required reshaping in order to permit it to function effectively as a vehicle for the spread of this information. It became increasingly apparent as the Meiji Period advanced that modernization of the written language would be a prerequisite for the smooth attainment of modernization across the board. Certain supporters of political reform during the 1860s and 70s became conscious of the potential of the colloquial style as a weapon in their campaign of mass education in the theories of western representative government, and employed it to further their aims with the deliberate intent of expanding the range of their works.

The first two decades of the Meiji Period were a time of intense political debate in Japan as the introduction of western political theories shook traditional views of society and government. As intellectuals attempted to fathom the implications of the Restoration and contact with the west for the future stability of the nation, a large number of books, essays, tracts, and journal and newspaper articles put before the reading public the many facets of one major theme – the nature and forms of political leadership. Of particular concern was the concept of representative government, introduced through expository works by intellectuals who had observed its workings abroad and through translations of important works of western political philosophy. As the debate intensified, spokesmen for varying approaches to the issue of bridging the gap between past and present gathered their supporters. Tetsuo Najita identifies three modes of political thought of particular importance: the materialistic liberalism of Fukuzawa Yukichi and Nishi Amane, which bolstered the Meiji cult of advancement through personal effort; the natural-right theory of Ueki Emori (1857–92) and Nakae Chōmin (1847–1901), which fostered the spirit of idealistic protest in Japan;

and the theory of social evolution espoused by Katō Hiroyuki and Nishimura Shigeki, which provided a new synthesis between past and present.[1] Politics preoccupied the major newspapers in this early period of their development, the question generating the most heated argument being that of an elected assembly. Disagreement over the timing and electoral range of such an assembly led to a decade-long period of agitation by disaffected liberals, commonly called the civil rights movement (*jiyū minken undō*), during which efforts were made to spread Rousseau's doctrine of the natural rights of man throughout the country in support of the idea of an immediate assembly, in the face of equally fierce rhetoric from supporters of the government's gradualist approach to the matter.

At the same time, the *gembun'itchi* movement for reform of the written language was also gaining ground. Although the new government legislated to abolish class barriers in 1871, soon after its inception, the continuing use of classical Chinese syntax and vocabulary in official documents, education, and intellectual discourse perpetuated Tokugawa Period class distinctions in so far as the years of study required to master their intricacies prevented access by the people at large to printed debate on the issues of the day. While the concept of style reform did not gain any significant and widespread acceptance until the adoption of colloquial style as the medium of the modern novel after 1888, some of those involved in the political education of the Japanese public contributed to the *gembun'itchi* movement in its early stages by their deliberate and pioneering use of spoken grammar in writing, so that names prominent in the political debate also appear in histories of the development of modern written Japanese.

What intellectuals such as these did, in effect, was to break with traditional class-bound attitudes to the written word, defying the accepted canons of scholarship by couching their message – to varying degrees – in the language of the masses in a bid to reach an extended readership, thereby acknowledging the newly-proclaimed legal equality of Japanese citizens and encouraging participation in public life by former commoners who had been firmly excluded from politics under the hierarchical Confucian social order. To these men it was becoming obvious that it was not appropriate to address the potential future electorate on matters concerning its possible admission to the decision-making process in a language which that electorate could not understand. Those such as Fukuzawa and Fukuchi Gen'ichirō who, while convinced of the necessity to simplify written Japanese, could not overcome their training to the extent of experimenting with colloquial grammar, nevertheless contributed to the cause of increased intelligibility by simplifying the vocabulary and phrasing of their works and to public awareness of the problem by discussing openly in print the unfortunate situation prevailing in written Japanese.

The experiments by political educators with stylistic simplification were an attempt to break the deadlock between the dominance of Sino-Japanese and the demands of a changing society by writing in a manner calculated to convey their theories more rapidly and to a wider readership than might be expected were traditional literary conventions observed. By thus admitting the importance of reader-oriented language, they provided an impetus for the growing movement for style reform.

FUKUZAWA YUKICHI AND *SEZOKU TSŪYŌ NO BUN*

First to invoke the aid of a simpler style in his efforts to educate his countrymen in both the details of western customs and institutions and also their philosophical underpinnings was Fukuzawa Yukichi, enlightenment scholar and bestselling author. Believing that superficial westernization was not enough, that the Japanese must re-evaluate the very different western approach to man's relationship with the universe which underlay the development of western science, Fukuzawa set out to disseminate western philosophy in an attempt to inculcate that spirit of independence lacking in Japan which he perceived as crucial to western success. Fukuzawa's early works were practical guidebooks either to elementary science, e.g. *Kyūrizukai* (*The Uses of Science*, 1868), or to the practical details of life in the west – *Seiyō Jijō* (*Conditions in the West*, 1866); *Seiyō Tabi Annai* (*Guide to Travel in the West*, 1867); *Seiyō Ishokujū* (*Food, Clothing, and Housing in the West*, 1867), based on notes taken during his two trips to the West in 1860 and 1862. His later works, in line with his post-Restoration realization that surface changes were perilously fragile without concomitant intellectual transitions, were serious academic treatises dealing with such issues as the status of women, civil rights, state rights, the nature of civilization, and the new view of learning, among others.[2] Fukuzawa was quick to realize the value of style reform in propagating popular education. *Conditions in the West*, an account of the running of social institutions of various types encountered during his visits to America and Europe, enjoyed bestseller status, due as much to the unusual clarity and simplicity of its style as to the information it contained.

Fukuzawa scorned the stylistic gymnastics practised by Japanese scholars, accusing them of deliberately using unnecessary, complicated Chinese characters for the sake of appearing erudite. Motivated by a desire to reach the widest possible readership, Fukuzawa himself went to considerable trouble to ensure the intelligibility of his work for those possessing the basic tools of literacy, even going so far as to enlist the services of his maid as proof-reader to identify obscure passages – what was not immediately clear to her, he rewrote. The result was a greatly simplified style, not fully colloquial as it retained the classical *nari-beshi* terminations not used in speech, but sufficiently straightforward and unconvoluted to represent a significant departure from the literary norms of the day.

As Nishio Minoru points out, even such contributors to *Meiroku Zasshi* as Nishi Amane, whose 'Yōji o mote Kokugo o shosuru no Ron' ('On Writing Japanese with the Western Alphabet') was published in the first issue in 1874 and who was aware of the style problem, wrote their articles in *kambun*; Fukuzawa alone made bold to put his theory into practice, creating a vigorous style which was neither classical Japanese nor Sino-Japanese but a judicious mix of Japanese, Chinese, elegant and colloquial elements with the primary aim of intelligibility for the masses.[3] Certainly one has only to compare the text of 'Tsūzoku Minkenron' ('On Civil Rights'), his 1878 essay on civil rights, with that of, say, Nakae Chōmin's 'Kokkairon' ('On a National Assembly', 1888) to observe the difference in terms of vocabulary (Nakae uses *kata* and *ikuta* to mean 'many' where Fukuzawa uses *ōi*, for example), syntactical complexity, frequency of Chinese idioms (e.g. *iwaku*), and number and intricacy of Chinese characters. For Fukuzawa, the primary purpose of writing was the communication of a message, not its obscuring through unnecessary ornamentation. In his own words:

> In my writing, I broke with the old-time scholarly style and adopted the simplest and easiest of styles. This was indeed distasteful to the scholars of the time. But fortunately both my own works and my translation were accepted eagerly by the public – like 'water to the thirsty' or 'a shower after a drought'. The number of copies sold was really surprising.[4]

In the preface to his collected works, Fukuzawa recalls the early impression made on him by Ogata Kōan (1810–63), a physician and instructor in Dutch language and medicine with whom he studied in Osaka as a youth. Ogata's attitude to translation was that it was a task undertaken for the benefit of those unable to read the original; to adhere rigidly to the structure of the original text and to stud the translation with unnecessary Chinese characters could ultimately result in something impossible to comprehend without reference to that same original supposedly being translated. The aim of translation was to provide the reader with information; to that end, Ogata avoided ostentatious writing, preferring instead a simpler text unadorned with difficult characters. Fukuzawa records his gratitude to Ogata for this lesson, ascribing his later adoption of a simple style as a translator in Edo to the influence of his mentor.[5]

With the clearly stated aim of enabling the new thought of *bummei* to be comprehended as widely as possible by using a quickly and easily understood form of prose, Fukuzawa violated the accepted literary canons of the day with a fine disregard for the scorn of his contemporaries. He had observed the limitations imposed on translations by *yōgakusha* in Edo by their insistence on using Chinese words and concern for stylistic elegance, disdaining as they did the use of colloquial language in prose. Fukuzawa believed that, although this had been accepted in practice for a century, it would not do for his own times. It was not enough merely to insert *kana* between the Chinese characters in Sino-Japanese style; the *kambun* foundation of any such attempt would still make the meaning hard to grasp, whereas a style based on the spoken language would be easily comprehended by all. Where the colloquial did not have the vocabulary to express a particular concept, the Chinese words could be used to fill the gap, mixing the two freely. Fukuzawa, trained from childhood in Sino-Japanese, did not find it easy to achieve his stylistic aims, and wryly recounts his struggle to free himself of old influences by rewriting phrases and substituting simpler characters. To Takaya Ryoshu, a scholar of Chinese who remonstrated with him after the Restoration for his failure to use Sino-Japanese, he replied that he had early on made a deliberate decision to employ a contemporary idiom in his texts, in order thereby to guide the masses to true civilization. This was the reasoning behind his adoption of what he called *sezoku tsūyō no bun* (familiar, common writing) in *Conditions in the West, The Uses of Science*, and other popular works.[6]

Fukuzawa's view of the rights of man, expounded in his later philosophical works, was contrary to the accepted Confucian doctrine of society as essentially hierarchical, reflecting the hierarchical nature of the larger universe, and therefore entertaining no notion of individual equality. The oft-quoted opening words of the first pamphlet of 'Gakumon no Susume' ('The Encouragement of Learning') – 'Heaven created no man higher than another, and no man lower than another'[7] – dismissed this view: Fukuzawa believed that all men were equal in the matter of rights, regardless of their widely varying situations. The concept of rights itself was difficult to explicate in the Japanese context; it had not existed in the traditional philosophy wherein rulers possessed unlimited power whether in the family or political sphere, and the ruled owed the duty of obedience. The language could not even supply a word for it; the words *kenri* and *minken* were first used by Mitsukuri Rinshō in his translations of the French Penal and Civil Codes respectively.[8] The rights which Fukuzawa assigned to the individual were those of preserving his life, property, and honour. In order to ensure that his explanation of this new and puzzling idea reached as many segments of society as possible, Fukuzawa again couched his text in what we might call laymen's terms, since he was addressing not just scholars but the nation as a whole.

'The Encouragement of Learning' was published as a series of seventeen brief pamphlets between 1872 and 1876; the first edition sold 200,000 copies, and in Fukuzawa's own lifetime the total number of copies sold throughout seventeen printings reached 3,400,000.[9] Its success may be attributed just as much to the attraction of its style for the people at large as to the novelty of its exhortations on useful education, the equality of men and nations, and personal independence. Sections 4 and 5, Fukuzawa noted, being essays aimed specifically at scholarly audiences, employ more learned vocabulary than the other sections meant for the general public; but he apologized for this, promising to return in later sections to the common words used in the first three pamphlets.[10]

Fukuzawa's style, as previously noted, was not a true colloquial style in so far as he retained the classical sentence finals *nari* and *beshi* rather than substituting *de gozaru* or other terminations found in speech. However, his resolute and consistent use of contemporary vocabulary and phrasing in those of his works meant for mass consumption rendered his prose instantly more readable than the Sino-Japanese of other Enlightenment writers. Yamamoto Masahide, doyen of scholars of the development of the modern colloquial style, comments that, while other early Meiji Sino-Japanese writings were bookish in tone, the modern reader of Fukuzawa's prose is not particularly aware of the difference in period, and is struck by both the familiarity of its vocabulary and its logical clarity.[11] The other members of the Meirokusha, Japan's first academic society founded in 1873 by Fukuzawa and nine other prominent Enlightenment intellectuals with the twofold aim of furthering Enlightenment scholarship and establishing new moral standards, may be presumed to have been aware of the problems posed by the existing literary conventions, since the first issue of the society's journal *Meiroku Zasshi* (*Meiji Six Journal*) carried Nishi's previously mentioned essay calling for the reform of written Japanese through both romanization and the adoption of a colloquial style. Of them all, however, only Fukuzawa, addressing the masses rather than fellow intellectuals alone, committed himself to practical endeavour in this field, something which Nishio Minoru attributes to the fact that Fukuzawa was attempting by his rejection of Chinese studies to bring about a re-evaluation of Japanese traditions, and to this end used language as a means of achieving an intellectual revolution.[12]

KATŌ HIROYUKI AND NISHI AMANE: IN THE STEPS OF HIRATA ATSUTANE

A second member of the Meirokusha dedicated, like Fukuzawa, to the enlightenment of his countrymen was Katō Hiroyuki. Katō, the first Japanese to study German language and thought, introduced German studies into Japan in the course of a long and distinguished career as a political theorist and educator which included a position as lecturer on western books to the Emperor, two terms as President of Tokyo Imperial University, and the headship of the Imperial Academy from 1905 to 1909. Originally a supporter of people's rights based on Rousseau's doctrine of the natural rights of man, in early works such as *Shinsei Tai-i* (*An Outline of True Government*, 1870) Katō expounded western theories of constitutional government and equality in law. Later, however, becoming more conservative as his involvement with the bureaucracy increased, he changed tack, assigning greater importance to state rights (*kokken*) than popular rights (*minken*). Whereas in *Kokutai Shinron* (*A New Debate on National Polity*, 1875), he had gone so far as to speak favourably of republican government, resulting in the book's withdrawal, in *Jinken Shinsetsu* (*A New Theory of Civil Rights*, 1882) he withdrew his support for the doctrine of natural rights, under the influence of both his new-found enthusiasm for Social Darwinism and a German-inspired belief in the supremacy of the state. While Katō had been the first to advocate constitutional government in Japan in his unpublished 1862 essay 'Tonarigusa', an attack on the shogunate disguised as a discussion of the unconstitutional nature of Chinese politics, he opposed the 1874 appeal by liberals for an elected legislature, on the grounds that a national assembly would be premature in the Japanese context until the Japanese people had achieved a degree of enlightenment sufficient to render their participation in representative government effective. What was needed, he argued, was a caretaker government of intellectuals, aristocrats, and wealthy businessmen until such time in the future as a parliament elected from the people became feasible.

Katō's desire to widen reader access to his political theories in his early period led him to publish two works in a *de gozaru* colloquial style, *de gozaru* being the form of the copula then used in speech by members of the *samurai* class of which he was a member.[13] These were *Kōeki Mondō* (*A Debate on Trade*, 1869), which was written as a two-person dialogue on the benefits of foreign trade, and *An Outline of True Government*, a colloquial reworking of *Rikken Seitai Ryaku* (*An Outline of Constitutional Polity*) which Katō had already published in *kambun kuzushi* style in 1868. *An Outline of True Government* took the form of a first-person discourse on constitutional government and the equality of man. Katō, like all the other founder members of the Meirokusha, was proficient in a European language and had no doubt remarked the versatility of the German colloquial style and its advantages in facilitating communication. He was the first scholar of the Meiji Period to publish a work in a style using one of the colloquial forms of the copula, albeit the high-toned *de gozaru* rather than the more mundane *da* or *de aru*. Given that the message of *A Debate on Trade* was presented as dialogue, its use of a colloquial style was not unreasonable; but *An Outline of True Government* was a straightforward narrative exposition of his personal views, and to adopt *de gozaru* rather than the classical *nari-beshi* was a departure from normal practice. Not even Fukuzawa had gone as far. Shindō Sakiko notes, however, that despite the colloquial terminations, early *de gozaru* works such as

An Outline of True Government and later Nishi's *Hyakuichi Shinron* (*New Theory of the Hundred and One*) retained bookish vocabulary and were strongly Sino-Japanese in tone,[14] in contrast to Fukuzawa's approach of adopting colloquial vocabulary and phrasing while retaining classical terminations. Nishio Mitsuo, analysing the text of *An Outline of True Government*, also comments on the frequency with which Katō uses Chinese words and quotations by comparison with colloquial vocabulary, and the preponderance of Sino-Japanese verbs made by adding *suru* to a word made up of two or more Chinese characters (e.g. *bemmei suru*) over Japanese composite verbs such as *oyobikaneru*.[15] Nevertheless, Katō's experiment resulted in a comparatively readable style, so that parts of *An Outline of True Government* were used as readers in elementary schools during the early years of the new education system.

Katō modelled his use of colloquial grammar on the *kōshakuhon* (lecture books) of Hirata Atsutane, Shinto theologian, scholar of the Japanese classics, and leader of the Shinto Restoration movement aimed at purifying Shinto of what Hirata regarded as deleterious Buddhist and Confucian influences. Hirata made national lecture tours of Shinto shrines, winning a following among farmers and village officials with his lectures on *kodō*, the ancient way. In 1811, a series of lecture books were issued, verbatim notes of Hirata's lectures written down by his followers in the identical *de gozaru* style in which they were delivered. These books, which included *Kodō Tai-i* (*An Outline of the Ancient Way*), *Zoku Shintō Tai-i* (*A Further Outline of Shinto*), and *Butsudō Tai-i* (*An Outline of Buddhism*), dealt with many topics, among them Shinto, Chinese studies, the ancient way (Japanese practices before the introduction of Chinese thought), and Buddhism.

As to whether Katō adopted colloquial style in these two works from any deep-seated conviction of the need for style reform or merely with the utilitarian aim of educating the masses, opinion is divided. Maruyama Masao concludes that there is a fundamental difference between the approach to colloquialization of Katō and Fukuzawa in that Katō adopted the *de gozaru* style as a temporary expedient for introducing new ideas, while Fukuzawa's fresh approach to writing was intimately connected with his much deeper concern with bringing about an intellectual revolution in Japan.[16] It is true that of all Katō's output, only these two do not employ classical syntax. Katō himself recalled in a 1901 lecture on *gembun'itchi* to the Gembun'itchi Club, however, that he had long been convinced of the efficacy of a conversational colloquial style in communicating ideas, and that for this purpose he found the *de gozaru* style of Hirata Atsutane's lecture books most suitable.[17] That his interest in the reform of written Japanese was keen, at least in his later years, is demonstrated by his appointment as head of Kokugo Chōsa Iinkai (National Language Research Council), set up by the government in 1902 with the investigation of orthographic and style reform as two of its four major charter points.

A second Enlightenment scholar to adopt the *de gozaru* style was Nishi Amane, educator, government official, and charter member of the Meirokusha. Nishi, on the orders of the Tokugawa shogunate, had spent three years studying law and economics in Holland, where he also developed an abiding interest in western philosophy, in particular the utilitarianism of John Stuart Mill which he sought to introduce to Japan through translation. His major original works were *Hyakugaku Renkan* (*Encyclopaedia*, 1870), a classification of the branches of scholarly knowledge based on lectures given by Nishi at the Ikueisha, a private academy he ran which offered a western-oriented education; *Hyakuichi Shinron* (*New Theory of the Hundred and One*, 1874), an attack on the Confucian tenet of the indivisibility of morals and politics; and *Jinsei Sampō Setsu*, (*Theory of the Three Human Treasures*, 1875), Nishi's outline of a moral programme for modern society. Of these, it is *New Theory of the Hundred and One*, widely circulated in the Meiji Period, which demonstrates Nishi's concern with the part to be played by language in mass education.

As noted earlier, Nishi had already revealed his awareness of the problems involved in literary Japanese with the publication in the first issue of the *Meiji Six Journal* in 1874 of 'Yōji o mote Kokugo o shosuru no Ron' ('On Writing Japanese with the Western Alphabet').[18] He began this essay by expounding upon the important roles played by scholarship, science, and writing in bringing enlightenment to the people. Since both scholarship and science were dependent upon the written word, the situation prevailing in Japan, where the grammars of speech and writing were different, presented an obstacle to the spread of learning which must be overcome. Nishi proposed that Japan should adopt the western alphabet to replace her existing orthographic conventions. One of the advantages of such a step, he believed, would be the eventual abandonment of artificial literary forms and the development of a more natural style, as the phonetic roman letters were more suited to the reproduction of the spoken language than the Chinese ideographs. While not yet a full-blown advocate of the *gembun'itchi* colloquial style, preferring a working compromise between literary and colloquial elements, Nishi foreshadowed its later appearance with this appeal. As the circulation of each issue of the *Meiji Six Journal* averaged 3,000 during its first year,[19] Nishi's theories on style reform may be assumed to have been widely read by Japanese intellectuals, at least in the capital. Indeed, Mozume Takami (1847–1928), who became an influential advocate of colloquial style with the publication of his essay 'Gembun'itchi' in 1886, recalled that it was the influence of Nishi's essay and his subsequent visit to Nishi to discuss the matter further which first sparked his interest in the subject.[20]

At about the same time as this article appeared in the *Meiji Six Journal*, Nishi published *New Theory of the Hundred and One*, a critical discussion of traditional moral teaching in which he attempted to sever the tie between politics and morality and to distinguish between the principles of science and those of mankind. Nishi had early been influenced by the thought of Ogyū Sōrai (1666–1728), who challenged the accepted Confucian orthodoxy which represented human society as a reflection of the cosmos, thus investing the hierarchical social structure with the authority of natural law. In *New Theory of the Hundred and One*, he sought to repudiate the doctrine that virtue and morality were the preserve of political leaders alone, attempting to develop in its stead a position on the importance of morals to a modern society divorced from traditional ethics. The debate was structured in the form of a dialogue between teacher and student, again using the *de gozaru* style of Hirata's lecture books. Like Hirata, Nishi's aim was to reach as wide a readership as possible with his new concept of the separation of ethics and government. 'On Writing Japanese with the Western Alphabet' had been couched in the Sino-Japanese style appropriate to the intellectual readership of the *Meiji Six Journal*. Nishi now sought a wider audience by publishing *New Theory of the Hundred and One* in book form, and this intent to enlighten consciously influenced his choice of style.

The twenty-third issue of the *Meiji Six Journal* in December the same year carried another piece by Nishi debating the issue of travel by foreigners within the country ('Travels in the Interior'), written in colloquial style which combined the common *da* termination with the more aristocratic *de gozaru*. This was the text of a speech given by Nishi on 16 November, it being the habit of Meirokusha members to hold fortnightly discussion meetings and monthly debating sessions at which papers were presented and subsequently published in the group's journal. While most members rewrote the notes of their speeches in Sino-Japanese before publication, Nishi chose to leave this one in the style of the spoken language in which it had been presented.

UEKI EMORI AND THE CIVIL RIGHTS MOVEMENT

The colloquial style of *New Theory of the Hundred and One* influenced the subsequent decision of civil rights activist Ueki Emori (1857–92) to try a similar tack in spreading his theories of representative government among the masses. The civil rights movement spread throughout the provinces in the decade between 1874 and 1884.[21] Translations of the works of John Stuart Mill, Rousseau, and Locke had introduced the concept of representative government to Japanese intellectuals, some of whom seized upon the issue of a national assembly as a means of attacking the monopoly of government by former Satsuma-Choshō *samurai*. Tosa dissidents led by Itagaki Taisuke (1837–1919) and Gotō Shōjirō (1838–97), unhappy with their departure from government in 1873 as a result of political machinations by other factions arising from the question of war with Korea, saw in western liberalism a chance to foment discontent with the government's gradualist approach to the question of representation. The resulting civil rights movement began with the formation by Itagaki and Gotō of the Aikokukōtō (Public Society of Patriots), which group presented a memorial to the emperor on 17 January 1874 condemning the influence of officials in the administration and arguing for the establishment of a representative assembly to broaden the base of power. His underlying motive being to unseat the present government rather than enable true popular participation in government, however, Itagaki's proposed electorate was not universal, being limited to *samurai* and wealthy commoners. In effect, despite the catch-cry of 'civil rights', political rights were not seen as extending to the masses.

The Itagaki memorial sparked a great deal of discussion among intellectuals, with Katō Hiroyuki, defender of the gradualist approach, arguing against the premature establishment of an assembly in a nation where the people as yet did not possess a developed political consciousness. Undeterred, Itagaki and his supporters continued their campaign, organizing the Risshisha (Self-Help Society) and the Aikokusha (Patriotic Society) to secure a political base. As the movement gained momentum, similar societies mushroomed in the provinces, where commoners – that is, wealthy merchants and farmers wishing to protect their traditional local power base against the encroachment of centralized government by gaining control of the prefectural assemblies established in 1878 – began to play a role in leadership. Newspapers and journals served to spread civil rights thought, as did the speeches of supporters who travelled around Japan and the influential writings of political theorists Ueki Emori and Nakae Chōmin. By the time of the formation of the Jiyūtō (Liberal Party) in 1881, there were 149 local political groups which affiliated with the new party and there had been a shift both in leadership class, from *samurai* to upper-class commoner, and geographical focus, from Tosa in the south-west to the Kantō area, along with a shift in ideological emphasis towards a more serious belief in the necessity for a parliament to implement the doctrine of natural rights.[22]

The government had not remained silent in the face of this campaign, taking steps in 1873 and 1875 to muzzle the press and in 1880 to restrict public political meetings by requiring permits and police supervision and forbidding communication between associations.[23] Such measures proved ineffective against the strength of public opinion. The press continued to debate the assembly issue; and 1881 and 1882 saw the formation of two national opposition political parties, the Jiyūtō and the Rikken Kaishintō. The Jiyūtō, led by Itagaki, advocated the more radical ideals of popular sovereignty and responsible parliamentary government, finding inspiration in the works of Rousseau; whilst the Kaishintō, led by Ōkuma Shigenobu (1838–1922), followed the more moderate line of Fukuzawa Yukichi, derived from the British utilitarians, urging a gradual extension of citizen participation in the process of government. The threat posed by the increasing vitality of these two opposition parties led the government to frame ordinances placing further and harsher restrictions on their activities, and to revise the press law in 1883 to further hinder opposition newspapers. The two parties, which together might have formed a united front, were weakened both internally and in the eyes of the public by a government-manipulated squabble over the departure of

Jiyūtō leaders on a study trip through Europe. In addition, rural unrest over economic factors led to the formation of inflammatory local peasant organizations which, under the influence of a radical wing of the Jiyūtō which advocated reform on the social and economic as well as political fronts, adopted terrorist tactics to achieve their aims, culminating in the Chichibu and Kabayama incidents of 1884 when angry farmers resorted to violent confrontations with government officials and landlords.

The Jiyūtō, split from within, was formally dissolved not long after, in October 1884; and the Kaishintō, weakened by the resignation of the Ōkuma faction over a policy disagreement in December, faded into insignificance. With the loss of these two major organizations, the decade of organized popular rights protest came to an end.

Despite the self-seeking political expediency of Itagaki and others in the early stages of the movement, they were supported in their ostensible aims by able political theorists such as Ueki Emori, Nakae Chōmin and Fukuzawa Yukichi, sincere in their desire to transplant liberal western political doctrines to Japan, who took upon themselves the task of educating the masses by publishing popular works dealing with representative government. Fukuzawa, representing the more conservative element, published *On Civil Rights* in 1878; Nakae translated Rousseau's *Social Contract* as *Min'yakuron* in 1882; Ueki wrote widely on the doctrine of natural rights, *Minken Jiyūron* (*On Civil Liberties*, 1879) being a treatise on the doctrine of natural human rights to independence and freedom and the consequent desirability of constitutional government. Of these three, the adoption of colloquial style as an aid in mass political education does not appear to have concerned Nakae, who published *Min'yakuron* in pure Chinese and other works in *kambun kuzushi*; while Fukuzawa's half-way house attitude, at the same time both progressive and conservative, has already been documented. It was Ueki who was most aware of the pragmatic benefits of style reform. Living and studying in Tokyo from 1873 to 1877, Ueki had become a great admirer of Fukuzawa. He had attended Meirokusha meetings, subscribed to the *Meiji Six Journal*, and visited Nishi Amane. It is reasonable to conclude that in addition to the political influence of the Meirokusha enlighteners, the idea of using colloquial style came to Ueki from Fukuzawa and Nishi, whose works he read.[24] As he was one of the few who had neither studied abroad nor studied a foreign language, gaining all his knowledge of western political philosophy from translations, he would not have observed at first hand the advantages of western colloquial styles; his decision to adopt this tack was therefore presumably influenced solely by the views of his Japanese mentors.

Ueki, in his *de gozaru* style foreword to *On Civil Liberties*, addresses the essay to farmers, merchants, fishermen, *samurai*, doctors, and new commoners (former members of the *eta*, or outcast group, denied even recognition as a social class under the earlier four-tiered feudal class structure), declaring its aim to be to spread people's rights and extend their freedoms. The main body of the text, five chapters in all, employs a number of colloquial terminations (*arimasu, ja, gozaru, de wa nai*) with occasional reversions to the literary *nari* and *bekarazu*. In a postscript, Ueki apologizes for the unevenness, explaining it as the result of hasty writing due to pressure of work. His text is studded with Japanese composite verbs (e.g. *tobisaru*, 'fly off', *uchikakaru*, 'strike out'), with relatively infrequent use of *suru* with Chinese compounds. Nishio Mitsuo comments that, Japanese composite verbs being more definite than the more abstract Chinese character compounds, their frequent use implies a will be to understood, either conscious or unconscious, on the part of the author.[25] In Ueki's case, the will may be taken to have been conscious, *On Civil Liberties* being a mass-oriented version of the theories he had previously expounded in *Kaimei Shinron* (*A New Debate on Civilization*, 1878) in literary style for educated upper class readers.

The fact that Ueki chose two different styles for two different readerships would seem to indicate that his adoption of colloquial style was motivated by pragmatism rather than by a desire for the reform of the written language *per se*. Believing as he did that sovereignty resides in the people, he selected that mode of expression which would be most familiar to his target audience, employing the terminations used by the common people in addition to the aristocratic *de gozaru* of Nishi and Katō's works as a powerful weapon in his campaign. *Minken Jiyūron Nihen Kōgo*, a continuation of this essay published in 1882, again employed a conventional *masu /de gozarimasu* style as Ueki continued his exposition of the nature of freedom, although a comparison of the texts of *On Civil Rights* and its sequel reveals in the latter a higher proportion of bookish Chinese-influenced vocabulary in contrast to the more straightforward tone of the earlier essay, with its greater number of words in daily use among the masses.[26] Within the civil rights movement proper, apart from the editors of opposition party newspapers, only Ueki took any practical stylistic initiative to reach the common people, his fellow advocates continuing to write in Sino-Japanese.

POLITICS AND THE STYLE OF THE PRESS

The newly emergent Japanese press played a significant role in political education in the early Meiji Period in two ways: the serious press provided a forum for the debate of the burning political issues of the day, while the party-affiliated popular press offered a means of propagandizing the masses. Fukuchi Gen'ichirō, editor of the *Tōkyō Nichi Nichi Shimbun* from 1874 to 1888, was one of the major figures debating the popular assembly issue in the serious press, and was chief supporter of the government's gradualist position on the matter. His main opponent in the verbal duel was Kurimoto Joun (1822–97) of the *Yūbin Hōchi Shimbun*, leading supporter of the liberal position. Fukuchi early realised the power of the press to mould public opinion, and introduced many western devices, such as the editorial, to upgrade its effectiveness, using the *Nichi Nichi* as a platform from which to participate actively in shaping political issues. The *Nichi Nichi* editorials took precedence in his view over news reporting; and in 1874–75 he penned forty in support of the government position that while representative government was desirable as the ultimate goal of political development, progress towards it should be made in a series of gradual steps, educating the populace slowly in self-government by creating first local and then prefectural assemblies rather than immediately placing control of a national assembly in the hands of a people not sufficiently trained in the political arts to handle it competently.[27] Unlike the civil rights campaigners, who despite their grand theories of the natural rights of man envisioned only an electorate restricted to *shizoku* (*samurai*), Fukuchi asserted that the assembly must be truly representative, open to commoner and aristocrat alike. The exchange between the *Nichi Nichi* and the *Hōchi* stirred up considerable interest and debate, delineating in the public mind the respective positions of the government and liberal camps.

Fukuchi's editorial 'Bunron' ('On Writing') of 29 August 1875, wherein he remarked upon the obstacles presented by written Japanese to the achievement of universal literacy through the education system and called for a return from the archaic to the familiar in writing, has already been discussed in the preceding chapter. Like other intellectuals in the early Meiji Period, Fukuchi had received the standard Confucian *samurai* education, with literary instruction consisting of rote recitation of Chinese classics, Chinese composition, and training in calligraphy. Again like many of the prominent figures of his time, he had studied foreign languages (Dutch and English) and had travelled to the west four times between 1861 and 1873. He read widely in English literature and history, through which he first became aware of the advantages of the colloquial style in western languages. In 1868, he launched the short-lived *Kōko Shimbun* to revile the Satsuma-Choshu forces in the new government as usurpers of power; his editorial policy was to use a simple colloquial style which even the minimally literate could read, the kind of style he had observed in western newspapers. The *Kōko Shimbun* lasted only a few months, but Fukuchi's attitude to the matter of its style clearly indicates his concern for making political comment accessible to the lower ranks of society.

Other untitled editorials followed, in 1874 and 1875, pointing out in general terms that a simpler style would enable the creation of a truly great Japanese literature without going into the matter in any great detail. Then, in 1881, Fukuchi again took up the style theme in a more explicit manner in 'Bunshōron' ('On Writing'), an editorial published in two parts on 23 and 24 May, in which he called unequivocally for the adoption of a modern colloquial style while at the same time lamenting his inability to achieve this in his own writings. Despite his self-confessed failure to abandon the literary canons of his upbringing, however, Fukuchi did much to simplify his own editorial style, eschewing esoteric vocabulary in favour of familiar, and long-windedness in favour of brevity despite his continued use of literary grammar. His aim at all times was simply to make people understand what he had to say, without unnecessary and confusing flourishes. In a scene from Takase Ukō's *Zenkoku Shimbun Zasshi Hyōbanki* (*Who's Who in Japanese Newspapers*, 1883), travellers in a carriage at night discuss the *Nichi Nichi* which one of them is carrying, praising the soundness of its moderate editorials and mentioning that Fukuchi's style makes it the easiest to read of all newspapers.[28] As a result of his understanding of the relationship between effective political education and style reform, Fukuchi took deliberate steps to ensure that his political opinions were presented in easily digestible form. In his position as head of an influential newspaper, he was well placed to reach a large number of intellectuals with his editorials on both subjects. And their effect was great, prompting Yano Fumio (1850–1931) of the *Hōchi Shimbun* to remark, 'I have not in all my life seen a time that a newspaper's editorials have so guided society'.[29]

In contrast to this serious attitude to the role of the press in society, the tabloid papers dealt in human interest stories and serialized fiction, aiming thereby to reach a mass readership and boost circulation. In pursuance of this objective, *furigana* glosses were placed next to Chinese characters to assist in deciphering the text and the colloquial style often replaced the Sino-Japanese found in *daishimbun*. The *Yomiuri* published colloquial versions alongside Sino-Japanese official notices; social snippets were written in colloquial style, employing a variety of terminations. As we have seen in Chapter 3, the trend towards using colloquial style in these newspapers continued until 1879, then began to fall off and dwindled to almost nothing by 1884.

The various branches of the civil rights movement saw in the format of *koshimbun* a means of spreading their political theories among the people at large, and indeed the press, whether serious or popular, was the main means of dissemination of liberal theory during this period.[30] After the formation of the opposition political parties in 1881 and 1882, each party began to produce its own press organs. The Jiyūtō launched *Jiyū Shimbun* in 1882, followed by two *koshimbun*, *E-iri Jiyū Shimbun* (1882) and *Jiyū no Tomoshibi* (1884). The Kaishintō controlled three of the already established major papers, these being the *Yūbin Hōchi Shimbun*, *Chōya Shimbun*, and *Tōkyō Yokohama Mainichi*. In addition, it published two *koshimbun*, the *E-iri Chōya Shimbun* (1883) and *Kaishin Shimbun* (1884). These politically-affiliated *koshimbun* adopted as part of their tactics the editorial, hitherto seen only in *daishimbun*, and from 1884 until 1886 the *E-iri Jiyū Shimbun*, *Jiyū no Tomoshibi*, and *Kaishin Shimbun* broke new ground by presenting editorials written in colloquial style. Whereas in earlier non-political *koshimbun* the focus of colloquialization had been the *zappō* (news items), to widen circulation and provide easily accessible entertainment, the editors of party papers now saw the value of abandoning Sino-Japanese as an expedient in spreading serious political concepts. This was both the first time editorials had been written for the people and the first time they had appeared in colloquial style. *Jiyū no Tomoshibi* led the way, publishing Sakasaki Shiran's fifteen-part *de arimasu* style editorial *Kyōdai Dōkenron* (*On Equal Rights for Siblings*) under the pseudonym of Ō Dōjin in 1884.

May to December that year saw a spate of such editorials. Yamamoto lists some of them: 'Gozennokami nado no Mukashi Banashi' ('Old Tales of the Emperors' 21 and 22, Angai Bō, *de gozaimasu*); 'Moshihogusa' (Anthology 38–70, Nobujo, *de arimasu* and *de gozarimasu*); 'Shinkō no Jiyū' ('Freedom of Religion' 62–5, Ō Dōjin, *de arimasu, de gozaru*); 'Oyaoya no Kokoroe' ('Hints for Parents' 77, Ō Dōjin, *masu*); and 'Kinka no Hanyake' ('Singed in a Nearby Flame' 78–111, anonymous, *de arimasu*). In all, 15 colloquial style editorials appeared, in 55 daily instalments.[31] The writer in charge of editorials was Sakasaki Shiran (1853–1912), political novelist and civil rights activist, who published six of his own under the pen-name of Ō Dōjin. As a result of an inflammatory speech made in his home province of Kochi in 1881, Sakasaki had been barred from making political speeches there for a period of one year, and had hit on the device of circumventing the ban by forming a company of storytellers which then performed accounts of European liberals and the French Revolution. Not surprisingly, parts of his speeches were deemed treasonous, and he was arrested and imprisoned. The advantages of the conversational style found in story-telling as a means of disseminating political education were not forgotten when he later joined *Jiyū no Tomoshibi*, however, and no doubt this experience led him to encourage colloquial style in its editorials. Yamamoto points out that the pen-name 'Asanebō' under which appeared an editorial 'Tōkyōgo no Tsūyō' ('The Common Use of the Tōkyō Dialect' 299, 30 June 1885, *masu*), urging the development of a standard form of Japanese based on Tokyo speech as a prerequisite for establishing a *gembun'itchi* colloquial style, is attributed to Sakasaki, which implies that Sakasaki's adoption of the colloquial style in editorials was motivated by a real desire for style reform in itself in addition to an appreciation of the pragmatic benefits of the moment for his cause.[32]

E-iri Jiyū Shimbun adopted the colloquial editorial about four months after its sister paper, publishing scores between 1884 and 1886, some using a mixture of classical and colloquial grammar, others purely colloquial. The editor-in-chief of this paper was Wada Izumi (died 1893), political novelist and literary critic who wrote colloquial editorials under a variety of pen-names and was presumably responsible for the decision to abandon literary artifice. Wada had worked in Kōchi with both Sakasaki Shiran and Ueki Emori on the staff of the *Kōchi Shimbun* (1880), and had been a member of Sakasaki's short-lived troupe of storytellers, the Tōyō Ippa Minken Kōshaku, influences which no doubt shaped his decision to colloquialize editorials. Colloquial-style editorials continued to appear in the *E-iri Jiyū Shimbun*, along with some in literary style, well into 1886.

The *Kaishin Shimbun*, under the leadership of Shigemura Itsuga, employed a slightly more conservative approach to the use of the colloquial style. It began with expository editorials written in simplified literary style and progressed in late 1884, for a period of two years, to the dialogue format earlier favoured by the enlightenment writers, casting editorials as discussions between two or more people and adopting a more humorous, familiar vocabulary than the more formal discursive editorials of its Jiyūtō counterparts. Examples which appeared in 1885 were: 'Konban wa ari akemashite omedetō' 8 January, *masu*), 'Gomen Asobase' ('By Your Leave', 9 January, *de gozaimasu*), 'Tora no Kawa no Urimono' ('Tiger Skins for Sale', 10 January), and 'Chōsen wa sunda, Shina wa mada da' ('Korea Is Done For, China Isn't Yet', 16 January, *da*).[33] The dialogues were written in the humorous, slangy speech of the masses, featuring characters familiar to them from *rakugo* (comic storytelling) presentations. The dialogue format was presumably adopted because it was more likely to appeal to a mass readership. From the point of view of style reform, however, these editorials were a step behind those of the Jiyūtō press, restricting the use of the colloquial to dialogue as had been done in the popular fiction of the Tokugawa Period rather than employing it in narrative.

Public interest in the civil rights movement declined sharply in the 1880s, as a result both of the 1881 pledge by the government to establish a parliament in 1890 and of the reaction against the escalating violence of the movement in 1883–84. The political argument which had been the mainstay of the serious press and party-affiliated organs lessened both as a result of the drop in interest and of the 1883 revision of the press law which severely limited the activities of opposition newspapers – in 1883 publication of 49 newspapers was suspended.[34] Internecine squabbles among the opposition papers led to a further weakening of their position. The *Jiyū Shimbun* ceased publication in January 1885, and the *E-iri Jiyū Shimbun* in September 1890. *Jiyū no Tomoshibi* survived through a number of name changes to become today's *Tōkyō Asahi Shimbun*. The Kaishintō, which although not disbanding like the Jiyūtō nevertheless sank into obscurity after the resignation of Ōkuma in 1884, continued to publish the *Kaishin Shimbun*.

We have no means of judging exactly how effective the use of colloquial style in political tracts and party *koshimbun* was in disseminating political theories to the people at large. The national education system was still in its infancy during the decade of vigorous political debate between Itagaki's memorial of 1874 and the dissolution of the Liberal Party in 1884, and was experiencing teething troubles in the form of untrained teachers, makeshift textbooks, and peasant resistance to compulsory attendance which placed a financial burden on poor families as well as taking away the important contribution of labour made by children to the family livelihood. The Fundamental Code of Education (1872) had made universal literacy its aim; but what new textbooks there were in the early years were often translations of foreign readers and moral texts, which employed Sino-Japanese or epistolary style, although some of Fukuzawa's simplified works were also used. A measure of the difficulty experienced by schoolchildren as a result of this adherence to Sino-Japanese is to be found in the previously-mentioned 1886 comment by Mozume Takami that his son had been unable to explain to him the content of his Confucian ethics text because of an inability to construe its language.[35]

The slow progress of formal schooling notwithstanding, a factor arguing for the probable wide reach of colloquially-phrased political argument is the previously mentioned relatively high rate of literacy in Japan at the beginning of the Meiji Period. The degree of literacy varied from the bare essentials to an advanced ability to read and write, of course, and some parts of Japan were more active in this area than others; however, given even an average base rate of 20 per cent among the more isolated segments of the populace, it seems likely that written political propaganda would have been accessible to many commoners either through their own ability to read or through the medium of other literate residents of the same village. The oral approach also played a substantial role, with activists travelling the country making speeches; songs carrying the theme of popular rights, among them Ueki's *Minken Kazoe Uta* (*People's Rights: A Counting Song*, c.1878) and *Minken Inaka Uta* (*People's*

Rights: A Rustic Ditty, 1879), were popular among rural people. Roger Bowen, in his study of the civil rights movement, examines evidence relating to the literacy or otherwise of participants in the Chichibu, Fukushima, and Kabayama incidents of 1884, concluding that there is reason to assume that a large number were literate, some to an advanced degree.[36] That being the case, one may assume that the calculated adoption in writing of the spoken grammar of the target audience would have facilitated the absorption of the information by those able to read but not versed in the intricacies of Sino-Japanese.

There are other names prominent in both liberal politics and the *gembun'itchi* movement – among them Taguchi Ukichi (1855–1905), economist, publisher, and civil rights activist who edited the *Jiyū Shimbun* for a time, and Yano Fumio, novelist, Progressive Party strategist, and editor of the *Yūbin Hōchi Shimbun* – but time and space do not permit their inclusion. The activities of men such as Fukuzawa, Nishi, Katō, Ueki, Fukuchi, and the others, committed to the modernization of their society, formed an important strand in the processes of both intellectual and linguistic growth and change through the dissemination of ideas.

Communication involves the transmission of information and ideas from one person to another. When this escalates to the level of mass communication from one person to a wide audience, the communicator, in order to be successful, must evaluate the means of expression available and choose that mode most likely to deliver the message with maximum effect. It is clear from the continued use of Sino-Japanese by most early Meiji enlighteners and political theorists that they clung still to the pre-Restoration view that serious writing, both in content and style, was the province of the educated élite. Those few intellectuals who recognized the need for linguistic disengagement with the highly refined literary forms of the past in order to communicate their ideas to ordinary Japanese people were for the first time visualizing the importance of the people as a whole to the modernization effort, and giving credence in a practical way to the officially-promulgated declaration of the dissolution of the class structure. No longer were the masses to remain ignorant of developments affecting their lives. The use by men like Fukuzawa and Ueki of the vocabulary and grammar of the spoken language extended to readers an opportunity to become conversant with the major issues of the day by removing much of what is known in communication theory as 'semantic noise',[37] interference which occurs when a message cannot be understood by the receiver because of some particular difficulty with the form in which it is sent.

The movement for the reform of written Japanese, spasmodic, fragmented, and basically utilitarian in thrust during the first two decades of the Meiji Period, was about to receive a boost from the adoption of colloquial style as the medium of the modern realistic novels which appeared at the end of this period, beginning with Futabatei Shimei's *The Drifting Cloud* in 1887–89. The modelling and refining of the new style in fiction over subsequent decades did much to establish its credibility in other sectors of public and private life and prepare the way for the eventual conversion to colloquial style of newspapers, school texts, and, last of all, government documents. The importance of the contribution to this process of early exponents of western political theory, whether motivated by localized pragmatism or a genuine belief in the validity of the overall reform of the written language as a factor in expediting the modernization process, cannot be underestimated; their words and actions revealed their awareness of the new status of the commoner as a political entity, and of the limitations of class-bound language in mass-oriented politics, and they demonstrated a willingness to break down the traditional strictures against the use of spoken language forms in writing by intellectuals in recognition of the new social order. By recognizing in practical fashion the expanded range of their readership due to the newly possible participation in public life of the former lower classes, these men, whether through advocacy in influential organs or practical implementation in popular works, played an important role in the development of modern written Japanese, adding to the slowly growing recognition that élitist attitudes to writing were no longer appropriate in the context of a now professedly egalitarian society.

5 The role of literature

In society at large, debate on the language issue had become quite widespread among educated men by 1884, with actual experimentation with colloquial style prose being undertaken in some cases. In the next few years, the experimentation was to spread and develop into fully-fledged implementation in the pages of the modern novel by a crop of new, young authors influenced by western literary theories. By modelling and polishing colloquial style in literature which was widely read by fellow intellectuals, these men did much to help dispel the fears of those who saw only deficiencies, thereby preparing the way for the eventual spread of the new style to other areas. Popular novels in the Tokugawa Period, as we have seen, were one of the few areas where colloquial style was to be found in writing, with narrative text being couched for the most part in *wakankonkōbun* and dialogue in colloquial style, to a greater or lesser degree depending on the author. The new writers of the Meiji Period, motivated by a desire to create realistic fiction in a serious attempt to depict the human psyche and environment rather than to provide entertainment or to moralize, were now to argue that the literary conventions of bygone ages were insufficient to do justice to the minute descriptions of the working of the modern mind in narrative as well as dialogue, and that the only possible substitute was colloquial style.

There had been one or two earlier pairs of eyes turned on the matter of style in literature. Fukuchi Gen'ichirō had suggested in 1874 and 1875 editorials[1] that a more practical, simpler style would do much to alleviate what he perceived as the contemporary degeneration of the literary arts by enabling the creation of really great literature. At a time when the idea of style reform was just beginning to be mooted by a very few people, his suggestion attracted little support. Ten years later, however, attitudes were beginning to soften; the concept of *gembun'itchi* was gaining wider acceptance despite pockets of bitter opposition, so that Taguchi Ukichi's 1885 essay[2] stressing that colloquial style was not only desirable but essential to the modern novel was published in a much more favourable climate than Fukuchi's editorials had been. While classical diction was appropriate for expressing the sentiments of bygone ages, Taguchi argued, modern ideas demanded a flexible modern language. The multiplicity of styles in literary Japanese was in his view responsible for the immaturity of Japanese literature by comparison with that of Europe. It would be well nigh impossible, he felt, to blend them all into one composite style capable of communicating the entire spectrum of emotions and ideas; the obvious choice for modern literature was colloquial style, which alone had a vocabulary range adequate to the task. Taguchi was to see the realization of his theories only two years later when the first colloquial style novels were published.

TSUBOUCHI SHŌYŌ

In September 1885, Tsubouchi Shōyō, critic, novelist, and dramatist,[3] published the first chapter of his landmark work of literary criticism, *Shōsetsu Shinzui* (*The Essence of the Novel*), in which he presented the then radical idea of the novel, hitherto considered beneath the dignity of serious authors, as an art form worthy of high regard in a civilized society. This essay, in addition to discussing theoretical aspects, offered practical advice on the mechanics of writing a good novel. In line with the accepted practice of publishing books in parts, the whole work appeared in instalments, in all a total of nine between September 1885 and April 1886. Tsubouchi had studied English literature as an undergraduate at Tokyo Imperial University. At the time *The Essence of the Novel* appeared, he was teaching at what was to become Waseda University and had already published a translation of Shakespeare's *Julius Caesar* as well as two translations of works by Sir Walter Scott. By virtue of his innovative suggestions for the future development of Japanese fiction, stemming from western literary theories which were no longer new in Europe but represented a startling departure from tradition in Japan, Tsubouchi, though never gaining particular prominence as a novelist himself, was to exert a profound influence on the emerging young writers of the time.

The novel in Japan had long been ostensibly considered frivolous and unworthy of the attention of the educated, although in practice they often proved voracious readers, Tsubouchi himself admitting that it was through eager reading of novels as a child that he learned sufficient of the state of Japanese fiction to make possible his later comparisons with western literature and to enable him to formulate, through invidious comparison, his theory of the true purpose of the novel. Certainly novel *writing* was deemed beneath the dignity of men of quality, and the social status of writers of popular fiction was low, whereas in England esteemed statesmen such as Disraeli and Bulwer-Lytton were famous for their fiction. One of the major contributions of *The Essence of the Novel* was to challenge this view by arguing that the novel could be transformed into an art form worthy of serious consideration by intellectuals. Deploring both the artificial didacticism of certain genres of Tokugawa Period fiction (the *kanzen chōaku*[4] syndrome) and the often almost pornographic sensationalism of others equally with the openly pragmatic motives of Meiji Period political novels,[5] Tsubouchi contended that a novel in which realism replaced moralizing as the aim of both characterization and plot would be able to hold its own as a respectable art form, the equal of poetry, music, and painting. The sole function of the novel, he insisted, should be to describe the human condition in accurate and unbiased terms. Realism should replace expediency as the goal of future writers.

The first, largely theoretical section of *The Essence of the Novel*, consisting of five chapters, sought to trace the historical development of the novel and to define the aims, types, and benefits of the true novel. The second section of six chapters offered Tsubouchi's practical guidelines for writing novels, dealing with plot, style, characterization, and narrative. Chapter 2 of this section dealt at length with the issue of style, being mainly a copiously-illustrated description of the three main styles found in the Japanese novel to date: *gabuntai* (classical Japanese, also known as *wabun*), *zokubuntai* (colloquial style), and *gazoku setchū buntai* (a blend of the other two). The first Tsubouchi dismissed as indeed beautiful and elegant, but lacking the vitality for the portrayal of modern life:

> *The Tale of Genji*,[6] written in *wabun*, won lasting fame for Murasaki Shikibu because its style and content, both charming, complemented each other well, and also, I think, because the

quality of her writing so well matched the spirit of the era. The style of the novel is not immutable, of course. When human nature and social customs advance further, style must be adjusted accordingly. It must make appropriate allowances for changes in language and strike out in new directions, because the stuff of which the novel is made is the portrayal of contemporary human nature and behaviour. Even Murasaki's talent would be hard pressed to produce a description of our present society in the pure *wabun* of her day.[7]

The second, on the other hand, while remarkably easy to understand and ideal for realistic dialogue because of its ability to reproduce class-bound variations in speech, was condemned as inappropriate in narrative prose because of its wordiness, its complex system of honorifics, and its lack of standardization. After pointing out these disadvantages, however, Tsubouchi softened his criticisms by pointing to the future possibilities for a new refined version of colloquial style:

> My readers are very much mistaken if they think that I have been surreptitiously denigrating the spoken language by saying that it lacks euphony and is full of linguistic corruptions. Language is spirit; style is form. Emotions are expressed with complete frankness in speech, whereas in writing they are overlaid with a veneer which to a certain extent camouflages their reality ... Dialogue is one area where a colloquial style does have advantages. Unfortunately, though, there is no getting around its defects. Perhaps one of my clever friends will discover a means of doing so. I shall wait impatiently for the day when a new version of the colloquial style appears.[8]

The best interim solution, Tsubouchi concluded, was to continue with *gazoku setchū buntai*, with narrative passages in *wabun* (referring only tangentially to the fact that it was really *wakankonkōbun* by conceding that 'Even Chinese words are occasionally employed to compensate for deficiencies in our language'[9]) and dialogue in colloquial. Within this general classification he distinguished two variants: *yomihon*[10] style, in which classical words account for 70–80 per cent of the whole in narrative and 50–60 per cent in dialogue, and *kusazōshi*[11] style, almost identical to *yomihon* style except for a higher proportion of colloquial vocabulary than Chinese words, understandable in light of the fact that these were written as entertainment for relatively uneducated women and children while *yomihon* were not. The *kusazōshi* style he recommended for novels of modern manners, the *yomihon* for historical fiction.

Tsubouchi's interest in the possibilities of colloquial style had been growing for several years. He was particularly impressed by its use in published versions of the stories of the great raconteur San'yūtei Enchō. Enchō's stories featured people from all walks of life, and such was his concern for realism in detail that he went to the locales in which his tales were set in order to study the customs and speech habits of the locals. In 1884, Wakabayashi Kanzō (1857–1938), who with several others had graduated the previous year from the fledging Japanese Shorthand Training Course set up by Tagusari Tsunaki (1854–1938) in the belief that recording speech verbatim would greatly enhance the prospects of achieving the *gembun'itchi* principle, was approached by the Kyōbashi firm, publishers of novels, to take down Enchō's live performance stories in shorthand for publication. Enlisting the aid of a fellow graduate, Wakabayashi attended performances of *Botan Dōrō* (*The Peony Lantern*) for 15 nights, sitting in the dressing room to take down what was being said on stage and later transcribing the text into a faithful reproduction of Enchō's words. One instalment was published each week. These were well received; they enabled people to read the words of the famous storyteller exactly as he had delivered them, without leaving home and without being hampered by a difficult style.

Wakabayashi and others formed a society for the study of shorthand in Tokyo, which published further Enchō stories obtained in the same manner in 1885–6 as a means of publicizing shorthand. At the same time, Enchō's friend and patron Jōno Saigiku began to serialize shorthand-recorded versions of his stories as a drawcard for his own new newspaper, *Yamato Shimbun*, launched in November 1886. Ten such stories appeared between then and May 1890, and as expected their popularity boosted circulation. The realism of the stories and the simplicity and aptness of their colloquial style had a marked influence on young novelists Futabatei Shimei (1864–1909) and Yamada Bimyō (1868–1910), who were later to model the first colloquial style novels on them. They also impressed Tsubouchi, who in a preface to the second edition of *The Peony Lantern*[12] praised the skilful and penetrating character delineation made possible by the use of the colloquial. He himself had at that time already published an essay on the style of the novel the previous year, in which he expressed interest in the potential of colloquial style.[13]

Despite his own reservations, expressed in *The Essence of the Novel*, about the use of colloquial style in its unvarnished state in the novel, Tsubouchi's advocacy of realism in fiction provided the impetus for its spread into literature. Whereas in other areas such as popular education and the press colloquial style had been adopted primarily because of a desire to facilitate comprehension, in fiction a second and even more compelling reason was the need to be able to portray in detail the subtleties of human nature without the restrictions imposed by stereotyped, archaic rhetoric and inadequate classical vocabulary. The ins and outs of an ordinary person's psyche cannot be documented in any convincing fashion in a language alien to that person's usual mode of communication. To attempt to do so would be to run the risk of unintentional humour; indeed, just such an effect has been deliberately achieved by humorists or satirists relying on the contrast between form and content to make their point. For a writer not thus motivated, however, a more realistic mode of expression is essential, a point not lost on the new generation of novelists in Japan.

Tsubouchi himself, however, continued to employ his favoured *gazoku setchū* in his own work, *Tōsei Shosei Katagi* (*The Characters of Modern Students*, 1885–86) and *Saikun* (*The Wife*, 1889) among others; as his style clung to the past, so did their content, *Modern Students* in particular containing several improbable incidents of the type favoured in earlier popular fiction. It was not long, however, before his protégé Futabatei Shimei took up the challenge issued in *The Essence of the Novel* and attempted to polish the colloquial into a fit literary medium in a novel.

FUTABATEI SHIMEI

Futabatei, son of a low-ranking *samurai* family, had begun his schooling with the study of the Chinese classics. Later, in 1881, he entered the Tokyo School of Foreign Languages, specializing in the study of Russian with the intention of becoming a diplomat. The closure of the school during a reorganization of the education system in 1885, however, prompted a reconsideration of his plans. Rather than transfer to the commercial school where students of Russian were to be relocated, Futabatei abandoned his diplomatic ambitions and, both impressed by Tsubouchi's ideas on realism and influenced by his own study of Goncharov, Turgenev, Dostoevsky, and the Russian critic Vissarion Belinsky, resolved instead to become a writer. In order to seek direction as to the best way of embarking on this career, he visited Tsubouchi in January 1886. Futabatei himself, recalling how he came to write in colloquial style, described what happened:

> I decided I should like to try my hand at writing something. I had never been able to write well, however, and had no idea of where to start. Accordingly, I went to Tsubouchi's house to ask his advice. He said, 'You know Enchō's stories. Why not try writing the same way?'[14]

Futabatei took his mentor's advice, he continued, producing a novel written in a style which sought to reproduce the Tokyo dialect. Although he does not mention it by name, it is probably *Ukigumo* (*The Drifting Cloud*, 1887–89), his first novel, he was referring to; this novel is generally recognized as his first attempt at colloquial-style fiction, his earlier works being translations of Russian literature. His main problem, he recalled, was trying to decide between the polite *de gozaimasu* copula or the more common *da*. Tsubouchi's advice was to steer clear of honorifics; Futabatei, though not entirely convinced, capitulated and adopted the *da* style. In so doing, however, he found it difficult to avoid a suggestion of vulgarity in his text, and was advised by Tsubouchi (advocate, it will be remembered, of *gazoku setchū*) to make his writing more 'refined'. On this point, Futabatei dug in his heels. He refused to use Chinese words which had not been completely assimilated into the Japanese language; nor would he use such classical words as *haberu* which were no longer part of the spoken language, or set phrases and stereotyped idioms. For his model, he took the *Fukagawa-kotoba*[15] of Shikitei Samba (1776–1822, Tokugawa Period novelist) which he believed were common but poetic and embodied, to him, the spirit of the spoken language.

> I resolved to use modern words throughout and trust to their natural development – I would wait for the flower to bloom and the fruit to grow. It is futile to try to force a mixture of Japanese and Chinese styles ... At the time, Tsubouchi advised me to make my writing a little more elegant, but I had no wish to do so. Indeed, it might be closer to the mark to say that I did my

utmost to keep elegance out of my work, endeavouring instead to polish commonplace words.[16]

The influence of Russian writers and the desire for realism combined with the desire for a simple, flexible style – in a 1907 article, 'Bundan Gosoku', he attributed his initial use of colloquial style to the wish to be able to put his thoughts down easily – as factors in Futabatei's choice of colloquial style in his novels. *The Drifting Cloud*, which appeared in three parts between 1887 and 1889, is generally regarded as Japan's first major modern novel, both for its application of the theory of psychological realism and its pioneering use of the Tokyo dialect throughout the text. It was with this work that the language modernization movement came together with the evolution of modern Japanese fiction in a powerful compact which was to have considerable consequences for both. The novel told the story of the effect upon Utsumi Bunzō, a young man of integrity, of the new pressures of Meiji society; beneath a sketchy plot, it was Bunzō's inner struggle which formed the real stuff of the novel. Bunzō's musings could not have been realistically conveyed in any idiom but that used in his everyday life.

Despite Futabatei's claim to have rejected the idea of 'elegant' writing, however – a claim made retrospectively almost 20 years after the event – he did not find it easy to write in colloquial style. It was difficult for him to shake off the influence of his early education in classical Chinese, and the first volume of *The Drifting Cloud* shows frequent traces of an earlier tradition. It has the *bungotai* preface favoured by Tokugawa Period writers, for example, something not found in the other two volumes,[17] and chapters are given titles as well as numbers, another carryover from the past. Stock epithets and word plays of the type described in Chapter 2 as well as Chinese expressions figure in the text to a much greater extent than in later volumes, so that on first reading there is not at first a particularly abrupt sense of disjunction with older literary forms. What was new was his use of colloquial grammar and vocabulary outside dialogue, and the spatial organization of the text itself, with dialogue separated out from narrative and more punctuation than was customary at that time. By his own admission, Futabatei modelled the first volume after Shikitei Samba and other Tokugawa Period novelists, the second on the prose of Dostoevsky, and the third on that of Goncharov. He is said to have written the draft of Volume 2 in Russian and then translated it into

140 *Language and the Modern State*

simple Japanese in an effort to rid himself of a tendency to use Chinese expressions. Figure 5.1 is an example taken from this volume.

The Drifting Cloud established Futabatei's reputation as a leading modern writer. It was followed by *Aibiki* (1888) and *Meguriai* (1888–89), translations of Turgenev's *The Rendezvous* and *The Three Meetings*, in which Futabatei used the colloquial in so skilful and polished a manner that literary circles were greatly impressed by its effectiveness. Though these were his first published *gembun'itchi* translations, they were not his first attempt: Marleigh Grayer Ryan recounts that in the early days of Futabatei's friendship with Tsubouchi he had shown him a colloquial-style translation of part of a Gogol story, which later disappeared. He had also translated, by March 1886, part of Turgenev's *Fathers and Sons* under the title of *Kyomutō Katagi* using, on Tsubouchi's advice, a more refined middle-class variety of the colloquial in preference to the down-to-earth language of the Gogol effort. While this translation was never published, for reasons now unknown, an advertisement printed by

Figure 5.1 Colloquial style and western punctuation in Futabatei's *Ukigumo* (*The Drifting Cloud*)

文三が二階を降りて、ソットお勢の部屋の障子を開けるその途端に、今迄机に頬杖をついて何事か物思ひをしてゐたお勢が、吃驚した面相をして些し飛上ッて居住居を直ほした。顔に手の痕の赤く残ッてゐる所を観ると、久敷頬杖をついてゐたものと見える。
「お邪魔ぢや有りませんか。」
「イヽエ。」
「それぢやア。」
ト云ひ乍ら文三は部屋に這入ッて坐に着いて
「昨夜は大に失敬しました。」
「私こそ。」
「実に面目が無い、貴嬢の前をも憚らずして……今朝その事で慈母さんに小言を聞きました。アハヽヽ。」
「さう、オホヽヽ。」
ト無理に押出したやうな笑ひ、何となく冷淡い。今朝のお勢とは全で他人のやうで。

Source: Futabatei Shimei '*Ukigumo*' *Gendai Bungaku Taikei* 1, Tokyo: Chikuma Shobō, 1967, p. 281.
Note: For translation see Appendix.

the publishers before negotiations ceased suggested that while cynics would regard Futabatei's translation style as an idle imitation of Enchō, admirers would regard it as heralding a new literary style for Japan.

The style of *The Rendezvous* and *Three Meetings* aroused particular enthusiasm among those young men who were later to become the writers of the Naturalist School, notably Tayama Katai (1871–1930) and Shimazaki Tōson (1872–1943). Earlier Japanese translations of foreign works had been for the most part free adaptations, often abridged, rather than faithful renderings. Futabatei strove to reproduce the natural rhythm of the Russian original, even going so far as to attempt to reproduce its punctuation. The freshness and delicacy of the descriptions of nature made possible by the use of colloquial style enthralled the budding Naturalists, among them Tayama Katai, who wrote:

> It was such a marvellous new style. I may not have been able to appreciate it fully at that age, but still the subtle description of nature made my heart leap ... Having been raised on the stiff Chinese classics and other ancient Chinese and Japanese texts, I was deeply moved by the precise, startling descriptive passages in this story. Could this be good style? I wondered. Yet I realized that such a clear-cut style was the strongest characteristic of western writing and that, in the future, the style of Japanese literature would most certainly have to move in this same direction.[18]

It is possible, as Ōta Saburō observes,[19] that Futabatei's more successful use of colloquial style in the third volume of *The Drifting Cloud* stemmed from his efforts to perfect *The Rendezvous*. The first volume of *The Drifting Cloud* was published, as we have seen, in 1887, the third in 1889; *The Rendezvous* and *Three Meetings* appeared in between, in 1888. Futabatei's concentration on their style may have helped him rid his writing of the antiquated expressions found in the first part of his novel. To translate foreign material into colloquial style was a much simpler proposition than original composition in Japanese, where lapses into traditional modes of expression triggered off by familiar connotations might be expected to occur with greater frequency. The translations may have provided a valuable experimental anvil on which to hammer out and remove anachronistic expressions and clichés.

Futabatei's career as a writer of fiction was neither long nor prolific. Forced by financial considerations to take a post on the government gazette in August 1889, he produced only three more novels: *Chasengami* (*Widow's Coiffure*, 1906), *Sono Omokage* (*An Adopted Husband*, 1906), and *Heibon* (*Mediocrity*, 1907), preferring to concentrate after 1904 until his death in 1909 on essay writing. Unlike many of his contemporaries, he did not publish long theoretical essays on the *gembun'itchi* issue. His importance in the language modernization movement stems from his being the first to demonstrate the possibilities of colloquial style in the new fiction.

The mentor–protégé relationship between Tsubouchi and Futabatei was by no means a one-way street. The benefits to Futabatei were obvious: Tsubouchi gave of his time and ideas in discussion, helping the younger man to round out his still immature theories and envision the means of their application; he prodded Futabatei into abandoning what he considered the vulgar lower-class colloquial of the *Fathers and Sons* translation in favour of the middle-class idiom of Enchō's stories; he introduced him to professional writers, so that Futabatei grew familiar with the workings of the literary world; and he read Futabatei's manuscripts, arranged with publishers to take them, and even lent his own name to the first two parts of *The Drifting Cloud* when it was published. This last was a fairly common practice of the times; young writers would publish under the name of an established author in an effort to ensure the work would sell. Tsubouchi's recent success with *The Characters of Modern Students* meant that his name on *The Drifting Cloud* would attract attention to it.

On Tsubouchi's part, the association between the two men led him to the realization as he watched Futabatei's achievement that he himself would never be able to write the truly realistic novel he espoused; the influence of the Tokugawa Period fiction he had loved to read in his youth proved too strong, as can be seen in *The Characters of Modern Students*. Made thus aware of his limitations by comparison, he turned from fiction to his great strengths of translation and teaching, becoming renowned for his renderings of Shakespeare's plays. He was also influenced by his discussions with Futabatei on colloquial style into moving away from his belief in *gazoku setchū* as the best style for the novel. Several months after the two men met, and soon after *The Essence of the Novel* appeared, Tsubouchi published *Bunshō Shinron* (*A New Theory of Writing*, 1886), in which he conceded that as the primary task of writing was to express thoughts and emotions, this could best be done in the kind of colloquial style found in the works of Samba and Ikku, with natural speech the standard. This was not to be construed, he went on, as an out and out advocacy of the *gembun'itchi* principle; whereas its supporters wanted speech and writing to be identical (a perception in which he may have been mistaken), he felt that a certain amount of polishing and refining was essential. Even an absolutely faithful reproduction of speech in writing, if it did not succeed in communicating emotion, would achieve nothing; so long as the emotion behind the words was conveyed to the reader, it was not important whether the style was the same as everyday speech or not. He made three practical suggestions: outdated classical expressions should be replaced with modern equivalents; writers should concentrate on meaning rather than form and stop trying to fit the sense to the style, as in the rhythmic 7–5 metre of Bakin; and the stereotyped clichés favoured in old styles should be avoided.

Tsubouchi attempted to write a novel to embody his new approach, *Koko ya Kashiko* (*Here and There*, 1887). Like Futabatei, he improved with practice; while the first part, though basically colloquial style, retained quite a few traces of genre fiction, these were not nearly as evident in the latter half. Tsubouchi himself, reminiscing to Yanagida Izumi in 1934, described his intentions in moderate vein:

> Researchers have apparently been attracted to its style as *gembun'itchi*, but I tried to emphasize that it was instead a kind of 'middle-of-the-road' style. I came to attempt this new style in response to the stimulus of Futabatei's new devices, but nevertheless I had my own ideals. I did not write in pure colloquial style, as Futabatei and Yamada [Bimyō] advocated; inwardly, I determined on an intermediate style somewhat akin to literary style. I was privately opposed to Futabatei's theory, and decided to make an experiment in writing my own style. The result was *Here and There*.[20]

This novel was Tsubouchi's only attempt at colloquial style. He gave up writing fiction in 1889; his last story, *The Wife* (1889), saw him retuen to the *gazoku setchū* style.

YAMADA BIMYŌ

The next major champion of the *gembun'itchi* cause in the novel was Yamada Bimyō, a childhood friend of Futabatei, who published his first full length colloquial style novel, *Fūkin Shirabe no Hitofushi* (*Notes from an Organ Melody*) in July 1887.

Bimyō had begun writing while still at school. In 1885, together with Ozaki Kōyō (1867–1903), Maruoka Kyūka (1865–1927), and others, he became a foundation member of the Ken'yūsha society, a small group of student writers who were disturbed by the blatant propaganda of the political novels which circulated in the early Meiji Period and who advocated a return to the literary styles of the late Tokugawa Period, in particular those of Saikaku and Bakin. In 1885, they began circulating among themselves a small, handwritten journal, *Garakuta Bunko* (*The Trash Library*), which contained offerings of their own work for group perusal and discussion; this journal was put on public sale two years later. Part of *Tategoto Zōshi* (*Tale of a Harp*), Bimyō's first novel dealing with England's King Alfred and written in the style of Bakin, appeared in its pages in 1885. So too did his first published attempt at a colloquial-style novel the following year, *Chōkai Shōsetsu Tengu* (*The Conceited Demon: A Satirical Novel*), an unfinished work which in form resembled the *kokkeibon* ('comic novels') of Samba and Ikku. Though written in the *da* style, its sentences, extremely long and sparsely punctuated, were reminiscent of those of Tokugawa Period light fiction. Bimyō did, however, introduce certain forms of punctuation which had not been seen in a Japanese work before, separating dialogue and narrative with the symbol + and using the device . . . . . . to suggest admiration or retrospection. *The Conceited Demon* was never completed; Bimyō himself considered *Notes from an Organ Melody* his maiden vernacular work.[21]

Bimyō's decision to switch from *wakankonkōbun* to colloquial style was brought about by several factors. Like Futabatei, he had been profoundly affected by the influence of a European literature, in his case English rather than Russian. At the time of the Ken'yūsha's formation, he was avidly reading Milton's *Paradise Lost*, Chaucer's *Canterbury Tales*, and Lamb's *Tales from Shakespeare*. He had been particularly impressed with Chaucer's brilliant handling of colloquial English. In his own words:

> I observed that the colloquial style was used in western writing. In my study of the history of English literature, I was deeply impressed by the poet Chaucer's marvellous achievement in bringing into being a modern English style; and also by the regrettable fact that although this took place several hundred

years ago, there has not yet appeared in Japan anyone to suggest establishing our own colloquial style.[22]

Then Futabatei passed on Tsubouchi's advice on patterning his colloquial style on that of the Enchō stories, advice which Bimyō accepted, explaining in the preface to *Notes from an Organ Melody* that its style was a slightly more ornamental version of that of the raconteur's love stories. A third influence was that of the lectures, both entitled 'Gembun'itchi', given by Mozume Takami and the English scholar Basil Hall Chamberlain at meetings of the Kana and Rōmaji Clubs in 1886 and 1887 respectively. Both men urged that writing be brought closer to speech as a matter of national urgency at just the time when Bimyō was beginning his first novels. Recalling his decision to adopt colloquial style, Bimyō wrote that these two lectures (he had heard about Chamberlain's, and had read the published text of Mozume's) had caused him to realize that the time was ripe to put his English-inspired plans into practice, and he had therefore attempted to do so in *Notes from an Organ Melody*. Despite his good intentions, however, he added, the somewhat old-fashioned tone of the narrative sections and the old-fashioned title were proof of his inability to rid himself completely of ingrained habits.[23]

While Futabatei had chosen colloquial style against the advice of his mentor Tsubouchi, Bimyō was actively encouraged to experiment with that medium in a novel by friends with a commitment to modernizing written Japanese. In 1887, he left *Garakuta Bunko*, where he had been one of the editors, to write for the feminist magazine *Iratsume* which was first published in July that year with a twofold aim – to bring the problems faced by Japanese women to the notice of society, and to publish vernacular novels in order to help disseminate colloquial style. *Iratsume* was produced by Bimyō and four associates, all students,[24] helped by Shimpo Iwatsugu, a member of the Kinkōdō publishing firm which had earlier put out the first colloquial-style primary textbook. Two of the students, Nakagawa Kojūrō and Masaki Naohiko, had the previous year won an essay competition run by Education Minister Mori on achieving a uniform style for both men and women with their proposal of *gembun'itchi*. Nakagawa related in later years that he and Masaki, emboldened by their win, had resolved that they themselves would strive towards the realization of the *gembun'itchi* principle; knowing of Bimyō's literary propensities through his activities in the Ken'yūsha group at the school which all three attended, they persuaded him to join their own circle as a writer of colloquial-style novels for Iratsume.[25]

Unfortunately, sales of *Iratsume* did not come up to expectations. Despite injections of cash from Shimpo, Nakagawa, and Masaki, the latter two donating their competition prize money, a more saleable format had to be found in order to stay in circulation. Eventually Bimyō took over the editorship and abandoned the feminist theme in favour of a purely literary approach, having by that time dropped out of school in order to devote all his time to writing. In 1888, he became editor of *Miyako no Hana* (*The Flower of the Capital*), a new literary magazine also published by Kinkōdō, and embarked upon a period of great literary activity, publishing his work in *Miyako no Hana, Kokumin no Tomo* (*The People's Friend*), *Jogaku Zasshi* (*The Female Student*), and other journals. *Natsukodachi* (*A Summer Grove*), a collection of short stories, was published by Kinkōdō in 1888, one of the best known pieces, *Musashino* (*The Plain of Musashi*), having earned him public attention when it appeared the previous year in the *Yomiuri Shimbun*. In all of them he used colloquial style to a greater or lesser degree, save for the dialogue of historical pieces which he strove to make authentic for the period in question. Figure 5.2 is an example from *The Plain of Musashi*.

Figure 5.2 Colloquial style in Bimyō's *Musashino* (*The Plain of Musashi*)

夜は根城を明渡した。竹藪に伏勢を張ッて居る村雀はあらたに軍議を開初め、闇の隙間から斫込んで來る曉の光は次第に、四方の闇を追退け、遠山の角には茜の幕がわたり、遠近の溪間から朝雲の狼烟が立昇る。

Source: Yamada Bimyō '*Musashino*', *Gendai Nihon Bungaku Zenshū* 2, Tokyo: Chikuma Shobō, 1954, p. 240.
Note: For translation see Appendix.

Despite his prolific output, Bimyō was overshadowed in literary circles by Futabatei after the appearance of *The Drifting Cloud*. Whereas Futabatei had the backing of the influential Tsubouchi, *Iratsume* was a small student-produced journal of small impact and narrow circulation. Bimyō did not attract very much attention, recalled Nakagawa, until the appearance of his *Kochō* (*The Butterfly*) in 1890,[26] which caused a considerable stir with its accompanying illustration of the semi-nude female body. If this was a calculated ploy on Bimyō's part to stimulate interest in his work, it backfired, the general reaction from literati being one of disapproval. His works continued to decline in popularity thereafter and in 1892 he turned from writing novels to poetry and theory, although he later wrote several more novels between 1896 and his death in 1911.

Apart from an understandable pocket of resistance from Ken'yūsha members aggrieved at his desertion and unlikely to praise his use of the colloquial style in the light of their own espousal of *gazoku setchū*, literary circles discussed Bimyō's offerings widely but with a fairly non-committal reaction. If there was no scathing denunciation, neither was there much overt approval. There was no strong conflict over the relative merits of colloquial style *vis-à-vis* other styles. The main reason for his loss of popularity seems to have been his over-enthusiastic adoption of European rhetorical devices which struck a jarring note during the early period of colloquial style in literature, though successfully incorporated by writers of a later period. These included inverted word order with the verb preceding the subject, innovative European punctuation such as the dash and the question mark, exclamation, personification, ultra-modern vocabulary, abbreviation, and similes so novel as to startle – the famous passage from *Hana no Ibara, Ibara no Hana* (*The Thorn on the Flower, The Flower on the Thorn*), for example, in which he describes the perfume of flowers as boarding the train of the wind and rushing among the groves of hair in the tunnels of the nostrils! While such stratagems certainly imparted an enticing novelty to Bimyō's work at the outset, his tendency to overdo them resulted eventually in mannered writing which held no great appeal for the public.

In this regard, Bimyō was in fact a man ahead of his time. A certain period of exposure was required to accustom the reading public to seeing colloquial style in fiction before further innovations could be successfully introduced. Whereas Futabatei strove for a simple, realistic style, Bimyō went to the other extreme, attempting to make his writing as arresting and 'interesting' as possible; but it was Futabatei's attitude which was the more appropriate to the real nature of *gembun'itchi* as a necessary adjunct to the new-style novel. Bimyō was at heart an artist rather than an impartial observer and recorder of life; he was keenly interested in poetry, and was one of the first to begin writing modern free verse in Japan. He did not look deeply enough into the reasons which made colloquial style important to the modern novel, but turned instead to premature polishing and manipulation. While his efforts in this direction did bring him attention for a short time, they were responsible for the eventual decrease in his popularity.

A second reason suggested by Muramatsu Sadataka for Bimyō's decline was his confusion over what variety of colloquial style to use.[27] He began by writing in the plain *da* style, using the least polite form of the copula. His critics pronounced this vulgar, however, and it offended his own artistic sensibilities, so that, beginning with *Sora Iku Tsuki* (*The Moon Above*, March 1888), he changed to the more polite *desu* style in both fiction and literary criticism. A factor in his decision may have been that *Iratsume* was a magazine for women and he feared they would find *da* too coarse. He did not succeed with the *desu* style; by the time he began to use it, Futabatei had already become famous for his use of *da* in *The Drifting Cloud*, and Bimyō's work suffered by comparison.

Although Bimyō may have run second to Futabatei in the actual practical application of colloquial style in novels, he was much more vocal in defending the *gembun'itchi* principle by means of theoretical essays. 'Gembun'itchi no Gairyaku' ('An Outline of the Gembun'itchi Argument', 1888) refuted three of the main arguments against colloquial style, which were that it would not be understood throughout the country because of dialectal variations in the spoken language; it would eventually become dated; and it possessed no grammatical coherence. Bimyō argued that a standard style based on the Tokyo dialect could be understood everywhere; *any* style would date; and the colloquial style certainly did have rules of syntax if people only looked for them. Two years later, he produced an essay entitled 'Wareware no Gembun'itchitai' ('Our Gembun'itchi Style') in response to Mori Ōgai's 'Gembunron' ('On Speech and Writing'), wherein it had been suggested that even those who supported *gembun'itchi* in prose still used classical syntax in poetry because the colloquial lacked as yet sufficient refinement,

The role of literature 149

and that perhaps this deficiency was sufficiently serious to justify a reversion to traditional styles in prose as well. To this suggestion, Bimyō replied that while classical styles were used in poetry because of their superior rhythm, no such requirement for tonal variation existed in prose. The elegance of a style, he argued, depended not on its age or beauty but on the meaning it expressed. Further polishing, he was sure, would impart to the colloquial style a satisfactory rhythm for poetry as well.

There has been disagreement among Japanese scholars as to which of the two men, Bimyō or Futabatei, was the creator of the colloquial-style novel. In so far as we have evidence, although not all were published, the earliest *gembun'itchi* works of literature were: Futabatei's Gogol translation (January–March 1886); Futabatei's *Fathers and Sons* translation (March–April 1886); Bimyō's *The Conceited Demon* (November 1886); Tsubouchi's *Here and There* (May 1887); Futabatei's *The Drifting Cloud* Part 1 (June 1887); Bimyō's *Notes from an Organ Melody* (July 1887); and Bimyō's *The Plain of Musashi* (November 1887). Although Tokuda Shūsei claims in *Meiji Shōsetsu Bunshō Hensen Shi (History of Stylistic Change in the Meiji Novel,* 1914) that Hirotsu Ryūrō was using colloquial style earlier than Bimyō, Ryūrō's first novel, published in 1887, was in *bungotai*; he did not attempt colloquial style until *Futa Omote (Back and Front)* in December 1888, eighteen months after *Ukigumo* appeared.

THE SPREAD OF *GEMBUN'ITCHI* IN THE NOVEL

After 1888, a growing number of novelists began to try their hand at the new style, among them Saganoya Omuro (1863–1947), who had known Futabatei at the Tokyo School of Foreign Languages and through him was introduced to Tsubouchi in 1886. Soon after, in the traditional mentor–protégé arrangement, he moved into Tsubouchi's house, was introduced by him to literary circles, and began to publish stories with his help. Saganoya was thus present during Futabatei's discussions of style with Tsubouchi during the writing of *The Drifting Cloud*. Under their influence, he began publication in 1888 of *Hakumei no Suzuko (Poor Suzuko)*, a novel written in the *de aru* form of colloquial style which had not before appeared in literature. Saganoya experimented with other terminations, using the *da* style in his extremely popular *Hatsukoi (First Love,* 1889) and the same -*masu* style later that year in *Nozue no Kiku* (*The Chrysanthemum at the Edge of the Field*).

A temporary convert to colloquial style was army doctor and writer Mori Ōgai (1862-1922), who supported the *gembun'itchi* principle for some time after his return from four years study in Germany. Under the influence of Futabatei's *The Rendezvous* and *Three Meetings*, he began his literary career by publishing several colloquial translations between January 1889 and March 1890, among them *Ryokuyō no Nageki* (*A Lament of Green Leaves*) and *Kōzui* (*The Flood*). He also used the colloquial style, mostly in its *da* form, in literary and drama criticism and topical essays. In 1980, however, he came under the influence of Ochiai Naobumi (1861-1903, classical scholar and poet), staunch opponent of *gembun'itchi*. Ochiai, while desirous of a written language much closer to speech, deplored the vulgarity of colloquial style and proposed instead a *shinkokubun*, a new toned-down version of *wabun*. Mori agreed; his novella *Maihime* (*The Dancing Girl*, 1890) was written in what was basically *gabuntai*, although at the time the style was christened *wakan'yō* because of the German elements dotted throughout.[28]

Several of the young members of the Ken'yūsha followed Bimyō's example in experimenting with colloquial style. Iwaya Sazanami (1870-1933) used it in children's stories such as *Shinnyo no Tsuki* (*The Light of Truth*, 1888), as did Kitagawa Makei in *Shimbijin* (*A True Beauty*, 1888). Hirotsu Ryūrō (1861-1928) began with *Futa Omote* (*Back and Front*, 1888), and Ishibashi Shian (1867-1927) with *Hana Nusutto* (*The Flower Thief*, 1889). Ōta Zuiken produced both novels and literary criticism in colloquial style from 1889 onwards. Outside the Ken'yūsha, Ishibashi Ningetsu (1865-1926), literary critic, writer, and admirer of the work of both Bimyō and Futabatei, wrote *Inga* (*Fate*) and *Tsuyokohime* (*The Little Dew Princess*), two *gembun'itchi* novels, in 1889. Uchida Roan (1868-1929), also an active literary critic and supporter of colloquial style, employed it in both fiction and critical works, while Wakamatsu Shizuko (1864-96) excelled in *gembun'itchi* translations, notably her 1890-92 version of *Little Lord Fauntleroy*.

In all, about 30 novelists were using colloquial style in 1888-89, a remarkable figure indicative of the new willingness to experiment prevalent among those younger writers. Many of their works were published in *Miyako no Hana* or *Iratsume*. Colloquial-style translations also appeared, among them *Seiyō Kaidan: Kuroneko* (*The

Black Cat), an 1887 translation from Edgar Allan Poe by Aeba Kōson (1855-1922); *Ōsama no Shin'ishō* (*The Emperor's New Clothes*, 1888), from Hans Christian Andersen by Kawano Saiichi; and *Ōkami* (*The Wolf*, 1889), from Grimm by Ueda Kazutoshi. Acceptance seemed assured; but difficulties still lay ahead.

A TEMPORARY SETBACK

At this seemingly favourable juncture, the burgeoning enthusiasm for realistic language in literature fell victim to the upsurge of nationalism which swept Japan at the end of the first two decades of the Meiji Period. Since the opening of the ports, the fad for things European had yearly increased in fervour as western technology, institutions, customs, and ideas were avidly transplanted. Now the loss of national identity seemed to present all too real a threat, and voices urging the preservation of uniquely Japanese characteristics and traditions were raised in a bid to stem the flow. In literature, the trend to a revival of Japanese studies was reflected by a return to the styles of Tokugawa Period authors Saikaku and Bakin. Novels in *gazoku setchū* style were produced by Mori Ōgai, Tsubouchi Shōyō, and Higuchi Ichiyō (1872-96), one of the few women writers of this time. It was during this period that those writers of the Ken'yūsha group who had not forsaken *gazoku setchū* for colloquial style came into their own, led by Ozaki Kōyō and Kōda Rohan (1867-1947).

Kōyō, leading light of the Ken'yūsha, was an outspoken opponent of the *gembun'itchi* principle. He believed that the prosaic nature of colloquial style made it inappropriate to fine writing, remarking scornfully that if circumstances should force him to use it he need only station a stenographer beside his bed and rattle off five novels a day for the newspapers.[29] If Muramatsu Sadataka's assertion that Kōyō considered Yamada Bimyō a traitor after the latter's desertion of the Ken'yūsha for *Iratsume* and *Miyako no Hana* is correct, the personal antagonism thus generated may have contributed to Kōyō's hostility towards the style favoured by Bimyō. Be that as it may (and Nakagawa Kojūrō, who was personally involved in these events and knew the principals, refused to believe that Bimyō's later decline stemmed from harsh treatment by vengeful Ken'yūsha members, describing Kōyō as neither small-minded nor cold-blooded but known for his tolerance[30]), Kōyō's main desire was to see a revival of *gazoku setchū*. He himself was fanatically meticulous in his writing; loving stylistic grace and beauty, he did not care how hard he worked to achieve them. In April 1890, he published *Ninin Bikuni Irozange* (*Two Nuns' Confessions of Love*), a *gazoku setchū* novel which immediately established him as a popular author. The enthusiasm with which the novel was greeted was indicative of the renewed eagerness in literary circles for traditional conventions. Taking Saikaku as his model, Kōyō strove by careful study of his works to create as elegant a style as possible.

From this time on, enthusiasm for traditional styles escalated, so that from 1890 until 1895, the application of *gembun'itchi* in prose fiction went into a decline. During this period, Futabatei stopped writing and translating, and left literary circles altogether to take up a government position. Ōgai left off experimenting with colloquial-style translations and developed a modernized form of *gabuntai* combining Japanese, Chinese, and European elements. Bimyō turned from novels to literary criticism and research into the grammar of the spoken language in 1892. The imitation Saikaku style dominated the literary scene; other than Kōyō, its major exponents were Kōda Rohan and Higuchi Ichiyō, neither of whom were Ken'yūsha members. Kōda is best known for the novels *Fūryū Butsu* (*The Buddha of Elegance*, 1890) and *Gojū no Tō* (*The Five-Storied Pagoda*, 1892). Higuchi wrote several novels between 1891 and her early death at twenty-four in 1896, the most famous of which, *Takekurabe* (*Comparing Heights*, 1894), was highly praised by both Ōgai and Kōda for the elegance of its style.

The few who continued to use colloquial style in this period included Wakamatsu Shizuko, whose *Shōkōshi*, a translation of *Little Lord Fauntleroy*, was serialized in *Jogaku Zasshi* from 1890 till 1892; Iwaya Sazanami, who continued producing children's stories; and Uchida Roan, whose *Tsumi to Batsu* (1892) was a *de aru* translation of Volume 1 of Dostoevsky's *Crime and Punishment*.

Oddly enough, another who produced *gembun'itchi* works during the lull was arch-critic Ozaki Kōyō himself. His *Ninin Nyōbō* (*Two Wives*) was serialized in *Miyako no Hana* from August 1891 to December 1892; from Part 4 on, Kōyō chose to write in the colloquial style. Other works included *Tonari no Onna* (*The Woman Next Door*, 1893), *Reinetsu* (*Cold Fever*, 1894), *Murasaki* (1894), and *Tajō Takon* (*Passions and Griefs*, 1896), of which the most important was the last-named. Kōyō chose to write in the *de aru* form of colloquial style; in *Passions and Griefs* he perfected a colloquial style much more polished than that of Futabatei and Bimyō. The temporary switch on the part of one of the most vehement detractors of *gembun'itchi* was apparently due to Kōyō's desire to prove he could master any medium he chose, one of the most outstanding characteristics of his literary output being his diversity of style. He tried his hand at many different varieties, and during this period was publishing both *gazoku setchū* and colloquial-style novels at the same time, his use of the latter being motivated by curiosity rather than by belief in its appropriateness as a medium for modern fiction. Unlike Futabatei, who regarded colloquial style as an intrinsic necessity for the type of novel he was attempting to write, Kōyō's main interest lay in the mechanics of its production for their experimental value.

Kōyō himself discussed his attitude to colloquial style in his essay 'Gembun'itchiron' ('On Gembun'itchi', 1905). His first impression was that it was amazingly simple; by comparison with pseudo-classical style, using colloquial style seemed to him like bounding lightly down a hill up which he had previously toiled with a heavy burden. Closer acquaintance, however, revealed this seeming simplicity to be deceptive. Taking the expression *gembun'itchi* literally, he had begun by writing down everything that entered his head, as if he were speaking, with no attempt at restraint. In this respect, he reflected, colloquial style required careful handling; while it allowed much greater freedom of expression than classical styles, it also carried the danger of garrulity. With this caveat in mind, he had set out to find a means of investing colloquial style with the elegance of *gazoku setchū*, but soon discovered himself to be expending just as much time and effort in the attempt as ever he had on traditional styles. This was no exaggeration. It was said that he kept a pair of scissors beside him; if something he had written displeased him, he would cut out a piece of paper, stick it on top of the offending phrase, and write the new version on it. This happened so many times that his manuscript ended by being too bulky to fold.[31]

While Kōyō felt that the flexibility of colloquial style offered unlimited possibilities given proper polishing, the one area in which he felt it to be vastly inferior to *gazoku setchū* was its lack of refinement. While its simplicity and clarity made it admirably suited for general use, he found its tone to be laconic and flat, rather like talking to a businessman. He rejected the arguments of those who felt that it *did* have a certain elegance, albeit repressed; in his opinion, colloquial style *as it was at that stage* could not compete with older styles and the subtle advantage of their underlying rhythm. It was this lack of rhythm which caused him eventually to abandon his experiments after *Passions and Griefs*. While he concluded that *gembun'itchi* was perfect as an everyday business style, he remained convinced that literature was a thing apart from everyday life, that it should be *bibun* (elegant prose), and so his 1897 masterpiece *Konjiki Yasha* (*The Demon Gold*) was written in *gazoku setchū*.

Transient though his colloquial phase was, Kōyō's services to the language modernization movement were great. Whereas Bimyō had jarred his readers by his too fanciful use of rhetorical devices, Kōyō proved that these could be skilfully blended into Japanese writing to enrich its expression. He showed by example that colloquial style could be polished and refined into an acceptable literary medium. The spread of the *de aru* termination, now the most common, is ascribed by Nakamura Mitsuo to his example;[32] other Ken'yūsha members such as Iwaya Sazanami adopted it after 1893, and its use became widespread outside the Ken'yūsha after 1895, later exponents including Tayama Katai and Shimazaki Tōson. Kōyō was a prominent literary figure, and his temporary espousal of *gembun'itchi* was no doubt one of the factors in its subsequent revival.

THE REVIVAL OF INTEREST

For revive it did, after a five year lull, reappearing in literature in 1895. In that year, Ōnishi Hajime (1864–1900, philosopher and critic), published an essay entitled *Bungakujō no Shinjigyō* (*A New Project in Literature*) in *Taiyō* (*The Sun*), making the point that the major task facing modern writers was to develop a new style, it being in his view ridiculous to pattern contemporary writing on archaic styles. It would be by no means impossible to realize *gembun'itchi* were influential writers to turn their hands to creating a standard style based on everyday language. Ōnishi's essay came at a time when, following victory in the Sino-Japanese War of 1895, attention was beginning to be focused on the Japanese language, which was now for the first time to be used in territories outside Japan. Once again the question of language modernization arose; script reform re-emerged as an issue, and the concept of a colloquial style began once again to capture the interest of intellectuals and writers.

In 1896, Futabatei once more appeared in print with *Katakoi* (*Unrequited Love*), a translation of Turgenev's *Asya*, followed in 1897 by *Ukikusa* (*The Floating Weed*), Turgenev's *Rudin*. Both were written in a flowing *de aru* version of the colloquial style, even more polished than the style of his earlier *The Rendezvous*, which again excited rising young writers such as Tayama Katai and Kunikida Doppo. Hirotsu Ryūrō was also writing colloquial style novels at this time, and under the combined influence of his work and that of Futabatei and Kōyō, *gembun'itchi* again began to spread in the novel.

In 1900 there arose a new literary movement which accelerated its expansion, the *shaseibun* school led by Masaoka Shiki (1867–1902). Shiki, impressed by the works of such western-style painters as Asai Tadashi and Shimomura Kanzan, wanted to introduce a similar technique to literature, to portray places, people, and events in the objective manner of an artist. Himself a poet, he attempted to apply the *shasei* (sketching) method to the traditional verse forms of *haiku* and *tanka*.[33] Prose pieces written by his followers thus came to be called *shaseibun* (sketches in prose).

Shaseibun writers turned their backs on the traditional techniques and style favoured by Kōyō, Rohan, and Ichiyō, choosing instead colloquial style as the most appropriate for their portrayal of everyday life and personal experience. Shiki expounded on this theme in his 1900 essay 'Jojibun' ('Descriptive Writing'), emphasizing that authors should forsake ornamental stylistic devices in favour of recording events just as they happened, simply but well. *Shaseibun*, he averred, was the most appropriate form for modern literature, and it required a style which could fulfil the special needs of realism. He himself had begun using colloquial style in mid-1889, but had not succeeded in throwing off entirely the influences of traditional forms. Another prominent supporter of *shaseibun* was Takahama Kyoshi, longtime friend of Shiki; together with Takahama's brother Yoshi, the two began in 1897 to publish the journal *Hototogisu* (*The Cuckoo*), which became the focal point of the group's activities. Takahama also published an essay on the style theme in 1900, entitled *Gembun'itchi*, wherein he stressed the absolute necessity of colloquial style to *shaseibun* objectives. His own first colloquial work was 'Hannichi Aruki' ('A Half-Day's Journey', 1899).

Shimazaki Tōson, who began his literary career as a Romantic poet and later became one of the leading novelists of the Naturalist school, wrote a collection of short stories under the influence of *shaseibun*; later published as *Ryokuyōshū* (*Collection of Green Leaves*) in 1907, these were short sketches of a country area in which Tōson attempted to apply the principle of objective descriptions. It was Natsume Sōseki (1867–1916), however, who really perfected the *shaseibun* method. Like Tōson, he too had first become known as a poet, but as a *haiku* poet of Shiki's school; he was another close friend of Shiki. In 1905, he published in *The Cuckoo*, at the invitation of Takahama Kyoshi, his first novel, *Wagahai wa Neko de aru* (*I am a Cat*), a satirical view of a group of Meiji intellectuals through a cat's eyes which was suddenly to focus public attention on *shaseibun*. The conciseness and freedom of its *de aru* colloquial style (Figure 5.3) was praised in a contemporary review which credited Sōseki with having managed to overcome the wordiness which had hitherto been a constant problem in *gembun'itchi* prose. Sōseki's success prompted other writers to publish their own attempts; some, among them Itō Sachio (1864–1913), Nagatsuka Takashi (1879–1915), and Terada Torahiko (1878–1935), managed to produce reasonably polished versions of colloquial style.

While the *shaseibun* movement was thus instrumental in helping to revive waning interest in colloquial style as a literary medium by espousing it as the only style appropriate for that particular approach to literature and demonstrating it in an increasingly acceptable form, the group which really established its primacy in the novel was the Naturalist school which dominated Japanese literature between 1905 and 1912. *Shaseibun* had advocated a totally objective, neutral, observer's attitude from author to subject, with the author's personality kept out of his work. Naturalism in its original European form also required an objective approach coupled with a delving into and a frank exposure of the truths of human life, in particular the less palatable, hidden aspects; but in Japan the quest for objectivity led paradoxically to deep subjectivity, Naturalist authors coming to believe that the only subject of which they could speak with total lack of fabrication was themselves. First-person narrative thus being the closest thing to total realism in their eyes, self-confession came to be a striking feature of their works, resulting in the development of the 'I-novel' which has been a distinctive feature of modern Japanese literature ever since. It was thus a matter of course that Naturalist writers would employ colloquial style, the closest approach to the language of everyday

Figure 5.3 Colloquial style in Sōseki's *Wagahai wa Neko de aru* (*I am a Cat*)

吾輩は猫である。名前はまだ無い。どこで生れたか頓と見當がつかぬ。何でも薄暗いじめじめした所でニャーニャー泣いて居た事丈は記憶して居る。吾輩はこゝで始めて人間といふものを見た。然もあとで聞くとそれは書生といふ人間中で一番獰悪な種族であつたさうだ。此書生といふのは時々我々を捕へて煮て食ふといふ話である。

Source: Natsume Sōseki '*Wagahai wa Neko de aru*', *Sōseki Zenshū* 1, Tokyo: Iwanami Shoten, 1965, p. 5.
Note: For translation see Appendix.

life, which allowed full and free expression of the often tortuous meanderings of the author's psyche and, lacking the artifice and 'artistic' aspect of traditional styles, was suited to the unvarnished revelation of man's darker side. More than any other group, these men, by their uniform adoption of colloquial style, helped ensure its continuing presence in the modern novel. In 1905, at the beginning of the period of Naturalism, 78 per cent of novels were written in colloquial style. By 1906 this figure had increased to 91 per cent, rising to 98 per cent in 1907 and reaching 100 per cent in 1908.[34]

The representative writers of Naturalism were Shimazaki Tōson, Tayama Katai, and Tokuda Shūsei (1871–1943). Tōson was already halfway to Naturalism through his work with *shaseibun*. His first Naturalistic novel, *Hakai* (*The Broken Commandment*, 1906) was written in a very simple colloquial style, which he strove to make as natural and uncontrived as possible (Figure 5.4). He made skilful use of European-derived constructions, blending them comfortably into his writing with no hint of incongruity. His style matured further in such later works as *Haru* (*Spring*, 1908) and *Ie* (*The Family*, 1910). Katai, who established himself as a Naturalist with *Futon* (*The Quilt*, 1907), had been impressed early in his career by the freshness and vividness of Futabatei's *gembun'itchi* translations.

Figure 5.4 Colloquial style in Tōson's *Hakai* (*The Broken Commandment*)

蓮華寺では下宿を兼ねた。瀬川丑松が急に転宿を思ひ立つて、借りることにした部屋といふのは、其蔵裏つゞきにある二階の角のところ。寺は信州下水内郡飯山町二十何ヶ寺の一つ、眞宗に附属する古刹で、丁度其二階の窓に倚凭つて眺めると、銀杏の大木を経てて飯山の町の一部分も見える。さすが信州第一の佛教の地、古代を眼前に見るやうな小鄒會、奇異な北國風の屋造、板葺の屋根、または多期の雪除として使用する特別の軒庇から、ところ〲に高く顕れた寺院と樹木の梢まで――すべて舊めかしい町の光景が香の烟の中に包まれて見える。たゞ一際目立つて此窓から望まれるものと言へば、丑松が奉職して居る其小學校の白く塗つた築物であつた。

Source: Shimazaki Tōson 'Hakai', *Gendai Nihon Bungaku Zenshū* 8, Tokyo: Chikuma Shobō, 1953, p. 36.
Note: For translation see Appendix.

In 1904, in his essay *Rokotsunaru Byōsha* (*Candid Description*), he had urged writers to abandon utterly traditional forms of writing and strive for frank and fearless realism. Later works included *Sei* (*Life*, 1908), *Tsuma* (*The Wife*, 1909), *Inaka Kyōshi* (*A Country Schoolmaster*, 1909), and *En* (*The Bond*, 1910). Tokuda, third member of the trio, had been a follower of Kōyō in his earlier career. While his style, concise and inclined to over-economy, was not sufficiently ornamental to rate much notice in the Ken'yūsha, its lack of ostentation made it appropriate to Naturalism. His first Naturalist work was *Shinjotai* (*The New Household*, 1908), followed by *Ashiato* (*Footprint*, 1910), *Kabi* (*Mildew*, 1911), and *Tadare* (*Festering*, 1913).

Once the most important hurdle had been cleared and the principle of *gembun'itchi* had been accepted as an inevitability in the novel, the attitude of its users changed. Colloquial style was no longer regarded merely as a simpler and more realistic alternative to *gazoku setchūbun* but became something to be worked on, to be carved and polished into a smooth, urbane vehicle for fiction. Those defects which had caused Tsubouchi and others to hesitate over its appropriateness in literature were now to be eradicated as individual writers began to evolve their own characteristic versions. The shock of unfamiliarity had been absorbed and was gone; as confidence in manipulating the new style grew, so novelists began to stamp their individual personalities on their work, so that it became no longer a question of using the suffix '-style' (*-chō* or *-tai*) to differentiate between discrete sets of conventions of syntax and lexicon as in the past but that of using the substantive 'style' (*buntai*) to refer to the collective characteristics with which a particular author imprinted a common medium.

This final stage in the process of acceptance of colloquial style in literature came about through the writings of members of the Shirakaba (White Birch) group, one of the several new schools of writing which succeeded Naturalism. The Shirakaba writers, who included Mushakōji Saneatsu (1885–1976), Arishima Takeo (1878–1923), Satomi Ton (1888–1983), and Shiga Naoya (1883–1971), rejected the purported objectivity and seaminess of Naturalism in favour of idealistic subjectivity, believing self-development to be man's ultimate contribution to humanity. The pessimism of Naturalism was replaced with optimism, its scepticism with faith in humanity, its nihilism with positive individualism, and its materialism with idealism. All these authors, with the exception of the 32 year-old Arishima, were in their twenties when they began publication of their journal *Shirakaba* (*The White Birch*) in 1910. Children when the first colloquial-style novels appeared, they had grown up during the maturation period of colloquial style as the modern literary medium. They were accustomed to its presence and relatively free of clinging loyalties to older styles in literature; it is hardly surprising then that it was these men who developed it to its full potential. Where the writers of Naturalism had established and polished colloquial style in their work, making of it an intellectually acceptable medium capable of conveying wit and elegance, Shirakaba members now built on that base, adding further substance and interest with the subtle and harmonious inclusion of European-derived constructions,[35] using foreign elements in a free and natural manner which far surpassed Bimyō's earlier premature experiments and the later more successful but still restricted efforts of Tōson and Sōseki.

Mushakōji made bold and clever use of everyday expressions in his writings. His work was completely free of lingering traces of traditional styles; for the first time, an author's work was entirely colloquial (Figure 5.5). His style attracted favourable comment in literary circles, and he exerted a considerable influence on other writers. Among his works are *Omedetaki Hito* (*An Innocent*, 1911),

Figure 5.5 Colloquial style in Mushakōji's *Yūjō* (*Friendship*)

野島は杉子とは殆んど話をしなかつた。杉子が芝居を感心して見てゐるらしいのに不愉快を感じた。しかしそれは無理もないとも思つた。仲田も感心してゐるやうなことを云つたが、それはむしろ彼にたいするお世辞のやうに見えた。
「矢張り新しいものは、我々に近い感じがするね」
そんなことを仲田が云つた時、彼は別に反對する氣にはなれなかつた。
「飯を食はう」

Source: Mushakōji Saneatsu 'Yūjō', *Gendai Nihon Bungaku Zenshū* 19, Tokyo: Chikuma Shobō, 1955, p. 84.
Note: For translation see Appendix.

Seken Shirazu (*Naivety*, 1912) and *Yūjō* (*Friendship*, 1919). The author most flamboyantly successful in incorporating western devices smoothly into his style was Arishima, who is said to have often written in English and translated back into Japanese to ensure a 'modern tone'. For the first time, European constructions lost their exotic air and became fully assimilated into Japanese prose. While the style of *Kankan Mushi* (*The Clamorous Insects*, 1910) was perhaps a trifle showy, in later works such as *Kain no Matsuei* (*Descendants of Cain*, 1917) and particularly *Aru Onna* (*A Certain Woman*, 1919), Arishima achieved a fresh, natural expression characterized by striking similes and skilful personification. Shiga Naoya, like Sōseki, succeeded in eradicating the verbosity and vagueness which had so often marred colloquial style, producing a compact, frank, and forceful style in such works as *Aru Asa* (*One Morning*, 1908), *Kamisori* (*The Razor*, 1910), and *An'ya Kōro* (*A Dark Night's Passing*, 1921–37) which has made him one of the most revered of contemporary writers.

In the works of the Shirakaba writers, then, the modern colloquial style reached perfection as a literary medium. Although it was not to displace traditional styles outside the literary world until 1946, from this time on it held unchallenged supremacy in the novel, successive authors moulding it to their individual patterns. The stages of its progress in literature may be simplistically but succinctly summed up by saying that Futabatei introduced it, Bimyō spread it, Kōyō polished it, Naturalism established it, and the Shirakaba writers perfected and individualized it.

The development of the modern Japanese novel thus played an important role in the language modernization process. The desire on the part of young, western-influenced writers to establish a new mode of psychological realism in fiction, thereby elevating it to the status of a respectable pursuit for educated men, helped underline the necessity of jettisoning those archaic literary and stylistic conventions which were no longer either appropriate to or capable of expressing modern concepts in writing. While intellectuals outside literary circles debated the broader issues of the *gembun'itchi* concept, the novelists pushed up their sleeves and got down to the detailed task of actually shaping and manipulating colloquial styles in descriptive writing as well as dialogue, facing and ironing out through practice and perseverance the difficulties perceived by critics and supporters alike. In fact, there existed a relationship of mutual dependence between the process of stylistic reform and the emergence of realistic fiction. The new novel could not have succeeded without the colloquial style so suited to its objectives; and the progress of acceptance of colloquial style outside literary circles was significantly aided by its modelling in the novel. The first of these assertions is undeniably true; the second is more difficult to substantiate. Whether the colloquial style would have eclipsed its precursors or the later *futsūbun*[36] in general circles by 1946 without the influence of its success in the novel is open to debate, but given the role of literature in modelling what so frequently transmutes from the avant-garde to the subsequently accepted norm, it seems a reasonable assumption that the one helped the other. There is no doubt that Tokugawa Period styles would eventually have been abandoned regardless of literary trends; the western example proved for those who were willing to see that a written language which approximated the contemporary spoken language offered enormous benefits to the citizens of a modern nation such as Japan was striving to become. School-books and newspapers were already turning back in that direction by the beginning of the Taishō Period. Had intellectuals not given the stamp of approval by first breaking with tradition to use colloquial style in narrative fiction and then demonstrating how it could be developed into a viable medium, however, a much longer period would have elapsed before its acceptance in society at large.

6 The final stages

Outside the literary world, a considerable amount of time was to elapse before *bungotai* was replaced by colloquial style in all areas. Because of entrenched views on the nature of the written language appropriate to the press, the style of most newspapers remained traditional until the 1920s, while it was not until the 1940s that official documents and government decrees were converted. In education, however, considerable progress had been made in the simplification of textbook style by 1910, thanks largely to the efforts of a group of linguists and educators dedicated to language modernization.

As Donald Keene has pointed out in his discussion of the Sino-Japanese War of 1894–95,[1] the Japanese victory was a turning point in the flagging struggle for the reform of written Japanese. We have seen that in the renewed climate of interest in the nature of the language problems faced and their possible future solution, the colloquial style reappeared in the novel and went on from there to consolidate a position from which it was never afterwards dislodged. The nationalistic sentiment resulting from the victory over the large nation which had provided such a formative influence in Japan's history prompted a reappraisal of the language reform issue in other areas as well, coinciding as it did with the appearance on the scene of Ueda Kazutoshi (also known as Ueda Mannen), the first Japanese to have studied western linguistics overseas. Ueda worked tirelessly to realize his aim of a government body set up to oversee research into and implementation of a standardized form of written Japanese based on the contemporary spoken language. As a result of his activities, the first few years of the twentieth century were to see the beginning of serious, co-ordinated examination of language policy at the national level through the agency of the

Kokugo Chōsa Iinkai (National Language Research Council), established under the auspices of the Ministry of Education in 1902.

Ueda (1867–1937) was a fervent supporter of government-directed language planning on both pragmatic and nationalist grounds. As an undergraduate in the Japanese Literature Department of Tokyo Imperial University, Ueda had studied under English scholar Basil Hall Chamberlain, whose views on the urgency of stylistic and orthographic reform (he was an advocate of romanization) were influential in stimulating his interest in the future development of his language. After graduating in July 1888, Ueda proceeded to postgraduate studies, and in 1890, through the influence of his academic mentors Toyama Masakazu (1848–1900) and Katō Hiroyuki (then head of the university), was sent by the government to study linguistics in Germany and France for four years. He returned to his Alma Mater in 1894, and was promptly given charge of the linguistics course, where he lectured on western linguistics, conducting similar classes also at Tokyo Normal School and Tokyo Special School. Many of his students later became prominent in Japanese linguistic circles, among them Hashimoto Shinkichi (1882–1945), Shimmura Izuru (1876–1967), and Hoshina Kōichi. In the course of his long and distinguished career, Ueda produced two major dictionaries, the *Daijiten* (1917) and the *Dai Nihon Kokugo Jiten* (1915–19, in collaboration with Matsui Kanji), in addition to many discursive essays on the Japanese language.

Ueda had arrived home from Germany to find nationalistic sentiments burning high. A return to things Japanese was being advocated on all fronts, not least of them writing. Ueda, fresh from his studies, was quick to suggest several ways in which his mother tongue might be improved, among them the adoption of a standard form of Japanese and the use of colloquial style in writing. In an 1894 lecture entitled 'Kokugo to Kokka to' ('Our Nation and Its Language'), he referred to Japan's language as the spiritual blood binding her people together. The national language, as the identifying mark of a state and the mother of its people, must be respected and protected, he argued, citing the movement for the purification of the German language as an example of what could be done by a people bent on refining their mother tongue. The next twelve months saw him deliver a number of addresses and write several essays on the theme of language reform,[2] always stressing his twin themes of standardization and colloquialization as being mutually interdependent and essential to the smooth future development of Japanese.

Japan was about to embark at bureaucratic level upon what Neustupný has termed the policy approach to language problems, characteristic of a modernizing society.[3] The issues of a standard language, colloquial style, and orthographic reform were being debated by intellectuals with increasing urgency. Two groups dedicated to the reform of the national language were now set up which were to prove instrumental in inducing the government to set up an agency to oversee co-ordinated language planning.

The first was Gengo Gakkai, a linguistics society established by Ueda in May 1898, which published the journal *Gengogaku Zasshi* (*Journal of Linguistics*) between 1900 and 1902, offering a forum for advocates of language reform to air their views. The founding members of the society included graduates of Ueda's courses, among them Shimmura Izuru, Hoshina Kōichi, and Fujioka Katsuji. In addition, its many contributors included Okakura Yoshisaburō (1868–1936, scholar of the English language), Shiratori Kurakichi (1865–1942, Professor of Oriental History at Tokyo Imperial University), and Okada Masayoshi (1871–1923, Professor of Japanese Literature at Tokyo School of Foreign Languages), who had published in 1895 a long essay advocating the total phasing out of Chinese characters and their replacement with *kana*.[4] The primary concern of these men was the further implementation of colloquial style; a secondary but equally pressing concern was the issue of standardization.

A second pressure group committed to the same objective was the Gembun'itchikai (Gembun'itchi Club), formed in March 1900 under the auspices of the country's most influential body of educators, the Teikoku Kyōikukai (Imperial Society for Education), with the aim of promoting the spread of colloquial style outside literature. The Teikoku Kyōikukai had the previous year set up a Kokuji Kairyōbu (Script Reform Section), headed by Maejima Hisoka who, it will be recalled, had first raised the issue of reform of the written language with his 1866 petition to the shogun calling for the replacement of Chinese characters with phonetic script and a concomitant simplification of style as steps in facilitating education. In addition to four subsections dealing with the examination of various script reform options, this section subsumed a fifth, known as the Kokubun Chōsabu (Language Investigation Section) which was commissioned to investigate ways and means of implementing colloquial style, a move which reflects the serious light in which the issue had come to be regarded by educators. When the more high-powered Gembun'itchi Club began its activities, indicating the increased importance being accorded to language reform, the Kokubun Chōsabu ceased to operate and its members were absorbed by the larger body.

The members of the Gembun'itchi Club, while drawn mainly from amongst educators and scholars, also included a smattering of journalists, among them Nakai Kitarō, editor-in-chief of the *Yomiuri Shimbun* which carried frequent items on the activities of the Club. Club chairman was Maejima Hisoka; many members were also members of the Linguistics Society and/or contributors to the *Journal of Linguistics,* among them Ueda Kazutoshi, Okada Masayoshi, Okakura Yoshisaburō, Ōtsuki Fumihiko, Shiratori Kurakichi, Shimmura Izuru, Hoshina Kōichi, and Fujioka Katsuji. Shiratori and Shimmura served as members of the fifteen-man committee; Shimmura was further entrusted with the task of editing model compositions in colloquial style, while Shiratori addressed the club on historical factors pointing to the need for colloquialization at its second public lecture meeting in February 1901. Ōtsuki, Shimmura, Fujioka, and Hoshina, with nine others, were appointed as investigators. In addition, Ōtsuki addressed the club at its third public lecture meeting on the topic 'Gembun'itchi no Hyōjungo' ('A Standard Language in Colloquial Style'). It may be seen, therefore, that the Linguistics Society and the Gembun'itchi Club worked together to achieve the same objective, namely the adoption of a standardized colloquial style, and to this end brought pressure to bear upon the government to extend official sanction to subsequent language planning efforts. The first issue of the Gembun'itchi Club's journal *Gembun'itchikai no Kaishi* in February 1902 listed the club's aims as twofold. Members would conduct research on *gembun'itchi* by rewriting difficult prose in colloquial style; reviewing colloquial-style writing which appeared in books, newspapers, and magazines; inviting famous writers to tell them of their experiences with colloquial style; and by deciding upon a standard form of Japanese. They would also seek to help disseminate *gembun'itchi* by writing contributions for newspapers and magazines in colloquial style wherever possible, using colloquial style in their correspondence, and recruiting new members for the club.[5]

In January 1900, a month before the formation of the Gembun'itchi Club, its parent body, the Imperial Society for Education, had presented to both Houses of the Diet a petition entitled 'Kokuji Kokugo Kokubun no Kairyō ni kansuru Seigansho' ('A Petition for the Reform of our Script, Language, and Style'), requesting the establishment of a government agency to oversee the implementation of script and style reform. The following month, the petition was passed in the Upper House. Instrumental to its success was Ueda Kazutoshi, who, in his capacity as Ministry of Education parliamentary councillor, had defended it during question time in its passage through the Lower House. Ueda had been agitating for the establishment of a national body for some time. In 1890, while continuing in his appointment at Tokyo Imperial University, he had been further appointed both head of the Education Ministry's Special Education Bureau and its parliamentary councillor, and in 1899 was awarded the title of Doctor of Literature. As a result of both diligent lobbying on Ueda's part and the petition from the Imperial Society for Education, the government announced the appointment in April 1900 of a seven-man team to begin preparatory investigation to determine the direction of future language planning. The commissioners were Maejima Hisoka (head), Ueda, Naka Tsūsei, Ōtsuki Fumihiko, Miyake Setsurei (1860–1945, educator and publisher), Tokutomi Sohō (1863–1957, journalist and publisher), and Yumoto Takehiko (1857–1925, educator and publisher).

Ueda was not yet satisfied. As head of the Special Education Bureau, he had been working within the Education Ministry for the improvement of Japanese language education, in co-operation with Sawayanagi Masatarō (1865–1927), head of the General Education Bureau. As a result of their collaboration, the Elementary School Ordinance of August 1900 limited the number of Chinese characters to be used and stipulated revisions of phonetic script orthography, to take effect from the publication of new readers in 1902. Convinced of the need for a national language research council with a clearly defined charter to bring about changes which would shore up these initiatives, Ueda and other members of the Gembun'itchi Club now began a period of intensive lobbying, concentrating their efforts on Kikuchi Dairoku (1855–1917), Education Minister from 1901 till 1903. Kikuchi was a noted mathematician and educational administrator who after studying mathematics and physics at Cambridge had founded the Mathematics Department at Tokyo

Imperial University in 1881, going on to become president of that institution from 1898 until 1901. He was a known supporter of language reform; in January 1901, prior to taking up the Education portfolio, he addressed the first public meeting of the Gembun'itchi Club, attended by over a thousand people, on the importance of style reform to education. Ueda and his supporters therefore resolved to appeal to Kikuchi to press for the establishment of a national body. To this end, they adopted several tactics, including a further, already drafted petition to the Diet, pressure on Kikuchi himself, and active lobbying of other influential groups within the government.

Ueda's views on language as a unifying national force were well known from his early lectures and essays. The connection between language and state had been further stressed by Shiratori Kurakichi in an address to a meeting of the Gembun'itchi Club in December 1900 during which he related the degree of development of a language to the state of its country's fortunes, citing Manchuria, Turkey, Korea, and other places as illustrations of his thesis that a strong nation has a developed, pure language, while a weak nation's language shows signs of corruption by outside influences. It was at this meeting that the decision was taken to petition the Diet the following year for the immediate establishment of a national language advisory council, a petition which was to stress the importance of language modernization to national unity and request the implementation of colloquial style as a national enterprise. Journalist Nakai Kitarō was commissioned to draft the petition, entitled 'Gembun'itchi no Jikkō ni tsuite no Seigansho An' ('Petition regarding the Implementation of Colloquial Style'), which was then submitted to both Houses in February 1901. Its gist was as follows: The development of a nation's language is intimately connected to both the unity and the destiny of that nation. The fact that the written form of European languages was based on the contemporary speech of the country was one element contributing to the degree of civilization and strength attained in the west, contrasted with the horrible example of certain Oriental countries whose failure to take steps to strengthen and develop their own language was linked with their eventual political decline. Japanese children must not only master their own very difficult language but also Sino-Japanese and various European languages in order to proceed to higher education. The time and energy thus wasted in struggling with the form before being able to extract the content constituted not only a personal loss but also a serious economic threat to Japan, now in the arena of world competition. It was therefore both urgent and imperative that colloquial style be brought into use so that students could divert the time thus saved into attaining other valuable knowledge. The implementation of such a style must be achieved before other educational reforms could be carried out. Previous representations concerning the setting up of a national language research council had been made, without success. In the belief that there is a strong connection between the state of the language and the fortunes of the nation, and that the implementation of colloquial style was a matter of the utmost urgency, this present petition renewed the request for the formation of such a body and urged that style reform be made a national enterprise.

The petition was passed in the Lower House in March, and forwarded to the Upper. Gembun'itchi Club members, aware that this second stage was crucial, kept up the pressure. In June, Kikuchi was invited to a Club meeting where several influential members expressed the hope that he would do his utmost to plead the case in the forthcoming Diet session, and to see that funds would be earmarked for the council. Kikuchi indicated his approval of the project, referring in the manner of politicians to the difficulty of obtaining funding but reaffirming his willingness to try, and suggested that Club members might themselves do the necessary research into how to put colloquial style into general use. A few months later, deputations of Club members made an official visit both to Kikuchi and to the Finance Minister to urge their case for funding, as well as to the offices of other influential bodies.

These efforts were crowned with success when in March 1902 the Diet approved funds for the immediate setting up of the Kokugo Chōsa linkai (National Language Research Council), established under the auspices of the Education Ministry to carry out a full-scale investigation of the state of the language. Its members were: Chairman Katō Hiroyuki, Ueda Kazutoshi, Kanō Jigorō (1860–1938, head of Tokyo Higher Normal School), Maejima Hisoka, Sawayanagi Masatarō, Ōtsuki Fumihiko, Tokutomi Sohō, Mikami Sanji (1865–1939, historian), Inoue Tetsujirō (1855–1944, philosopher and pioneer of new-style poetry), Takakusu Junjirō (1866–1945, educator and Buddhist scholar), Watanabe Tōnosuke, Kimura Masakoto (1827–1913, scholar of classical Japanese literature), and Shigeno Yasutsugu (1827–1910, historian). Educators were prominently represented: Ueda, Inoue, Takakusu, and Mikami were all professors at Tokyo Imperial University. Auxiliary members appointed were Hayashi Yasunori, Hoshina Kōichi, Okada Masayoshi, Shimmura Izuru, and Ōya Tōru (1850–1928, linguist), who worked under the guidance of Ōtsuki and Ueda. Many members were also members of the Linguistic Society and the Gembun'itchi Club.

Following a series of meetings debating policy and methodology, the council published its proposed plan of action in the government gazette of 4 July 1902, under the title 'Kokugo Chōsa Iinkai Ketsugi Jikō' ('Resolutions of the National Language Research Council'). Four major problem areas in the language were identified. The tasks of the Council, it was announced, would be: to investigate the relative merits of *kana* and *rōmaji* with a view to adopting a phonetic script; to examine ways of bringing colloquial style into widespread use; to examine the phonemic system of Japanese; and to survey the dialects and settle upon a standard language.

In one sense, the establishment of this body may be seen in a negative light as merely a matter of a rubber-stamp operation, much of the spadework having already been done by those early advocates of colloquial style discussed in Chapter 4 and by the novelists of Chapter 5; the Council was certainly not starting from scratch but rather consolidating and giving the official stamp of approval to initiatives already in operation. In another, it may be viewed in a positive light as bringing together earlier, uncoordinated, isolated attempts in various fields motivated mainly by pragmatic concerns under the one umbrella of a co-ordinated, bureaucratic, scientific approach to language planning motivated by an awareness not only of the instrumental benefits to be gained from language modernization but also of the significance of the national language as a unifying force on the sentimental level.

The influence of the National Language Research Council made itself felt in the publication in 1903 of the first state-compiled school texts, after control of textbooks reverted to the government following cases of alleged bribery by publishers attempting to subvert members of textbook selection committees. Earlier textbooks, with the exception of a few tentative forays into colloquial style as a stepping stone to more advanced methods of writing, had adhered to classical literary modes. The Education Ministry had given initial support to a programme of standard language education in 1900, when Clause 3 in the 'Shōgakkō Rei Shikō Kisoku'

('Rules for the Enforcement of Elementary School Regulations') designated practice in *futsūgo* (another term referring to a standard form of Japanese) as part of *kokugo* (Japanese language) education. In 1901 it was announced in 'Kōtō Shihan Gakkō Jinjō Shōgaku Kokugoka Jisshi Yōryō' ('Higher Normal School Outline for the Implementation of Japanese Language Teaching at the Elementary Level') that henceforth the Japanese taught in schools would be that of middle- and upper-class Tokyoites. The third national meeting of education associations that year unanimously accepted a petition from the Imperial Society for Education's Gembun'itchi Club which urged the adoption of colloquial style as a matter of policy in the primary curriculum.

The Ministry's first series of state primers, *Jinjō Shōgaku Tokuhon* (*Elementary Primers*, 1903–04), contained a high proportion of colloquial style and a vocabulary adhering to the stipulated range with the stated aim of spreading a standard form of Japanese. The Imperial Society for Education's Script Reform Section had had a hand in this, petitioning that the style to be used in the new primers would be that endorsed by the October 1901 meeting of the Section, i.e. a colloquial style based on the Tokyo dialect as the standard. The emphasis of this first series was on spreading the Tokyo dialect, with more stress placed on teaching varieties of honorifics used in speech through dialogue than on the application of colloquial style in plain description.[6] The 1909 revised series, *Kaitei Kokutei Shōgaku Tokuhon* (*Revised National Primers*), achieved an even greater proportion of colloquial style, this time emphasizing its development as a neutral narrative medium unencumbered by honorifics. It was during this period that Naturalist writers were polishing *gembun'itchi* in literature, so that progress was occurring simultaneously in both literary and educational spheres. From this time on, with Ministry blessing, classical styles began to disappear from textbooks, except as subjects for special study, and colloquial style gradually became the normal mode of expression.

The Gembun'itchi Club, having achieved two of its aims with the setting up of the National Language Research Council and the extended use of colloquial style in textbooks, began to scale down its activities after 1904 and finally disbanded in December 1910. It had not been the only group working towards the dissemination of *gembun'itchi* during this time; three other groups with similar names had been formed in 1901–02, but had proved unable to weather internal schisms to present the united front necessary for success. One of the officials of the Gembun'itchi Club, Hayashi Mikaomi, who had been instrumental in its inauguration, had alienated fellow members by his fanatical patriotism, eccentric behaviour, and unwillingness to allow others a say in the running of the group. He was therefore replaced in his official capacity in 1901, and was ostracized by former supporters. Annoyed by this cavalier treatment, Hayashi formed a second Gembun'itchi Club, which published as its bulletin the journal *Shimbun* (*New Writing*) with the avowed aim of disseminating colloquial style nation-wide. Whereas the parent Gembun'itchi Club pursued a strategy of holding meetings to study various aspects of the theory and practice of *gembun'itchi*, the splinter group planned to publish books on the subject. Its members included novelists, journalists, and writers of many kinds, whereas those of the parent group were mainly educators and intellectuals.

Yet another Gembun'itchi Club, the third of the same name, was set up soon after when Hayashi clashed with Yamakawa Naonobu, a fellow official of the second Gembun'itchi Club, over Yamakawa's preference for helping to develop colloquial style in utilitarian writing rather than literature. Hayashi was not alone in his dissatisfaction; other members were also alienated by Yamakawa, not so much by his preferred sphere of application as by his high-handed and dictatorial behaviour in the running of the club. In February 1902, they therefore resigned in a body from this second Gembun'itchi Club and formed the Gembun'itchi Kyōkai (Gembun'itchi Association), with the monthly bulletin *Shinkigen* (*The New Era*). Fifty-two members were listed in the inaugural issue of *The New Era*, most of them businessmen, lawyers, journalists, and company employees. The chairman was a lawyer, Asakura Gaimotetsu; councillors included economist Taguchi Ukichi, novelist Ozaki Kōyō, critic Shimamura Hōgetsu, and journalist Kōtoku Shūsui. Their primary aim as expressed in *The New Era*, was, like Yamakawa's, to encourage the use of colloquial style in practical writing outside the area of literature. This group approached the original Gembun'itchi Club soon after its inauguration, in March 1902, with the suggestion that the two groups work together with a view to achieving the same aim, a proposal unanimously accepted by the older group. Another group also active at this time was the Shōnen Gembun'itchikai (Young People's Gembun'itchi Club), with the journal *Gembun'itchi*, set up in 1903 to encourage the future adults of the nation to adopt *gembun'itchi* in their formative years. The journal ceased publication at the end of 1903 and the club's other activities likewise dwindled. Of all the groups, the original Gembun'itchi Club did most to bring about the realization of its objectives; the others suffered the fragmentation of disharmony caused in the main by personality clashes, which reduced their ability to concentrate effectively on the business in hand.[7]

In addition to a crop of *gembun'itchi*-oriented organizations, these first few years of the twentieth century also saw the publication of a large number of 'how-to' manuals which offered practical instruction in the technique of using colloquial style. These included Yamada Bimyō's *Gembun'itchi Bunrei* (*Model Gembun'itchi Compositions*, 1901–02), Sakai Karekawa's *Gembun'itchi Futsūbun* (*Gembun'itchi for General Use*, 1901), Wada Masao's *Gembun'itchi Ōfukubun* (*Gembun'itchi Correspondence*, 1901), Kusano Shibaji's *Gembun'itchi Bunshū* (*Collection of Gembun'itchi Writings*, 1902), Nakamura Kō's *Gembun'itchi Bumpan* (*Model Gembun'itchi Compositions*, 1901), Kawamura Hokuen's *Gembun'itchi Kiji Ronsetsu Bunrei* (*How to Write Articles and Editorials in Gembun'itchi*, 1901), Horie Hideo's *Gembun'itchi Bumpan* (*Model Gembun'itchi Compositions*, 1907), and many others. One of the earliest and most popular was Bimyō's *Gembun'itchi Bunrei*, a four-volume work which ran into nine printings within a year of publication. The first volume was given over to four chapters containing examples of various types of correspondence, on a rich variety of topics ranging from wedding congratulations to invitations, introductions to enquiries after sick friends, job-seeking to requests for loans, in Chapter 1; announcements of various events or situations in Chapter 2; official documents, laws and regulations of different kinds in Chapter 3; and such miscellaneous communications as public notices, petitions, and guarantees in Chapter 4. Having presented the examples, Bimyō then went on to address the twin problems of how to redeem the verbosity of colloquial style and how to express one's meaning clearly in that medium, enumerating a number of rhetorical devices by which these aims might be achieved such as inversion of word order, abbreviations of sentences, and repetition of words or phrases. The second volume contained eight chapters. The first dealt again with correspondence, presenting twelve types of letters and appropriate replies, this time in both plain and honorific versions. Other chapters illustrated topics as diverse as diaries, colloquial translations of Buddhist scriptures, and satirical prose, followed at the end of the volume with a discussion of each. Volume 3 contained a discourse on plain and polite language, followed by some of his own revised stories. In the final volume was to be found a sample collection of miscellaneous writings, the continuation of his discourse on rhetoric in colloquial style, a discussion of the ending of sentences with the noun *koto*, and a comparison of the original and colloquial-style versions of various statutes.

The following is an example of part of Bimyō's rewriting of a directive issued by the governor of Kanagawa in 1901.[8] The original text reads:

Bareisho yakubyō wa bareishobyōchū mottomo osorubeki jinsoku no densensei o yūshi sono higai no gekijin naru wa zenkoku o gaishi nobite ichichihō moshikuwa ikkokunai agete kaikei o fuhai shi sarani shūkaku nakarashimetaru wa kaigai kakkoku ni sono rei sukunashi to sezu. (Potato plague is the most dreaded, fastest spreading of potato diseases. The severity of the damage it causes harms the whole country. It has been known overseas to rot all tubers in a province or country, and cause the harvest to fail.)

This Bimyō rewrote as:

Bareisho yakubyō wa osoroshiku hayaku densen suru mono de, hanahadashii no wa hatake zentai no kaikei o kusarase, tsui ni ikkokunai ni made gai o oyoboshita no wa gaikoku ni mo mezurashiku nai.

Orthographically, the colloquial version does not have the long strings of Chinese characters so noticeable in the original and it is punctuated, while the original is not. In other changes, the Chinese *jinsoku* and its linking *no* have been replaced by the Japanese adjective *hayai* for 'fast'; the literary attributive *osorubeki* (verb *osoru* followed by auxiliary *beki*) by the adverb *osoroshiku* for 'dreaded'; the formal *sono higai no gekijin naru wa* (where *higai* and *gekijin* are Chinese-derived) by the adjective *hanahadashii* followed by *no wa* to mean 'in severe cases'; the Chinese verb *fuhai su* by the Japanese *kusaraseru* for 'rot'; the four-character *kaigai kakkoku* by the two-character *gaikoku* for 'overseas', and so on. Overall the rewritten version is shorter, after condensing into a word what in the original was a clause or phrase; Chinese loanwords are replaced by Japanese words except where the loanwords have become part of everyday Japanese (e.g. *gaikoku*, and *densen*, 'epidemic'); literary grammar features have been replaced by their spoken language equivalents or omitted when Bimyō has condensed information (e.g. *shūkaku nakarashimetaru*, 'has caused the harvest to fail', or more literally 'has caused there to be no harvest' has been rephrased as *gai o oyoboshita*, 'has caused damage'). The final phrase 'it has been known overseas' or 'there have been cases overseas' is in Bimyō's version *gaikoku nimo mezurashiku nai*, using the simple negative of the adjective *mezurashii* ('unusual, unknown'), whereas the original was the Sino-Japanese *sono rei sukunashi to sezu*. The original contains many more Chinese characters than phonetic Japanese symbols, and the *kana* used are *katakana*, whereas in the second version the phonetic script is *hiragana* and it is present to a much greater extent. In addition, commas and full stops are used to indicate phrasing and sentence finals.

Sakai Karekawa's *Gembun'itchi Futsūbun* appeared in two parts. The first contained a general discussion of what Sakai termed as a most important reform for the first year of the twentieth century. After an initial overview of older styles, he outlined a truncated history of *gembun'itchi*, ascribing the spread of colloquial style to its successful modelling in the Meiji novel and the influence of verbatim transcripts of raconteurs' performances published in newspapers. A second section dealt with methods by which colloquial style might be disseminated. Sakai believed that if laws, school textbooks, and newspaper editorials and articles were to be written in colloquial style, all other spheres of writing would follow suit within ten years. Newspapers in particular he described as reflecting the society they served; this being the case, supporters of colloquial style must do their utmost, through exhortation and practical example, to change the attitude of society to writing so as to bring about a change in journalistic writing. The first part concluded with his statement that he had undertaken to publish this collection of model compositions in the hope of making converts to his cause, followed by a short description of how *gembun'itchi* should be written: by bringing both speech and writing closer to the other by an equivalent degree, rather than attempting an exact reproduction of the spoken word in writing or attempting to speak in the elevated terms used in writing.

Part 2 consisted of four chapters. The first contained a discussion of letter-writing in general, and offered specific examples of various types of letters between friends, business communications, social correspondence, and postcards; Chapter 2 discussed and modelled diary writing; Chapter 3 newspaper article and editorial writing; and Chapter 4 the writing of certain miscellaneous communications such as statements of income, placards, receipts, notifications of absence, and various other possibly useful types of correspondence. While admitting that there were still problems to be solved in the use of colloquial style (it must be remembered that this was 1901, before the writers of the Shaseibun, Naturalist and Shirakaba schools had polished and refined it), Sakai hoped by providing these examples to encourage others to adopt a modern approach to writing. Certainly these manuals which appeared in 1901–02 contributed in a practical way to publicizing the matter of style reform, at a time when the government was still considering whether or not to set up the National Language Research Council.

The years following 1901 also saw the publication of many grammars of the spoken language. Betweeen 1901 and 1906 alone appeared *Nihon Zokugo Bunten* (Matsushita Daizaburō, 1901); *Nihongoten* (Maenami Nakao, 1901); *Nihon Zokugo Bunten* (Kanei Tomozō, 1901); *Hanashikotoba no Kisoku* and *Hanashikotoba no Kisoku no Furoku* (Ishikawa Kuraji, 1901); *Nihon Zokugo Bumpōron* (Irie Shukuei, 1902); *Nihon Kōgohō* (Suzuki Nobuo, 1904); *Nihon Kōgohō* (Yoshioka Gōhō, 1906); and *Nihon Kōgo Bunten* (Suzuki Nobuo, 1906). In addition to these private initiatives, the task of codification of the desired norm proceeded under the auspices of the National Language Research Council with the compilation of the first official normative grammars. The Council published several surveys on dialects, phonology, aspects of the spoken language, and colloquial style, among them *Kōgohō Chōsa Hōkokusho* (*Report on a Survey of the Grammar of the Spoken Language*, 1906), which led eventually to the appearance in 1916 of the *Kōgohō* (*A Grammar of Spoken Language*) in 1916, edited by Ōtsuki Fumihiko, Ueda Kazutoshi, and others. It was followed a year later by a supplementary volume, the *Kōgohō Bekki*. Although these volumes were the result of work carried out under the auspices of the National Language Research Council, that body had already ceased operation in 1913 as a result of administrative shuffles. It was later replaced between 1921 and 1934 by the Rinji Kokugo Chōsa linkai (Interim National Language Research Council), which was charged with carrying out a survey of *kanji*, revising *kana* usage, and modifying colloquial style.[9] This was in turn replaced in 1934 by the Kokugo Shingikai (National Language Council), likewise an organ of the Education Ministry, set up to advise the government on matters pertaining to the teaching, development, and romanization of the language. Its activities have related to *kana* usage and romanization, and the specification of the *tōyō* and more recently the *jōyō kanji*.[10] In 1948, an additional body, the National Language Research Institute, was set up to carry out detailed and wide-ranging research into theoretical and applied linguistics, particularly socio-linguistics, a task it continues today.

In the newspaper world, the adoption of colloquial style across the board was not achieved until as late as 1926. One early starter was the *Shin Nihon (The New Japan)*, which in 1900 adopted colloquial style in both news items and editorials, in fact throughout the entire paper. Elsewhere, however, conservative elements remained strong in the conviction that colloquial style was unsuitable for serious reporting. Sporadic use of the new style did occur in human interest stories in the *Yomiuri Shimbun* after 1901, but it was not until the Taishō Period that this became a widespread trend, in line with 'Taishō democracy'. Editorials, the last area to change, remained stubbornly *futsūbun* or *kambun kuzushi*. The *gembun'itchi* style was still viewed as flawed and unpolished. It was during these years, however, that the writers of the Shirakaba school were working on eradicating its defects and shaping it into a sophisticated medium for literary expression, with such success that their efforts went a long way towards breaking down such prejudices by example.

In 1916, the magazine *Nihon oyobi Nihonjin (Japan and the Japanese)* published a special issue entitled *Gendai Meika Bunshō Taikan (A Survey of the Views of Eminent People on Writing Today)*, in which upwards of one hundred and sixty prominent figures gave their views on how Japanese should be written, indicating a considerable degree of support for colloquial style as a necessary adjunct to the dissemination of information nation-wide in an open society. Under the combined weight of growing public acceptance and the influence of progress in both educational and literary spheres, the editorials of major newspapers gradually began to abandon their traditional mode of expression. A few *de aru*-style editorials appeared in 1919 in the *Tōkyō Asahi Shimbun* and the *Tōkyō Nichi Nichi Shimbun*. The *Yomiuri Shimbun*, which had long shown interest in the language reform issue by carrying news of developments as they occurred and by the active part played by some of its journalists in those developments, adopted colloquial style in its editorials in November, 1920. It was followed two months later by the *Tōkyō Nichi Nichi Shimbun*, from whose editorial pulpit Fukuchi Gen'ichirō had fulminated upon the serious deficiencies of written Japanese almost fifty years earlier, and in 1922 by the *Tōkyō Asahi Shimbun*. Once the use of colloquial style became a matter of editorial policy, *futsūbun* was no longer seen in any section of these newspapers. As major organs of the press, their example led others to follow, until by 1926 all newspapers had followed suit. The *de aru* termination was chosen as the journalistic form of colloquial style because of its neutrality in the matter of honorifics (a problem which had long vexed both opponents and supporters of *gembun'itchi*), its relative conciseness, and its perceived superiority in terms of dignity to the *da* termination.

After World War One, colloquial style was used in writing in a growing number of fields, among them history, science, criticism, and expository prose. Eventually, the only area in which the older literary conventions remained firmly entrenched was that of official government documents and Imperial proclamations – the latter were not even punctuated until 1946. Within the Education Ministry, always the leader in language initiatives, colloquial style had been used in notices, written reports, certificates and the like from 1918 till 1922 under Education Minister Nakahashi, but this trend was later reversed. The Ministry's *Kōgobun Yōreishū* (*Collected Examples of Colloquial Style*, Volume 1), published in 1921, offered guidelines on appropriate forms of colloquial style to be used in particular situations, at the same time emphasizing the importance of using punctuation and voice marks. Topics covered included written reports, requests, and certificates; notifications, enquiries, and responses; invitations and instructions; statements and letters of advice; modes of greeting, thanks, and condolence; introductions and requests; and advertisements – the entire range of communications its staff might be expected to encounter.

An Imperial proclamation issued on New Year's Day 1946 incorporated two orthographic innovations not seen together in earlier proclamations which represented the first step towards making such texts more readable. These were the use of punctuation, never before found here, and the addition of *nigori* marks to distinguish between voiced and unvoiced consonants in *katakana* portions of the text. The latter had been seen a few times before, but this was the first time it had been undertaken in conjunction with improved spatial organization of the script. As Imperial proclamations provided the model for other official documents, it was not long before these were reproduced in the text of the revised draft of the constitution.

In April 1946, a significant victory was achieved in the area of officialese when the draft of the revised constitution was published in colloquial style. Not only style but orthography was different; where earlier legal and official documents had been written in a mixture of *kanji* and *katakana*, the *katakana* now gave way to *hiragana*, albeit in the historical usage as the modern format had not yet been worked out.[11] One of the prime movers behind this change to colloquial style was Yamamoto Yūzō (1887–1974), a novelist and dramatist with a keen interest in language issues, who in 1945 had been instrumental in setting up the Mitaka Language Research Institute at his private residence to work for the democratization of the Japanese language.[12] The connection between democracy and language was the major theme of the arguments of Yamamoto and his supporters, among whom was Andō Masatsugu (1878–1952, Japanese language scholar). An editorial in the *Mainichi Shimbun* on 20 November 1945, had urged those involved in drafting the constitution to seize this chance to change the style to one which could be easily understood by the entire populace, on the grounds that the constitution was the source of the nation's laws and that an understanding of its contents was vital in a society where democracy was becoming a reality with the enfranchisement of women and the lowering of the voting age.

In January 1946, Yamamoto arranged a meeting of representatives from various groups dealing with language issues, among them the Kokugo Gakkai (Language Society), Nihon Gengo Gakkai (Linguistics Society of Japan), Kokugo Kyōiku Gakkai (Language Education Society), and *kana* and *rōmaji* pressure groups, in order to discuss whether Japanese might work together to solve the language problem, rather than have a solution imposed from outside. The resulting body styled itself the Kokumin no Kokugo Undō Remmei (Federation of National Language Movements); its brief was to work for the simplification of *kanji* and the adoption of colloquial style in all fields. Members devised a petition describing in no uncertain terms their view of the importance of language reform in official documents. They were critical of the past failure to present documents relevant to the whole population in a style which all could read. The coming push to build a new Japan could not succeed unless this were remedied; the people must be absolutely clear as to what the nation required of them. The new constitution and all statutes should be written in colloquial style, with a minimum of difficult Chinese-derived words and esoteric expressions; in orthography there should be fewer Chinese characters, and increased use of punctuation and voice marks.[13] The day after this was submitted by Yamamoto, Andō and others to Minister of State Matsumoto Jōji and Legislative Bureau Head Irie Toshio, an addendum further requesting the replacing of *katakana* with *hiragana* and the use of indented paragraphing was appended.

There ensued an unsettled period of argument. Minister Matsumoto felt the proposal to be too radical, believing that although colloquial style was now dominant outside official circles, it still possessed defects which rendered it inappropriate for use in a document of this kind. He remained unconvinced by the arguments advanced by Yamamoto and Andō, but agreed to discuss the matter in Cabinet. Irie, on the other hand, had been interested in the issue of colloquialization for some time, and agreed that now was the time for decisive action. At his urging, Matsumoto was persuaded to allow Yamamoto Yūzō to prepare a draft colloquial-style version of the constitution; after some revision, this was tabled at a Cabinet meeting in early April. Lobbying before the meeting resulted in support from a number of Ministers, in particular Minister for Home Affairs Mitsuchi Chūzō, who spoke strongly in favour of the proposal and elicited agreement from the meeting. The colloquial-style draft constitution was then made public on 17 April.

Matsumoto's switch from opposition to support has been explained as resulting from his feeling that the use of colloquial style might at least save the constitution from seeming too much like a translation of an English original.[14] Matsumoto's original draft of the constitution had been rejected by SCAP (Supreme Commander of the Allied Powers) in February, and replaced by the 'MacArthur draft'. While the content was thus fairly firmly spelled out by the Americans, Irie asserted, the idea of using colloquial style originated on the Japanese side and not, as has been claimed, with SCAP. SCAP in fact were at first suspicious of the proposal, suspecting that by 'colloquialization' was intended the use of words of unclear meaning which would allow the Japanese loopholes in interpretation; only after several rounds of negotiation did they accept that the purpose was to present the constitution in language familiar to most Japanese. Mystery writer Takagi Akimitsu offers an interesting sidelight on the reactions of those not involved, in his novel *Zero no Mitsugetsu* (*Honeymoon to Nowhere*): a character who is a lawyer comments that while under normal circumstances the proposal to write the constitution in modern language instead of the traditional style would have created a prolonged argument, the contents of the constitution were themselves so revolutionary that the phraseology did not really matter, and the idea was adopted without fuss.[15] In May 1946, a colloquial-style Imperial proclamation was broadcast, and from that time on colloquial style came to replace its literary precursors in the language of public life.

Shiraishi Daiji, writing in 1947, recalled that the day after the draft of the constitution appeared, a meeting of vice-ministers drew up a document entitled 'Kakukanchō ni okeru Bunshō No Buntai nado ni kansuru Ken' ('Matters Relating to the Style of Documents in Government Offices'), which laid down that the style, vocabulary, script, and punctuation of future documents and newly enacted laws would henceforth conform to the example of the constitution in a bid to achieve simplification.[16] Existing laws, however, were to remain as they were for the time being. The Ministry of Education, too, called a preliminary meeting to discuss the reform of its terminology, at which it was arranged that this Ministry would circulate to others suggestions for simplifying the orthography and terminology of statutes and documents. Further meetings were attended by representatives from the Legislative Bureau; after a total of four discussion sessions, the assembly was thrown open to attendance by other ministries. The end result was the document 'Kanchō Yōgo o Hei-i ni suru Hyōjun ni kansuru Ken' ('Matters Pertaining to Standards for Simplifying Government Terminology'); its implementation was then discussed at a meeting of vice-ministers. The section on standards dealt with style and orthography, giving concrete examples, within a broad policy framework of simplicity and conciseness. It having been decided that the Cabinet and all ministries would then collaborate in producing actual examples of script and terminology in a *Handbook of Official Terminology*, the Education Ministry then held a special conference for this purpose, attended by representatives from Cabinet, the Legislative Bureau, and the Ministries.

One problem which had to be addressed before colloquial style could be successfully adopted as the medium of government documents was which of the several forms of the copula used in the spoken language should be employed. This matter had been the focus of considerable debate since the first *gembun'itchi* novels had appeared in the late 1880s. The aristocratic *de gozaru*, although used often in colloquial works written by scholars during the first ten years of the Meiji Period when the feudal influence remained strong, was seldom seen after about 1885. *De gozaimasu*, although later often found in children's literature between 1897 and 1907, was both too respectful and too lengthy for the new realistic novel, and likewise fell out of general use. *De arimasu* had been used consistently in school readers after 1886, starting with Shimpo Iwatsugu's *Nihon Tokuhon* (*A Japanese Reader*), until displaced in the 1903 state series by *desu* and *de aru*. Saganoya Omuro first used it in the novel in *Nozue no Kiku* (*The Chrysanthemum at the Edge of the Field*, 1889), and continued to do so in all his *gembun'itchi* novels until 1892. It was not particularly popular in fiction because of its length and its non-neutral overtones, and Saganoya himself later abandoned it. Writers of popular historical novels serialized in newspapers between 1906 and 1913, however, often employed this termination.

The *desu* style was adopted in Nishi Tomisada's textbook *Yōgaku Tokuhon* (*A Child's Reader*, 1887) in a bid to replace *de arimasu* (used in other contemporary textbooks in which the colloquial was beginning to appear) with a form more widely used in speech. The 1903 state primers adopted *desu* in preference to *de arimasu*. It was the termination preferred by novelist Yamada Bimyō, who used it in a total of six novels between 1888 and 1892 (when he stopped writing fiction) as well as in his critical and expository essays. Another ten or so novelists also used *desu* in their works during this period, among them Hirotsu Ryūrō (*Back and Front*, 1888), Ishibashi Shian (*The Flower Thief*, 1889), and Wakamatsu Shizuko (*Little Lord Fauntleroy*, 1890–92).

Da, the plain form of Tokyo speech, was often used in the popular press but not in other colloquial-style writing until Futabatei Shimei chose it for his novel *The Drifting Cloud* in 1887. The probable reason for its lack of exposure in writing was the impression of coarseness it imparted; it was not a polite form, being short and abrupt and used when speaking to inferiors. Its one advantage was its refreshing brevity in comparison with other longer, politer terminations. This no doubt influenced Futabatei's decision in his quest for realism; with *da* he could avoid those characteristics of the spoken language – long-windedness and excessive emphasis on honorifics – which had led Tsubouchi Shōyō to the conclusion that the colloquial style as it stood in 1886 was not a suitable medium for literature. Shōyō himself employed *da* in his own sole attempt at a colloquial-style novel, *Here and There*. The only other authors to experiment with *da*, Yamada Bimyō in 1887 and Saganoya Omuro in 1889,[17] later abandoned it in favour of *desu* and *de arimasu/de aru* respectively. Bimyō's critics decried his use of *da* as vulgar and abrupt, and it offended his own poetic sensibilities.

De aru, while a slow starter in early attempts at colloquial style, emerged from obscurity when it was adopted in the novel. Several novelists experimented with it in 1890–91,[18] and Ozaki Kōyō developed and polished this style in his *gembun'itchi* period, achieving his best results in *Passions and Griefs*, 1896. His success influenced others to employ *de aru*; they included Uchida Roan, Iwaya Sazanami, Hirotsu Ryūrō, Futabatei Shimei, Yamada Bimyō, Saganoya Omuro, Tayama Katai, and others. From this time on the *de aru* termination became that most commonly used in colloquial style in both the novel[19] and other areas, including education, where it was used in primary textbooks after the 1903 series of state texts appeared. *De aru* had been used as a translated version of the English *be* or the Dutch *zijn* in early Meiji renderings of science books and histories; like the classical *nari*, it was a neutral expression, unencumbered with problems relating to the level of honorifics and suitable for objective description.

When the time came to consider which variety of colloquial style should be used in legal documents and government statutes, then, its neutrality and already widely-entrenched usage made the *de aru* style, in which *de aru* is the copula and other verbs appear in their plain forms, the obvious choice, particularly in documents and correspondence dealing with government offices of the same rank. There remained, however, the problem of what style should be used in documents circulating between departments of greater or lesser importance. Some sort of ruling was necessary to establish a policy on the use of honorifics. At a meeting of vice-ministers on 17 June 1946, it was decided that while *de aru* would be the standard form of colloquial style in public documents, the semi-formal *-masu* style could also be used in cases such as reports or enquiries where some degree of deference was deemed necessary.

7 The opposition

The preceding three chapters have outlined the positive steps to achieving stylistic reform, the milestones along the way, the famous names who through their efforts brought the goal a step nearer with each initiative. Lest it be thought that these gains were easily made, however, let us now turn our attention to those who opposed what was being proposed and gradually implemented, who fought a bitter rearguard action against what they perceived as the loss of traditional literary standards. There was much discussion among interested parties on alternative solutions to the language problem. Some, such as that proposed for literature by Tsubouchi Shōyō in *The Essence of the Novel* and Ozaki Kōyō, and other Ken'yūsha group members, were simply reactionary, advocating a return to tradition at all costs. Others, as we shall see, were more responsive to the changed social climate: the *futsūbun* solution, for instance, or Mori Ōgai's *wakan'yō*. I shall now examine the objections of the major critics, look at several of the alternative suggestions, and discuss the most notable of the controversies carried on in print over the issue of colloquial style, the 1889 *Bun* wrangle which lasted several months.

Suggested alternative solutions to full-scale adoption of colloquial style ranged from outright rejection in favour of traditional literary conventions to more moderate proposals for a blend of old and new which sought to retain the best of the past while injecting into it the necessary vitality of the present. One of the earliest in this latter category was contained in an editorial, 'Nihon Bunshōron' ('On Written Japanese'), which appeared in the *Chōya Shimbun* on 25 February 1876. Its writer advocated replacing *kambun kuzushi* with a style based on the common speech of Tokyo but also incorporating the graceful expression of Heian Period classics and the splendour and vigour of the medieval war chronicles. While this fell far short of addressing the problems faced in written Japanese, it was a step in the right direction, with the use of the grammar of the spoken language in writing being at least envisaged as reasonable even if not to be attempted on its own. Almost a year later, on 16 January 1877 in the same newspaper, Ōtsuki Fumihiko published a similar conservative suggestion for a style consisting of medieval Japanese vocabulary, Sino-Japanese syntax, and expressions found in modern conversation. What these two men wanted was in effect a modernized literary style, revitalized by the incorporation of elements of the spoken language but still a thing apart from everyday speech. In this they were much of a mind with Fukuzawa Yukichi, although Fukuzawa, as we have seen, took considerable pains to replace archaic expressions with those in common use wherever possible.

The first definite anti-*gembun'itchi* statement published in the newspapers was 'Bunshō Kogoto' ('A Grumble about Writing')[1] by Narushima Ryūhoku (1837–84, writer of *gesaku* fiction), who strongly advocated maintaining the dichotomy between speech and writing. A longer, more reasoned rejection of the push towards colloquial style was published in 1886 by Yano Fumio (1850–1931, politician, journalist, and novelist). Two years earlier, in 1884, Yano had written a short essay entitled 'Buntairon' ('On Style') as a preface to the second part of his novel *Keikoku Bidan* (*Fine Tales of Statesmanship*), in which he classified the styles in current use under the four headings of *kambun*, *wabun*, *ōbunchokuyaku* (the name given to the kind of writing which attempted as far as possible to reproduce the structures found in European languages in *kambun*, *wabun*, or *gembun'itchi*), and *zokugo-rigen* (colloquial and dialect). After discussing the pros and cons of each, he concluded with a plea that all four elements be combined into one new composite style, believing writing which was out of accord with its times to have little point. While he admitted that there was nothing to be gained by clinging stubbornly to the old styles, Yano was critical of the growing tendency to value clarity above all else, censuring those who abandoned Sino-Japanese and classical Japanese as self-indulgent and undisciplined while still nevertheless to be praised for their efforts to find a new style. To him, it made more sense to make the most of what was already there rather than to reject it utterly.

In 1886, his essay 'Nihon Buntai Moji Shinron' ('A New Discourse on Japan's Style and Script') was published. Yano himself was in England at the time studying, among other things, the newspaper business; he had observed in the Japanese newspapers sent to him the growing debate on the question of script and style reform, and had sent this essay home to add his opinions to the pot. Two chapters dealt with script reform, four with style. The second chapter set out his reasons for rejecting colloquial style. For one thing, it was too wordy. While this did not matter in speech, which was transient, it became annoying in print. Sino-Japanese, while it might be hard to understand if read aloud, was at least concise and pleasing to the eye. Then there was the over-abundance of honorifics in spoken Japanese which made it much more difficult to use in writing than, say, the English colloquial. For example, one would use *itashimashita* ('I did it') to a superior, *shimashita* to an equal, and *shita* to a subordinate. The first was too polite for writing, the second too familiar, and the third too disrespectful to the reader. Literary styles, on the other hand, were comparatively free of honorifics; those which did appear, such as *tamau* ('deign') or *haberu* ('serve'), were relatively concise. A third reason was his fear that the unavoidable differences in expression between speech and writing which he had observed even in Europe, where the *gembun'itchi* principle ostensibly applied, would be still further magnified in the case of Japan where the two were regarded as different. Then, too, it would be impossible to avoid boring the reader without the aid of special literary devices to replace the visual and aural stimuli of gesture and tone of voice; it would by no means be sufficient to record speech verbatim and leave it at that. And finally, the obvious simplicity of the colloquial style, which needed no special study, was negated by dialectal differences; before it could be successfully used, a standard language would have to be selected and taught in the nation's schools.

The essay was not a blind reaction against new ideas by a traditionalist; it was well thought out and logically argued. Yano, having studied and visited England, had first-hand experience of the advantages of colloquial style in that country, and must therefore have been aware of the possibilities which would be opened up should a similar situation come to exist in Japan. He was, however, clear-sighted enough to realize that the differences between the spoken English language and the spoken Japanese language were such that Japan could find herself in a worse plight than before were she to rush into emulation of the European languages, as advocated by keen supporters of the *gembun'itchi* principle, without first taking proper cognizance of the difficulties involved. It would be foolish, he argued, to deny that there were serious problems inherent in colloquial style – far better to examine them and make a rational decision on the results.

In spite of his rejection of colloquial style, Yano did recognize the need for a modern style with the emphasis on simplicity. He went on in the third chapter[2] to discuss the relative merits of five styles, referred to as pure *kambun*, *hentai kambun* (*wakankonkōbun*), *zatsubuntai* (*kambun kuzushi*), *ryōbuntai* (*zatsubuntai* with *kana* glosses given for Chinese characters, as seen in popular newspapers) and *kana* style. Of them all, Yano concluded, the most convenient was what he called *ryōbuntai* (two-in-one style): while its glosses made it as easy to read as *kana* styles, it retained the visual aid of Chinese characters to help distinguish between homophones, thereby also avoiding the tendency to ramble inherent in *kana* texts. As shown by its success in popular fiction and the popular press, it could be read by those with little education, and would therefore be the best choice for an everyday style. He further classified the *zatsubuntai* (mixed style, or *kambun kuzushi*) which was the basis of *ryōbuntai* into three streams and listed their strengths: the *kambun* stream, a more or less direct translation of Chinese into Japanese, which had the advantage of being concise; the *wabun* stream, basically everyday Japanese vocabulary and classical grammar, which possessed great evocative power; and the *yōbun* (western style) stream, a direct translation of European languages, which permitted the writer the freedom to describe things in great detail. Of the three, Yano favoured the second as the basis for a general-purpose style, believing the first to be too difficult and the third not yet sufficiently assimilated to seem natural. Above all, the style chosen should be easy to understand, with the more difficult styles being reserved for literature. In this he departed from the critical stance he had earlier adopted towards the desire for simplicity.

In conclusion, Yano recommended that the Ministry of Education have the Tōkyō Gakushi Kaiin, or Tokyo Academy,[3] study the question of style, and further that it encourage public discussion of various styles in the newspapers. A solution to the problem could thus be arrived at by combining scientifically-conducted research with the weight of public opinion. In this he foreshadowed the eventual setting up sixteen years later of the National Language Research Council in the Ministry of Education. His own preferred solution was to adopt a middle-of-the-road policy, concentrating on scaling down what was already to hand rather than rushing off full tilt into unfamiliar territory, an attitude not surprising perhaps in one who had earlier been a student of Fukuzawa Yukichi.

THE *FUTSŪBUN* MOVEMENT

Yano's essay was the starting point for what became the major contender against colloquial style in the search for a new way of writing: the *futsūbun* (general style) movement, which began to attract support after 1886, as support for colloquial style increased among intellectuals and novelists, from those opposed to the idea. Its supporters were men who, while recognizing the need for change, remained convinced that the demand could be met by modification of existing styles. The term *futsūbun* essentially means merely the most commonly used style of an era. In the Meiji Period, however, it came to designate the Classical Standard, the special style which came into use after about 1897 in newspapers, magazines, textbooks, and government business; the term was probably first used in education circles to indicate the styles used in textbooks, its first documented appearance being in the third clause of the 'Kaisei Shōgakkō Rei Shikō Kisoku' ('Revised Rules for the Enforcement of Elementary School Regulations') issued by the Ministry of Education in 1900.[4]

The stylistic diversity which had still been so prized during the first two decades of the Meiji Period had begun to pall by this time; there had arisen a desire for one uniform style which would be easily understood without being either too elegant or too vulgar. Accordingly, those elements of older styles considered most appropriate to this end were selected and taught in schools. Magazines and newspapers gradually adopted the resulting hybrid in place of the more difficult *kambun kuzushi*, until with the passage of time it became established in general use. What was eventually settled on was a blend of the most familiar idioms and grammatical features of *kambun*, *wabun*, *wakankonkōbun*, and *sōrōbun*, with a simplified vocabulary and a certain proportion of European-derived expressions as well.[5] Like the colloquial style, *futsūbun* did not spring full-blown into being but experienced a similar period of groping after its final form. It was a direct result of the desire for a standard language which began to become evident after 1878. The aims of its supporters were basically the same as those of the *gembun'itchi* movement: to develop a uniform, reasonably simple style which could be understood throughout the country and would facilitate communication and education. The difference between the two lay in their envisaged solution, the one being the Classical Standard, the other the Colloquial Standard.

Yano's ideas on *futsūbun* were echoed eight months later by Suematsu Kenchō (1855-1920, politician and lawyer, who had worked on the *Tōkyō Nichi Nichi Shimbun* with Fukuchi Gen'ichirō) in a nine chapter essay *Nihon Bunshōron* (*On Japanese Writing*), which dealt with both script reform and with style. Referring back to Yano's preface to *Fine Tales of Statesmanship*, Suematsu reiterated its classification of styles into four categories and, lamenting the confusion caused by such diversity, supported Yano's suggestion of a blending of elements from all four into one smooth, composite style. Unlike Yano, however, Suematsu saw this operation in terms of an important intermediate step in the transition to colloquial style.

> Because our ultimate aim is *gembun'itchi*, in order to make writing easily comprehensible for as many people as possible, we must strive in blending the various styles to attain a smooth and flowing result. We must also, in choosing vocabulary, take care to use those words in common use in society.[6]

Despite Suematsu's ultimate commitment to achieving the implementation of colloquial style, his advocacy of the intermediate *futsūbun* added to Yano's was sufficient to set *futsūbun* research in motion. The project was eagerly received by conservatives because it was reasonably easy to put into practice; all the material was there to hand, whereas the attainment of colloquial style, beside offending their sensibilities, would require hard work to fashion the comparatively unfamiliar (in prose) raw material into an acceptable medium. Suematsu's willingness to spend some time on the *futsūbun* plateau *en route* to his goal of *gembun'itchi* was in tune with the newly cautious mood of the times; in literature, the first flush of enthusiasm for colloquial style in the novel was about to fade in favour of a return to *gazoku setchūbun*.

Other advocacies of a non-colloquial general business style around this period included Hagino Yoshiyuki's *Wabun o ronzu* (*On Wabun*, 1887) and Sekine Masanao's *Kokugo no Hontai narabi ni sono Kachi* (*The True Japanese Language and Its Value*, 1888),[7] both of which called for a new modernized version of *wabun* as a general-purpose style instead of Chinese or European influenced styles. In May 1888, these two men, both classical scholars, together with Ochiai Naobumi (1861–1903, poet and classical scholar), Nishimura Shigeki (1828–1902, bureaucrat), Takasaki Masakaze (1836–1912, poet), and several others formed a group known as the *Nihon Bunshōkai* (*Society for Japanese Writing*) with the intention of creating a standard *futsūbun*. The society held monthly meetings at which members were encouraged to read submissions for discussion by colleagues. Two collections of writings were published in March and August 1889, in which members aired their opinions on the style question. The group's own favoured style was a kind of *wabun* modernized with familiar expressions and also incorporating a proportion of Chinese words.

One of the group's members, Ochiai Naobumi, who was later to launch a movement for a return to elegant classical Japanese prose as a reaction against Europeanization and the *gembun'itchi* movement, delivered a lecture on the topic 'Bunshō no Gobyū' ('Errors in Writing') in July 1889, deploring the grammatical errors which had been appearing with increasing frequency in styles of all kinds in magazines, newspapers and novels. Classifying contemporary varieties of writing into the four categories of Sino-Japanese, the style used in translations, the style used in novels, and colloquial style, Ochiai discussed the shortcomings of each. Errors were often to be found in *kambun* texts because of confusion over the manner in which they should be read in Japanese; particular attention should be paid to the correct usage of *kunten*, the guiding diacritics used to show how to construe Chinese into Japanese. The style found in translations had been a hastily put-together affair in its earliest period, about the time of the Restoration, which later scholars had accepted as it stood without bothering to improve on it. It incorporated some extremely odd expressions which were literal translations of constructions found in European languages: un-Japanese expressions such as *atta beku* (*beku* should follow the form *aru*, not *atta*), and the misuse of particles, in particular the conjunctive particle *tsutsu* which is added to the stem of a verb to indicate continuing or repetitive action as in *yuki wa furitsutsu* ('the snow is falling') but was now being used with a following *aru* in such phrases as *oshietsutsu aru* ('he is teaching') and *ikitsutsu aru* ('he is going') to indicate action in progress. In the third category, he found that although novels were enjoying a period of great popularity they contained many grammatical errors and possessed no dignity, mainly because their style was modelled on the vulgar idiom of *gesaku* writers such as Tanehiko, Shunsui, Ikku and Samba; novelists would have to raise their standards. And finally, while recognizing the colloquial style's great advantage of simplicity to which he attributed its current popularity, Ochiai cautioned his readers against moving too far in the direction of colloquialization of writing, believing the colloquial style as it was currently being used to be over-vulgar. His own policy would be to 'make speech slightly more dignified and lower the tone of writing a little.'[8] Whatever happened, he averred, it was imperative to fix upon a standardized *futsūbun*, to avoid confusing readers with errors, or worse, causing them to imitate them. The Nihon Bunshōkai, with its emphasis on preserving the best elements of traditional styles, paved the way for his later *shinkokubun* movement.

And so the *futsūbun* initiative gathered strength, gaining ground in newspapers and textbooks until it became the colloquial style's most formidable rival. In 1905, the Ministry of Education issued 'Bumpōjō Kyoyō ni kansuru Jikō' ('On Approved Grammar'), a sixteen-clause document which sought to update those elements of Heian Period grammar still in use and achieve a modernized literary grammar; for example, it sanctioned the use of *shi*, traditionally the participial form of the perfective auxiliary, as a conclusive form able to end a sentence.[9] Other departures from classical grammar which had by then achieved wide currency included certain euphonic changes (*sezuwa arazu* had become *sezumba arazu*, for example); the relaxing of the *kakarimusubi* rules characteristic of older styles which decreed that where certain emphatic particles occurred near the start of a sentence a particular verb form must be used at the conclusion; and the adoption of certain features of the spoken language, such as attaching the indefinite conditional connective *ba* to the *izenkei* (conditional) rather than the *mizenkei* (negative) form of the verb. It is interesting that this occurred three years after the National Language Research Council was set up to look into, among other things, the implementation of colloquial style; its many vocal supporters had obviously not yet carried all before them. *Futsūbun* had by this time replaced *kambun* in textbooks. Mikami Sanji (1865–1939, historian) recalled that he was frequently required to travel to the provinces on official trips to gather records for the university in the late Meiji Period, at about the time the National Language Research Council was set up. On each occasion, he was required to write a report for the official gazette. Once, when he wrote his report in colloquial style, it was returned by the gazette office with a curt note to the effect that the style was unacceptable and it should be rewritten in *futsūbun*.[10] Obviously the language policies of the upper levels of the Ministry had not yet filtered down throughout the hierarchy.

Tobiyama Junko, in an attempt to analyse the precise characteristics of *futsūbun*, has examined twelve pieces of critical writing produced between 1892 and 1912 by Mori Ōgai, Tsubouchi Shōyō, Tokutomi Sohō, Miyake Setsurei, and Takayama Chogyū, all of whom were involved in writing for newspapers and journals.[11] Her research shows that in terms of *vocabulary*, Chinese words accounted for a large share, averaging between 40 per cent and 50 per cent depending on the author, with many examples of four-character compounds. About 40 per cent of verbs were of the *sagyō henkaku* type (i.e. Chinese words and *su*), and she found no examples of auxiliary verbs of the type 'stem + (e.g.) *kakeru*'. Most adjectives, however, came from classical Japanese. Its *rhetorical touches* included various forms of couplets typical of Sino-Japanese; forms of exclamation and personification characteristic of classical Japanese, but none of the traditional pivot words, linked forms, or stock epithets beloved of *wabun* writers; and some newer forms derived from European rhetoric. With regard to *structure*, the most common sentence endings were the *shūshikei* (final form) of verbs or the copula *nari*. Present-tense verbs were often used to conclude sentences even when the past was under discussion. Average sentence length was longer than Sino-Japanese but shorter than classical Japanese. Tobiyama's analysis of *grammatical forms* shows that those of Sino-Japanese preponderated: of the conclusive forms *tsu*, *nu* and *tari*, the Sino-Japanese *tari* outnumbered the classical *tsu* and *nu*; *bekarazu* and *zarubeshi* were used as negatives in preference to *maji*; and *shimu* occurred rather than *su* or *sasu* when a causative auxiliary was required. Case particles were often used in the same way as in the spoken language, with the use of *ga* to mark the subject becoming more frequent. The most often-used connective particles were *ba* and *te*, with *tomo*, *domo*, *wo*, *tsutsu* and *de* hardly seen at all. *Mo* was used often as an adverbial particle, but almost never with its traditional significance of emphasis or excitement, more often to indicate a paradox. Overall there was a heavy bias towards Sino-Japanese, toned down and made easier to understand by an admixture of elements of classical Japanese and the contemporary spoken language.

Futsūbun was not destined to last. The polishing and refining of colloquial style which was taking place within the literary world during this period succeeded in convincing many former detractors of its wider possibilities, so that colloquial style began slowly to supplant *futsūbun* outside literature. Kembō Gōki quantifies the comparative rates of advancement of colloquial style and decline of *futsūbun* in the magazine *Taiyō* (*The Sun*) as shown below. *The Sun* being a general magazine rather than a purely literary journal, it may be taken to reflect general stylistic trends in society as a whole rather than in one small segment. The following are the figures for the proportional percentage of colloquial-style articles and stories published between 1897 and 1907, the balance being *futsūbun*:

May	1897	13.6%
May	1898	3.3%
May	1899	18.5%
May	1900	27.6%
April	1901	16.9%
April	1902	31.6%
May	1903	30.2%
May	1904	38.0%
May	1905	44.7%
May	1906	43.5%
May	1907	45.9%

By May 1917, the proportion had risen to 92.5 per cent. Kembō points out that as novels accounted for only about 10 per cent of the total content, the growth rate cannot be attributed to the spread of colloquial style in fiction.[12]

Although ostensibly a rival of colloquial style, *futsūbun* may in a sense be said to have actually helped smooth the way for its ultimate victory. Its emphasis on simple vocabulary, combined with the influence of the new, polished colloquial style of Naturalist and Shirakaba writers, probably helped to weaken the remaining anti-colloquial prejudice among intellectuals, preparing them for the later transition to full colloquialization.

OTHER PROPOSALS

In a departure from the retrospective approach of *futsūbun* advocates, Morita Shiken (1861–97, journalist and man of letters) suggested in *Nihon Bunshō no Shōrai* (*The Future of Japanese Writing*, 1888) a simplified version of *ōbun chokuyakutai* which would allow a detailed meticulous expression of the subtleties of thought. *Ōbun chokuyakutai* was the name given to a style which had an air of being a direct translation of European languages because of its incorporation of European-type constructions. The question of style, Morita averred, was one of the most important issues facing Japanese society. There was too much variety in the range of styles available; what was needed was a *futsūbun*, a single general-purpose style for education, government, and the ordinary business of society. It would not replace old styles, but would instead be a composite of their best elements. The problem was, however, that both society and human thought had become intricate and sophisticated. Any new style, therefore, must likewise possess these characteristics in order to do justice to its users. *Kambun*, however great its popularity, had originated in antiquity when people thought in a simple and straightforward manner, and was thus too restricted for modern purposes. Morita himself had conducted an experiment to verify this several years earlier; examining Chinese written by Americans, he had observed that in order to express western thoughts in a natural manner they had used the style of the Chinese colloquial novel, literary Chinese proving insufficient.

In the absence of any Japanese- or Chinese-derived medium which would fit the specifications, Morita suggested patterning a modern style on those employed in Europe. By this he meant not that colloquial style should be adopted but that European constructions should be copied in Japanese, while still writing in Chinese characters according to the rules of *kambun*.

> While it might appear to be very difficult to arrange characters in the Chinese way while using European expressions, this is not really the case at all ... Among contemporary styles, the 'direct-translation style familiar to people' is akin to the one I should choose as the future style for Japan, because its mode of expression is modelled directly on European styles and its character usage follows Chinese rules.[13]

There was indeed a style known as *ōbun chokuyakutai* which had originated in early Meiji translations of European works. Morita himself had helped develop it in his own translations, striving for a *shūmitsu buntai* (careful detailed style) based on European modes of expression. However, he conceded, this would require some modification before it would serve as a *futsūbun*, in the form of a weeding out of the gratuitously difficult Chinese characters with which it was normally studded.

As for the concept of *gembun'itchi*, Morita rejected the idea that speech and writing could ever be identical:

> Speech and writing are two different things; they cannot be made into one. It is impossible to make even Western writing, in which the two can be said to be almost the same, into an exact replica of speech. The gap between the two has merely been narrowed considerably; anyone who has studied ordinary Western writing knows that it is not completely the same as speech. It is thus not logical to call for absolute *gembun'itchi*. The essence of the matter is that speech and writing are merely to be brought as close together as possible.[14]

Thus he rejected colloquial style, or at least the kind of no-holds-barred colloquial style he believed was being advocated by *gembun'itchi* supporters, inclining instead towards a simpler, more polished version of the *kambun*-based *ōbun chokuyakutai*.

One of the more extreme solutions mooted, again involving European elements but this time of an archaic nature, was that proposed by Nishimura Shigeki in his 1884 essay 'Bunshōron' ('On Style'). Nishimura (1828–1902, Enlightenment scholar and bureaucrat) was an unyielding opponent of colloquial style, having eleven years earlier successfully blocked progressive Education Minister Ōki Takatō's plan to introduce colloquial style into school textbooks by reporting, as head of the working party set up to investigate the feasibility of the scheme, an inability to settle upon a workable means of putting the plan into action. While recognizing the inevitability of a certain amount of western influence in developing a modern Japanese culture, Nishimura believed fervently in preserving the purity of Japanese tradition, and for that reason rejected the idea of a colloquial style modelled on the European example. As head of the textbook compilation bureau, he was an influential man, and as a result of his negative appraisal the scheme was shelved, not to reappear in education for almost fifteen years.

Colloquial style was not mentioned at all in 'Bunshōron'. Instead, Nishimura suggested that scholars should study the syntax of classical Japanese and Chinese and also European languages, in particular Greek and Latin, carefully perusing the literary masterpieces of each language. They should then choose the most pleasing elements of each, to be blended into a new style which would contain the best that Japan, China, and Europe had to offer. This, declared Nishimura, was a simple exercise which could be carried out with a minimum of fuss in a reasonable time. Scholars, after all, had traditionally devoted their youth to the study of *kambun*, many giving over their entire lives to writing; why should they not now switch the focus of their labours from Chinese to Japanese and concentrate on developing a new style for Japan? He himself being too stupid and too old to learn new ways, he commended the task to others.[15]

Four years later, in an 1888 lecture at the Tokyo Academy, Nishimura reiterated his hope that scholars would become proficient in his *wakan'yō* (Japanese-Chinese-European) style. This time he did mention the *gembun'itchi* argument, rejecting it on the grounds that it would be impossible to achieve in practical terms and would further seriously disadvantage Japanese literature in some unspecified way. Writing in Japan had always been glorified and exalted in literary circles, whereas speech, left to develop as it would, had come to be regarded as vulgar. Those who claimed that speech and writing were the same in western countries were mistaken: they were not. Even if they were, why should Japan follow suit? Keeping the two separate and distinct was to Nishimura proof of a much greater degree of civilization and sophistication than seeking uniformity. Advocates of *gembun'itchi* could solve their problem in one of two ways: they could raise the tone of the spoken language, making it more like the written, or lower the tone of writing, bringing it close to speech. Nishimura found both ideas laughable. The first was impossible, because of the essentially vulgar nature of speech. On the other hand, it was certainly possible to lower the tone of writing, but at what point was one to stop? He trotted out a few other arguments against the adoption of colloquial style, pointing out the inconsistency in using it in readers for lower grades while sticking to literary language at higher levels, and finished by reiterating his conviction that even were *gembun'itchi* a feasible goal, it would bring no benefits and the progress of Japanese literature would be impeded because of it. Scholars and educators should stop wasting their time on such a useless project.

Other supporters of non-colloquial styles around this time were Fujii Sei and, of course, Ozaki Kōyō and other Ken'yūsha members. Fujii aired his views in an essay 'Shōrai no Nihon Bunshō' ('The Japanese Style of the Future') which appeared in the *Yomiuri Shimbun* on 2–3 November 1888. Like Nishimura, he supported a blend of Japanese, Chinese and European elements for an all-purpose *futsūbun*. While he did not level the usual charge of vulgarity against colloquial style, he dismissed it on the grounds of verbosity:

> *Gembun'itchi* is advocated by a school of novelists. Certainly it is in many cases very convenient in the novel, but writing which imitates speech is long-winded and complex. It is not suitable for practical purposes, so how can we use it?[16]

What he envisaged was a blend of the conciseness and grandeur of *kambun*, the elegance and grace of *wabun* and the subtlety and attention to detail of *ōbun* – the best of the old spiced with the best of the new.

It was only to be expected that Kōyō, leading light of the conservative Ken'yūsha group of novelists with their desire to revive Saikaku's style,[17] should take a dim view of colloquial style except in the dialogue sections of the novel. His 1889 essay 'Dokusha Hyōbanki' ('The Reader's Who's Who') discussed the comparative merits of colloquial style and his own preferred *gazoku setchū* style. Kōyō summed up the arguments of the opposing factions as follows: *gembun'itchi* supporters dismissed *gazoku setchū* as reactionary and anti-progressive. If one were to draw a parallel between composition and sculpture, with style as the chisel, then colloquial style would prove dagger-sharp by comparison with the blunt and ineffective *gazoku setchū*. Their opponents, on the other hand, denounced colloquial style as 'heretical' and 'Christian', and claimed it gave the impression of being shorthand notes of a raconteur's recital, or the language used by prostitutes. While it was popular because of its practical simplicity, it was not even worth considering in rhetorical prose. Kōyō, taking up the sculpture metaphor, went on to leave no doubt as to which side he aligned himself with:

> Are sketching and photography all there are to art? Reference has been made to a sharp chisel. That chisel can indeed do minutely detailed work; but when it carves uncalled-for hairs in the nostrils of a beautiful woman, or eyebrows which could just as well have been left off, when it carves on downy hairs on the assumption that even beautiful women have hairs on their legs,

then the finished sculpture becomes that of a personable goblin – can we, in all conscience, say that it is the likeness of a beauty? It may indeed appear as a belle or a nymph to the sculptor; but to the onlooker, it is a goblin.[18]

Abhorring the stringent, warts and all realism which colloquial style could be made to serve, Kōyō preferred instead to gloss over the more prosaic aspects of life with the less flexible but more elegant, less earthy and more removed from the ordinary, *gazoku setchū* style.

Kōyō did a good deal to prevent the spread of colloquial style. He expostulated against it in theoretical essays, and was also one of those responsible for the swing away from *gembun'itchi* in the novel between 1890 and 1895, when his beautifully-polished *gazoku setchū* works, written during the period of national recoil from Europeanization towards a revival of tradition, captured the imagination of literary circles and led to a temporary halt in the burgeoning of colloquial style in the novel. It is all the more ironic, then, that Kōyō's temporary experimenting with colloquial style during the five-year lull, motivated by curiosity rather than by conviction, should result in a smooth, polished version of that medium which impressed its critics and helped re-establish it in fiction, despite his own later return to *gazoku setchū*.

THE CONTROVERSY OF 1889

The year 1889 saw a heated debate on colloquial style carried out in a spate of articles published for the most part in *Bun* (*The Written Word*), a journal headed by *gembun'itchi* supporter Miyake Yonekichi, and the *Yomiuri Shimbun*.

An early sign of the impending outbreak of hostilities had come in 1887, with the publication in *Gakkai no Shishin* (*Guide to Scholarship*) of Tatsumi Kojirō's 'Baku Gembun'itchiron' ('An Attack on Gembun'itchi'). The essay was a response to the lecture given to the Rōmaji Club several months earlier by Basil Hall Chamberlain,[19] in which Chamberlain had advocated the immediate adoption of colloquial style. Tatsumi's intent was to discuss further those issues raised by Chamberlain which he himself either supported or found confusing, mainly the latter. What he admired most about colloquial style was the ease with which it could be read in comparison with *kambun*. He was also impressed by the manner in which Chamberlain contrived to use it so that it was not vulgar.[20]

These sources of satisfaction notwithstanding, Tatsumi began in the second section of his essay to find fault. His main disagreement with Chamberlain stemmed from the latter's advice to Rōmaji Club members to use the colloquial as it stood, advice which Tatsumi found unacceptable: speech and writing, though originating from the same inner source, had mutual differences in their external manifestations which made attempts at uniformity inadvisable. Whereas speech was usually private in nature, its reception restricted – except in the course of public speaking – to a few hearers, writing was of a more public aspect, as in government ordinances which informed or commanded a much wider audience. Speech varied with the speaker's dialect; written Japanese, or at least the written language of public life, did not, its words being required to convey a fixed meaning. Speech was transient, and explained what could be seen with one's own eyes; writing endured, communicating to the present the things of the past and to future generations the things of the here-and-now. Speech appealed to the senses; writing to the mind. And finally, while speech conveyed emotion well, writing expressed scholarship.

Tatsumi rejected the claim made by supporters of *gembun'itchi* that the spoken and written languages of European nations were really identical, giving as an example the long, complex sentences of the German philosopher Kant, surely unlike any ever uttered in the course of normal conversation. Even in England, Chamberlain's homeland, he argued, years of study of English books would not provide a vocabulary useful for everyday discourse; in that country, too, speech and writing were clearly not the same. The true proof of civilization, Tatsumi believed, lay in a written language which was not prey to transient fads. It was a matter of course that speech and writing would grow further and further apart as a result of cultural development. Why hope to achieve such an intrinsically worthless objective as *gembun'itchi*? He concluded with a firm rejection of Chamberlain's proposal.

Tatsumi's emphasis on a static written language, preserved as it were in the amber of tradition, as proof of true civilization is evidence of the intransigently ivory-tower attitude of many educated men towards language reform at this time. Surrounded though he was by a multitude of new factors underlining the unsatisfactory nature of the existing situation, chief among them newly developed systems of education and communication, he clung nevertheless to the entrenched intellectual view of writing as a thing apart from the mainstream of everyday life, an ornament rather than an instrument. He was of course quite right in pointing out the awkwardness of dialectal differences in speech, a handicap not suffered by literary styles, but appears not to have given any serious consideration to the alternative of settling upon a standard form of spoken Japanese which would become the basis of a modern colloquial style. He was likewise justified in pointing out that the concept of *gembun'itchi* could not be taken literally to mean that speech and writing should be identical, but appears to have entertained no notion that an acceptably polished form of colloquial style *based on* rather than an identical reproduction of contemporary speech might offer a viable alternative to tradition. Civilization, to Tatsumi, meant only one thing when it came to writing: classicism.

In March 1889, Kojima Kenkichi (1866–1931, scholar of Chinese literature) published an essay 'Bunshōron' ('On Writing') in *The Written Word* which echoed Tatsumi's comments: colloquial style was uncivilized; truly civilized nations had separate spoken and written languages. Kojima was motivated to make this claim by alarm at the increase in numbers of *gembun'itchi* supporters and by the encroachment of colloquial style in literature. His essay sparked off a storm of anti-*gembun'itchi* criticism in articles contributed to *The Written Word*, essays in one issue provoking responses in the next. Following an overload of correspondence in the mid-May issue, the editors opened a special *Gembunron* (abbreviated from *Gembun'itchiron*) section to contain the discussion. The first appeared at the end of May, its presence justified by the volume of correspondence which continued to pour in. In eight issues of *The Written Word* over a period of three and a half months, there appeared eleven articles rejecting *gembun'itchi*, ten supporting it, and four adopting a middle-of-the-road stance on the issue. The main defender of colloquial style was Yamada Bimyō, who had by that time published several *gembun'itchi* novels, and who accounted for 60 per cent of the defences published in *The Written Word*. Perhaps the criticisms levelled at colloquial style by *futsūbun* supporters can best be summarized by examining Bimyō's rebuttals in his critical essays.

A year prior to the *The Written Word* controversy, in 1888, Bimyō published 'Gembun'itchiron no Gairyaku' ('An Outline of the Gembun'itchi Argument') in *Guide to Scholarship*, an essay in which he argued point by point the four major objections of *futsūbun* advocates to colloquial style. The first was that advanced in 1887 by Tatsumi: that if the colloquial were used as it stood, it would not be understood by all Japanese because of regional dialects. But the Tokyo dialect was understood in most areas and would continue to spread, Bimyō reasoned, and colloquial style based on this as the standard would be easily comprehensible everywhere. A second objection was that today's colloquial would be out of date tomorrow. Were that theory to be taken seriously, Bimyō retorted, by logical extension there would be no point in producing new inventions of any kind, let alone in reforming the language. The same could be said of *futsūbun*, and was certainly not a valid excuse for marking time. Then there was the belief, quite commonly held by supporters of the established order around this period, that the colloquial had no grammar. So-called 'scholars' who believed this, Bimyō replied, had obviously not researched their subject thoroughly enough. The spoken language did indeed have its own grammar, he asserted, giving examples of verb tenses; the trouble was that it had not yet been exhaustively identified and codified. The fourth and final criticism was perhaps the most commonly heard: the spoken language was coarse and vulgar, lacking the beauty of refined expressions. This depended on the basis on which the criticism was made. Bimyō thought it related to rhythm:

> Most of the things which have been handed down to us as examples of archaic styles have been *waka* (Japanese poetry), in which rhythm is paramount. The special vocabulary and syntax used in writing of this kind naturally sound more elegant than those used in writing which is not concerned with euphony. Of course, the latter sound frank. Dust in sugared water is sweeter than dust in brine. It is not that the first kind of dust itself is sweeter than the others – the difference is only in the flavour it has absorbed. We are very familiar with rhythm-oriented *waka*. They contrast sharply with colloquial style, which does not have melody as its main object. *Waka* are the sugared water, colloquial style the brine. The dust – i.e. the quality of their syntax and vocabulary – is different in both cases.[21]

Bimyō deplored the prevailing belief that the added factor of rhythm imparted elegance to all classical styles.

Later, irritated by the anti-*gembun'itchi* stance of articles by Kojima Kenkichi and Yoshimi Keirin which appeared in *The*

Written Word on 31 March 1889, Bimyō replied with *Gembun'itchi Kogoto* (*Finding Fault with Gembun'itchi*) in the next issue. In format this was substantially the same as *Gembun'itchiron no Gairyaku*, tackling the argument point by point, but it dealt with an additional three objections which had not appeared in his earlier article, bringing the total to seven. The extra three were: that there would be no advantage to be gained from using colloquial style; that in the event of its implementation, Japan would no longer have any *bun* (used here to mean elegant writing in the old tradition); and that writing possessed a dignity which speech lacked. Bimyō replied as follows: the English example provided proof of the untruth of the first assertion. Vernacular literature had flourished with the advent of Chaucer and Shakespeare, as had writings on the physical sciences. The greatest advantage of colloquial style was not that it was easy to read and to learn but that it met the requirements of the age; older styles, rooted in previous eras, were not able to express the fullest complexities of sophisticated modern thought. The second he dismissed as unworthy of argument, based as it was on the untenable premise that speech and writing must always be dissimilar. Supporters of the third he accused of confusing content with tone. If one regarded talent and material as the same thing, then anything at all would be capable of achieving excellence. Not even a middle-school student, if he had studied something of rhetoric, would subscribe to such a theory.

The controversy between the two sides in *The Written Word* eventually grew so heated that it degenerated into a confused jumble of ill-considered abuse, with no prospect of victory for either side. Accordingly, the special *Gembunron* column was discontinued in mid-July and no further correspondence was entertained by the editors, so that the debate was left hanging with no gains made.

A second, shorter exchange of views took place in 1888-89 in the pages of the *Yomiuri Shimbun*. First to appear was an editorial, 'Omoitsukitaru Koto (Gembun'itchi)' ('Reflections – Gembun'itchi'), on 13 December 1888, whose author remarked upon the popularity then being enjoyed by colloquial style as a result of Bimyō novels and in general exhibited goodwill towards the idea. He deplored, however, the use of such rough expressions as *subetta* ('I slipped'), *koronda* ('I fell'), and *aruita* ('I walked'), the plain past forms of the verb, which, although undoubtedly admirable when seen in their true perspective, still left something to be desired by their abruptness. The argument had hitherto turned on bringing writing into a closer approximation of speech, and this had led people to reject the ideal of colloquial style because of what they perceived as the ineradicable vulgarity of the spoken word when written down; were the tone of the spoken word rather to be lifted and refined, however, the ideal of *gembun'itchi* would be achieved much more quickly.

In knee-jerk reaction to this criticism, there appeared in the contributors' columns of 16 and 18 December 'Omoitsukitaru Koto Sono Ichi (Gembun'itchi)', written by a *gembun'itchi* supporter styling himself 'Subetta Koronda' in defiance of the editorial's comments. The writer defended colloquial style on the grounds that it was still in its formative stages and was a long way from perfection. He disagreed vehemently with the suggestion of making speech closer to writing: how on earth could this be done? An individual might manage it, but on a national scale? The article ended with a reassurance to the editorialist that writing in colloquial style involved much more than mere unconsidered recording of speech; while it was undeniably based on the spoken language, it followed the laws of rhetoric.

Next came three articles which appeared in supplement to the main body of the paper on three occasions. The first was Yoshikawa Hide's 'Gembun'itchi' (20 March 1889) in which the writer supported the view that *bun* ('writing') and *gen* ('speech') being fundamentally different, to ignore this by attempting to achieve uniformity would be to make the one no more than a reproduction on paper of the other. The idea of *gembun'itchi* had been introduced by scholars over-enthusiastic about western customs without regard for the relative merits of the proposal; once the novelty wore off, no more would be heard of it. In Yoshikawa's view, while colloquial style purported to be intelligible even to the uneducated, its European elements rendered it both complex and uninteresting; while it did have some merits, it needed to be polished and to be pruned of unfamiliar foreign expressions.

This was followed by Hoshinouchi Teruko's 'Gembun'itchi to iu Koto ni tsuite' ('About Gembun'itchi') on 24 March 1889. The writer took exception to Yoshikawa's avowal that speech and writing were fundamentally different in purpose. Such a priori reasoning was designed to preserve the differences; if everyone thought that way, there would never be any new inventions, she said, echoing Bimyō. To suppose that *gembun'itchi* supporters aimed at using nothing but colloquial expressions was a mistake;

their real aim was to dispense with archaic grammar, not to abandon refined vocabulary. The writer concluded by reiterating her belief that colloquial style was the true style of modern society.

Yoshikawa came under attack again in the third article, Shian Gaishi's 'Gembun'itchi ni tsuite' ('About Gembun'itchi') on 31 March 1889, in which he praised the convenience of and detail permitted by colloquial style:

> A gas light sheds the brightness of gas, an electric light the brightness of electricity; since of the two, electric light is by far the better and the more convenient, it is gradually replacing gas everywhere. By the same token, colloquial style is far superior to and more convenient than traditional writing, so why should we not adopt it?[22]

Colloquial style was not difficult to understand, as Yoshikawa claimed; it only seemed strange because it was still unfamiliar. Shian did, however, decry the use of such odd European devices as personification, commenting that once they were removed colloquial style would truly be fit to replace the old style.

The *Yomiuri* exchange, though much smaller in volume and more spasmodic in appearance than the *The Written Word* debate, nevertheless indicates the degree of interest in society at large on the matter, an interest which was about to go underground for the five-year period of reaction to western influences. After the closing of the special column in *The Written Word* in July 1889, no more was heard for some years, until renewed debate broke out after the Sino-Japanese war when Ueda Kazutoshi and his colleagues took up the issue again.[23] This time it was not possible to dismiss support for colloquial style as merely a passing fad. The growing enthusiasm in education circles, the frequent advocacy of *gembun'itchi* in newspaper articles, and the increasing use of colloquial style in literature all combined to indicate that it was fast gaining ground as an acceptable medium not only for general business but for more specialized tasks as well. Its detractors in this period therefore accepted it as a *fait accompli*, concentrating their criticism now on what they perceived as its clumsiness and the lack of polish. Nishimura Shigeki, while acknowledging that colloquial style had become an established convention, again denounced the coarseness of the spoken language on which it was based, reiterating his belief that the tone of speech must first be raised to give a needed elegance if *gembun'itchi* were to be successful.[24]

A surprising article entitled 'Gembun'itchi no Fukanō' ('The Impossibility of Gembun'itchi') appeared in the *Yomiuri Shimbun* on 17-19 December 1902 – surprising because it was a rejection of *gembun'itchi* by Mozume Takami, whose essay 'Gembun'itchi' had been instrumental in leading the way from the theory to the practice of colloquial style in 1886 and had inspired interest in others such as Yamada Bimyō. Mozume now retracted his argument, referring to his earlier advocacy as superficial, written in an excess of youthful enthusiasm when he had not yet researched the subject sufficiently thoroughly. His mistake had been borne in upon him during his 1890-91 writing of *Nihon Bunten* (*A Grammar of Japanese*), when he had become convinced of the inescapable differences between *kaiwabun* (used in letters and dialogue) and *kirokubun* (narrative, i.e. everyday writing, except letters). The former used second person and present tense most frequently, with sentences ending with second-person-oriented honorifics; the latter used the third person most frequently, used all tenses, often completed sentences without honorifics, and used third-person-oriented honorifics. With so many dissimilarities between the two types of writing, how could one style serve for both? Mozume had therefore reached the conclusion that it was impossible to make writing the same as speech; the most that could be achieved was to simplify writing by abandoning archaic expressions in favour of familiar modern ones. His remarks indicate a rather narrow view of the colloquial style, predicated upon the then widely held assumption that it was really a conversational style in which the user employed honorifics in the same way as in speech; no real understanding of the possibility of polite and plain forms for use in the two areas of vocative prose and narrative had yet been reached.

In 1902, the Hi-Gembun'itchikai (Anti-Gembun'itchi Club), a group of *futsūbun* supporters who had followed the example of their opponents and banded together to form a pressure group, published *Dainippon to Bunshōteki Kokumin* (*Japan and a Literate Populace*), a collection of arguments against colloquial style containing such essays as 'Gembun'itchi wa Shoseiron nari' ('Gembun'itchi: An Impractical Theory'), 'Gembun'itchi Ronsha no Futsūbun to Gojin no Futsūbun to no Taishō' ('A Comparison of Our View of Futsūbun and that of Gembun'itchi Advocates'), 'Gembun'itchi to Mumi-Kansō' ('Prosaic Gembun'itchi'), and 'Byōteki Bunshōka' ('Unsound Writers'). The titles alone reveal their writers' stylistic bent, with the literary *gojin* ('we'), *mumi-kansō* ('bald, dry as dust'), and the copula *nari*. This was followed in May by a counter-attack volume, *Gembun'itchi Ronshū* (*Collection of Pieces on Gembun'itchi*), a collection of transcripts of lectures given at the Gembun'itchi Kōsetsukai (the Gembun'itchi Lecture Club) in which advocates of colloquial style took issue with the points raised by its detractors in the earlier volume. These two works marked the peak of the debate over colloquial style; after 1902, with the establishment of the National Language Research Council which included in its charter the across-the-board implementation of colloquial style, public criticism and discussion tailed off sharply as it became obvious that, with government backing to shore up not inconsiderable existing initiatives, it was only a matter of time before *futsūbun* was supplanted. A decade later, after colloquial style had been polished into a sparkling, cultivated medium by the novelists of the Naturalist and Shirakaba schools, its detractors could no longer ridicule its roughness. It possessed two great advantages which *futsūbun* did not, in its simplicity and the flexibility which allowed writers to convey on paper any thought capable of expression in speech. Although the use of *futsūbun* persisted in newspapers and magazines for several years to come, the swing to colloquial style could no longer be halted.

The major cause of dissension among opponents of the new style appears to have been their too-literal interpretation of the term *gembun'itchi* itself. As their arguments show, many took this to mean that what was being proposed was that writing should be an exact reproduction of speech, and attacked this idea on the perfectly valid grounds that this would result in verbose, disjointed, vulgar prose, pointing out, quite rightly, that the written European languages which were being held up as examples were not in fact mirror images of the spoken languages of those countries. The concept of a colloquial style *based on* but not a verbatim reproduction of contemporary speech had not yet taken firm enough hold to lure them from their devotion to the elegance of traditional literary rhetoric, resulting in a preference for *futsūbun* or some other similar blend of the best of classical elements from both east and west, or in impractical, hazy suggestions for 'refining speech'. It was thanks to the later labours of novelists in polishing and refining colloquial style and to the collections of model compositions by *gembun'itchi* supporters that these twin ghosts of verbosity and vulgarity were eventually laid to rest and the advantages of colloquial style allowed to stand clear.

8 The standardization debate

An important issue upon which depended the success of plans to remodel the written language was that of standardization. This chapter will examine the manner in which the standardization of written Japanese as part of the language modernization process in the Meiji Period was effected as a result of both purely pragmatic developmental concerns, such as the facilitation of communications and education and other necessary trappings of a modernizing nation, and of nationalistic sentiment.

INSTRUMENTAL FACTORS IN LANGUAGE MODERNIZATION

On the instrumental level, an important motivating force in the achievement of a standard colloquial style was that of communication, both between the centralized bureaucracy and its constituency and between individuals. The replacement of autonomous feudal domains in 1871 with prefectures ruled by governors appointed by Tokyo; the inauguration of the postal service under Maejima Hisoka (1835–1919) in the same year; the lifting of restrictions on individual travel and choice of occupation; the development of mass-communication printed media after 1870 – these elements combined to make communication an important consideration in the new order. The smooth and rapid transmission of information is an essential attribute of a modern state. In order to both disseminate and receive information, a standard modern colloquial style divorced from dialectal variation is desirable, a style versatile and flexible enough to express advanced concepts and nuances of feeling and allow its users to participate fully in public life.

It seems logical to assert that for colloquialization of writing to be successful on a national scale as an aid to social change, it must be predicated upon standardization. It is true that the two processes developed at virtually the same pace and at almost the same time in Japanese language history, with the former arising as a topic of debate among supporters of language modernization almost a decade earlier than the latter; but as support for the *gembun'itchi* principle grew in the second half of the 1890s, so too did awareness that a standard language was essential to its eventual realization. A colloquial style based on regional dialects, differing with locality, would serve less well as a uniform means of transmitting information from a centralized controlling agency such as the Ministry of Education than the existing Classical Standard (*futsūbun*) which came into general use in education and the press after about 1897 as opponents of colloquialization sought an alternative solution to the language issue by synthesizing elements of classical varieties of writing into an all-purpose literary idiom. In order to achieve the smoothest and easiest means of disseminating knowledge, the problem of dialectal variations had to be addressed before colloquialization could be truly effective. In Japan at the time of the Meiji Restoration, these were in some cases extreme. Hattori Shirō, writing in 1960, noted that the Kagoshima and Sendai dialects were still mutually unintelligible.[1] Not all fell into this category, of course; a kind of limited communication was possible between many. Within each feudal domain, needless to say, the local dialect *was* the standard, fulfilling the primary function of language, i.e., communication. Farmers, fishermen, and forestry workers had no need of any other medium of communication, since strictures on travel made it unlikely that they would have occasion to communicate with speakers of other dialects. It was the governing élite and later the merchants and artisans who followed the shifting centre of power from west to east who felt the need for a common language.

Perhaps some clarification of terminology is necessary at this juncture. The terms *kyōtsūgo* (common language) and *hyōjungo* (standard language) are both found in socio-historical descriptions of the Japanese language. *Kyōtsūgo* refers to a common or standard (cf German *Gemeinsprache*) language in the sense of a supradialectal language of convenience which admits of the existence of dialects and is not concerned with their eradication. *Hyōjungo*, while still referring to a language which is standard in that it can be used throughout the country, incorporates further the idea of a standard of excellence to which users of that language should aspire, and thus designates an idealized and perhaps unattainable form of the language. By virtue of the implication of some sort of moral superiority inherent in *hyōjungo*, the use of this term as the goal of language planning in the late Meiji Period led in time to the 'dialect complex', a result of efforts to wipe out dialects through the teaching of *hyōjungo* in the education system. Where *hyōjungo* involves a value judgement, *kyōtsūgo* does not. The *Kokugogaku Jiten* (*Dictionary of Japanese Language Studies*) defines *kyōtsūgo* as 'the language in which ideas can be exchanged in common throughout any one country', while *hyōjungo* is 'an ideal language controlled by fixed standards, a polished *kyōtsūgo*'.[2] *Hyōjungo* was used from the time standardization first became an issue in the Meiji Period until after the Second World War, when *kyōtsūgo* replaced it in the usage of some scholars in referring to the standard form of Japanese, as it was felt that no true *hyōjungo* yet existed in Japan.[3]

EAST-WEST RIVALRY

Prior to the Meiji Period, the problem of a standard form of written Japanese did not arise, the classical style being relatively fixed and unchanging, as well as being the province of the educated élite. Behind this highly literate class lay the mass of common people who spoke various dialects but whose functional literacy was usually sufficient only for the daily business of life. Written communication among the upper class was governed by a strait-jacket of rigidly classical form which permitted little deviation and constituted in itself a written norm, or rather several different norms depending on context. Until the mid-Tokugawa Period, the common language used to facilitate spoken communication among those sections of society where mobility was possible was the speech of the capital, Kyoto. There had long been a dialectal rivalry between eastern and western Japan – examples may be found in the *Tale of Genji* which show the scornful attitude of capital dwellers to the speech of the east. It was Kyoto speech written down which formed the basis of what in later centuries became classical Japanese, used in *kana* literature written in Japanese and *waka* and *nō* chants, and meriting the appellation of *gagen* (refined language). No active attempt was made on the part of any agency to establish Kyoto speech as *hyōjungo*; it functioned by virtue of being the dialect of the capital as a common language for communication among those whose business took them there and was perceived as the 'best' form of spoken Japanese by virtue of the exalted status of its speakers. Despite the Kamakura Period shift of power to the east, Kyoto remained the imperial city and the centre of culture so that its dialect – or rather the upper-class variant – retained its aura of prestige and was alone regarded, in a country of increasingly sharply differentiated dialects, as the 'correct' form of Japanese.

This situation continued until the mid-Tokugawa Period, by which time the language of Edo, seat of shogunal power, had achieved sufficient cohesion to become a second contender in the common language stakes. Edogo (the language of Edo) had evolved since the building of the city some 150 years earlier from a mixture of the Kantō dialect used by the original inhabitants of the area; the Mikawa dialect brought in by Tokugawa *samurai* from their home province of that name; and the Kamigata dialect of the Kyoto – Ōsaka area (also known as Keihango) brought from the capital by merchants, courtesans, and court ladies and their waiting women who came to Edo castle.[4] The Kamigata influence was particularly strong because of the continuing cultural dominance of the Kyoto–Ōsaka area. By around 1750, these three elements had blended into a characteristic Edogo used at that time mainly within Edo itself, surrounding districts still retaining relatively unadulterated Kantō dialects.

Edo now began to develop its own distinct culture in opposition to that of the Kamigata area. The growth of a popular literature in the city saw the language of Edo employed in written form in dialogue in genre fiction, and it was at about this time that Edogo began to exert an influence on other parts of Japan. The *sankin kōtai* system instituted by the Tokugawas, whereby *daimyō* from all areas of the country spent alternate years in Edo, leaving their families there as hostage against their pledged return from their home fiefs, played a part in spreading knowledge of Edogo to distant provinces. The fact that the families of *daimyō* were kept in Edo meant that future heirs were brought up there and learned early to speak the *samurai* variant (as opposed to the townspeople's variant) of Edogo in order to acquit themselves honorably in future dealings at the castle. The practice of sending *hatamoto* (direct retainers of the shogun) from Edo to areas under direct shogunate control such as Nagasaki, Uraga, and Fushimi further contributed to the spreading influence of Edogo outside its immediate point of origin,[5] as did the constant traffic along the Tōkaidō of those drawn to the city on business affairs, while the upsurge in literary production established the townspeople's variant of Edogo as a language for literature in its own right.

It should be noted here that the Edogo which was beginning to rival Kyōtogo (the language of Kyoto) as a language of wider communication was the upper-class variant; two distinct class-bound streams had developed in the process of maturation, the *samurai* variant owing most to its Mikawa heritage and the townspeople variant stemming from the marked influence of the Kyoto dialect on that of the Kantō.

One side effect of the *sankin kōtai* system was to encourage the publication of books dealing with dialects, and these serve to illustrate the changing status of Edogo as a language of wider communication. The earliest such works measured dialects against the standard of Kyoto speech, ranking that of Edo among the dialects at large. After 1750, however, mention of Edogo as a central standard became increasingly frequent, as in *Tsukushi Hōgen*, and *Shimpen Hitachi Kokushi*.[6] Edogo was by this time established as an independent language of authority functioning in an ever widening sphere as a *kyōtsūgo*, so that many scholars believe that in the late Tokugawa Period there were in fact two languages of wider communication operating in Japan, representing the east–west split of political, cultural, and economic power – Edogo, functioning as a common language among the educated élite, and Kyotogo, also a *kyōtsūgo* but regarded further in the light of a *hyōjungo*, the 'best' form of Japanese.

Various foreigners entering Japan in the late Tokugawa – early Meiji Period remarked on the extent to which the speech of Edo (and later Tokyo) was understood in other parts of Japan. The American missionary, James Curtis Hepburn (1815–1911), writing in 1867, had commented in the section on 'Dialects' in the first edition of his *A Japanese – English and English – Japanese Dictionary* that the language of Kyoto was considered the standard. Five years later, however, updating this section for the 1872 second edition, he noted that since the removal of the capital to Edo, renamed Tokyo, it was the dialect of that city which now took precedence and was understood throughout Japan among the educated classes. Since this change could hardly have been effected within so short a time in the absence of both conscious language planning on the part of the élite and a centrally co-ordinated education system, the Edo dialect may be assumed to have been widely understood for some considerable period before the Restoration. The Japanese studied by foreigners wishing to acquire the most widely understood form of the language in this period was the upper-class variant of Edogo/Tōkyōgō. Two decades later, Basil Hall Chamberlain (1850–1935), in *A Handbook of Colloquial Japanese* (1888), commented that 'the dialect of Tokyo ... has gained an overwhelming importance as the general medium of polite intercourse throughout the country'.[7]

The ascendancy of Tōkyōgo over Kyōtogo both as the language of wider communication of the Meiji Period and its perceived standard language was in part the natural outcome of the formalization of the shift of power (in this case the new imperial administration) to the east by the relocation of the capital in 1868. Other early factors were the abolition of the feudal class system in 1871, leading very gradually to the eventual relaxation of class-bound speech variants; the establishment of a national education system the following year, though literary styles continued to dominate textbooks in early decades and it was not until conscious language planning began thirty years later with the establishment of the National Language Research Council in 1902 that the classroom became significant in the dissemination of Tōkyōgo as the literary norm; the beginning of national conscription in 1873; the development of a modern transport and communications system; the lifting of the restrictions on travel; and the increased coming and going between capital and prefectures under the centralized bureaucracy. In both education and communications, language standardization played a pivotal role.

During this early period of upheaval, the speech of Tokyo was itself undergoing internal evolution from Edogo into a form characteristic of the modernization period which was later to form the basis for standard Japanese. Certain typifying features developed in the first two decades of Meiji, as the result of exposure to foreign influences and in the wake of internal upheavals; these included the coining of numerous neologisms, an influx of foreign loanwords, the adoption of certain European-derived constructions in writing, and a proportional increase in dialectal expressions stemming from demographic change. Thus, by the time intellectuals brought their attention to bear on the matter of a standard language both as a convenient practical help in modernization and as a focus for a sense of national pride and unity, Tōkyōgo had developed a unique character of its own. Over the same period, debate had begun on the issue of replacing classical literary styles with a modern colloquial style based on, though naturally not a verbatim transcript of, everyday spoken Japanese. As the focus of the colloquialization debate in time shifted away from the initial exchange between progressives and conservatives towards a general, if uneasy, acceptance of its necessity, the question then became which form of spoken Japanese should serve as model in the implementation of the new style. The language of the capital came under immediate scrutiny as a matter of course.

EARLY VOICES

In January 1874, Assistant Minister for Education Nishigata Takashi published in the first issue of *Mombushō Zasshi* (*Journal of the Ministry of Education*) an article discussing the content and aim of subjects taught in the fledgling education system. The section on the teaching of *kotobazukai* reveals Nishigata's concern for standardization: instructing school children in a common form of Japanese, he pointed out, was a step towards removing the inconvenience caused by the dialectal fragmentation of Japanese. In pursuance of this aim, the Education Ministry had in 1873 published glossaries and phrase sheets for use in *kotobazukai* lessons. Two of the earliest were *Rengohen Ichi* (*A First Phrasebook*), a series of short questions and answers, and *Shōgaku Kyōjusho* (*Elementary Lesson Book*), which began with a glossary and progressed to short sentences. In addition to Tokyo vocabulary, these materials employed colloquial grammar.

The following year, on 3 September 1875, Watanabe Shūjirō (1855–1945) presented in the *Tōkyō Akebono Shimbun* an essay entitled 'Nihombun o Seitei suru Hōhō' ('Steps to Regulating Written Japanese'), advocating emulation of the west's example in colloquialization and standardization of the written language. In his opinion, the basis for the standard should be the most commonly used form of Tokyo speech and scholars should at once set about the codification of that norm into dictionaries and grammars.

Two rather more conservative approaches to the problem appeared in the *Chōya Shimbun*, roughly a year apart. The first was an editorial on 25 February 1876, whose author, after first reporting the current division of opinion between a standard based on contemporary speech, a modern language, and one based on *gagen*, a return to the Japanese of the past, proposed a compromise: into the speech of Tokyo, centre of government, should be woven the best elements of the classics – the grace of the Heian romance, the vigour of the Kamakura war chronicle – resulting in a blend of the best linguistic aspects of each age in Japan's history. Echoing this on 16 January 1877 came Ōtsuki Fumihiko's 'Nihon Bunten Henshū Sōron' ('Editing Japanese Grammars'). Ōtsuki (1847–1928), upon entering the Education Ministry in 1872, had been set to compile an English–Japanese dictionary and later a Japanese dictionary. Possessed of a keen interest in the grammar of his language, and convinced of the need for suitable grammars and dictionaries to facilitate education, Ōtsuki, too, advocated a mixture of modern and medieval elements, adding however that in the event of colloquialization the difficult choice between the speech of Kyoto and that of Tokyo as the basis for the new style could only be made in Tokyo's favour, by virtue of its position as the capital.

In the 1880s, supporters of one of two methods of orthographic reform – by romanization or by replacing Chinese characters with phonetic *kana* – began to cite standardization as a step towards achieving their ends. In 1882, Yatabe Ryōkichi (1851–99), botanist and pioneer of new-style poetry, advocated the use of *rōmaji* (the western alphabet) in a style based on the language of Tokyo in his essay 'Rōmaji o mote Nihongo o tsuzuru Setsu' ('A Theory on Romanizing Japanese').[8] Yatabe, a founding member of the Rōmajikai (Rōmaji Club) established in 1885 to pursue the realization of the romanization goal, was one of forty members chosen as a committee to investigate the practical details of the plan. He and five other committee members drafted a motion, published under the title 'Rōmaji nite Nihongo no Kakikata' ('How to Romanize Japanese'), which contained nineteen clauses, one proposing that romanization be based on the pronunciation of normally educated Tokyoites. Fellow member Hikami Kakutarō, writing in the club's journal on the colloquialization issue in 1888, observed that while regional isolation and its consequent linguistic fragmentation may have suited the feudal authorities, it was imperative for modern Japan, in contact with the west, to have a uniform language and a colloquial written style.[9] In Hikami's view, standardization was an essential prerequisite to colloquialization.

A similar concern with *hyōjungo* was expressed by members of the other arm of the script reform movement, who in 1883 amalgamated four earlier groups to form the Kana no Kai (Kana

Club). Miyake Yonekichi (1860–1929), educator and secretary of the club, was another in the increasing band of supporters of the *gembun'itchi* theory of style reform. In his *Kuniguni no Namari Kotoba ni tsukite* (*On Regional Dialects*, 1884),[10] he unfolded a three-point plan for the future of Japanese: standardization, colloquialization, and script reform, in that order. Adopting a conservative approach to the first of these, Miyake favoured an indirect method of natural selection rather than direct intervention by artificial manipulation, believing that any attempt to decide arbitrarily on a standard and implement it forthwith could only end in failure. He identified and discussed three approaches to standardization then current: the *gagen* theory, that all dialects should be replaced with a single form of speech based on classical Japanese; the *gendaigo* or modernist theory, favouring the adoption of a dialect currently in use but divided over the merits of that of Tokyo or Kyoto; and the *hōgen tasūketsu* or majority-dialect theory, which postulated that the standard should be that dialect with the largest number of speakers, arguing that the speech of big cities was a hotchpotch of dialects brought from all over Japan by members of the socially mobile élite. None of these seemed to Miyake a workable plan; he believed that the continuing encouragement of social intercourse between formerly isolated (in terms of human geography) regions would result in a gradual blending and smoothing out of dialectal variations. All that was needed was the improvement of communications and the passage of time, although he did at the same time acknowledge that all dialects should be surveyed with a view to deciding a later standard. What Miyake did not realise, or chose to ignore, was that naturally occurring environmentally-induced linguistic change is dependent upon the luxury of time, a luxury not high on the list of priorities of a developing nation jerked suddenly from a fully-fledged feudal system into the modern industrialized world without the period of evolution experienced in the west. Given his enthusiastic advocacy of artificial intervention in language development in the form of script reform and colloquialization, his *laissez-faire* attitude to standardization seems inconsistent with his overall approach to the modernization of the language.

Three other members of the Kana Club advocated a more direct approach to the fashioning of a uniform *hyōjungo* as a prerequisite to colloquialization and script reform. Shimano Seiichirō, in *Kanabumi o Mitōri ni wakuru Ron* (*On Three Ways of Writing in*

Kana, 1885),[11] promoted middle-class Tokyo speech as the obvious base for a universal colloquial style, not merely because of its prestige as the dialect of the capital, but also because it was a composite of expressions from many other dialects and therefore already qualified to a large extent as a *kyōtsūgo*. By deleting from it all traces of vulgar expressions and further blending in more of the 'best' expressions from other dialects, it could be made into an ideal standard, which should be codified in dictionaries and used at all times. Concurring with this view was Katayama Atsuyoshi, who in *Kanazukai o Aratamen ka, Kotoba o Tadasan ka* (*Language and Script Reform*, 1886)[12] examined standardization in terms both of its effect on facilitating education and of national prestige. Were Japan to follow the English example of publishing primary texts in the language of the capital, suitably combined with appropriate expressions from regional dialects, teaching would be simplified, a colloquial style could be more easily spread, and Japan, with a uniform language, would become a truly civilized country in the western mould. Further stressing the instrumental aspect of standardization, though reversing the usual order, Mozume Takami, in *Gembun'itchi* (1886),[13] suggested the modern postal system as an agent in spreading *hyōjungo*, and regarded the achievement of the *gembun'itchi* objective as offering the ancillary benefit of a uniform language.

By 1886, then, the overall consensus among those concerned with language reform was that some form of standard was necessary as a basis for colloquial style. The Education Ministry, with whom so many in the *gembun'itchi* movement were associated, published a reader in 1887 whose first, introductory volume was written almost entirely in colloquial style based on Tokyo speech.[14] Of the three approaches to standardization discussed by Miyake, the modernist theory had gained most ground, with educated Tokyo speech finding more favour than Kyōtogo. The speech of the capital seemed the logical choice: not only did it carry the prestige associated with the centre of the nation's government, commerce, industry, and culture, but it was also known in other areas, the capital being the centre of the country's communications network as well. It would obviously be easier to polish and legitimatize an already existing *kyōtsūgo* than to set about fashioning a new one. Further, this was the form of Japanese studied by foreigners, invested thereby with the function of representing the language of Japan on the international front.

Given that the premier position of the capital as a focus of the arts helps to disseminate its dialect through literature, the ascendancy of Tokyogo was about to become further and finally assured by its adoption as the basis for the new colloquial style in the modern novels which began to appear in the late 1880s. Jespersen notes that 'literature plays no small part in the rise of a great common language', ascribing the chief importance of such European figures associated with national language movements as Dante, Luther, and Chaucer to their roles as literary models which gave a certain impetus to what was already in train.[15] In the Japanese case, the need for a new literary language, already recognized from its instrumental aspects by forward thinkers in the preceding two decades of the Meiji Period, was further highlighted by the attraction for young authors of western literary theories of realism and, later, naturalism. Rigid classical styles were no fit medium for the sensitive examination of modern dilemmas and psychological intricacies. First to attempt a modernization of style in line with approach and content, as we have seen in Chapter 5, was Futabatei Shimei, who used Tokyo speech as the basis for a colloquial style in *The Drifting Cloud* (1887–89). His example was followed by other writers in such numbers that Tōkyōgo was soon well on the way to acceptance as the new literary norm. Surviving the temporary five year (1890–95) setback which resulted from a revival of Japanese studies on an inward swing of the pendulum away from what many perceived as excessive adulation of the west, the colloquial style flourished in later mainstream literary movements, and its influence in this sphere did much to advance the cause of style reform in other areas. Hand in hand with colloquialization in literature went the adoption of educated Tokyo speech as its basis, strengthening the claims of that particular idiom as the matrix for the standard language by modelling it on the modern novel.

NATIONALISM AND LANGUAGE PLANNING

The catalyst in accelerating both the return to *gembun'itchi* in the novel and elsewhere and the beginning of serious, co-ordinated examination of language policy at the national level was Japan's victory in the Sino-Japanese War in 1895. It was at this point that the issue of the national language assumed significance as a unifying force on Kelman's sentimental level. Hitherto, discussion on the subject had centred upon the pragmatic benefits to be gained from a standard language acting as a kind of cultural glue, bonding together formerly disparate communities into the larger social unit of the nation-state, facilitating communications at all levels of its sphere of influence. With victory over China, however, came an upsurge of nationalistic fervour, an awareness of and pride in the potential of Japan as a force in world affairs which led to a re-examination of the Japanese language in an attempt to disencumber it of the classical Chinese influence. Modernization of the language, now beginning to be called *kokugo* (a term delineating a single language representing Japan), came to be seen as an important element in fostering a spirit of national identity and unity, a factor contributing much to the sense of authenticity necessary to social cohesion in a developing power. While the Swiss example proves the fallacy of the assertion that a single national language is an essential requirement of nationhood, in the Japanese case there was on hand just such a single linguistic heritage used by the nation within the borders of the state which could, with extensive modification of its internal inconsistencies, serve as a focus of national pride. The time had now come for government-sanctioned language planning to provide official encouragement and direction for the already considerable inroads made upon the task of reform.

It has been pointed out that the active co-operation of the intellectual élite of a speech community is required for the standardization of its language.[16] Advocates of *hyōjungo* after the Sino-Japanese War adopted a centralist approach to the problem, paving the way for policy decisions at bureaucratic level. An early supporter of direct intervention in language planning on both pragmatic and nationalist grounds was Ueda Kazutoshi, who took advantage of the nationalistic sentiments inspired by the war with China to stress the connection between a strong nation and an effective language. His early lecture 'Kokugo to Kokka to' has already been described in Chapter 6.

A few months later, in January 1895, Ueda published 'Hyōjungo ni tsukite' ('On a Standard Language')[17] wherein he discoursed on the concept of *hyōjungo* as that language among those spoken in a given country which is understood by most people throughout that country, as opposed to regional dialects used only in circumscribed areas, giving the English *standard language* and German *Gemeinsprache* as examples and adding the rider that a standard language acts as the model for the country. In order to establish the standard satisfactorily, attention must be paid to both its oral and written forms. It must be based upon a dialect actually in current use somewhere within the country, and must then become the literary norm. Writing reaches a wider audience than speaking; it remains for posterity. The written word in various forms was now capable of swift dissemination. The speech of educated Tokyoites had the potential to become the *hyōjungo* of the future, given considered polishing. Particular areas deserving both academic study and the best efforts of those engaged in their associated linguistic activities were the language of education, the courts, the Diet, the theatre, and literature. Ueda larded his text with European examples supporting his thesis, mentioning among others the role of the French theatre and Académie Française in working for the improvement of the French language.

In the same month, Ueda addressed the Dai Nihon Kyōikukai (Japan Education Society) on the necessity of establishing a standard language as a plank in the education system in his lecture 'Kyōikujō Kokugogakusha no Hōki shi-iru Ichidaiyōten' ('A Major Oversight by Language Scholars in Education').[18] Expressing his whole-hearted support for a co-ordinated centralist approach to language planning, Ueda pointed out that as the national language formed the basis for universal education, its future development must be carefully structured to further that object. Teachers must themselves first be trained in the standard language, for example at what was later to become Tokyo University, before attempting to impart it in the classroom. Ueda stressed the interdependence of colloquialization and standardization, asserting that true education could not begin until Japan had achieved a uniform colloquial style.

Next to call for direct intervention was Okakura Yoshisaburō (1868–1936), linguist and English language scholar credited with being the first to use the term *hyōjungo* in 1890,[19] who in *Ōyō Gengogaku Jukkai Kōwa* (*Ten Lectures on Applied Linguistics*, 1902) spoke of the unification of the national language as essential to national progress. Decrying the decentralist approach – allowing several main dialects in place of one standard language – as ultimately harmful to national solidarity, Okakura rejected Miyake's earlier indirect method of natural selection, conceived in a less nationalistic day, as carrying dangers in that it was by no means certain that only the most desirable elements of different dialects would intermingle. Okakura's own preferred option was to use the classroom as a forum for correcting and eradicating dialectal usage and inculcating a standard language, making education the vehicle for propagating the norm. Common to both his and Ueda's platforms was the notion that dialects were a social evil, which should be rooted out rather than allowed to coexist with *hyōjungo*.

As we have seen in Chapter 6, the efforts of Ueda, Okakura, and others in the language reform pressure groups 'Linguistics Society' and Gembun'itchi Club were instrumental in persuading the government to set up a national body, the National Language Research Council, to decide and direct official planning input into future developments. While the primary concern of the members of both societies was the implementation of colloquial style, they also recognized the necessity of choosing a standard variant of Japanese as its base, and many of the articles published in the *Journal of Linguistics* reflected this concern. 'Gembun'itchi ni tsuite' ('About Gembun'itchi'), an unsigned piece appearing in April 1900, called for Japan to follow the European example in establishing a uniform colloquial style, advocating as the standard a polished and refined form of the language used by middle-class Tokyoites. The following year came Fujioka Katsuji's 'Gembun'itchi', part of which stressed the need for standardization, referring to the envisaged colloquial style as the standard language written down. Citing the commonly held opinion that the standard should be the speech of educated Tokyoites, Fujioka went on to outline steps to achieving his aim. Provincial primary school teachers should be brought to Tokyo to learn to speak the Tokyo dialect; future primary texts should be written in colloquial style, and existing books rewritten. A programme aimed at gradually standardizing the dialects to that of Tokyo should be devised; dialect dictionaries should be published. Scholars must research the nature of the standard language, and publish guidebooks; their essays and model compositions could be issued by the Education Ministry in a monthly bulletin. Through these and other avenues, every effort should be made to achieve reform of the written language.[20]

One of the four areas identified by members of the National Language Research Council soon after its establishment in 1902 as major problem spots in language reform was the matter of standardization. The proposed plan of action gazetted in July of that year included a commitment 'to survey the dialects and settle upon a standard language'. The wording of this programme drew comment from Hoshina Kōichi in the form of an article entitled

'Kokugo Chōsa iinkai Ketsugi Jikō ni tsuite' ('Concerning the Resolutions of the National Language Research Council'), published in the *Journal of Linguistics* in August 1902. Hoshina was concerned by the brevity of the mission statements, which gave no concrete details as to methodology and objectives. More information was particularly important in the case of the fourth point, as procedures and results would differ greatly depending on which of the two current approaches to standardization was adopted. If the dialects were to be widely surveyed and the most attractive elements of each extracted to create an artifical *hyōjungo*, using perhaps honorifics from Tokyo, negative forms from Kyoto, and so on, no one could predict what the end result would be. Although many scholars espoused this method, Hoshina himself opposed it, on the grounds that such a survey would prove impossibly time-consuming and the standard language thus created would be too unnatural and stilted to survive for long in everyday use. He favoured a second approach, which held that a survey of the dialects, rather than being viewed as the matrix from which a man-made standard would spring, should be no more than an auxiliary step in the process of deciding upon a *hyōjungo*. One dialect would first be chosen in its entirety to become the norm; it would then be polished and refined, with reference to other dialects, which would be surveyed to assist in this process. The safest choice for the standard, Hoshina felt, was the language of middle- and upper-class Tokyoites. That in its present form, however, was not suitable, requiring much work to smooth over the rough edges and make up deficiencies. As a reference for this refining process, the dialects should be surveyed for pronunciation, morphology, syntax, and vocabulary.

Hoshina's support for Tōkyōgo was echoed by a second article in the same issue of the *Journal of Linguistics*, 'Hyōjungo ni tsuite' ('Concerning a Standard Language') by Okano Hisatane. Of the language problems then faced in Japan, Okano stated, the most important was the matter of a standard form of Japanese for the colloquial style. The speech of middle-class Tokyo males should be that standard, in polished form. These endorsements of the speech of the capital as the norm followed sustained discussions on the subject at meetings of the Gembun'itchi Club the previous year. Nakai Kitarō had addressed the club on the issue, and a subcommittee of thirteen members, including Ōtsuki Fumihiko, Fujioka Katsuji, and Hoshina Kōichi, set up to carry out general research into all aspects of the colloquial style, made the adoption of simple, middle-class Tokyo speech the starting point for their draft of ground rules relating to writing. The Script Reform Section of the Imperial Education Society meanwhile arrived at a similar consensus, resolving to develop a colloquial style based on the tidied-up speech of educated Tokyoites. By the time the National Language Research Council published its resolutions, there was substantial support among interested parties for the choice of the Tokyo dialect as the standard form of Japanese.

The first state textbooks to be published under the auspices of the Council in 1903 reflected this concern. In 1900, the Education Minstry had stipulated practice in a standard form of Japanese as part of Japanese language classes, and had announced in 1901 that from then on the Japanese taught in schools would be that of middle- and upper-class Tokyo dwellers. The first series of state primers therefore adhered to these earlier directives, keeping vocabulary within the prescribed range. The 1909 series continued the initiative, further disseminating the Tokyo variant, so that from then on standardization of the written language accelerated both in and out of the classroom, with the Tokyo dialect adopted as the medium not only of formal education but also of literature and, to an increasing extent, the mass media. Standardization of spoken Japanese was, of course, a different matter, not rapidly achieved; *hyōjungo* education was for a long time largely a matter of reading and writing, with little attention paid to training in the spoken language.

Under the auspices of the National Language Research Council, the first official normative grammars were published. The preliminary publication of several surveys on dialects, phonology, and aspects of the spoken language and colloquial style culminated eventually in the appearance of the *Kōgohō* (*A Grammar of the Spoken Language*) in 1916, edited by Ōtsuki Fumihiko, Ueda Kazutoshi and others, followed a year later by a supplementary volume, the *Kōgohō Bekki*. The *Kōgohō* clearly defined the standard language as that currently spoken by the educated people of Tokyo. (Given that universal education was by then into its fifth decade, 'educated people' accounted for a much higher proportion of the population of Tokyo than was the case in Edo, when formal, officially-sponsored education remained the privilege of the élite). There had been earlier grammars of colloquial Japanese,[21] but these were the first to carry the weight of state authority; although by the time they were published the National Language Research Council had already been disbanded, they were the outcome of research conducted under its sponsorship, and with their prescriptive definition of the Tokyo dialect as the standard ended this phase in the modernization of the language.

Garvin and Mathiot have identified three functions of a standard language; the unifying function, in that it unites speakers of different dialects into a single speech community with which the speakers then identify; the separatist function, in that by its opposition to other languages as a separate entity it becomes a powerful and emotionally charged symbol of national identity; and the prestige function, whereby its existence enables a nation to claim equality, in terms of linguistic unity, with another admired nation.[22] These three factors did indeed loom large in the arguments of advocates of standard Japanese in the Meiji Period, who were struggling in part to provide a linguistic element in that sense of national pride necessary to fuel the modernizing nation for its ventures into international relations. Language standardization was important on both the instrumental and sentimental levels in the Japan of that time. Those products of the modernization process which offered the avenues for the implementation of standardization – the education, communications, and media systems – were at the same time dependent upon that implementation to enable them to reach their own full potential, a situation providing a powerful incentive for the selection of a norm. The nationalism of the 1890s and 1900s aided in the achievement of this goal; the activities of committed scholars who played upon the theme of the relationship between language reform and national destiny added fuel to the debate, reinforced existing initiatives, and eventually brought about government intervention in future language development, resulting in the first formal state-backed language planning initiatives. Which was the more important aspect in the final analysis is difficult to gauge; nationalism provided the impetus leading to action which enabled the instrumental agencies to become fully-realized agents of social change by virtue of their role in spreading that standard Japanese so necessary to their own effective operation.

9 The problem of orthography

Two further changes needed to improve the ease with which Japanese could be written and read were script reform and the development of a system of punctuation. The first of these, script reform, was already being discussed in the late Tokugawa Period; during the first twenty years of the Meiji Period, two separate campaigns aimed at replacing Chinese characters with either the phonetic *hiragana* script or the roman alphabet developed parallel to, and to a certain extent dependent on, the *gembun'itchi* movement itself.

The first to feel the need for script reform were students of the west (*yōgakusha*), who could not help noticing the conciseness of the 26-letter Latin alphabet compared with the more than 10,000 characters available in Japan. Noted Confucian scholar Arai Hakuseki (1657–1725), although not himself a *yōgakusha*, wrote a book titled *Seiyō Kibun* (*A Transcript on the West*, 1715), based on his interrogation of an Italian missionary priest, Giovanni-Battista Sidotti, who had landed at Yakushima in Kyushu in 1708. In this account, Arai commented on the remarkable conciseness and flexibility of the alphabet.[1] His remarks were confined to simple observation of the fact, however; he did not suggest that Japan should adopt the foreign system.

Dutch studies (*rangaku*) had begun in Japan around 1720 when the shogun Yoshimune lifted the earlier ban on western scientific texts, provided that they contained no reference to Christianity, which had been proscribed since 1614. Twenty years later, he commanded two of the prominent scholars of the day, Noro Genjō (1693–1761) and Aoki Kon'yō (1698–1769), to begin the study of the Dutch language. From that time on, an increasing number of scholars bent their minds to the new learning. Dutch studies influenced the thinking of Japanese scholars on the way their own language was written both by reinforcing the discovery of the alphabet's simplicity and by bringing to their notice criticisms of the Japanese writing system made by foreigners. Among these latter were a Dutch book mentioned by Morishima Chūryō in *Oranda Zatsuwa* (*Idle Tales of the Dutch*, 1787) which ridiculed the vast network of characters used in Chinese and the consequent inability of most people to read their own written language; and *Nihon Fūzoku Bikō* (*Notes on the Customs of Japanese*, 1833), a Japanese translation of a book published in Amsterdam by J. F. van Overmeer Fisscher after a sojourn at the Dutch trading post on Deshima in which he decried the use of Chinese characters, declaring that the Japanese considered them the flower of writing and failed to realize the extent to which they hindered learning.[2]

The study of Dutch led several Japanese scholars to comment on the western system whereby any word could be written down by using a simple and concise alphabet. Gotō Rishun (1702–71), in *Orandabanashi* (*Tales of Holland*, 1765), wrote out and briefly described the Dutch alphabet; Ōtsuki Gentaku (1757–1827), in *Rangaku Kaitei* (*A Guide to Dutch Studies*, 1783), remarked on how easily it could be learned; Shiba Kōkan (1747–1818), in *Oranda Tensetsu* (*Tales of Holland*, 1796), praised the ease afforded reading by the use of a phonetic script. Shiba suggested that Chinese characters be replaced by *kana*, an idea supported by Yamagata Bantō (1748–1821) in *Yume no Shiro* (*The Value of Dreams*, 1802), and Honda Toshiaki (1744–1821) in *Sei'iki Monogatari* (*Tales of the West*, 1798). Honda even recommended the use of the western script itself, which, he noted, was more flexible than *kana* and had the advantage of being internationally recognized. From these proposals, between 1796 and 1802, came the seeds of the ideas which would later lead to the formation of the Kana Club and Rōmaji Club.

Nothing more was heard on the subject of script reform until 1866, when Maejima Hisoka presented to the shogun his petition calling for the replacement of Chinese characters with *kana*. From that time on, the idea of ridding written Japanese of its heavy burden of characters began to take root in the minds of a small group of intellectuals. Some believed their purpose could be accomplished by restricting the number of characters to reasonable dimensions, others by using only *kana*, and still others by using only *rōmaji*.

LIMITING THE NUMBER OF KANJI

Not many espoused this particular cause, to do so being to fly in the face of tradition, for Chinese characters had formed the basis of written Japanese since the sixth century. More than merely a form of writing, the characters had become a value-laden cultural institution, the yardstick against which scholars measured their erudition. Their very difficulty was prized for the mystique with which it invested writing; their formality appealed to Japanese officialdom, who buried the often simple gist of official communications under a bewildering number of symbols. To phase them out completely would have involved much more than just a change in writing habits – it would have meant a radical rethink of the art and aims of writing itself, and a reversal of traditional ideas on the true nature of learning. Nevertheless, it was clear that the system as it stood was detrimental to modernization. The difficult Chinese script was just as great a barrier to understanding as the archaic literary styles used in contemporary prose. Lower-class education extended to little more than the *kana* scripts; even upper-class children, ostensibly receiving a thorough Confucian education, often merely learned to recite passages by heart rather than actually read and understand them. Hours of concentrated study were required to memorize characters before the contents of books could be absorbed.

One of the first to speak seriously of limiting the number of characters in use was Fukuzawa Yukichi in *The Teaching of Characters*, 1873. Realizing that to phase them out altogether would take time, and aware of the dangers inherent in rushing into sweeping reforms without allowing time to adjust to the changes, Fukuzawa suggested that a start be made by avoiding the more difficult characters wherever possible. Having calculated that most business could be carried on with a total of just under a thousand characters, he put his theory into practice in *The Teaching of Characters*, which was written for children and used no more than 928 different *kanji* in its three volumes. Patterned on western readers, it began by introducing single words, then gave examples of the words in short sentences, and gradually progressed to more complex constructions. *The Teaching of Characters* was used in the early days of the new education system as a stopgap textbook before the Ministry of Education had organized production of its own readers. Like his approach to style, Fukuzawa's attitude to script reform was gradualist; despite his acknowledgement of the desirability of phasing out Chinese characters, he approached the problem in a rational, formalistic manner, in the belief that the intermediate step of reducing the number of characters in daily use was preferable to the radical excision of all.

In July 1872, the first Minister of Education, Ōki Takatō, a progressive *yōgakusha* who believed strongly in the necessity for script simplification, set Tanaka Yoshikado (1841–89) and Ōtsuki Shūji (1845–1931) the task of compiling a selection of the characters used most often by ordinary people in everyday affairs. The result of their deliberations was a two-volume dictionary, *Shinsen Jisho* (*A New Dictionary*), which contained 3,167 characters.

There were few calls for the restriction of characters after this, as the emphasis of the developing script reform movement gradually shifted away from improving the existing system toward replacing *kanji* altogether with one of the phonetic scripts.

EARLY *KANA* ADVOCATES

The first move in this direction came from Maejima Hisoka, then a translator at the Kaiseijo, when he presented to the shogun Yoshinobu in 1866 a petition titled 'Proposal for the Abolition of Chinese Characters', calling for the replacing of *kanji* with *kana*. Maejima believed that the path to strong nationhood was through the education of the populace as a whole. Once the Japanese people were able to learn for themselves about conditions abroad, they would soon realize that they themselves were inferior to no one, and would develop the national pride and self-esteem so important to Japan's development and prosperity. One of the major hindrances to the rapid spread of that education, Maejima believed, was the use of Chinese characters, for the inordinate amount of time needed to master them could be better spent on other study.

> The abolition of *kanji* in general education would curtail the time wasted in memorizing and learning to write characters. For the ordinary primary-school child it would save at least three years; for students of specialized higher studies, between five and eight years. Beyond doubt, it will be an immeasurable advantage if they use the time thus gained in scholarship or industry, each according to his own inclination.[3]

Scholars, he was sure, would oppose his suggestion, but needlessly – Japan had its own unique language, easily the equal of western languages, and fifty phonetic symbols to record it. The loss of *kanji* would not mean that writing would stop, merely that it would be done differently.

Maejima realized that without Chinese characters, confusion would result from the large number of homophones in the Japanese language – how to distinguish between the three words 'bridge', 'chopstick', and 'edge', all pronounced *hashi*, for example – and also that word boundaries might be wrongly interpreted without the visual aid of *kanji*, so that *kasumi. so nohe . no . nihohi . kana* might be wrongly read as *kasu . miso . no . heno. nihohi . kana*.[4] He was confident, however, that these problems could be overcome by codification of the grammar system and by the compilation of new dictionaries. In an 1869 document, 'How to Implement Japanese Language Education', which together with 'A Personal View on the Abolition of Chinese Characters' was a rider to his 'Petition Concerning a Proposal for Japanese Language Education', he set out steps to be followed in teaching a simpler form of written Japanese in schools. The first phase would last two years, during which eminent scholars in each of the fields of Chinese, western, and Japanese studies would be chosen to devise and formulate rules for a *kana*-only writing system; they would also compile new dictionaries. This would be followed by a second two-year period of intense preparatory activity during which, among other things, new textbooks would be compiled, Japanese classics and books dealing with world affairs would be rewritten in *kana*, and important Chinese and western works would be published in *kana* versions. Next would come two phases of one year each: in the first, each district would send to Tokyo a minimum of two people to study the new grammar books; in the second, these people would return to their homes to disseminate the information, paying particular attention to certain specially selected students who would then become the second wave of teachers. The fifth phase was also to last two years, and would involve setting up schools around the country. By the end of this period, the important people in the nation would have finished their education in the new script and the task of spreading it to every corner of Japan could begin in earnest as the sixth and final, open-ended phase of Maejima's scheme.

Maejima appealed in this submission for an Imperial edict to decree that, from the beginning of his first phase, official documents should be written in *kana* and that *kana* should be used wherever possible in private texts. This, he felt, would overcome much of the natural doubt that would be entertained by many regarding the feasibility of replacing Chinese characters with *kana* in only eight years. Maejima was convinced that people would be totally accustomed to using *kana* by the end of the fifth phase. He concluded his remarks by observing that replacing characters did not mean that their use would thenceforth be proscribed. Although the characters would not be employed in official documents or future books, they could still be used for private business if a person so desired. At colleges, they could be studied in special courses, after the manner of a foreign language.

The meticulous detail in which Maejima planned his campaign reveals the depth of his concern with script reform, a concern most unusual in an era when mastery of difficult characters was a badge of erudition among scholars. His first petition, 'Proposal for the Abolition of Chinese Characters',was presented when the Tokugawa Government was still in power; such were Maejima's patriotism and conviction that they led him to risk the disapproval of the authorities and the ridicule of his colleagues. However, his petitions which were supplemented in 1873 by another, 'Gakusei Goshikō ni sakidachi Kokuji Kairyō Ainaritaki Hiken Naishinsho' ('A Report on my Humble Opinion that Reform of our Written Language Should Precede the Establishment of an Education System'), evoked no response. Traditional attitudes were too strongly entrenched in the Confucian-educated bureaucracy, and political matters took precedence in the government order of priorities at that time. The petitions were not heard of by the general public until they were published by Maejima and Konishi Nobuhachi (another *kana* advocate) in 1899.[5]

In 1872, undaunted by the lack of official interest, Maejima established a company, the Keimōsha, which began in 1873 to publish the *Mainichi Hiragana Shimbun*, a newspaper written entirely in *kana* with the intention of making news available to lower-class people not educated in *kanji*, in accordance with his belief that Japan's future progress depended upon the universal education of her populace. Publication ceased in the same year, however, in part, Maejima recalled in later years, because the practice of reading newspapers was not yet established, and also because many people were irked by the complete absence of *kanji*. Maejima offered the newspaper free when subscriptions dwindled, but decreasing capital eventually forced him to close it down.

Maejima was one man, fired by a vision inspired by his study of the west of what his country could become given the means of universal education, pitted against a solid block of conservatism in an area important to the modernization effort – the achievement of a democratic written language. Despite their lack of success in this early period, his efforts indicate that there was at least a dawning awareness of the problem.

Next to advocate the use of phonetic script was Shimizu Usaburō (1829–1910) in *Hiragana no Setsu* (*A Theory on Hiragana*, 1874). Shimizu, who had studied Dutch, Russian, French, German, and English, had earlier published in 1860 an English conversation book titled *Engirishi Kotoba* (*English Conversation*) and written entirely in *hiragana*, as was his translation 'Kishūsan Sekitan Kantei no Setsu' ('Expert Opinion on Coal from Kishu') published in the *Chūgai Shimbun* under the pen-name Mizuhoya Usaburō (after his bookshop Mizuhoya) on 26 August 1869. In *A Theory on Hiragana*, he defended this practice, and argued against the theories of others who favoured using a mixture of *kana* and *kanji*, or *rōmaji* only, or even completely new characters yet to be devised. Shimizu, like Maejima a believer in educating the masses, felt that the use of the simple *hiragana* script would best achieve this aim. He was also a defender of civil rights, believing that script reform would help improve the lot of the common people. Again like Maejima, he put his theories into practice. Two months before the appearance of *A Theory on Hiragana*, he published *Monowari no Hashigo* (*The Ladder of Physics*), a three-volume translation of a German science primer written entirely in *hiragana*, with spaces between words, in a simple colloquial style. Given the urgent necessity of mastering western technology in the early Meiji Period, physics was an important subject, and Shimizu tried to demonstrate that training in its principles could be facilitated by script and style reform.

Shimizu and Maejima shared several points in common. Both men saw the spread of education as the prime mover in script reform; both advocated a colloquial style used in conjunction with *kana*; both practised their theories; and both were ardent patriots who saw the use of *kana* script as a way of freeing Japan from a cumbersome foreign system.

A third advocate of *kana* was Watanabe Shūjirō, whose *Nihombun o Seitei suru Hōhō* (*Steps to Regulating Written Japanese*, 1875), dealt primarily with the problem of style reform but also mentioned script. He suggested that written Japanese could be simplified by first replacing literary styles with a simple colloquial style and then making *hiragana* the national script, the only Chinese characters to be retained being those for numerals. The knowledge contained in even the most academic treatises would then be readily accessible to anyone with a knowledge of *hiragana*.

Maejima, Shimizu, and Watanabe were the three major early-Meiji advocates of *kana*. As they were all following individual trains of thought and did not unite in a combined front, their calls for script reform aroused little response, and it was not until several years later that a group was formed to work toward the practical application of their theories.

THE KANA CLUB

In 1881, a number of interested people from various backgrounds came together to consider the problem of script reform, resulting in the formation of three support groups over the following eighteen months. Kana no Tomo (Friends of Kana), begun as an informal meeting of friends in 1881 and officially named as a club a year later, included among its members Nambu Yoshikazu (1840–1917), Katayama Atsuyoshi, Shimizu Usaburō, Mozume Takami, and Ōtsuki Fumihiko; Mozume and Ōtsuki, with assistance from Shimizu, began publishing the group's own paper, *Kana no Michibiki* (*Guide to Kana*), in 1883. The members of the Irohakai (Iroha Club), also inaugurated in 1882 after two years of discussion, were in the main educators, among them Gotō Makita, Miyake Yonekichi (1860–1929), and Nakamigawa Yūjirō. Those involved in formal education were naturally more enthusiastic than others about spreading popular education, and the object of the Iroha Club was to search out a way of more efficiently achieving this objective through script reform. The third group, the Irohabunkai (The Irohabun Club), was started in the same year by businessmen, journalists, and graduates of Keiō Gijuku,[6] among them Takahashi Yoshio, Watanabe Osamu, and Motoyama Hikoichi.

While the general objective of the three groups was the same, their motives and idea on *kana* usage differed markedly. *Kana* was not just a simple phonetic script. A proper phonetic script matches one symbol to one sound, but *kana* had already been in use for several hundred years, and several symbols reflected changes in pronunciation during that time. For example the symbols

い and ゐ

were both pronounced 'i'; the symbol for *ha* could also be pronounced *wa* when functioning as topic marker; there were two ways of writing both *ji* and *zu*; and three possible representations of the sound *e*, depending on context. The problem facing *kana* advocates was how to deal with these discrepancies; should they be labelled 'historical usage' and tolerated as such, or rejected as contradictions of a one-to-one phonetic system? It was division of opinion on this matter which led to the formation at first of three separate groups of *kana* supporters rather than one larger association. Friends of Kana members were classical scholars who believed in retaining the historical usage, whereas their Iroha Club counterparts, mainly concerned with smoothing the path of education, wanted the simplest possible, strictly phonetic script. The journalists and businessmen who made up the Irohabun Club and yet a fourth small club, Itsura no Oto, being a varied group of journalists and businessmen with no other motive for supporting script reform beyond the practical benefits which would accrue to them, were impartial on the issue, desiring only simplification without having strong views on the details of the process.

The universities were one of the motivating forces in the formation of both *kana* and *rōmaji* groups. Scholars studying European civilizations were spurred by their observation of the western script to contemplate their own system. As knowledge of western culture spread from a scholastic élite to society at large, some patriotic Japanese, pondering the question of how to make Japanese culture the equal of European, began to develop the idea of spreading education through simplifying script. Many of those who had personally undertaken western studies, university lecturers in particular, supported the idea of romanization; others advocated *kana*. Contemporary society was ablaze with curiosity about things western, and those who had visited Europe were accorded a gratifying respect. The pronouncements of university lecturers, who enjoyed a high social status, carried much weight, and it was thus under their influence that educators formed the Iroha Club.

In July 1883, the three groups eventually banded together to form the Kana no Kai (Kana Club). They retained their differences of opinion, however, splitting into three factions within the parent club, so that in effect all that had been achieved by uniting was to bring together under a common name those seeking to replace Chinese characters with Japanese phonetic script while still leaving them free to pursue their individual theories within the group. The old Friends of Kana became the Tsuki no Bu (Moon Faction, historical usage), the Iroha Club and Irohabun Club the Yuki no Bu (Snow Faction, phonetic usage), and the middle-of-the-road Itsura no Oto the Hana no Bu (Flower Faction, no set views.) The aims of the club were to bring about both the use of *kana* as the only national script and the simplification of vocabulary. Membership increased annually until by 1887 there were over thirty regional branches with a total membership of more than 10,000.[7]

Between 1883 and 1891, the club published a total of six journals through which to disseminate its various theories. First came *Kana no Michibiki* (*A Guide to Kana*, May 1883–May 1884), published originally by Friends of Kana, later the Moon Faction of the Kana Club. It was followed closely by *Kana no Manabi* (*The Study of Kana*, August 1883–June 1884), the organ of the Snow Faction section. When Snow, Moon, and Flower factions united in 1884, they published *Kana no Shirube* (*Guide to Kana*, July 1884–May 1885). The union proved brief, however, the old problems resurfacing after a year, and the club was again divided internally, this time into the Moto no Tomo (formerly the Moon Faction, advocates of historical usage) and the Kakikata Kairyōbu (formerly the Snow Faction, progressives wanting purely phonetic *kana*). This latter group put out the *Kana no Zasshi* (*Kana Journal*, July 1885–January 1886), while the former published the *Kana Shimbun* (*Kana Newspaper*, July 1885–June 1886). After July 1886, the Club's only bulletin was *Kana no Tekagami* (*The Kana Model*, August 1886–March 1891).

As the Kana Club had been established with the aim of script reform rather than style reform, and script reform bent on replacing Chinese script with Japanese, the articles published in its magazines were written in a style based on classical Japanese grammar and vocabulary. Club members in the main attributed the difficulty of the written language to the nature and diversity of the scripts in use rather than to the divergence between speech and writing, thereby addressing only one part of the overall problem. They failed to realize that literary Japanese was just as difficult to read when written in *kana* as when written in *kanji* – more difficult, in fact, without the visual clues afforded by characters to help pinpoint meaning and indicate certain word boundaries. Rather than simplifying matters, therefore, their manner of writing actually compounded the difficulty of reading Japaese. Not all were blind to what was happening, however, and some members began to put forward proposals for a dual approach combining script *and* style reform. Influential advocates of this approach were Miyake Yonekichi, Hirata Azumao, Ōtsuki Fumihiko, and Mozume Takami, all of whom wrote articles calling for stylistic simplification as a prerequisite to script reform.

Miyake was secretary of the Kana Club and editor of *The Study of Kana*, *Guide to Kana*, and *Kana Journal*. A member of the Snow Faction, he advocated a one-to-one phonetic correspondence in *kana* usage. Writing under the pen-name of 'Nakama no Hitori' ('One of the Group'), Miyake published 'Bun no Kakikata ni tsuite' ('On Writing') in the *Study of Kana* on 20 February 1884, making the point that adoption of a simpler script was not in itself a remedy for what ailed the written language – without concomitant style reform, orthographic reform would achieve nothing. The gap between the written and the spoken forms of the language should be closed as far as possible; while the use of widely-known Chinese words could continue, archaic words and expressions should be dropped. Some might voice the widely-held fear that the use of expressions from the spoken language in writing would cheapen the latter; but if hearing another person speak could move and inspire a listener, then seeing the same words on paper ought also to be capable of producing a like reaction in the reader. In Miyake's view, a colloquial style written in phonetic script could succeed in skilfully and fully expressing the entire gamut of thought and emotion.

Five months later, on 30 July, a second article entitled 'Tegami no Kakikata' ('On Letter Writing'), this time in *Guide to Kana* under the pen-name 'Mi Yo', narrowed the focus of similar remarks to correspondence. Criticizing the traditional epistolary style *sōrōbun* for its strongly Chinese tone, difficult stereotyped idioms, and too rigid patterns of expression, Miyake urged people to try to express their own personal feelings in letters by taking advantage of the much greater freedom offered by colloquial style, concluding by emphasizing the need to reshape and polish the written Japanese language to the point where it could compete on equal terms with the best of western writing. Miyake's third sally was an essay which appeared the following month in *Guide to Kana* and extended over three issues: 'Kuniguni no Namari Kotoba ni tsukite' ('On Regional Dialects') in which he again urged *kana* supporters to adopt colloquial style, this time also emphasizing the need to decide upon a standard form of Japanese as its basis.

Miyake's articles, which were not themselves written in colloquial style, made little impact on the ingrained habits of club members, although a few colloquial-style articles did appear the next year in *Kana Newspaper*, organ of the Moto no Tomo faction. Nevertheless, he persevered within his own group. His next effort was 'Zokugo Iyashimu Na' ('Don't Despise the Vernacular', *Kana Journal*, November–December 1885 and January 1886), in which he classified writing into the two subsections of practical and ornamental. Among useless ornamentation which should be eradicated from *kana* prose he included esoteric Chinese and classical Japanese words, declaring that ordinary writing needed none of these fripperies; it should be modelled on the everyday spoken language, not the vulgar colloquial of the lower classes but the normal speech of middle-class society. The purpose of writing he deemed to be not adornment but communication. Rhetoric ought to be reserved for specialized areas such as literature, leaving letters, scientific prose, and all practical writing simple and unadorned. Realizing that true educational progress depended on a more democratic view of the written language, what Miyake sought was a reversal of the traditional view of writing, a repudiation of the veneration of classicism and form over content. The concept of writing as a rarefied art had to yield to a new respect for practicality and convenience; in short, scholars had to accept that the feudal period had passed and that to cling to an outmoded and inappropriate set of linguistic conventions and attitudes was to risk becoming obstructive and anachronistic.

Hirata Azumao had been concerned with style as well as script reform since the Kana Club's formation. His 'Fumi no Kakisama ni tsuite' ('On Writing Letters', *Kana no Michibiki*, June 1883) argued that writers ought to select the simplest, most widely-used words wherever possible, and blend them together smoothly. The resultant text would be easy to read, understand, and study, so that all Japanese people would soon be able to read and write their own language. Three years later, on 15 October 1886, *The Kana Model* carried the transcript of a lecture given by Hirata the previous month at a club meeting ('Wagakuni no Gakujutsu no Ishizue o sadamu beshi' ['On the Need to Establish a Foundation for Scholarship in Japan']), in which he reiterated the interdependence of script and style reform, addressing them as two of the major issues facing Japan in an era of comprehensive reform. The true nature of writing as a simple means of communication, he believed, had been forgotten, resulting in the widespread gap between it and the contemporary spoken language. He urged the Kana Club and the Rōmaji Club, as the two bodies most actively concerned with the reform of the written language, to take up the issue of style as well and co-operate in selecting vocabulary and standardizing grammar. Hirata was sensitive to the incongruity of a situation whereby so many aspects of Japanese life were undergoing scrutiny and undergoing a reshaping to fit the changing needs of society while the linking thread which ran through all of them – the written language – was allowed to stagnate in a mire of anachronism and difficulty. The measure of his concern is his willingness to put aside partisan differences over phonetic scripts between supporters of *kana* and romanization and seek their co-operation in working to bring written Japanese into line with the times.

Ōtsuki Fumihiko, one of the great scholars of the Japanese language in the Meiji and Taishō Periods, was keenly interested in the modernization of written Japanese, making his views known on issues of standardization, colloquialization, and orthographic reform. In 1884, he and six others, including Mozume, Shimizu, and Hirata, formed a group to study the Japanese language called Kotoba no Tomo (Friends of Language), which joined forces with the Kana Club in July that year. A strong advocate of *kana* as the national script, he had earlier published a long article in which he attempted to field the objections of its opponents.[8] In 1888, however, abandoning traditional forms of writing and suiting the action to the word in a refreshingly practical manner, Ōtsuki published 'Tegami no Kakikata' ('How to Write Letters') as a sixty-page supplement to issues 23 and 25 of *The Kana Model*, further distributing copies to Kana Club members. This was a collection of model letters and answers appropriate as invitations, New Year greetings, congratulatory notes, and so on, written out in *kana* in simple colloquial style rather than *sōrōbun*.

Mozume, a lecturer in literature at Tokyo Imperial University, had also been a member of the club since its inception. His best known work is the 1886 essay 'Gembun'itchi' which enumerated the arguments in support of colloquial style and was the first attempt at providing practical illustration of the theory. He did not mention the issue of script reform in this text, which was itself written in a comparatively simple mixture of *kanji* and *kana*; as he was a councillor of the Club, his views on the matter could presumably be taken for granted. What he sought to hammer home here was the importance of tackling the stylistic difficulties which were hindering the smooth progress of the *kana* movement. This theme was repeated two years later in a lecture to the Yokohama branch of the club, exhorting members to write in a style which could be easily understood when read aloud.

The importance of stylistic reform to the script reform movement was therefore not unnoticed by several men influential in the organizational hierarchy of the Kana Club, whose interest had doubtless been further stimulated by the press debate of 1884-89 on *gembun'itchi* and by the appearance in 1887 of the first colloquial-style novels and translations of literary works. Some colloquial-style articles did begin to appear in club magazines in reponse to their urging, but it was at best a slow business, and most contributors continued to use classical Japanese grammar. It was this general failure to realize that script and style reform could not be carried out independently, coupled with the lack of a cohesive approach owing to the inability of the Moto no Tomo and Kakikata Kairyōbu to agree on a unified policy of *kana* usage, that led to a decline of enthusiasm for the club's activities in 1889. In line with the desire to disseminate education and culture which motivated members' support for script reform, changes in the editorial policy of *The Kana Model* in November of that year meant that discussions of script and style were suppressed in favour of scientific and general articles, most of which were not written in colloquial style. The internal schisms finally proved too strong to maintain the club, and although publication of *The Kana Model* continued beyond 1889, that too came to an end on 25 March 1891.

EARLY *RŌMAJI* ADVOCATES

The movement for replacing *kanji* with *rōmaji* (the western alphabet) developed concurrently with the *kana* movement. First to call for a romanized script was Nambu Yoshikazu (1840-1917), who presented a petition to Yamanouchi Yōdō, head of the Daigakuryō.[9] He followed this with two petitions to the Minister of Education in 1871 and 1872, the second titled *Moji o Kaikan suru no Gi* (*Petition for the Reform of Characters*).

Nambu was followed by Nishi Amane (1826-97), a progressive scholar of the west who spoke three European languages and had travelled to Holland as one of the first students sent to study abroad. One of the foremost philosophers of the Meiji Period, Nishi was a foundation member of the Meirokusha, the intellectual society formed in 1873 which numbered among its members such luminaries as Mori Arinori, Fukuzawa Yukichi, and Katō Hiroyuki. The first issue of its bulletin, the *Meiji Six Journal*, in March 1874, carried his essay on romanization, 'Yōji o mote Kokugo o shosuru no Ron' ('On Writing Japanese with the Western Alphabet'), in which he stated his belief that learning, science, and writing played important roles in bringing enlightenment to the people. Given that writing was the instrument of the other two, the contemporary state of written Japanese was ridiculous. Nishi felt that recent proposals to limit the number of characters or to replace them by *kana* were both biased and unwieldy; the best plan for a Japan which was feverishly adopting western customs and technology was obviously to use the western alphabet (only the alphabet, he hastened to add, not the English language itself as proposed by Mori Arinori). *Rōmaji* should be introduced gradually. As a first step, influential supporters of the idea should band together in a Rōmaji Club to promote this aim. The benefits of using *rōmaji*, Nishi felt, would far outweigh the disadvantages; for one thing, a colloquial written style would automatically result from adoption of roman letters, as these were phonetic and would allow the reproduction of spoken Japanese in writing, which would be of tremendous benefit to women and children and the lower classes whose knowledge of Chinese characters was limited. Interestingly, he perceived the emergence of *gembun'itchi* as a direct result of romanization; in this he was more clear-eyed than other early advocates of colloquial style who, with the exception of Maejima and Shimizu, paid scant attention to script reform and failed to realize that colloquial grammar would be of little use if the script employed to write it down remained at its current level of difficulty. To solve the problem of settling on a method of expression neither too refined nor too colloquial, Nishi recommended spelling *rōmaji* words according to the rules of elegant diction but pronouncing them in the colloquial manner. For example, a phrase might be written in *rōmaji* in the traditional form *ikasama omosirosi* ('interesting in some way'), but pronounced *ikasama omosiroi*, as was normal in speech. His proposal seems rather inconsistent with his assurance that romanization would result in total colloquialization, but he may perhaps have seen it as an intermediate step to avoid causing alarm by too rapid a change.

It was to be eleven years before *rōmaji* advocates adopted Nishi's suggestion of banding into the Rōmaji Club. Nevertheless, his ideas reached a fairly large number of intellectuals, as each edition of the *Meiji Six Journal* sold an average of 3,205 copies. Shimizu Usaburō's 'A Theory on Hiragana' was published in the seventh issue, so that the two schools of script reform received roughly equal coverage and were equally well known by 1884, despite the relegation to obscurity of Maejima Hisoka's earlier petitions on *kana*. Nishi himself, though adopting colloquial style in his *New Theory of the Hundred and One* and *Travels in the Interior* (1874), did not apply romanization in his writing. His theories on romanization received no serious consideration until the formation of the Rōmaji Club, but his ideas on style reform did strongly influence several young men who later played their parts in the *gembun'itchi* movement. They were Mozume Takami, impressed by the 'Western Alphabet' essay, who visited Nishi to discuss the issue of style reform; Ueki Emori, who later wrote some of his civil rights treatises in colloquial style; and Mori Ōgai (1862–1922), who lodged in Nishi's house for some time.

In 1876, Ōtsuki Fumihiko contributed an article, 'Nihon Moji Henkakuron' ('On Reforming Japanese Script'), to *Chōya Shimbun*. Ōtsuki was known in particular as a compiler of Japanese grammars and dictionaries, and was deeply convinced of the need for adequate versions of both. In his article, he noted that he found the existing script system a hindrance to his work of compiling grammars. Chinese characters could have different meanings according to which readings were used, and *kana* letters were inadequate as phonetic characters. The best script to use in a grammar, he felt, was the western alphabet, which by allowing the separation of vowels and consonants could show pronunciation more efficiently than syllabic *kana*. He had entertained the idea of adopting the alphabet since going to Yokohama to study ten years earlier. Presumably he saw it as of use only in grammar books, however, as he later became one of the leaders of the Kana Club.

The last important essay on *rōmaji* before the formation of the Rōmaji Club was 'Rōmaji o mote Nihongo o tsuzuru Setsu' ('On Writing Japanese with the Western Alphabet'), which appeared in *Tōyō Gakugei Zasshi, The Journal of Oriental Culture,* 7 and 8, in April and May 1882. It was written by Yatabe Ryōkichi (1851–99), botanist and pioneer of the new style of poetry which appeared in the Meiji Period, and advocated the adoption of a *rōmaji* script and a written style based on the speech used in Tokyo.

THE RŌMAJI CLUB

In 1884, supporters of the adoption of the alphabet began to discuss joining forces to fight more effectively for the removal of Chinese characters. In July of that year, Toyama Masakazu published 'Rōmaji o Shuchō suru Mono ni tsugu' ('Advice to *Rōmaji* Advocates') in the *Journal of Oriental Culture*, calling for the formation of a club, and on 2 December a meeting attended by over seventy people was held to discuss strategy. They included Toyama (who gave a talk on the objectives of forming a Rōmaji Club), Yatabe, Terao Hisashi (1855–1923), and Yamakawa Kenjirō (1854–1931). The Rōmaji Club was officially inaugurated on 17 January 1885.

Forty members were chosen as a committee to inquire into *rōmaji* usage. Six of them – Toyama, Terao, Basil Hall Chamberlain, C. S. Eby, Yatabe, and Kanda Naibu (1857–1923) – drafted a motion and published it under the title 'Rōmaji nite Nihongo no Kakikata' ('How to write Japanese with the Alphabet'). It contained nineteen clauses, one of which proclaimed that *rōmaji* usage should be based on the pronunciation of Tokyo residents with standard education. In June 1885, *Rōmaji Zasshi* (*Rōmaji Journal*) was launched as the official club bulletin; it remained in publication until December 1892. Most of the essays and other items therein were written in *rōmaji*, but, as in the case of Kana Club publications, difficult literary style was used until about 1887.

Most members of the Club had studied foreign languages. When Tokyo Imperial University was founded in 1877, it was staffed almost entirely by foreigners, the few exceptions including Toyama, Yatabe, and Kikuchi Dairoku. English was used as the medium of instruction. Students thus seeing the foreign script in daily use could not help noticing its advantages, and it was natural that they should later advocate its adoption as the Japanese script.

In June 1885, membership of the Rōmaji Club totalled 2,908, of whom 2,734 were Japanese and 174 were foreigners. By March 1887, there were twenty-nine regional branches in addition to the main group in Tokyo, and the total membership had increased to 6,876; by the end of 1888, this number had risen to over 10,000.[10]

Like the Kana Club, the Rōmaji Club was divided over the issue of usage. An investigative committee had decided on the Hepburn system, but Tanakadate Aikitsu disagreed; the Hepburn system employed roman letters as they were used in foreign languages, whereas he wanted to find a way to use them in faithfully reproducing the sounds of Japanese. He and his followers therefore broke away from the main group and formed a splinter society, the Rōmaji Sinsisha. Using the system they favoured, the group published a journal *Rōmaji Sinsi* (*New Rōmaji Journal*) from May 1886 until August 1890.

Rōmaji supporters writing in the *Rōmaji Journal* fell into the same trap as had their counterparts in the *kana* movement in that they merely changed their script while continuing to use traditional literary styles. Again, this achieved the very reverse of their objectives; instead of becoming simpler, written Japanese actually became more difficult to read without the visual aid of characters in working out the meaning of complex Chinese words. It was an oversight which was to retard their progress severely, and which furnished non-supporters of the movement with material for criticism. Even the column of miscellaneous items of the early *Rōmaji Journal* was written in *kambun kuzushi*, although the vocabulary was simpler than that used in the essays in the main body of the magazine. Again, not all members were unaware of the problem. A small group of progressive thinkers, realizing that ordinary Club members were making heavy work of the *rōmaji* articles published by scholars, began to push for the use of colloquial style in conjunction with the roman alphabet.

First was Taguchi Ukichi, with 'Nippon Kaika no Seishitsu' ('The Nature of Japanese Culture'), published in seven instalments in *Rōmaji Journal* from June 1885 to June 1886. The essay was written in *rōmaji*, in colloquial style using the *de gozarimasu* termination. Taguchi criticized the *kambun kuzushi* style, arguing that a writing system should be based on speech for easy comprehension. He saw a combination of the roman script with colloquial style as the ideal form of written Japanese for the future. Four areas where the western alphabet would be particularly convenient were industry, where being able to write horizontally would allow the use of the convenient Italian industrial bookkeeping method; technology, where artisans such as carpenters and plasterers would be able to record the special jargon of their trades which could not be written in Chinese characters; science, where clarity was important to the expression of ideas in practical areas such as physics and chemistry; and such miscellaneous tasks as setting up print type, writing letters, and so on. The one possible disadvantage he conceded was that Japanese literature, having been written with Chinese characters for so long, might suffer during the stage of transition to the alphabet. Taken as a whole, however, he believed that a romanized colloquial style would be infinitely simpler and more convenient than *kambun kuzushi*, and would be much more in tune with modern society.

Nishi Amane had said basically the same thing in 'On Writing Japanese with the Western Alphabet' in 1874, but Taguchi was the first member of the Rōmaji Club itself to speak out in favour of style reform, not only advocating it but illustrating it with the style of his own essay. He followed 'Nippon Kaika no Seishitsu with Rōmaji nite Kakikata no Shinkufū' ('A New Method of Writing with the Alphabet'), another colloquial-style *rōmaji* essay published in *Rōmaji Journal* in August 1886 in which he identified certain difficulties he had encountered with romanization. Particularly annoying was the need to write *watakushi* ('I') and *gozarimasu* so often, and Taguchi suggested that these words be abbreviated to 'w' and 'g', although still read aloud in full.

The seventeenth issue of *Rōmaji Journal* in October 1885 carried two essays, both written in a romanized colloquial style, on the style-reform theme: 'Rōmaji o amaneku Yo ni okonawasuru ni tsuki Iken' ('An Opinion on the Dissemination of the Alphabet') by Kusano Mompei, and 'Rōmaji Zasshi no Kairyō o nozomu' ('A Wish for the Reform of Rōmaji Zasshi') by Amagai Yuzuru. The first asserted that the Japanese language could never develop satisfactorily until the use of Chinese characters was discontinued. Characters were essentially alien to the nature of Japanese, whereas *rōmaji*, being phonetic characters, could be used to reproduce any language. They were easy to read and easy to learn. Even *rōmaji* would be useless, however, unless *kambun kuzushi* were also ousted along with characters. Kusano suggested several steps to facilitate the spread of romanization, the first and most important being the development of a colloquial written style. Other proposals included taking notes in shorthand from lectures by famous people and publishing them in *rōmaji*; pushing for *rōmaji* education for children; and publishing *rōmaji* books written in a simple style for members of the middle and lower classes.

In the second essay, Amagai put forward two suggestions for encouraging the use of *rōmaji*. One was to simplify the style of the articles appearing in *Rōmaji Journal*, most of which were crammed with difficult Chinese words. As many of these were homonyms, romanizing them led to confusion over meaning. Critics of the Rōmaji Club, he noted, were amused that its members continued to use Chinese vocabulary while scorning Chinese characters. Second, the columns of miscellaneous items should contain more articles written in *rōmaji*. Amagai suggested publishing romanized versions of western novels and recent Japanese novels such as Tsubouchi Shōyō's *Characters of Modern Students* as well as articles such as Taguchi's 'Nature of Japanese Culture'.

The fourth warning came from a foreign member of the Club, the Englishman Basil Hall Chamberlain, then a lecturer in linguistics at Tokyo Imperial University. On 19 March 1887, he gave a lecture titled 'Gembun'itchi' at the second general meeting of the Club, the text of which was published in colloquial style in *Rōmaji Journal* in May. Chamberlain likened the Rōmaji Club to a ship trying to steer a safe course through uncharted waters full of hidden reefs. The dangerous reef, and the one which could well sink the ship, was the style habitually used by club members, which both Japanese and foreigners alike had difficulty in understanding. Particularly difficult were Chinese-derived neologisms which had been coined to describe devices imported since the Restoration, for nobody could understand these terms without seeing the *kanji*. To take away the visual clues offered by Chinese characters was merely to compound the difficulty of written Japanese. It was no use replacing Chinese words with classical Japanese expressions; the archaic language simply did not have the vocabulary to express modern concepts. The solution, he believed, lay in using colloquial style. Every civilized country followed this practice, yet Japanese scholars, taught to value stylistic complexity as a mark of erudition, were ashamed of simplicity – a situation similar to that in medieval Europe, when scholars wrote in Latin not understood by the common people. Important government announcements to the Japanese people went unread because of their wording.

Chamberlain did not advocate the adoption of colloquial style simply for the sake of aping the west. He saw it as the only sensible course to follow if education were to be spread among the people. Not a great deal of work was involved, he asserted; the colloquial was there to hand if only the prejudice against it could be overcome.

He suggested that members of the Rōmaji Club begin at once on a program of colloquialization by following the example of Molière, who was said to have read his works to his servants to ensure their intelligibility. If the Rōmaji Club resolved to adopt this practice for a year, newspapers such as the *Nichi Nichi Shimbun*, always favourably disposed toward the Club, would be encouraged to follow suit.

Partly in response to these theories and partly in response to the growing influence of the *gembun'itchi* movement in society at large, there did in fact occur a change from *kambun kuzushi* to colloquial style in the essays published in *Rōmaji Journal* after April 1887. Many lecture texts were also published in colloquial style in response to the demand by Club members for useful articles; and these came in time to outnumber original colloquial works. The trend to colloquialization was thus more pronounced in the bulletin of the Rōmaji Club than in those of the Kana Club, with communications to members from the secretary and treasurer being published in colloquial style from December 1886.

Eventually, despite this promising trend, the Rōmaji Club fell victim in 1892 to the backlash against over-enthusiastic adoption of western customs and was disbanded in December of that year, although sporadic discussions on the use of *rōmaji* continued for many years.

OUTSIDE PERCEPTIONS OF THE KANA AND RŌMAJI CLUBS

Outside the script reform movement, there appeared in newspapers and magazines a spate of essays dealing with the need for stylistic simplification, and many of these referred to the Kana and Rōmaji Clubs. Kanda Kōhei, in 'Bunshōron o yomu' ('On Reading Bunshōron', 1885), accused the clubs of taking a superficial approach to the problem in not attempting to preface script reform with style reform, a view which Fukuchi Gen'ichirō supported in three editorials published in the *Nichi Nichi Shimbun*: 'Bunshō no Shinka' ('The Evolution of Writing', 1885); 'Bunshō Kairyō no Mokuteki' ('The Purpose of Style Reform', 1886); and 'Bunshō no Kairyō' ('The Reform of Style', 1887). Fukuchi approved the clubs' aims as one element in a plan for modernizing written Japanese, but thought that the essential convenience of *kana* and *rōmaji* would be lost unless these scripts were used in a colloquial style. An editorial in the *Meiji Nippō* on 17 November 1885 also stressed the need for a *gembun'itchi* style, adding as a corollary that its absence actively prevented the Rōmaji and Kana Clubs from achieving their objectives.

In 'Nihon Bunshōron' ('On Written Japanese', 1886), Suematsu Kenchō (1855–1920) analysed the pros and cons of *kana* and *rōmaji*, and offered their supporters advice on improving their technique. For *kana* to be effective, he proposed, words should be separated by spaces (not hitherto done), capital letters and punctuation should be used to clarify meaning, and strictly phonetic *kana* usage should replace the historical method. He warned Kana Club members to settle their differences of opinion, fix on a definite and coherent approach to usage, and plan gradual steps for its application.

While roman letters needed no such remedies, Suematsu suggested, they too were as yet imperfect. The number of letters needed to write a sentence was double that required when *kana* was used – the sounds 'shi' and 'tsu', for example, each represented by a single *kana* symbol, required three letters to write in *rōmaji* so that to Japanese long used to the conciseness of *kanji*, *rōmaji* seemed unwieldy. In this respect, the alphabet was inferior to both characters and *kana*. He did not feel it necessary, however, to make a final choice between *kana* and *rōmaji* at that time, the most important task being to phase out characters. Both phonetic scripts possessed advantages and disadvantages; both should be allowed to develop, and the final decision left to natural selection. Meanwhile, colloquial style was a necessary adjunct. Rōmaji Club members normally wrote in *kambun kuzushi* – they would write, for example, *sono shinri o shikibetsu sezaru mono* ('those who do not understand the truth of it'), which Kana Club members, favouring classical Japanese, would render as *sono kotowari o wakimae shiranu yakara*, in which the Chinese words *shinri* and *shikibetsu* are replaced with Japanese equivalents. While the use of Sino-Japanese was merely a matter of habit and could be easily discontinued, that of classical Japanese by Kana Club members was part of a deliberate nationalistic plan to rid the Japanese language of the Chinese influence. Both clubs would come to grief if they did not encourage colloquial style.

An outright rejection of the aims of the two clubs came from Sugiura Shigetake (1855–1924), in *Nihon no Gengo Bunshō* (*Japanese Language and Writing*, 1887). Both scripts, he wrote, were difficult to apply and were actually harmful in that they exacerbated the inconvenience of written Japanese. Their supporters were not realistic in their outlook; they did not realize that it was impossible to get rid of characters, or that, even supposing there were benefits to be reaped from doing so, the task would take centuries to accomplish. Japan's most urgent need was a simple style for everyday use rather than a phonetic script.

The common theme linking all the foregoing attacks was the need for style reform. Other critics took a different tack by suggesting the existing writing system be continued in a modified form. Once again, the idea of reducing the number of characters in use surfaced. One of its supporters was Yano Fumio who in *Nihon Buntai Moji Shinron* (*A New Discourse on Japanese Style and Script*, 1886), stated his opposition both to colloquial style and to a completely phonetic script. The best style for Japan, he argued, was *kambun kuzushi* with added *kana* glosses to help with readings. Such a style would retain the visual clues to meaning afforded by characters, the lack of which handicapped readers of *kana* and *rōmaji* writings. In order to transform this into a general style understood by all, however, drastic reductions in the number of Chinese characters would have to be made. Yano divided writing into two categories. The first included government notices, textbooks, newspapers, and letters – documents whose intelligibility was of paramount importance. The upper limit on the number of characters used for these purposes should be three thousand of the most common forms; in practice, 1,500 or less would probably suffice. His second category was literary – novels, essays, specialized books, histories, and biographies – and here, too, he set the limit at 3,000 characters. Yano had found this number sufficient in his own experience to express even the most abstruse concepts. He concluded by deploring the recent confusion over script and style reform. It was important, he believed, to decide on a firm policy and begin at once to implement it.

Yano's main objection to the use of either phonetic script was the amount of time needed to make it a viable option. Years would be required to accustom people to using it, and Japan could ill afford the time or confusion. Why bother with such unwieldy schemes when the existing system could be tailored to fit modern needs with a minimum of time and fuss simply by reducing the number of characters? Characters were not altogether bad when used in moderation, Yano asserted; combined with *kana*, they made an acceptable and, more to the point, already familiar medium of communication.

From the point of view of script reform, Yano's approach was perhaps the most convincing and practical of all the theories circulated at that time, and pointed in the direction eventually taken. It took into consideration the real needs of the Japanese people and the urgency of the problem rather than chasing after attractive but impractical ideas of full-scale change. Yano followed Fukuzawa's lead in advocating a policy of moderation, making the best of available resources. Later, as the editor of *Yūbin Hōchi Shimbun*, he published several other articles expanding on the same theme, and on 16 September 1887, announced that the newspaper would from 1 October adopt a limit of 3,000 characters in essays, miscellaneous items, and so forth. Exceptions to the rule would be novels, proclamations, and geographical names. *Sanzenji Jibiki* (*A Three-Thousand Character Dictionary*) was published as a supplement to the 27 November issue.

Support for his idea came from 'N. N.', the initials used by the author of 'Nihon Bunshōron' ('On Japanese Writing'), a four-part essay published in *Kyōiku Zasshi* (*Education Journal*) from May to July 1886 which at the same time criticized the Kana and Rōmaji Clubs for attempting to abolish characters while still reproducing Chinese words in phonetic script, making reading twice as difficult as before. Characters had become an integral part of written Japanese and could not be just tossed aside after centuries of use. Yano's idea of a 3,000 limit, the writer believed, was sound and needed no time to implement. People should use characters and phonetic script in conjunction, striving always to choose only the most common Chinese characters. No other way of writing should be used in daily business.

Discussion of script reform continued for many years after the disbanding of the Kana and Rōmaji Clubs, becoming particularly vehement during the upsurge of national spirit following Japan's victory in the Sino-Japanese war of 1894–95 when many sought ways of throwing off the Chinese influence. A fresh spate of calls for the abolition or reduction of characters appeared in journals such as *Seinenbun* (*Young Writing*) and *Kokugaku* (*Classical Studies*). Perhaps one of the best of these later articles, one which summed up the arguments and discussed the various schools of thought, was 'Shinkokuji Kakutei no Jiki' ('Time to Decide on a New Script',

1898), by Inoue Tetsujirō (1855–1944), a philosopher and lecturer at Tokyo Imperial University, also known as a pioneer of new-style poetry.

Inoue prefaced his argument by drawing a gloomy picture of the contemporary state of written Japanese. There was a profusion of scripts. While *katakana* had fixed forms, both *hiragana* and *kanji* could be written as square or cursive characters, the cursive forms being very difficult for ordinary people to read. Reading characters was complicated by the several different pronunciations accorded to each character depending on context. Script, which should be merely a means to an end, had become an object of learning in itself, a situation which was seriously impeding Japan's attempts to catch up with the west.

Unlike most other critics of Chinese characters, Inoue did not regard them as altogether useless. They provided visual clues to meaning; their Chinese readings made a welcome contrast to the somewhat effeminate-sounding native Japanese; and they were concise, a major virtue in a busy society. On the debit side, their successful use depended entirely on prodigious feats of memory, whereas in the west, mastery of a simple alphabet was sufficient to allow any word in the language to be read. Characters could not show Japanese grammatical inflexions, and they had originally been developed to represent the mostly monosyllabic morphemes of Chinese whereas Japanese morphemes are to a large extent polysyllabic. They could not be conveniently used as phonetic characters for foreign names, and there were an amazing number of homophones among them.

If script reform was ever to take place, Inoue felt, the time at which he wrote was opportune. As a result of the Sino-Japanese victory, things Chinese were in low standing in Japanese eyes, and there were many foreigners then resident in Japan who could advise on the use of the western alphabet. Japan should capitalize on the opportunity to rid her written language of Chinese characters, but how was it to be done? Inoue considered the various options available.

He was not in accord with those who advocated a reduction in the number of characters. Chinese prose and poetry had a large following, and to reduce the number of characters would produce a deleterious effect on literature. Furthermore, future scientific developments would doubtless require complicated explanations, where characters would prove useful. It would be extremely difficult for even the government, let alone individual scholars, to prohibit further use of the accustomed medium of written expression. Using *kana* would not help the progress of Japanese culture; they resulted in prose of a length unacceptable to busy people, and they could not be used to represent all sounds. They could not, for example, distinguish between English 'l' and 'r', making it difficult to reproduce foreign names. The western alphabet, on the other hand, was ideal for this purpose, and would be particularly apt for foreign words in technical books. But it, too, had its pitfalls; the text became even more lengthy than when written in *kana*, requiring twice the number of symbols, and it was difficult to distinguish between homophones. Furthermore, Inoue wrote:

> Script develops along with the human mind and has a close connection with the history of the development of a people's spirit. It is therefore different from other foreign imports such as railways and steamships. Suddenly to abolish the script which has grown along with the development of ideas since our ancestors' times and replace it with the entirely different alphabet would be to destroy the inner foundation stone of the nation and do violence to the people's feelings.[11]

These difficulties had led to the decline of the Rōmaji Club, and had also given rise to a fourth proposal, which was to create a new script altogether; Shiratori Kōkan and Tanaka Hideho, for example, had suggested similar systems in which Chinese characters were combined with phonetic symbols.[12] Inoue himself, however, believed that it would be best to use an existing script, and suggested that *kana* letters would make a workable system if they were abbreviated, for instance

は to ま,

punctuated, and written horizontally to facilitate insertion of western scientific terms and names. Their one great advantage over the alphabet was that they halved the number of symbols needed.

Inoue's essay presented all sides of the problem in an impartial and thorough way. Perhaps better than any other, it summed up the need for a simplified script and presented the pros and cons of the alternatives. In the long run, as we know today, it was the policy of modification of the existing script which won out over the more radical suggestions for change. Chinese characters, despite their attendant difficulties, seemed preferable to other scripts by virtue of their semantic content and brevity, and also because of their long-standing tradition of use in Japan. Reduced in number and supplemented by *kana* script which had likewise undergone revision, they were moulded into an efficient means of writing Japanese, within the capabilities of anyone possessing a high-school education.

Paring down the number of Chinese characters came about initially through the Ministry of Education. In 1887, the *Jinjō Shōgakkō Chogen* (*Preparatory Remarks on Elementary Schools*) set the number to be used in primary-school textbooks at 2,000, a state of affairs which lasted until 1900, when the *Shōgakkō Rei Shikō Kisoku* (*Rules for the Enforcement of Elementary School Regulations*) further lowered the limit to 1,200. At the same time it decreed standardization of the *kana* syllabaries and replacement of the historical system of *kana* usage with the phonetic system earlier championed by the Kana Club's Snow Faction. This last decision proved unpopular with many, and was in fact countermanded eight years later, not to be revived until 1931 when the strength of public opinion again forced its postponement. It was not until 1946 that the government, in a post-war climate of reform more receptive to orthographic change than the also reform-oriented but less desperate situation of the Meiji Period, promulgated the rules for pronunciation-based *kana* usage which are employed today. At the same time, the National Language Council, a body set up by the government in 1934 to investigate ways of improving the language and promoting its teaching, presented a new list of 1,850 Chinese characters (the *tōyō* or 'currently-used' *kanji* list) which was also endorsed and adopted within a short time. This number was expanded to 1,945 in a 1981 revision, the present list being known as the *jōyō kanji* (characters for general use).[13]

The Meiji Period controversy over script reform was inevitable in the light of contemporary developments in Japanese society. While advocates of phonetic scripts may not have achieved their individual aims, they nevertheless performed a valuable service by drawing attention to the problem of Japan's unwieldy, élitist orthographic system. A further innovation during this period was the practice of punctuating Japanese texts, which had hitherto been either sketchily punctuated or not punctuated at all. No spaces separated words, which rendered the mainly *hiragana* classical Japanese style particularly difficult. To extract the sense of the passage, the reader had to recognise sentence finals and other grammatical signals indicating function. It is not uncommon to find page after page of texts of this period almost totally without punctuation or punctuated only by commas and full stops. Where these last *were* in evidence, there does not appear to have been any rigorous convention governing their use. Examination of nineteenth-century government documents, scholarly texts,[14] and novels shows that in some cases the symbols , and . were used to indicate clause and sentence boundaries respectively; in others, the symbol . fulfilled both functions; sometimes commas were used for both, varying the size from that ordinarily used today to others so small as to be barely visible. Often, long sentences were broken up with commas but contained no full stops. Documents written in pure *kambun* or *sōrōbun* were in many cases not punctuated at all. Paragraphing was often non-existent, or at least rudimentary, which meant that readers of Chinese-style texts in particular were faced with solid blocks of characters unrelieved by visual variation.

While it may be argued that no more than basic clause, sentence, and paragraph separation are needed in official documents, the same cannot be said of the novel, where dialogue and narrative need separation and where effective punctuation gives life to the text. Figure 2.10 is an extract from *By Shanks' Pony Through the West* (1870–76) by Kanagaki Robun (1829-1894). Its only punctuation is quotation marks to indicate dialogue embedded in the body of the narrative; this is true of the entire work with the exception of English words rendered in *katakana* which are separated from each other by full stops.[15]

In this area, as in many others, the need for reform was highlighted by exposure to the west. Those who came in contact with western prose could not help noticing, in addition to the clarity and versatility of its colloquial style and the conciseness and simplicity of its alphabet, the ease which punctuation imparted to the deciphering of its content. The first attempt at breaking Japanese prose into less formidable blocks took the form of word spacing. With the exception of the authors of Dutch and English language textbooks, the first to write phonetic script in such a fashion was Shimizu Usaburō. Shimizu, as we have seen, believed that Chinese characters should be replaced entirely with the *hiragana* script. His main concern was with the rapid dissemination of new knowledge; he felt that this could be greatly facilitated by simplifying script as well as style. A major problem in using the

252 *Language and the Modern State*

kana script was its lack of any visual method of signalling word boundaries. Shimizu demonstrated that this could be simply overcome by spacing words in the western manner in *Expert Opinion on Coal from Kishu* (1869), and later in *The Ladder of Physics*, (1874), a three-volume translation of a German science primer. Figure 9.1 is an example from the former, in which even postpositions indicating the syntactic function of the preceding word are separated from their head nouns.

Another who adopted the device of spacing words in *kana* prose was Watanabe Shūjirō (1855–1945), who had studied English and became eventually a renowned historian. He gave an example in *Nihombun o Seitei suru Hōhō* (*Steps to Regulating Written Japanese*, 1875) of how he thought *kana* should be written, suggesting the use of *katakana* (in a *hiragana* text) to indicate capital letters in personal and place names, and the insertion of commas and full

Figure 9.1 Western punctuation in Shimizu Usaburō's 'Kishūsan Sekitan Kantei no Setsu' ('Expert Opinion on Coal from Kishu')

Source: Shimizu Usaburō, 'Kishūsan Sekitan Kantei no Setsu', *Chūgai Shimbun*, 26 August 1869. *Meiji Bunka Zenshū V. 4 Shimbun-hen* (3rd edn), Tokyo: Nihon Hyōronsha, 1968, p. 435.
Note: For translation see Appendix.

stops. The Japanese should adopt European grammar as a model, he asserted with a fine disregard for the difference between grammar and orthography; they should emulate its best features, such as punctuation, paragraphing, parenthesis, dashes, and quotation marks. Unlike Shimizu, Watanabe was content to preach and did not practise his theories in his own prose, preferring to write in the traditional mode to which he had been educated. In the very early years of the Meiji Period, few of the scholars who espoused script and style reform actually departed from custom in their own essays, perhaps fearing the thrust of their argument would be lost in the scorn bound to be attracted from the intelligentsia at large by such departures.

One of the first areas in which these new ideas were put to the tests was, of course, education. The first use of punctuation outside translations of western literature was in a primary reader, *E-iri Chie no Wa* (*An Illustrated Puzzle Ring*, 1872), written by Dutch studies scholar and Enlightenment writer Furukawa Masao, who used full stops and commas. These symbols were later used in *Shōgaku Kyōjusho* (*Primary Textbook*), published by the Education Ministry in 1873, and in Tanaka Yoshikado's *Shōgaku Nihon Bunten* (*Japanese Grammar for Primary Schools*, 1874–75). Tanaka (1841–79), a scholar of the west, was appointed head of the Education Ministry's editorial office for Normal School textbooks in 1872. His book was a conscious imitation of English grammars, hence his adoption of the punctuation he found therein. *Japanese Grammar for Primary Schools* was written in a variety of Japanese characterised by heavy use of Sino-Japanese items which were conventionally associated with the rendering of Chinese-style texts into Japanese; texts of this type were normally left unpunctuated.

The following decade saw several instances of the advocacy and practical application of punctuation. Miyake Yonekichi (1860–1929), secretary to the Kana Club, called in *Bun no Kakikata ni tsuite* (*On Writing*, 1884) for the use of commas and full stops. Mozume Takami, while making no actual reference in the text of his 1886 *Gembun'itchi* to the need for punctuation, used commas and full stops liberally to clarify its meaning. That same year Suematsu Kenchō, politician and scholar who had studied for eight years in England, suggested in *Nihon Bunshōron* (*On Written Japanese*) that those who advocated replacing Chinese characters altogether with *hiragana* should use word spacing, capitals, and western-style punctuation to improve their texts. His views were echoed by Nishi Tomisada, physicist and leading member of the Dai Nihon Kyōikukai, in *Nihon Futsūbun no Zento* (*The Outlook for Written Japanese*, 1888). In *Nihon Futsūbun Dō* (*The Future of Written Japanese*, 1887), Shimpo Iwatsugu, a member of the Kinkōdō publishing firm who had earlier published the first colloquial-style primary textbook, suggested the use of punctuation as part of an overall progression towards a simple colloquial style, claiming that under the current system what stops were used at all were simply inserted after a certain set of number of characters regardless of meaning. Shimpo experimented with applying full stops and commas to the *Records of Ancient Matters* and other Japanese classics, and went on to illustrate his theory further in a primary school reader, *Nihon Tokuhon* (*Japanese Reader*, 1886). Two other school texts experimenting with punctuation at this time were Nakagawa Kenjirō's *Rika Tokuhon* (*Science Reader*, 1886) and Nishi Tomisada's *Yōgaku Tokuhon* (*Children's Reader*, 1887), both of which used commas, full stops, paragraph indentations, and large characters to begin each sentence. Nishi also used capitals for names.

Thus, thanks to the urging of men involved in western studies who realized that the success of colloquial style in western countries was due in part to the convenient division of writing into manageable segments, the practice of punctuating texts slowly gained a foothold in Japan. Much more influential in its eventual spread than the early scholars, however, were the novelists who began to use the colloquial style as a necessary adjunct to the new realistic fiction which appeared in the mid-1880s. Futabatei went so far as to attempt in his colloquial translations of Russian literature to reproduce the exact punctuation of the original:

> In translating foreign literature, one runs the risk of spoiling the original if one concentrates only on meaning. I myself was convinced of the necessity to grasp and reproduce the rhythm of the original text; I therefore did not dispense arbitrarily with even a single comma or period. If there were three commas and one period in the original, then I put the same into my translation, in an effort to convey its tone. When I first began doing a translation, in particular, I expended considerable effort on the matter of form, even going so far as to use the same number of words as the original in an effort to reproduce the rhythm with absolute fidelity; but this did not go at all as I

hoped, and there were times when I could not meet my own standards.[16]

The text of *The Drifting Cloud* itself, which appeared in three volumes, was sparsely punctuated in Volume 1, but better punctuated in the later volumes, with dialogue separated from narrative on separate lines as well as by quotation marks (see Figure 5.1). Futabatei's prose in the first volume showed frequent traces still of traditional literary styles, and no doubt this affected his attempts at punctuation too. When he became more proficient at using colloquial style in Volumes 2 and 3, which he patterned after the prose of Dostoevsky and Goncharov, his punctuation also became more complex. His diary for 1888, *Kuchibashū: Hitokagome* (*A Collection of Dead Leaves: First Basket*), is written in literary style and punctuated by only a few commas, lacking even full stops. By contrast, 'Yo ga Hansei no Zange' ('Confessions of Half a Lifetime'), an autobiographical essay published twenty years later in 1908, is replete with paragraph indentations, commas, full stops, dashes, lines of dots to suggest reflection, quotation marks, and exclamation marks.

Another who incorporated European punctuation into his novels was Yamada Bimyō, who began writing colloquial-style works at about the same time as Futabatei. His first published attempt at the new style was *The Conceited Demon*, an unfinished work published in 1886 in *Trash Library*, the journal of the Ken'yūsha group. Its extremely long and sparsely punctuated sentences were reminiscent of those of Tokugawa Period light fiction, but Bimyō did introduce certain forms of punctuation which had not been seen in a Japanese work before, separating dialogue and narrative with the symbol = and using the device .... to suggest admiration or lingering memories. In later works he adopted with enthusiasm all forms of European punctuation, including abbreviation, dashes, exclamation marks, question marks, and quotation marks, as well as the basic comma and full stop.

The use of punctuation in Japanese fiction accelerated from then on in direct proportion to the adoption of the colloquial style by Meiji Period authors. Because the one major drawback to the colloquial style was its wordiness by comparison with the much more concise Chinese style, it was essential that it be controlled and shaped by orthographic devices, and authors continued to hammer out a system of punctuation appropriate to Japanese as a necessary corollary to their successful use of *gembun'itchi*. The text of *I am a*

Cat (1905) by Natsume Sōseki (1867–1916), one of the most famous authors of this period, is studded with question marks, quotation marks, dashes, and lines of dots to indicate fragmented speech, in addition to the standard commas and full stops. Paragraphs are indented. In some sections dialogue and narrative are separated, with dialogue beginning on a new line; in others, Sōseki reverts to the older practice of leaving dialogue in the body of the narrative, separated only by quotation marks. *The Broken Commandment* (1906) by Shimazaki Tōson, a prominent writer of the Naturalist school, is similarly embellished, with the added refinement that Tōson used full stops as well as quotation marks to end sections of dialogue whereas Sōseki did not, relying instead on the closing quotation mark alone to indicate the end of an utterance. By that time the practice of punctuation was well established, and later writers continued to use it both as an indication of the sense of their text and as an aid in stamping their own individual styles upon the written language.

Not all European devices were adopted. Inverted commas as used to indicate quotation in the west were not appropriate in Japan, where the addition of " next to the top right-hand corner of certain of the phonetic symbols denoted a change from unvoiced to voiced consonant. In their place were used the symbols 「」. Nor was the use of capitals more than a passing fad among those who advocated replacing Chinese characters entirely with phonetic script; while it may have been possible in an all-phonetic text, it would have made typesetting a nightmare in the script situation which actually existed. Word spacing was not generally adopted; it is found today only in certain elementary textbooks, children's fairytales meant to be used as first readers, and some elementary Japanese language textbooks for foreigners. Despite these exceptions, however, once established, the practice of punctuating texts accompanied the use of colloquial style as it gradually spread from fiction to other areas of written Japanese, until by 1925 both had become permanent features in both education and journalism. While script reform had taken a different direction from that envisaged by Meiji Period proponents of *rōmaji* and *kana*, the face of written Japanese had by that time, irrespective of the influence of colloquial style, changed markedly for the better owing to restrictions on the number of Chinese characters and improved spatial organization of the text through punctuation.

Conclusion

After the post-war reforms of legal and official terminology, colloquial style held undisputed sway in textbooks, novels, newspapers, magazines, discursive and critical essays and books, official communications, and other forms of writing in common circulation in society. In substance, the desire of the early reformers for a simple, versatile, utilitarian style had been fulfilled, at least in so far as the written language was now officially based on the grammar of the contemporary spoken language, although nobody familiar with discursive intellectual writing in Japanese today would doubt that Japanese scholars still retain a fondness for obscurity, colloquial style notwithstanding.

The development of colloquial style was in no way the result of a natural evolutionary process, but rather a revolutionary reform undertaken deliberately as a result of exposure to the west. Had Japan remained in isolation under a feudal system, the commoner would have remained unimportant in the social order, education would have continued the privilege of the upper class, prohibition on the publication of information relating to government would have prevented the development of the serious press, and élitist attitudes to the function and status of writing would have persevered. Moves towards language reform were prompted by two things: observation of western practices, and growing awareness in the wake of social changes consequent upon the beginning of modernization that difficult classical literary conventions understood by only one section of society were not appropriate in times when mobilization of the entire populace for the national effort was essential. It became further apparent that before a single readily-understood mode of expression could be established as the norm across the nation, the issue of standardization must be addressed.

On the orthographic front, something had to be done about rationalizing the script situation and simplifying the reading process through improved spatial organization of texts by punctuation. Early reformers approached the issue initially from each of these perspectives in isolation, only gradually coming to realize that script and style reform were interdependent and that no effective style reform could be achieved without standardization.

The two most important facilitators of debate on the issue in the Meiji Period were the Ministry of Education and the press, both areas charged with informing the public. Many Education Ministers – Ōki, Mori, and Kikuchi, for example – were committed to language reform in one form or another. The National Language Research Council was set up under the auspices of the Ministry, and the expanded use of colloquial style in the subsequent first and second series of state primers put paid to the supremacy of *futsūbun* in school texts, disseminating colloquial style based on the Tokyo dialect as the standard form of written expression throughout the classrooms of Japan. In the serious press, the case both for and against language reform in various manifestations was thrashed out by intellectuals, while the popular and party-affiliated political press of the civil rights era demonstrated colloquial style in practice, albeit for partisan reasons not inspired by any overarching concern for language reform *per se*.

Although early advocates of style reform had broadly advocated that writing be made identical with speech, thus attracting much criticism from those who feared that what they perceived as the verbosity and 'vulgarity' of the spoken language would translate ill onto paper, time and experience revealed the pitfalls of this approach. It became obvious that despite the existence of colloquial style in European languages there still remained differences between written and spoken expression, made inevitable because of the nature of the two. Whereas in speech much could be conveyed by look, gesture, and tone of voice, in writing every word had to be included to make the meaning clear, resulting in unacceptable length. Slang terms used in speech were also not considered acceptable in public writing. Later reformers therefore came to realize that what was needed was not just colloquial style but a polished form of colloquial style, based on the spoken language but with the rough edges smoothed. They therefore bent their endeavours to achieving this aim, in the process silencing critics who attacked these aspects. Given that the merit of writing had for so long been judged on its artifice rather than on utilitarian value, it was particularly important to overcome prejudices against the mundane nature of colloquial style by demonstrating the extent to which it could be refined and improved before widespread acceptance was possible.

The bulk of the work of fashioning the new style into an acceptably polished medium was carried out by novelists of the new schools of fiction which emerged after 1887, in particular by the *shaseibun*, Naturalist, and Shirakaba schools of the first two decades of this century. The contribution made by these writers to the language modernization process cannot be stressed too heavily; by modelling the desired norm in fiction and by ridding it of its perceived defects, they did much both to increase public awareness of the issue through practical demonstration and later to overcome oppositions from critics. It was of course to their own benefit to do so, colloquial style being the only conceivable medium for the modern novel of psychological realism, so that a mutually dependent relationship existed between the novel and the process of style reform.

The significance of Japan's victory in the Sino-Japanese war likewise cannot be underrated. As a direct result of the consequent resurgence of interest in the flagging language issue because the language was now to be used outside Japan, men like Ueda Kazutoshi seized the opportunity to work on the emotive subject of pride in the national language to persuade the government to take a hand in co-ordinating and determining future developments in language planning. By that time, considerable headway had already been made in putting forward colloquial style as the most appropriate solution to what was by then generally recognized to be the problem of the inadequacy of the written language. The National Language Research Council built on these initiatives and attempted to establish a series of priorities for further action after empirical research. Whereas earlier individuals and groups had proceeded independently towards the same goal, the Council now provided an overarching framework of co-ordinated bureaucratic support for the attainment of that goal. Without the boost to support for language reform as a matter of national pride supplied by victory over China, a longer time may have elapsed before the government was convinced to intervene. Pressure groups such as the Linguistics Society and the Gembun'itchi Club were instrumental in accelerating the process by utilising the patriotic aspect.

Deliberation is perhaps the word which best sums up the hallmarks of the search for an answer to the problem. For the first time, people took thought in working towards the goal of developing and applying a style which would suit the needs of their own time rather than being restrained by a straitjacket of classicism. Older styles had been accepted in their ossified forms for so long that concerted examination of the way people wrote was something new. True, *gikobun* had involved a discussion of language and a planned return to classical Japanese by classical scholars, but it had been supported only by one section of the intelligentsia. In the Meiji Period, however, after initial shock at the idea of change had begun to abate somewhat, the question of a new style became a matter of interest for the intellectual community at large. Whether for or against, educated people debated this subject widely, and the concept of planned language reform took root, with consensus eventually being reached that some form of rationalization was desirable. Without this widespread background concern for simplification, the modernization of the written language would of course have proceeded more slowly than it did. Once the desirability of reform was established, however, the issue of whether the solution should take the form of colloquial style or *futsūbun* generated intense interest, and it was this climate of general interest which enabled proponents of colloquial style to obtain the government support necessary to the realization of their goal. In the end, it was the support of intellectuals which brought about the change rather than any groundswell of opinion from society at large.

If one accepts that the dissemination of information is essential to modernization, then it is clear that the modernization of the written language in Japan played an important, if somewhat delayed, role in facilitating the educatory process. It is clear from the comments of educators even as late as 1900 that much time was spent in schools grappling with the difficulties of form before content could be understood and absorbed. Once these difficulties were resolved, the hours saved could be spent in the pursuit of more profitable knowledge. Likewise the information contained in the pages of the press became freely available to the literate public with the removal of those modes of expression which had earlier hindered comprehension. In this sense the development of colloquial style with its satellite concerns of standardization and orthographic reform may be said to have played a pivotal role in opening up participation in public life to the ordinary Japanese.

Appendix

FIGURE 2.2 VARIETIES OF *KAMBUN*

Mencius answered, 'Your Majesty loves war. Allow me to illustrate with a military example. The drums are beating loudly, and battle has been joined. Two soldiers abandon their armour and run off, trailing their weapons. One stops after a hundred paces, one after fifty. If he who took only fifty were to jeer at him who took one hundred, what would you think?'

The King said, 'It would be wrong. He may not have taken a hundred paces, but he too ran away.'

2.2 (a) and (b)

Maushi	kotahete	iwaku	'Ō		tatakahi o
Mencius	answered and	said	'The king		war

konomu.	Kofu	tatakahi o	motte	tatohen.
loves.	I beg	war	using	illustrate.

Tenzentoshite	koshi,	heijin	sude ni
Loudly	drum, and	soldiers	already

sessu.	Kou o	sute	hei o
make contact.	Armour	abandon, and	weapons

hikite	hashiru.	Aruiwa	hyakuho	ni shite
drag, and	run.	One	hundred paces	taking

nochi	todomari,	aruiwa	gojūho	ni shite	nochi
then	stop, and	one	fifty paces	taking	then

todomaru.	Gojūho	o motte	hyakuho o
stop.	Fifty paces	on account of	hundred paces

warawaba,	sunawachi	ikan'	to.	Keiō
(if they) laugh at,	then	how'	he said.	King

iwaku,	'Fuka	nari.	Tada	hyakuho
said,	'Wrong	it is.	Only	hundred paces

narazaru	nomi.	Kore	mo	mata	hashiru
is not	only.	This	too	also	to run

nari'	to.
is'	he said.

2.2 (c)

Mōshi ga	(keiō ni)	okotae shite	itta.	'Ō wa
Mencius	king to	answered, and	said	'Your majesty

tatakai ga	osuki desu.	Dōzo	tatakai no	koto
war	loves.	Please,	military	thing

de motte	tatoesasete	kudasai.	Dondon to
by means	allow me to	illustrate.	Rub-a-dub

shingeki no	taiko ga	uchinarasare	(ryōgun no)
assault's	drums	are sounded, and	both armies

buki ga	majiwatte iru	saichū	desu.	(Sono toki
weapons	joining	in the midst	are.	Just then

futari no	heishi ga)	yoroi o	nagesutete,	buki o
two	soldiers	armour	threw away, and	weapons

hikizutte	nigedashimashita.	Hitori wa	hyakuho
dragging	ran away.	One	hundred paces

nigete	kara	tomari,	mata	aru	hito wa
fleeing	after	stopped, and	also	a certain	person

gojūho	nigete	kara	tomarimashita.	Sono toki,
fifty paces	fleeing	after	stopped.	Then

ippō no	hito ga	gojūho	shika	nigenakatta
one	person	fifty paces	only	fled

to iu riyū de,	(sono hito ga)	hyakuho	nigete shimatta
because	that person	hundred paces	fled

hito o	waratta	to shitara	dō	deshō?'
person	laughed at	suppose that	how	would it be?'

Keiō wa	itta.	'Ikenai.	Tada	hyakuho
The king	said.	'Wrong.	Only	hundred paces

(nigeta no)	de nakatta	dake	da.	Kono	hito
fled	was not	only	it is.	This	person

datte	onaji yō ni	nigete iru no da.'
also	in the same way	has run away.'

FIGURE 2.3 *SŌRŌBUN* IN MAEJIMA'S PETITION 'KANJI GOHAISHI NO GI' ('PROPOSAL FOR THE ABOLITION OF CHINESE CHARACTERS')

A proposal of this kind seems irrelevant in the extreme at a time when national affairs are pressing and people are scrambling to devise emergency measures. I hesitate to ask for your august attention to it; and yet because I believe that it will be hereafter of the utmost importance for Japan to be able to take her place alongside the other great powers, I venture to tender it despite my misgivings.

To simplify learning and to administer a common education is to open up the people's intelligence and to develop their minds. It is the initial gateway to all arts and reasoning. Therefore, I request your aid in order to accomplish this as simply, quickly, and widely as possible.

Mokka	onkokuji	gotatan	ni shite	hitobito
Now	national affairs	pressing	are, and	men

kisotte	kyūkyūsaku o	kōzuru	no sai,	kono gotoki
vying	emergency measures	devise	when,	this sort of

gi o	gonjō tsukamatsuri sōrō wa	hanahada	uen ni
proposal	I tender (humble)	very	circuitous

nite	gokeichō	oki kudasare sōrō	hodo mo
seems, and	close attention	give (polite)	state of affairs

ikaga	goza aru ka	to	habakari-iri
how	would it be?	that	hesitatingly

zonji tatematsuri sōraedomo,	mikuni o shite	hoka no
although I think (humble),	Japan	other

reikyō	to	heiritsu seshimerare sōrō wa	kore yori
powers	with	cause to stand alongside	hereafter

jū	katsu	dai naru wa	korenaki ya ni
important	moreover	serious	will it not be

zonji tatematsuri sōrō	ni tsuki	kaerimizu	kyōku
I think (humble)	because	in spite of	trepidation

aete	gonjō tatematsuri sōrō.	Gakuji o	kan
boldly	I tender (humble).	Learning	simple

ni shi	futsū	kyōiku o	hodokosu wa
make, and	common	education	administer

kokujin no	chishiki o	kaidō shi,	seishin o
people's	intelligence	open up, and	mind

hattatsu shi,	dōri	geijutsu	hyappan	ni okeru
develop, and	reasoning	arts	all kinds	in

shoho no mon	ni shite	kokka	fukyō o
first steps' gate	is, and	nation	wealth and strength

nasu no	soji	ni goza sōraeba,	narubeku
form	foundation stone	since it is,	as ... as possible

kan'i ni	narubeku	hiroku	katsu
simply	as .. as possible	widely	moreover

narubeku	sumiyaka ni	yukitodoki sōrō	yō
as .. as possible	quickly	accomplish fully	in order to

osewa	goza aritai	koto ni	zonji tatematsuri sōrō.
your aid	desirable	thing	I think (humble).

FIGURE 2.4 *SŌRŌBUN* IN AN OFFICIAL GOVERNMENT NOTICE, *CHŪGAI SHIMBUN*, 3 APRIL 1868

Proclamation to those in the Ueno temple compound

We wish to advise that word has come from the Kakuōin to the effect that the Prince is extremely grateful for the loyal exertions of the Shōgitai and their patrolling of this temple, and that he has since placed himself in the hands of the authorities.

Ueno sannai	e no	fukokusho	Shōgitai	chūgi
Ueno temple	to	proclamation	Shōgitai	loyalty
fumpatsu	narabi ni	tōgosan	moromuki	
exertions	and	this temple	in all directions	
gokeiei	ni tsuki	sekishin no	jōjō	
patrolling	with regard to	sincere	everything	
miyasama	gyokan	asakarazu		
prince	appreciation	is not superficial, and		
irai	osore-ōku-mo	sontai	tōkyoku	
since then	graciously	himself	the authorities	
e	goinin asobasaresōrō	dan	gosata no	
to	entrusts (polite)	inasmuch as	royal words'	
omomuki	kakuōin	yori	aitassare sōrō	aida
effect, gist	the Kakuōin	from	is notified	as
kono dan		kaitatsu ni oyobisōrō.		
regarding this matter		we advise.		

FIGURE 2.5 *SŌRŌBUN* IN A LETTER PUBLISHED IN THE *CHŪGAI SHIMBUN*, 6 APRIL 1868

The exposition ended on the eighth of October last. The sovereigns of various countries came to France to see it. Three Austrian princes were staying here at the time, so there were military drills to watch. There were three armies, with a total of 50,000 men. Among them were 10,000 cavalry, and 100 cannons. It was a remarkable affair.

Hakurankai mo	saru	jūgatsu	yōka
Exposition	last	October	eighth

owari ni ainari mōshi sōrō.	Hakurankai	ni tsuki
ended.	Exposition	because of

shokoku no	teiō	tōkoku	e
various countries'	sovereigns,	this country	to

mairaresōrō.	Tōji	ōchiri	teikyōdai	sannin
came (polite).	At the time	Austria	princes	three

tōryū itasaresōrō	ni tsuki,	chōren	ichiran
stayed (polite)	because,	military drill	sights

ni ainarisōrō.	Sampei	awasete	gomannin
there were.	Three armies	altogether	50,000 people

sono uchi	kikei	ichiman	taihō	hyakuchō
among them	cavalry	10,000	cannons	100

koreari,	mezamashiki	koto	ni gozasōrō.
there were, and	remarkable	thing	it was.

FIGURE 2.6 TWO VERSIONS OF A *SŌRŌBUN* LETTER BY FUKUZAWA YUKICHI, THE FIRST ABSTRUSE, THE SECOND REWRITTEN FOR CLARITY

(a) Original

I idled away three or four years in the above-mentioned circumstances. At present I have no means of making my own living, and have been a dependant in the house of an old friend since spring. His wife, however, is discourteous in her treatment of me. This secretly fills me with indignation; I want to leave, but there is nobody else I can turn to. I am utterly perplexed and discomfited. I beg you to look upon my situation with compassion and recommend me for some suitable government post. Actually, I hope for an imperially-approved appointment; a bird in distress has no time to choose a branch, however, and so for the time being I would naturally not decline a position as gate-keeper or night-watchman. As I wish to receive an appointment, however humble, I earnestly implore your good offices.

Migi no	shidai	nite	itazura ni
Above-mentioned	circumstances	in	idly

sanyonnen no	seisō o	sugi	jikon ni itatte wa
3 or 4 years	time	pass, and	at present

isshin	kakkei no	hōhō	mo	naku
self	livelihood's	means	even	don't have, and

shunrai	kyūyū no	ie	ni	shokkaku
since spring	old friend's	house	in	a dependant

ainari orisōrō	tokoro	naijitsu wa	dōke no
I am	although	in fact	the house's

saikun	kyaku o	taigū suru ni	rei o	shisshi
wife	guest	to treat	courtesy	lacks, and

boku	hisokani	fumman ni	taezu	saredomo
I	secretly	indignantly	constantly	am, although

ima	saran	to hosshite	hoka ni	irai subeki
now	to leave	wanting	other	can ask

tokoro mo	naku	shintai	ikoku no
place	there is not, and	utterly	perplexed

baai	ni ochi-iri	tōwaku no	shidai	ni sōrō.
situation	fall into, and	discomfited	state	in I am.

Nanitozo	migi no	jōjitsu	bizen
Kindly	the above-mentioned	circumstances	pity

oboshimesare	shikaru beki	kanto	e
think, and	suitable	government post	to

gosuikyo kudasaretaku	jitsu wa
I want you to recommend (polite), and	actually

sōnin	ijō o	kibō itashi sōraedomo
Emperor-approved appointment	above	I hope for, but

sashimuki no tokoro	kyūchō	eda o	erabu ni
for the time being	bird in distress	branch	to choose

itoma	arazareba	hōkan	gekitaku
time to spare	does not have, so	gatekeeper	night-watchman

motoyori	jisuru	tokoro ni arazu	tōgai shusshi
of course	to refuse	am not in a position, and	junior official

nitemo	tsutsushinde	haimei tsukamatsuritaku sōrō	aida
even	humbly	I wish to be appointed	as

ikue nimo	goshūsen	negaitatematsurisōrō nari.
earnestly	your kind offices	I implore (humble).

(b) Rewrite

I idled away three or four years in the above-mentioned circumstances. At present I have no means of making my own living, and since spring I have been a dependant in the house of a friend. His wife, however, regards me with disfavour. This secretly angers me very much, but there is nowhere else I can go. I am at a loss as to what to do. I hope that you will take pity on me and intercede for a good position as a government official for me. Actually, I hope for a good salary, but for the time being I am not in a position to dictate terms and am willing to work even as a gatekeeper or caretaker. I therefore earnestly implore your help.

Migi no	shidai	nite	itazura ni
Above-mentioned	circumstances	in	idly

san, yonnen o	sugoshi	tadaima	to narite wa
3 or 4 years	passing, and	this point in time	reaching

dokushin no	yowatari	ni	mo	komari
single	livelihood	for	too	am in difficulties, and

haru	irai	tomodachi no	ie	ni
spring	since	friend's	house	in

isōrō itashisōrō	tokoro	kanai	ni
I live at his expense	although	wife	by

ahiso o tsukasare	watashi	mo	kokoro no
am regarded with disfavour	I	too	heart's

uchi	ni wa	rippuku itashisōraedomo	imasara
interior	in	am angry, but	now

doko	e	to mōshi	yorisugaru beki	saki mo
where	to	say, and	can depend	destination even

naku		tohō ni kuresōrō	shidai	nanitozo	aware
do not have, and		I am at a loss	state	kindly	pity

to oboshimesare	yoki	yakunin no	kuchi
think, and	good	government official's	position

e	ontorimochi	kudasaretaku
to	your good offices	I want you to give (polite), and

jitsu wa	kyūkin no	ōki hō o	nozomisōraedomo
actually	wages'	a lot	I hope, but

sashimuki no tokoro	kane no	tashō o	mōsu beki
for the time being	money's	amount	can say

baai	ni	korenaku	momban	nitemo
circumstances	in	I am not, and	gatekeeper	even

kozukai	nitemo	kurushikarazusōrō	aida
caretaker	even	I am at liberty to do	as

ikue nimo	onsewa	negaitatematsurisōrō nari
earnestly	your help	I implore (humble).

FIGURE 2.7 WABUN WRITTEN IN THE EARLY MEIJI PERIOD

There once lived some frogs in a certain pond who did just as they pleased in all things, outdoing each other in their tolerant behaviour. In time, they began to have difficulty controlling themselves, and so one day they gathered together, looked up to heaven, and begged in unison, 'Grant us a good leader to govern us'. The gods, hearing this, laughed at the futility of it, and threw down a log from heaven.

Mukashi	aru	ike	ni	kahiru	sumite
Once	a certain	pond	in	frogs	lived, and

nanigoto mo	yuruyaka ni	kokoro makase	narikeru
everything	leniently	their own way	was

ni	tagai ni	gaman no	furumai	masarite,
since	mutually	tolerant	behaviour	excel at, and

tsuhi ni	osamarigataku	narikereba	aru
in time	difficult to control themselves	as it became	one

hi	kaherura	aiatsumari,	ama o
day	the frogs	gathered together and	heaven

aoide	morotomo ni	'wagatomogara o
looking up to	all together,	'us

subehiki yubeki	yoki	shujin o	tamaware'	to, negahiuttahe
can govern	good	leader	grant'	pleading

mōshitari.	Tenshin	kore o	kikitamahi,	yaku mo naki
said.	The gods	this	hearing (polite)	useless

koto	nari	to waratte,	tada	ippon no	maruhashira o
thing	is	laughed, and	single	one	log

tenjō	yori	nagekudashi tamafu.
heaven	from	threw down (polite).

FIGURE 2.8 A PASSAGE FROM IHARA SAIKAKU

'This is the first I have heard of it. It must be so,' he said. When he saw the corpse, it was that of the woman he was seeking. 'This!' he cried, clutching her tightly, 'What fate has brought us together in such bitter circumstances! If I hadn't taken you with me this would not have happened. This is all my fault.' Dissolving into tears, he writhed in anguish. Strangely, the woman opened her eyes, smiled, and then became again as she had been. 'I have lived twenty-nine years — I have no regrets!' he cried. His two companions restrained him from killing himself, and took him home. In that they showed good sense.

'Ima	made	shiranu	koto	nari	Samo
Now	until	unknown	thing	it is.	So

arubeshi'	to	shibito o	mireba	waga
it must be'	(he said)	corpse	when he saw	I

tazunuru	onna,	'Kore wa'	to
seek	woman	'This'	(he cried)

shigamitsuki,	'Kakaru	ukime	ni
clutching tightly, and	'Such	bitter circumstances	in

afu	koto,	ikanaru	inguwa no	mawarikeru zo
meet	that we...	what	fate	has turned?

Sono	toki	tsurete	nokazuba
That	time	together	if we had not left

samonaki	o,	kore	mina	waga
it would not be like this	since,	this	all	I

nasu	waza'	to,	namida	ni	kurete
do	deed'	(he said)	tears	into	dissolve, and

mimodae suru.	Fushigiya	kono	onna	ryō no
he writhed in anguish.	Strangely	this	woman	both

manako o	mihiraki	warahigao shite,	mamonaku
eyes	opening wide, and	smile, and	soon

mata	moto no	gotoku	narinu.	'Nijūkyū
again	as it was	like	became.	'Twenty-nine

made no	ichigo,	nani	omohinokosaji'	to
as far as	span of life	what	do not regret'	(he said)

jigai o suru o,	futari no	mono	iroiro
commit suicide	two	people	in various ways

oshitodomete	kaeru.	Fumbetsudokoro	nari.
restrain, and	went home.	Good sense	it is.

FIGURE 2.9 A PASSAGE FROM JIPPENSHA IKKU

Here a one-sided street of tea-houses, all of them two-storied and with balustraded flying galleries, commanded a fine view of the sea. Women stood at their gates, crying, 'Come in and rest! We have warmed-up cold rice! Cooled hot fish! Try our thick *soba*! Our *udon* is the fattest! Come in and rest!'

Koko wa	katagawa	ni	chaya	noki o
Here	one side	on	tea-houses	eaves

narabe		izuremo	zashiki	nikai
line up next to each other, and		all	rooms	2-storey

zukuri,	rankan tsuki no	rōka kakehashi	nado
construction,	balustraded	flying galleries	and so on

watashite	namiuchigiwa no	keishoku	itatte	yoshi.
crossing, and	waves	view	very	fine.

Chaya no	onna	kado	ni	tatte
Tea-houses'	women	gates	at	stand, and

'oyasuminasai yaase.	Attakkana	hiyameshi	mo
'come in and rest.	Warmed-up	rice	too

gozaiyaasu.	Nitate no	sakana no	sameta no
we have.	Boiled	fish	cooled down ones

mo	gozaiyaasu.	Soba no	futoi	no o
too	we have.	Buckwheat noodles	thick	ones

agariyaase.	Udon no	otsuki na	no	mo
eat.	Wheat noodles	thick	ones	too

gozaiyaasu.	Oyasuminasaiyaase.'
we have.	Come in and rest.'

FIGURE 2.10 *GAZOKU SETCHŪBUN* OF THE EARLY MEIJI PERIOD

We set sail from Shanghai (also known as Sanhai or Shanhai) and were able to make landfall in the English colony of Hong Kong after a voyage of four days. Hong Kong is a small island to the south-east of China. It is no more than a rocky mountain five *ri* wide and three *ri* long; vegetation is sparse, and there is no flat ground. It originally belonged to China, but since the English took it over recently they have by degrees moved in their houses, opened trading posts, built churches, and established schools. The population has gradually increased, and it has become a prosperous port.

Shina no	jaukai	(sanhai	tomomata	shanhai
China's	Shanghai	(sanhai	also called	Shanhai

tomo) o	shuppan shite	eiryōnaru	honkon
also called	set sail from, and	English territory	Hong Kong

made	funaji	yokka	nite	chakusubeshi
to	voyage	4 days	within	were able to arrive

somo	honkon wa	shina no	tōnan no	kata
!.	Hong Kong	China's	south-eastern	direction

ni	aru	kojima	nari	nagasa	go ri
in	which is	small island	is.	length	5 ri

haba	sanri	iwayama		nomi	nite
width	3 ri	a rocky mountain		only	it is, and

kusaki	sukunaku	hirachi	nashi
vegetation	is sparse, and	flat ground	there is no.

Moto	kara no	ryauchi	narishi	ga
Originally	China's	territory	it was	but

chikagoro	igirisu	ryau	to narishi	yori
in recent times	England	territory	it became	since

eijin	ohiohi	sumai o	utsushi
the English	by degrees	dwellings	move, and

kauekiba o	hiraki	tera o	tate
trading posts	open, and	churches	build, and

gakumonjo o	mōkete	hito no	kazu	mo
schools	establish and	people's	numbers	also

shidai ni	mashi	hanjau no	minato
gradually	increase, and	prosperous	port

to nareri.
it has become.

FIGURE 3.1 COLLOQUIAL STYLE IN A RECORDED SERMON OF SHIBATA KYŪŌ

His parents were not stupid but how wrong they had been about their child. When the document of disinheritance reached the old couple, the mother began to sob loudly. The father, clenching toothless gums, hung his head low. Soon he said, in a choked voice, 'Old lady, get the seal'. The mother could not answer. Weeping, she took the seal in its leather wallet from a drawer in the cupboard and put it in front of her husband. Outside the shutters their good-for-nothing son peeped in with bated breath. Inside his father slowly undid the wallet's string and took out the seal. Just as he was about to affix the seal, the mother grasped his hand and said, 'Wait, I beg you wait!'

Hito no	oya no	kokoro wa	yami	ni
His	parent's	hearts	darkness	in

aranedomo		ko o	omofu	michi	ni
although they were not		child	think about	way	in

mayohinuru	kana	Kano	oyatachi	fūfu no
went astray	how they ...	This	parent	couple's

mahe	ni	kandau no	guwansho ga	mawatte kuru
front	to	disinheriting's	application	was passed

to,	hahaoya wa ohogoe o	agete	naki-idasu.
when,	the mother loud voice	lifted, and	began to cry.

Teteoya wa	ha mo naki	haguki o	kuhishibatte
The father	toothless	gums	clenched, and

sashiutsumuite iraruru.	Yagate	kumotta	koe	de
hung his head.	Soon	blurred	voice	in

'Obaba	ingyau o	totte gozare.'	Hahaoya wa	henji
'Old lady	seal	get.'	The mother	answer

mo	idekane,	nakunaku	tansu no
even	could not give, and	weeping	cupboard's

hikidashi	kara	kawazaifu	ni haitta	ingyau o,
drawer	from	leather wallet	ensconced in	seal,

teteoya no	mahe	ni	oku	to,	kano
father's	front	in	place	when,	their
nora musuko wa,		amado no	soto	kara	iki o
good-for-nothing son		shutters'	outside	from	breath
tsumete	ukagaute iru.		Sono uchi ni	gotegote to	
held and	was peeping in.		Inside	slowly	
saifu no	himo o	toki,		ingyau o	toridashi,
wallet's	string	undo, and		seal	take out, and
niku o	tsukete,	sude ni	han o	osau to suru	
ink	apply, and	just as	seal	about to affix	
toki,	hahaoya ga sono		te	ni	sugatte,
when,	the mother his		hand	to	clung, and
'Matsu,	matte kudasare'		to ifu		
'Wait,	please wait'		said.		

FIGURE 3.2 A SECTION OF THE ORIGINAL TEXT OF HIRATA ATSUTANE'S *KODŌ TAI-I (OUTLINE OF THE ANCIENT WAY)* AND ITS MODERN RENDERING

Now, as I said in my lecture the other day, when the world began there was something hanging in the firmament from which the heavens sprouted up like a reed shoot, so that it became heaven's root. At the bottom of it there dangled another thing. Here were born Kuni-no-toko-tachi-no-mikoto and Toyo-kumunu-no-mikoto. The dangling thing was called 'ne no kuni' or 'ne no katasu kuni'. It later detached itself, and became the moon we know now.

(a) Original

Sate	senjitsu no	enzetsu	ni	mōshitaru
Now	the other day's	lecture	in	I said
tohori,	yo no	hajime	kano	ohosora no
as,	the world's	beginning	this	firmament's
naka	ni	tadayottaru	hitotsu no	mono	yori,
inside	in	hanging	a single	thing	from

ashikabi	no gotoku	moeagatte	ame	to nari,
reed shoot	like	sprouting up	heaven	became, and

sono	ama no	ne	to natte iru.	Hitotsu no
that	heaven's	root	became.	One

mono no	soko	ni	mo,	mata	hitotsu no
thing's	underpart	in	too,	again	one

mono ga	tarikudarinari	soko	ni
thing	dangled, and	there	in

kuni-no-toko-tachi-no-kami	to	toyokumunu-no-kami to ga
kuni-no-toko-tachi-no-mikoto	and	toyo-kumunu-no-mikoto

odekinasareta de gozaru.	Sono tarikudattaru	mono o,
were created (polite).	That dangling	thing

ne-no-kuni tomo	ne-no-katasu-kuni	tomo mōshitaru ga,
ne-no-kuni (is also called)	ne-no-katasu-kuni	is also called, and

kore ga	nochi ni	kirehanarete,	ima
this	later	detached itself, and	now

ma no atari	mitatematsuru	tsuki	to natta de gozaru.
before our eyes	see	moon	became.

(b) Modern

Sate	senjitsu no	enzetsu	ni	mōshita	tōri
Now	the other day's	lecture	in	I said	as,

yo no	hajime,	ōsora	ni	tadayou
the world's (polite)	beginning	firmament	in	hanging

hitotsu no	mono	kara,	ashi no	me	no yō ni
a single	thing	from	reed's	shoot	like

moeagatte	ame ga	deki	sono	ame no
sprouting up	heaven	was made, and	that	heaven's

ne	to natte iru	hitotsu no	mono no	soko
root	forming	single	thing's	underpart

ni	mo	mata	mō hitotsu no		mono ga	taresagari,
in	too	again	one more		thing	dangled, and

soko	ni	kuni-no-toko-tachi-no-kami		to
there	in	kuni-no-toko-tachi-no-mikoto		and

toyo-kumunu-no-kami	oumare ni natta.	Sono
toyo-kumunu-no-mikoto ga	were born (polite).	That

taresagatta	mono o	ne-no-kuni	to mo
dangled-down	thing	ne-no-kuni	(is also called)

ne-no-katasu-kuni	to mo	iimashita	ga,	kore ga
ne-no-katasu-kuni	is also	called	and	this

nochi ni	kirihanarete,	ima	me no atari ni
later	detached itself, and	now	before our eyes

mite iru	tsuki	to natta no de arimasu.
we see	moon	became.

FIGURE 5.1 COLLOQUIAL STYLE AND WESTERN PUNCTUATION IN FUTABATEI'S *UKIGUMO* (*THE DRIFTING CLOUD*)

Bunzō came down the stairs and quietly slid open the door to Osei's room. As he did so, Osei, who had been sitting deep in thought at the table with her head in her hands, started a little and straightened up. Judging by the red mark her hand left on her cheek, she had been sitting that way for some time.

'Am I disturbing you?'
'Not at all.'
'Well then.' Bunzō came in and sat down. 'I was very rude last night.'
'So was I.'
'No, really. I'm ashamed of myself, carrying on like that in front of you. Your mother told me off about it this morning.' He laughed.

Osei's answering laugh seemed forced and somehow cold. She seemed like a different person from the Osei of that morning.

Bunzō ga	nikai o		orite,		sotto
Bunzō	second floor		came down from, and		quietly

osei no	heya no	shōji o		hirakeru	sono	totan
Osei's	room's	sliding door		open	that	instant

ni,	ima made	tsukue	ni	hōzue o tsuite
in,	hitherto	table	on	sitting head in hands, and

nanigotoka	mono omohi o	shite ita	osei ga,
something	meditation	doing	Osei

bikkuri shita	kahotsuki o	shite	sukoshi
surprised	expression	made, and	a little

tobiagatte	izumahi o		nahoshita.	Kao ni
jumped up, and	sitting posture		adjusted.	Face on

te no	ato no	akaku	nokotte iru	tokoro o	miru
hand's	print's	red	remaining	place	look at

to,	hisashiku	hōzue o tsuite ita
when	for some time	was sitting head in hands

mono to mieru.	'Ojama	ja arimasen	ka'
it looked as though.	'A disturbance	it is not	?'

'Iie.'	'Sore jaa'	to ihinagara	bunzō wa	heya
'No.'	'Well then....'	saying	Bunzō	room

ni	haitte	za	ni	tsuite	'sakuya wa
into	entered, and	seat	on	sat, and	'last night

ohoki ni	shikkei shimashita.'	'Watakushi	koso.'
very	I acted rudely.'	'I	indeed.'

'Jitsu ni	memboku ga	nai,	anata	no mae o
'Really	credit	there is no,	you	in front of

mo	habakarazu shite...	kesa	sono	koto
even	acting inconsiderately	this morning	that	matter

de	okkasan	ni	kogoto o	kikimashita.
because of	your mother	by	a scolding	I heard.

Ahahahaha.'	'Sau,	ohohoho'	to muri ni	oshidashita
Hahaha.'	'Really,	hohoho'	willy-nilly	squeezed out

yau na	warahi	nantonaku	tsumetai.	Kesa no
seeming	laughter	somehow	cold.	This morning's

osei to wa	maru de	tanin	no yau	de.
Osei	exactly	another person	like	is.

FIGURE 5.2 COLLOQUIAL STYLE IN *BIMYŌ'S MUSASHINO* (*THE PLAIN OF MUSASHI*)

Night surrendered its citadel. The sparrows, who were laying an ambush in the bamboo grove, re-opened their councils of war. The glow of dawn, pushing its way through crevices in the bedchamber, gradually pushed back the surrounding darkness. A rosy curtain extended to the edges of the distant mountains; from ravines far and near arose the beacons of the morning clouds.

Yoru wa	nejiro o	akewatashita.	Takeyabu	ni
Night	citadel	surrendered.	Bamboo grove	in

fukuzei o	hatte iru	murasuzume wa	arata ni	
ambush	laying	sparrows	anew	

gungi o	hirakihajime,		neya no	sukima
council of war	began to hold, and		bedroom's	crevices

kara	kirikonde	kuru	akatsuki no	hikari wa
from	fighting in	coming	dawn's	light

shidai ni	atari no	yami o	ohinoke,	
gradually	surrounding	darkness	chased back, and	

tōyama no	kado	niwa	akane no	tobari ga
distant mountains'	edges	to	rosy	curtain

watari,	ochikochi no	keikan	kara wa	
extended, and	far and near	ravine	from	

asagumo no	noroshi ga	tachinoboru.
morning clouds'	beacons	arose.

FIGURE 5.3 COLLOQUIAL STYLE IN SOSEKI'S
WAGAHAI WA NEKO DE ARU (I AM A CAT)

I am a cat. As yet I have no name. I have no idea where I was born. All I remember is miowing in some dark, damp place. It was in this place that I first saw a human being. Later, when I made enquiries, I discovered that person to belong to the species known as 'student', by all accounts the most wicked of humans. It is rumoured that these students sometimes catch us cats, cook us and eat us.

| Wagahai wa | neko | de aru. | Namahe wa | mada |
| I | cat | am. | Name | as yet |

| nai. | Doko | de | umareta | ka | tonto |
| do not have. | Where | at | was born | ? | entirely |

| kentau ga tsukanu. | Nandemo | usugurai | jimejimeshita |
| have no idea. | Everything | dark | damp |

| tokoro | de | nyaanyaa naite ita | koto | dake wa |
| place | in | was miowing | fact | only |

| kioku shite iru. | Wagahai wa | koko | de |
| I remember. | I | this place | at |

| hajimete | ningen | to ifu | mono o | mita. |
| for the first time | human being | known as | thing | saw. |

| Shikamo | ato de | kiku | to | sore wa | shosei |
| And | later | I ask | when | that | student |

| to ifu | ningenchū | de | ichiban | dauaku na |
| known as | species | is, and | the most | wicked |

| shuzoku | de atta | sau da. | Kono | shosei |
| species | it was | it seems. | These | students |

| to ifu | no wa | tokidoki | wareware o | tsukamahete |
| known as | things | sometimes | us | catch, and |

| nite | kufu | to ifu hanashi de aru. |
| cook, and | eat | it is said. |

FIGURE 5.4 COLLOQUIAL STYLE IN TŌSON'S *HAKAI* (*THE BROKEN COMMANDMENT*)

Rengeji temple offered lodgings. The room Segawa Ushimatsu decided to rent after his sudden decision to change quarters was in the corner of the second floor of the priest's living quarters. The temple was an old one, affiliated with the Pure Land sect of Buddhism; it was one of twenty or more temples in the town of Iiyama in the Shimo-Minochi county of Shinshū. From its second-storey windows, part of the town of Iiyama could be seen beyond the big gingko tree. As might be expected, Buddhism having taken hold more strongly here than in any other area of Shinshū, everything appeared old and wreathed in fragrant incense, from the small town where the past still lived before one's eyes, the strange architecture of northern Japan, the shingled roofs, the special eaves used as snow shelters in winter, to the high temple roofs and the treetops which appeared here and there. The only thing not in tune with the scene from the window was the white-painted primary school where Ushimatsu was at present employed.

Rengeji	dewa	geshuku o	kaneta.	Segawa ushimatsu ga
Rengeji	at	lodgings	doubled as.	Segawa Ushimatsu

kyū ni	yadogahe o	omohitatte,	kariru
suddenly	change of lodgings	decided on, and	to rent

koto ni shita	heya	to ifu no wa
decided	room	(indicates a description following)

sono	kuritsu zuki	ni	aru	nikai no
its	priests' living quarters	in	is	second-storey

kado no	tokoro.	Tera wa	shinshū	shimominochi
corner's	place.	Temple	Shinshū	Shimo minochi

gun	ihiyama	machi	nijūnankaji no
county	Iiyama	town	twenty or more temples'

hitotsu,	shinshū	ni	fuzoku suru
one,	Pure Land Sect	with	affiliated

kosatsu	de,	chōdo	sono	nikai no
ancient temple	is, and	just	its	second-storey

mado	ni	yorikakatte	nagameru	to	itefu no
window	on	leaning	look	when	gingko

ōki o	hedatete	ihiyama no	machi no	ichibubun
big tree	beyond	Iiyama's	town's	part

mo	mieru.	Sasuga	shinshū	daiichi no
too	can see.	As might be expected	Shinshū	premier

bukkyō no	chi,	kodai o	me no mahe ni	miru
Buddhist	spot,	the past	before one's eyes	see

yau na	shōtokai	kii na	hokkoku	fū no
seeming	small town,	strange	North Japan	style

yazukuri,	itabuki no	yane,	mata wa	tōki no
architecture,	shingled	roofs,	or	winter's

yukiyoke	toshite	shiyō suru	tokubetsu no	kembi
snow shelters	as	use	special	eaves

kara,	tokorodokoro ni	takaku	arawareta	jiin
from,	in places	high	appeared	temples

to	shigeki no	kozue	made	subete
and	trees'	treetops	up to	all

furumekashii	machi no	arisama ga	ka no
old-looking	town's	scenes	fragrant

kemuri no	naka	ni	tsutsumarete	mieru.
smoke's	interior	in	being wreathed	appears.

Tada	hitokiwa	medatte	kono	mado
Just	conspicuously	standing out	this	window

kara	nozomareru	mono	to iheba,	gen ni
from	can see	thing	if we mention,	at present

ushimatsu ga	hoshoku shite iru	sono	shōgakkō no
Ushimatsu	is working	that	primary school's

shiroku	nutta	tatemono	de atta.
whitely	painted	building	it was.

FIGURE 5.5 COLLOQUIAL STYLE IN MUSHAKŌJI'S *YŪJŌ (FRIENDSHIP)*

Nojima hardly spoke at all to Sugiko. Sugiko, although appearing to watch the play with admiration, felt uncomfortable. However, it was only to be expected, she thought. Nakata made ostensibly admiring comments too, but they appeared to be merely flattery meant for Nojima.

'New things feel familiar to us after all, don't they!'

When Nakata came out with that sort of thing, he could not bring himself to take particular issue with it.

'Let's have something to eat.'

Nojima wa	sugiko	to wa	hotondo
Nojima	Sugiko	with	hardly

hanashi o shinakatta.	Sugiko ga	shibai o	hanshin shite
talked.	Sugiko	play	admiringly

mite iru	rashii	noni	fuyukai o	kanjita.
was watching	it seemed	although	discomfort	felt.

Shikashi	sore wa	muri mo nai	to mo omotta.
However	it	is understandable	she thought.

Nakata	mo	kanshin shite iru	yau na	koto o	itta
Nakata	too	admiring	seeming	things	said

ga,	sore wa	mushiro	kare	ni taisuru	oseji
but,	that	rather	him	aimed at	flattery

no yau ni	mieta.	'Yahari	atarashii	mono wa
like	appeared.	'After all	new	things

wareware	ni	chikai	kanji ga suru	ne.'
us	to	close	feel	don't they?'

Sonna	koto o	nakata ga	itta	toki,	kare wa
That sort of	thing	Nakata	said	when	he

betsu ni	hantai suru	ki ni narenakatta.
particularly	take issue	could not bring himself to.

'Meshi o   kuhau.'
'Rice   let's eat.'

FIGURE 9.1 WESTERN PUNCTUATION IN SHIMIZU USABURŌ'S 'KISHŪSAN SEKITAN KANTEI NO SETSU' ('EXPERT OPINION ON COAL FROM KISHŪ')

The word 'anthracite' originated in the Greek word 'anthrax' meaning charcoal. It is found in the mountains, has the characteristics of charcoal, and contains carbon and a little hydrogen. Its colour is black, and when sprinkled with a few drops of water it has a sheen like gold. Thus it is also called shining or sparkling charcoal. It burns quietly, without smoke. Hence it is also known as blind coal. Miners consider it to be ashes left over from the work of the gods, formed primarily from ordinary coke plant matter. It burns like coking coal ashes. It is plentiful in Ireland and also occurs in the coking coal fields of England, Scotland and Eastern Europe. It is found in very good supply in America.

| Antarashiito wa | girisha no | antarakusu | sunawachi |
| Anthracite | Greek | anthrax | i.e. |

| sumi | to ifu | kotoba | yori | idetari. | Kore wa |
| charcoal | called | word | from | originated. | It |

| sumi no | umaredachi | naru | yamairo |
| charcoal's | nature | is | mountain-variety |

| mono | nite | sumine | to | wazuka no | mizune o |
| thing | is, and | carbon | and | a little | hydrogen |

| fukumu. | Iro | kuroku, | horohoro to |
| contains. | Colour | is black, and | few drops |

| kakete | yaya | kane | no gotoki | hikari | ari. |
| sprinkle, and | a little | gold | like | sheen | it has. |

| Yorite | kagayakizumi | mata | hikarizumi |
| Thus | sparkling charcoal | or | shining charcoal |

| tomo ifu. | Shizuka ni | moete | keburi |
| is also called. | Quietly | burns, and | smoke |

nashi.	Yorite	mata	mekurazumi	tomo ifu.
doesn't have.	Thus	also	blind coal	is also called
Yamashi wa	kore o	tsune no	ishizumi no	kikusa o
Miners	it	ordinary	coke's	plants
tane	to shite	naritatsu	kamiwaza no	amari no
matter	taking as	formed	divine works'	left-over
yakegara	to su.	Sate	kore o	ishizumigara
ashes	consider as.	Now,	it	coke ashes
no gotoku	takimochifu.	Kore wa	irurando	ni
like	burns.	It	Ireland	in
ohoku	mata	egirisu	sukotorando	narabi ni
is plentiful, and	also	England	Scotland	and
europa no	higashi no	ishizumibara	ni	mo
Europe's	eastern	coke fields	in	too
izuru.	Amerika	niwa	ito	ohoku	izuru nari.
occurs.	America	in	very	plentifully	occurs.

Glossary

ateji	Chinese characters used as phonetic approximations in Japanese words
bibun	elegant prose – classical Japanese
bummei kaika	civilization and enlightenment, a Meiji Period slogan
bun	the written word
bungotai	umbrella term for classical literary styles
daishimbun	the serious press
engo	word associations
furigana	*kana* glosses of Chinese characters, showing pronunciation
futsūbun	general-purpose style. Also refers specifically to the late Meiji Classical Standard, a synthesis of watered-down classical and Sino-Japanese for general use.
ga	elegant
gabun	another name for *gikobun*
gabuntai	elegant writing – classical Japanese
gagen	refined language
gairaigo	foreign loanwords
gazoku setchū	a style blending classical narrative with colloquial dialogue
gebun	satirical writing of the late Tokugawa Period
gembun'itchi	the early term given to both the concept and practice of colloquial style, meaning literally 'unification of speech and writing'
gesaku	umbrella term for Tokugawa Period genre fiction

Glossary

gikobun	Tokugawa Period revival of classical Japanese
haibun	prose poems
hentai kambun	hybrid Chinese developed in Japan in the Middle Ages
hiragana	one of the two Japanese phonetic scripts
hyōjungo	standard language
jiyū minken undō	civil rights movement
jōruri	ballad dramas
jōyō kanji	the 1945 characters presently designated for general use by the Ministry of Education.
kaeriten	diacritics indicating reverse word order
kakari musubi	emphatic particles which require a particular kind of final inflection
kakekotoba	word plays
kakujoshi	case indicator
kambun	Sino-Japanese
kambun kakikudashi-bun	same as *kambun kuzushi*
kambun kundoku	Chinese read in the Japanese manner with the aid of diacritics and glosses
kambun kuzushi	*kambun kundoku* written out in full as Japanese
kambun chokuyakutai	a version of *kambun kundoku* aimed at a faithful rendition of the original
kanabun	texts in phonetic *kana* script
kangakusha	scholars of Chinese
kango	Chinese words
kanji	Chinese characters
kanji-kana-majiribun	texts combining Chinese characters with phonetic script/s
kanzen chōaku	praise virtue and castigate evil, the didactic motto of some genres of Tokugawa Period fiction
kashihonya	lending libraries
katakana	one of two Japanese phonetic scripts
katakana-majiribun	texts written in a mixture of Chinese characters and *katakana*

kodō	the ancient way. Refers to Japanese practices before the introduction of Chinese thought.
kōgotai	colloquial style
kokkeibon	comic novels of the Tokugawa Period
kokugo	the term used by Japanese to designate their language since the 1890s
kōshakuhon	lecture books
koshimbun	the popular press
kotobazukai	the term by which school classes in the Japanese language were known
kunten	diacritics and glosses added to Chinese to show how it should be read in Japanese
kusazōshi	picture books – genre fiction of the Tokugawa Period
kyōtsūgo	common language
makura kotoba	conventional epithets
man'yōgana	rebus writing, spelling out Japanese words using Chinese characters with pronunciations roughly corresponding to each syllable
mizenkei	negative base
monogatari	a long story; early form of the novel
nigori	marks added to *kana* symbols to indicate voicing
ninjōbon	love stories of the Tokugawa Period
noritobun	the style used in Shinto ritual prayers
ōbun	European-derived style
ōbunchokuyaku	an attempt to reproduce as far as possible the structures of European languages in Sino-Japanese, classical Japanese, or colloquial style
okototen	diacritics marked on an invisible square around a character to indicate inflections
okurigana	*kana* added to Chinese characters to show their Japanese inflections
ōraimono	copybooks used as manuals for teaching writing
rangaku	Dutch studies
ren'yōkei	conjunctive form

risshin shusse	Meiji Period slogan meaning 'getting ahead in the world'
rōmaji	the western alphabet
sagyō henkaku dōshi	verbs made by following a Chinese noun with the verb *suru*
sankin kōtai	the system of alternate years of attendance at the Tokugawa capital by *daimyō*
semmyōbun	the style used in Imperial proclamations
setsuwa	narratives
shaseibun	the 'sketches in prose' method of writing advocated by poet Masaoka Shiki in the early 1900s
shinkokubun	Meiji Period variant of classical Japanese
shōmono	Muromachi Period verbatim notes of lectures on the Chinese classics and Buddhist scriptures, printed by priests of the Rinzai sect
shūshikei	final form
sōrōbun	epistolary style
tōyō kanji	the 1850 characters chosen for general use by the Ministry of Education in 1949, replaced in 1981 by the *jōyō kanji*
ukiyozōshi	a type of Tokugawa Period genre fiction dealing with the pleasure quarters
wabun	classical Japanese
waka	Japanese poetry
wakan'yō	a style combining elements from classical Japanese, Sino-Japanese, and western languages
wakankonkōbun	a style blending classical Japanese and Sino-Japanese
yamato kotoba	native Japanese lexicon
yōbun	western style; a kind of direct translation of western language
yōgakusha	scholars of the west
yomihon	historical genre fiction of the Tokugawa Period
zappō	news items
zoku	colloquial
zokubuntai	colloquial style

Notes

1 LANGUAGE AND MODERNIZATION: THE JAPANESE EXPERIENCE

1. Rejai, Mostafa and Enloe, Cynthia 'Nation-States and State-Nations' in Smith, Michael; Little, Richard; Shackleton, Michael (eds) *Perspectives on World Politics*, London: Croom Helm and the Open University Press, 1981, p. 37–8.
2. Deutsch, Karl *Nationalism and Social Communication: An Inquiry into the Foundations of Nationality*, Cambridge: MIT Press and Wiley, 1953.
3. Fishman, Joshua A. *Language and Nationalism: Two Integrative Essays*, Rowley, Mass.: Newbury House, 1972, p. 5.
4. Kelman, Herbert C. 'Language as an Aid and Barrier to Involvement in the National System', in Rubin, Joan and Jernudd, Björn (eds) *Can Language Be Planned*? Honolulu: East-West Center Press, 1971, pp. 21–51.
5. Fishman, Joshua A. 'Language Problems and Types of Political and Sociocultural Integration: A Conceptual Postscript', in Fishman, Joshua, *et al.*, (eds) *Language Problems of Developing Nations*, New York: Wiley, 1968, pp. 491–8.
6. Ferguson, Charles 'The Language Factor in National Development', *Anthropological Linguistics* 4, 1, 1962, pp. 23–7; Fishman, Joshua *Language and Nationalism: Two Integrative Essays*, Rowley, Mass.: Newbury House, 1972. This work includes an extensive bibliography; Neustupný, J.V. 'Basic Types of Treatment of Language Problems', in Fishman, Joshua (ed.) *Advances in Language Planning*, The Hague: Mouton, 1974, pp. 37–48; Garvin, Paul 'Some Comments on Language Planning', in Fishman (ed.) *Advances in Language Planning*, pp. 69–78; Haugen, Einar 'Dialect, Language, Nation', *American Anthropologist* 68, 1966, pp. 922–35.
7. Ferguson, Charles 'Language Development', in Fishman *et al.* (eds) *Language Problems*, p. 31.
8. Garvin, Paul and Mathiot, Madeleine 'The Urbanization of the Guarani Language: A Problem in Language and Culture', in Fishman,

Joshua (ed.) *Readings in the Sociology of Language*, The Hague: Mouton, 1972, p. 365.
9 Haugen, Einar 'Linguistics and Language Planning', in Bright, William (ed.) *Sociolinguistics: Proceedings of the UCLA Sociolinguistics Conference 1964*, The Hague: Mouton, 1966, p. 53.
10 Smith, Wilfrid Cantwell *Modernisation of a Traditional Society*, London: Asian Publishing House, 1965, p. 26.
11 For an English account of the *risshin shusse* ethic, see Kinmonth, Earl H. *The Self-Made Man in Meiji Japanese Thought: From Samurai to Salary Man*, Berkeley: University of California Press, 1981.
12 See Yanagida Kunio 'Hyōjungo no Hanashi', *Yanagida Kunio Shū* 18, Tokyo: Chikuma Shobō, 1963, p. 510. Also Tōjō Misao 'Hyōjungo to Hōgen', *Kokubungaku Kaishaku to Kanshō* 4, 7, 1937, p. 100.
13 Andō Masatsugu 'Kokugoshi Josesu', *Andō Masatsugu Chosakushū* 2, Tokyo: Yūzankaku, 1974, p. 65.
14 Fukuzawa Yukichi 'Fukuzawa Zenshū Shogen', *Fukuzawa Yukichi Zenshū* 1, Tokyo: Iwanami Shoten, 1958, p. 6.
15 See Dore, R. P. *Education in Tokugawa Japan*, Berkeley: University of California Press, 1965.
16 Schramm, Wilbur *Mass Media and National Development*, Stanford : Stanford University Press, 1964, p. 25.
17 Anderson, C. Arnold 'The Modernization of Education', in Weiner, Myron (ed.) *Modernization: The Dynamics of Growth*, New York: Basic Books, 1966, p. 69.
18 Mozume Takami, *Gembun'itchi* (1886), in *Meiji Bunka Zenshū* 20, 2nd edn, Tokyo: Nihon Hyōronsha, 1967, p. 132.
19 Smith, *Modernisation*, p. 31.
20 Deutsch, Karl *Nationalism and Social Communication: An Inquiry into the Foundations of Nationality*, Cambridge: MIT Press and Wiley, 1953, p. 61.
21 Schramm *Mass Media*, p. 41.
22 Pool, Ithiel de Sola 'Communications and Development', in Weiner, *Modernization*, p. 99.
23 Nitobe Inazo et al. *Western Influences in Japan*, Chicago: University of Chicago Press, 1931, pp. 342–3.
24 Cited in Shibuzawa Keizō (ed.) *Japanese Life and Culture in the Meiji Era*, tr. Charles S. Terry, Tokyo: Ōbunsha, 1958, p. 17.
25 For an English translation, see Twine, Nanette, *The Essence of the Novel*, Department of Japanese, University of Queensland, Occasional Papers No. 11, 1981.
26 Shafer, Boyd, C. *Faces of Nationalism: New Realities and Old Myths*, New York: Harcourt, Brace, Jovanovich, 1972, pp. 40–1.
27 Passin, Herbert *Society and Education in Japan*, New York: Teachers College Press, Columbia University, 1965, p. 57.
28 ibid., p.12.
29 Keene, Donald *World Within Walls: Japanese Literature of the Pre-Modern Era, 1600–1867*, London: Secker and Warburg, 1976, p. 409.
30 Lerner, Daniel 'Towards a Communication Theory of Modernization: A Set of Considerations', in Pye, Lucian W. (ed.) *Communications and*

Political Development, Princeton: Princeton University Press, 1963, p. 341.
31 Black, Cyril Edwin 'Change as a Condition of Modern Life', in Weiner (ed.) *Modernization*, p. 20

2 PRE-MODERN STYLES

1 For detailed descriptions of these styles in Japanese, the reader is referred to Satō Kiyoji *Kokugogaku Kenkyū Jiten*, Tokyo: Meiji Shoin, 1977, and to Kokugo Gakkai (eds) *Kokugogaku Daijiten* (2nd edn), Tokyo: Tōkyōdō Shuppan, 1982.
2 See Murayama Yoshihiro 'Kambummyaku no Mondai', *Kokubungaku* 25, 10, 1980, pp. 40–5.
3 Saeki Umetomo *Kokugo Gaisetsu* (3rd edn) Tokyo: Shūei Shuppan, 1967, p. 208.
4 Miller, Roy Andrew *The Japanese Language* Chicago: University of Chicago Press, 1967, p. 99.
5 Saeki *Kokugo Gaisetsu*, p. 208.
6 ibid. p. 209.
7 Hashimoto Shinkichi *Kokugogaku Gairon*, Tokyo: Iwanami Shoten, 1946, p. 151.
8 Maejima Hisoka 'Kanji Gohaishi no Gi', *Maejima Hisoka Jijoden*, Hayama (Kanagawa): Maejima Hisoka Denki Kankōkai, 1956, pp. 154–5.
9 The form of the verb followed by, e.g. *nu, nai, reru* and *seru*.
10 For a detailed analysis of the characteristics of *kambun*, see Tsujimura Toshiki 'Meiji no Bungobun no Kaishaku to Bumpōjō no Mondaiten' in *Kōza Kaishaku to Bumpō 7: Gendaibun*, Tokyo: Meiji Shoin, 1960, pp. 190–218, and Takano Shigeo 'Kambun Kundokutai no Gohō', *Kokubungaku Ronshū (Jochidai)*, 1975, pp. 172–94.
11 Lensen, George Alexander *Russia's Japan Expedition 1852–55*, Gainesville: University of Florida Press, 1955, pp. viii–ix.
12 *Nari* being the classical copula and *keri* a perfective verb ending.
13 Kamei Takashi, Ōfuji Tokihiko and Yamada Toshio (eds) *Nihongo no Rekishi V. 6: Atarashii Kokugo e no Ayumi*, Tokyo: Heibonsha, 1965, p. 260.
14 Volume 23, for example, which consists of sixteen essays, contains seven such prefaces and three postscripts.
15 Twine, Nanette (tr.) *The Essence of the Novel*, Department of Japanese, University of Queensland, Occasional Papers No. 11, 1981, p. 51.
16 Reproduced in part in Yamamoto Masahide, *Kindai Buntai Keisei Shiryō Shūsei (Hasseihen)*, Tokyo: Ōfūsha, 1978, pp. 290–307.
17 'Gikobun', in *Bunshō Hyōgen Jiten* (7th edn) Tokyo: Tōkyōdō Shuppan, 1966, p. 100, and Hashimoto Shinkichi: *Kokugogaku Gairon*, Tokyo: Iwanami Shoten, 1946, p. 160.
18 Kembō Gōki 'Wakankonkōbun' to iu Meishō no Kigen', in Kokuritsu Kokugo Kenkyūjo (eds) *Kotoba no Kenkyū*, Tokyo: Shūei Shuppan, 1959, pp. 303–5.

19 For a Japanese account of the development of *wakankonkōbun*, see Nagazumi Yasuaki 'Wakankonkōbun no Keisei' *Bungaku* 12, 12, 1952, pp. 11–21. Also the 'wakankonkōbun' entry in Satō Kiyoji, *Kokugogaku Kenkyū Jiten*, Tokyo: Meiji Shoin, 1977, pp. 937–8.
20 Ekoyama Tsuneaki, *Nihon Bunshōshi*, Tokyo: Kawade Shobō, 1956, p. 2.
21 Nagazumi, 'Wakankonkōbun no Keisei', p. 17
22 Where *ga* means 'elegant' and *zoku* 'colloquial'.
23 Hirata Tomoko 'Gohōjō yori mita Meiji Shobuntai no Seikaku', *Bungaku* 18, 1962, pp. 40–58.
24 Emphatic particles attached to a word which require a particular kind of final inflection.
25 Twine, Nanette (tr.) *The Essence of the Novel*, pp. 67–8.
26 For example Katō Yūichi's *Bummei Kaika* (1873–74), Ogawa Tameharu's *Usagi no Mondō* (1873) and *Kaika Mondō* (1874–75), Okamoto Kōchū's *Shōgaku Kisoku Issekidan* (1874) and Ishii Nankyō's *Meiji no Hikari* (1875).
27 Nakamura Michio ' "De arimasu" Kotoba', *Kokugo Kenkyū* 9, 4, 1941, pp. 5–10.
28 Kojima Toshio 'Goki Edogo ni okeru "desu", "de arimasu", "masen deshita" ', *Kokugogaku* 39, 1959, p. 82.
29 ibid., pp. 76 and 77–8.
30 This was Shimizu Usaburō's *Monowari no Hashigo* (1874).

3 EARLY STIRRINGS: EDUCATION AND THE PRESS

1 The characters literally mean 'speech and writing united'. The term *gembun'itchi* was coined by Kanda Kōhei in his 1885 essay *Bunshōron o yomu*, in *Nishimura Shigeki* 2, Kyoto: Shibunkan, 1976, pp. 122–8, and widely used in the Meiji Period to refer both to the broad concept of developing a modern written language based on contemporary speech and to the colloquial style itself as it began to appear in writing, so that what today is known as *kōgotai* (colloquial style, i.e. modern written Japanese) was then often referred to as *gembun'itchitai*.
2 See Chapter 4 for a detailed discussion.
3 Tanabe Masao 'Hirata Atsutane to Kokugogaku', *Kokugakuin Zasshi* 74, 11, 1973, p. 52.
4 Yamamoto Masahide *Kindai Buntai Hassei no Shiteki Kenkyū* (2nd edn) Tokyo: Iwanami Shoten, 1982 (1st edn 1965), p. 87.
5 Maejima Hisoka 'Kanji Gohaishi no Gi', in *Maejima Hisoka Jijoden*, Hayama: Maejima Hisoka Denki Kankōkai, 1956, p. 153.
6 Nishio Mitsuo *Kindai Bunshōron Kenkyū*, Tokyo: Tōkyō Shoin, 1951, p. 41.
7 For an English account of the *Kokugo Haishiron* (*Proposal for the Abolition of Japanese*), as Mori's plan came to be known, see Ivan Parker Hall *Mori Arinori*, Cambridge, Mass.: Harvard University Press, 1973 pp. 189–95.
8 Fukuzawa Yukichi 'Fukuzawa Zenshū Shogen' (1897), in *Fukuzawa Yukichi Zenshū* 1, Tokyo: Iwanami Shoten, 1958, pp. 7–8.

294 *Language and the Modern State*

9 For an English biography of Fukuzawa, see Blacker, Carmen *The Japanese Enlightenment: A Study of the Writings of Fukuzawa Yukichi*, Cambridge: Cambridge University Press, 1964.
10 Translated in Braisted, William (tr.) *Meiroku Zasshi: Journal of the Japanese Enlightenment*, Cambridge, Mass.: Harvard University Press, 1976, p. 97.
11 ibid., p. 99.
12 See Chapter 4.
13 They included *Dōmo Tokuhon Kaiwa Hen* (*A Child's Reader: Conversation*, 1873–4, Ichioka Masaichi, *-masu* and *de gozaimasu*), *Ōtashi: Kaiwa Hen* (*Ōta's Conversation Primer*, 1873, Ōta Zuiken, *de aru*), *Kaiwa Tokuhon* (*Conversation Reader*, 1874, Kubo Fusō, *-masu* and *de gozarimasu*), and *Shōgaku Kaiwa no Shōkei* (*Short cut to Beginners' Conversation*, 1874, Ide Inosuke, *-masu* and *de arimasu*).
14 For a discussion of the development of the press, see Altman, Albert A. 'The Press' in Jansen, Marius and Rozman, Gilbert *Japan in Transition: From Tokugawa to Meiji*, Princeton, New Jersey: Princeton University Press 1986, pp. 231–47.
15 See Huffman, James L. *Politics of the Meiji Press: The Life of Fukuchi Gen'ichirō*, Honolulu: University Press of Hawaii, 1980.
16 Yamamoto Masahide *Kindai Buntai Hassei* p. 133.
17 Fukuchi Gen'ichirō 'Bunshōron' (1881), in *Meiji Bungaku Zenshū* 11, Tokyo: Chikuma Shobō, 1966, p. 369.
18 ibid. pp. 369–70.
19 These glosses are called *furigana*, and their abundant use led to these tabloids being known as *furigana shimbun*.
20 For an English translation of this journal, see Braisted, William *Meiroku Zasshi: Journal of the Japanese Enlightenment*, 1976.
21 English translation from Braisted *Meiroku Zasshi*, p. 13.
22 *Meiroku Zasshi* 23, December 1874.
23 Kamei Takashi, Ōfuki Tokihiko and Yamada Toshio (eds) *Nihongo no Rekishi 6: Atarashii Kokugo e no Ayumi*, Tokyo: Heibonsha, 1965, p. 89.
24 See Chapter 4.
25 See Chapter 5.
26 See Chapter 9.
27 Taguchi Ukichi 'Nippon Kaika no Seishitsō Yōyaku Aratamezaru Bekarazu', *Tōkyō Keizai Zasshi*, 1884, 239, pp. 608–10, 240 pp. 642–6, 241 pp. 675–8, 242 pp. 710–12, 243 pp. 746–9.
28 In this essay the term *gembun'itchi*, which was to become the slogan for the language modernization movement, appeared for the first time in print.
29 Kanda Kōhei 'Bunshōron o yomu', in *Meiji Bungaku Zenshū* 3, Tokyo: Chikuma Shobō, 1967, p. 229.
30 See Chapter 4, note 28.
31 See Chapter 2 for Mozume's first-hand experience of this problem.
32 Mozume Takami 'Gembun'itchi' (1886), in *Meiji Bunka Zenshū* 20, Nihon Hyōronsha, 1967, p. 134.
33 See Chapter 7 for an overview of the opposition.
34 Hall *Mori Arinori*, p. 338.

35 This was 'Nihon Futsūbun no Zento' ('The Outlook for Written Japanese'), *Dai Nihon Kyōiku Zasshi*, 1 January 1888.

4 LANGUAGE AND POLITICS

1 Najita Tetsuo *Japan: The Intellectual Foundation of Modern Japanese Politics*, Chicago: University of Chicago Press, 1974, p. 87.
2 For a discussion of Fukuzawa's life, thought, and works, see Blacker, Carmen *The Japanese Enlightenment: A Study of the Writings of Fukuzawa Yukichi*, Cambridge: Cambridge University Press, 1964.
3 Symposium with Nishio Minoru, Maruyama Masao, and Etō Jun 'Fukuzawa Yukichi no Buntai to Hassō', *Bungaku* 28, 12, 1958, p. 1563.
4 Kiyooka Eiichi (tr.) *The Autobiography of Fukuzawa Yukichi*, New York: Columbia University Press, 1966, p. 247.
5 Fukuzawa Yukichi 'Fukuzawa Zenshū Shogen' (1897), in *Fukuzawa Yukichi Zenshū* 1, Tokyo: Iwanami Shoten, 1958, pp. 4–5.
6 ibid pp. 5–8.
7 Fukuzawa Yukichi 'Gakumon no Susume' (1872–76), in *Fukuzawa Yukichi Zenshū* 3, Tokyo: Iwanami Shoten, 1959, p. 29. For an English translation of this work see Dilworth, David and Hirano Umeyo (tr.) *Fukuzawa Yukichi's An Encouragement of Learning*. Tokyo: Sophia University, 1969.
8 Blacker *The Japanese Enlightenment*, p. 105.
9 Fukuzawa, 'Zenshū Shogen', p. 38.
10 Fukuzawa 'Gakumon no Susume', p. 57.
11 Yamamoto Masahide *Kindai Buntai Hassei no Shiteki Kenkyū* (2nd edn), Tokyo: Iwanami Shoten, 1982 (1st edn 1965), p. 107.
12 Nishio, Maruyama and Etō 'Fukuzawa Yukichi' p. 1564.
13 Yamamoto Masahide ' "De gozaru" tai kara "de aru" tai e' *Buntairon Kenkyū* 12, June 1968, p. 18.
14 Shindō Sakiko 'Meiji Shoki no Gengo no Seitai', *Gengo Seikatsu* 90, 1959, p. 61.
15 Nishio Mitsuo 'Meiji Jidai Shoki no Bunshō', *Kokugo to Kokubungaku* 40, 2, 1963, p. 8.
16 Nishio, Maruyama and Etō 'Fukuzawa Yukichi', p. 1564.
17 'Gembun'itchi ni tsuite', *Yomiuri Shimbun*, 25 May 1901.
18 Found in *Meiji Bungaku Zenshū* 3, Tokyo: Chikuma Shobō, 1967, pp. 88–93. An English translation is 'Writing Japanese with the Western Alphabet', in Braisted, William (tr.) *Meiroku Zasshi: Journal of the Japanese Enlightenment*, Cambridge, Mass.: Harvard University Press, 1976, pp. 3–16.
19 Braisted *Meiroku Zasshi* p. xx.
20 Yamamoto Masahide 'Nishi Amane no Kokugo Kaikaku Katsudō', *Gengo Seikatsu* 196, 1968, p. 91.
21 I am indebted for the following discussion of the civil rights movement to Beckmann, George M. *The Modernization of China and Japan*, 1962, pp. 276–97; Hane Mikiso 'The Movement for Liberty and Popular Rights' and Huffman, James L. 'The Popular Rights Debate:

Political or Ideological?', in Wray, Harry and Conroy, Hilary (eds) *Japan Examined: Perspectives on Modern Japanese History*, Honolulu: University of Hawaii Press, 1983, pp. 90–7, 98–103; and Bowen, Roger W., *Rebellion and Democracy in Meiji Japan: A Study of Commoners in the Popular Rights Movement*, Berkeley: University of California Press, 1980.
22 Bowen *Rebellion and Democracy*, pp. 113–15.
23 For an English text of the 1875 and 1880 Acts, see *Meiji Japan Through Contemporary Sources* 3, Tokyo: Centre for East Asian Cultural Studies, 1972, pp. 32–43.
24 Yamamoto Masahide 'Jiyū Minken Shisōka to Gembun'itchi Undō', *Kokugo to Kokubungaku* 39, 11, 1962, p. 110.
25 Nishio Mitsuo 'Meiji Jidai Shoki', p. 9.
26 Yamamoto 'Jiyū Minken Shisōka', p. 109.
27 Huffman, James L. *Politics of the Meiji Press: The Life of Fukuchi Gen'ichirō*, Honolulu: University of Hawaii Press, 1980, p. 97.
28 Takase Ukō 'Zenkoku Shimbun Zasshi Hyōbanki', in *Meiji Bunka Zenshū* 4 (3rd edn) Tokyo: Nihon Hyōronsha, 1968, p. 72.
29 Huffman *Politics* p. 175.
30 Yamamoto *Kindai Buntai Hassei*, p. 210.
31 Yamamoto 'Jiyū Minken Shisōka', p. 112.
32 ibid., p. 113.
33 ibid., p. 115.
34 Beckmann *The Modernization of China and Japan* p. 295.
35 See Chapter 1, note 10.
36 Bowen *Rebellion and Democracy*, pp. 214–15.
37 Emery, Edwin, Ault, Phillip H., and Agee, Warren K. *Introduction to Mass Communications* (2nd edn), New York: Dodd, Mead and Company 1966, p. 6.

5 THE ROLE OF LITERATURE

1 Published in the *Tōkyō Nichi Nichi Shimbun* on 2 December 1874 and 26 April 1875.
2 *Ishōron-Bungaku no Bu* (*On Design – Literature*). See Chapter 3, note 27.
3 For a biography in English of Tsubouchi, see Ryan, Marleigh Grayer *The Development of Realism in the Fiction of Tsubouchi Shōyō*, Seattle: University of Washington Press, 1975.
4 Literally, 'praise virtue and castigate evil'.
5 For an English discussion of the political novel, see Donald Keene *Dawn to the West: Japanese Literature of the Modern Era* 1, New York: Holt, Rinehart and Winston, 1984, Chapter 4.
6 Famous novel of court life, c. 1005, by Lady Murasaki Shikibu.
7 Twine, Nanette (tr.) *The Essence of the Novel*, Department of Japanese, University of Queensland: Occasional Papers No. 11, 1981, p. 52.
8 ibid. pp. 59–60.
9 ibid. p. 60.

10 *Yomihon* were a genre of popular fiction, popular in the late eighteenth century. The title literally means 'reading books', i.e. they were meant to be read at home rather than heard at a recital hall or on the stage. They were adaptations of Chinese short stories and recreations of Japanese classics, with a leaning toward the supernatural and fantastic, and were often highly didactic.
11 A variety of entertaining fiction written mainly for women and children, usually in phonetic script and supplied with copious illustrations. This genre accounts for more than 60 per cent of pre-Meiji novels.
12 Published by Haishi Shuppansha in October 1884.
13 This was 'Shōsetsu Buntai' ('The Style of the Novel'), *Meiji Kyōkai Zasshi* 25–8, 20 September 1883–20 October 1883.
14 Futabatei Shimei 'Yo ga Gembun'itchi no Yurai' (1906), in *Futabatei Shimei Zenshū* 5, Tokyo: Iwanami Shoten, 1965.
15 The variety of Japanese found in the Fukagawa district of Tokyo.
16 Futubatei *Yo ga Gembun'itchi no Yurai*, p. 111.
17 Hara Shirō, however, suggests that this *bungotai* preface may also be seen as an attempt at striking a balance, in this very early stage of *gembun'itchi* in literature, between the old and the new, the familiar and the unfamiliar, which served to point out the experimental nature of the new style. Hara Shirō 'Futabatei Shimei, Naimen no Gengo e', *Kokubungaku* 25, 10, 1980, p. 91.
18 Tayama Katai *Futabatei Shimei Kun* (1909) and *Tōkyō no Sanjūnen* (1917). Translated in Ryan, Marleigh Grayer *Japan's First Modern Novel: Ukigumo of Futabatei Shimei*, New York: Columbia University Press 1967, p. 118 and pp. 123–4. Also see Ryan, p. 117–18 for a translation from an article by poet Kanbara Ariake (1876–1952) praising Futabatei's use of colloquial style in *Aibiki*.
19 Ōta Saburō 'Kōgo Buntai no Seiritsu to Honyaku Buntai', *Gengo Seikatsu* 74, 1957, p. 29.
20 Yanagida Izumi 'Koko ya Kashiko Sono Hoka', *Kokugo to Kokubungaku*, 11, 8, 1934, p. 73.
21 Muramatsu Sadataka 'Yamada Bimyō: Gembun'itchi Sōshisha toshite no Higekiteki Ummei', *Kokubungaku Kaishaku to Kanshō* 34, 1, 1969, p. 58.
22 Yamada Bimyō *Gembun'itchi no Yurai* (1906). Cited in Yamamoto Masahide *Kindai Buntai Hassei no Shiteki Kenkyū* (2nd. edn) Tokyo: Iwanami Shoten, 1982 (1st edn 1965), p. 519.
23 ibid., p. 520.
24 Okada Ryōhei (1864–1934), Ichiki Kitokurō (1867–1944), Nakagawa Kojūrō and Masaki Naohiko. Okada and Ichiki were studying philosophy and politics respectively at Tokyo Imperial University, while Yamada, Nakagawa, and Masaki were all students at the university's preparatory school.
25 Nakagawa Kojūrō ' "Iratsume" to Gembun'itchi' Pt 1, *Ritsumeikan Bungaku* 1, 6, 1934, p. 3.
26 ibid. Pt 2, *Ritsumeikan Bungaku* 1, 7, 1934, p. 17.
27 Muramatsu 'Yamada Bimyō' p. 60.
28 *Wa* = Japanese, *Kan* = Chinese, *Yō* = European.

298 Language and the Modern State

29 Homma Hisao 'Gembun'itchi no Hattatsu', in *Nihon Bungaku Kōza 12: Meiji Taishō-hen,* Tokyo: Kaizōsha, 1934, p. 288.
30 Nakagawa 'Iratsume', Pt 2, p. 28.
31 Homma 'Gembun'itchi' p. 288.
32 Nakamura Mitsuo, *Modern Japanese Fiction 1868–1926* (2nd edn) Tokyo: Kokusai Bunka Shinkokai, 1968, p. 59.
33 *Haiku* are short poems of seventeen syllables dating from the seventeenth century which attempt suggestion of the universal through concentration on the minute particular. The *tanka,* a five-line, thirty-one syllable form, dates from centuries earlier.
34 Yamamoto Masahide *Kindai Buntai Hassei* p. 51.
35 Specifying subjects of sentences, increased use of the passive voice, and such rhetorical devices as personification, for example, not often seen in written Japanese before exposure to the influence of Western languages.
36 See Chapter 7.

6 THE FINAL STAGES

1 Keene, Donald 'The Sino-Japanese War of 1894–95 and Japanese Culture', in *Appreciations of Japanese Culture,* Tokyo: Kodansha International 1981, pp. 259–99.
2 See Chapter 8.
3 Neustupný J. V. 'Basic Types of Treatment of Language Problems', in Fishman, Joshua (ed.) *Advances in Language Planning.* The Hague: Mouton 1974, p. 39.
4 This was 'Kanji Zempai o ronjite Kokubun Kokugo Kokuji no Shōrai ni oyobu', *Teikoku Bungaku* 1, 10, 1895, pp. 385–412.
5 See Gembun'itchikai (eds) *Gembun'itchikai no Kaishi* 1, Gembun'itchikai, 1902, pp. 1–2. Held in the Diet Library, Tokyo.
6 See Shiozawa Kazuko 'Meijiki no Kokutei Kokugo Kyōkasho', *Kokubungaku Ronshū (Jochidai)* 11, 1979, pp. 119–20.
7 For a detailed description of these groups and their activities, see Yamamoto Masahide *Gembun'itchi no Rekishi Ronkō,* Tokyo: Ōfūsha, 1971, Chapters 16 and 17, and *Gembun'itchi no Rekishi Ronkō: Zokuhen,* Tokyo: Ōfūsha, 1981, Chapters 11 and 12.
8 Yamada Bimyō *Gembun'itchi Bunrei* 1, Tokyo: Naigai Shuppan Kyōkai, 1901, pp. 58–9. Held in the Diet Library, Tokyo.
9 See Seeley, Chris 'The Japanese Script Since 1900', *Visible Language* 18, 3, 1984, p. 270.
10 The term *tōyō kanji* (*kanji* for current use) refers to a list of 1850 characters promulgated by Cabinet in 1949 for general use. This was replaced in 1981 by an expanded *jōyō kanji* (*kanji* for general use) list of 1945 characters. See Seeley op. cit. for full details of the development of these two lists.
11 See Seeley 'The Japanese Script' chapter 9, note 13, for an explanation of the difference.
12 See Nagano Masaru 'Yamamoto Yūzō Hyōden Shinshiryō 38: Koku-

min no Kokugo Undō Remmei to Nihon Kokkempō no Kōgoka', *Kokubungaku Kaishaku to Kanshō* 48, 15, 1983, pp. 187–95.
13 Two dots or a circle added to the top right-hand corner of a symbol representing a combination of vowel and unvoiced consonant to indicate that the consonant should then be voiced, e.g. *ta–da*, *sa–za*.
14 See Hayashi Shirō 'Nihon Kokkempō no Bunshō', *Gengo Seikatsu* 402, 1985, pp. 46–51, for a comparison of the English and Japanese versions of the constitution. Hayashi asserts that while the texts are so similar as to give the impression that one was translated from the other, the style of the Japanese version to him exhibits the definite, distinctive characteristics of legal Japanese.
15 An English translation of this 1965 novel is Takagi Akimitsu, *Honeymoon to Nowhere*, Brisbane: Anthos Press, 1972. See pp. 81–2.
16 Shiraishi Daiji 'Kanchō Yōgō no Hei-ika', *Kokugo to Kokubungaku* 24, 1, 1947, p. 40.
17 Yamada Bimyō in *Fūkin Shirabe no Hitofushi* and *Musashino*, both 1887, and Saganoya Omuro in *Hatsukoi*, 1889.
18 For example, Yamada Bimyō in *Togakureiyama Kikō* (1890) and Shian Gaishi in *Waga Koi* (1891).
19 After 1897, 90 per cent of colloquial-style novels used this variety. See Yamamoto Masahide ' "De gozaru'-tai kara" de aru'-tai e', *Buntairon Kenkyū* 12, 6, 1968, p. 26.

7 THE OPPOSITION

1 In the *Yomiuri Shimbun* 28 May 1881.
2 The third chapter is reproduced in Yamamoto Masahide *Kindai Buntai Keisei Shiryō Shūsei: Hasseihen*, Tokyo: Ōfūsha, 1978, pp. 290–308.
3 A body of graduates of the Imperial University established in 1879 to function as a scholarly society and a watchdog on the government's educational policies.
4 Kembō Gōki 'Meiji Jidai no Bungobun: Futsūbun ga dekiru made', *Gengo Seikatsu* 11, 1957, p. 35.
5 For example, the use of *sore* to represent the impersonal pronoun 'it', the increased use of the passive verb, and the use of abstract nouns as grammatical subjects.
6 Suematsu Kenchō *Nihon Bunron*, p. 256. Reproduced in Yamamoto *Kindai Buntai Keisei*, pp. 255–60. The page number refers to this version.
7 Both published in *Tōyō Gakkai Zasshi*, Hagino on 20 December 1887 (vol. 2, no. 2) and Sekine on 20 January 1888 (vol. 2, no. 3).
8 Ochiai Naobumi 'Bunshō no Gobyū', *Kōten Kokyūjo Kōen* 11, 1889, p. 36 (Keiō University Library).
9 Saeki Umetomo *Kokugo Gaisetsu* (3rd edn), Tokyo: Shūei Shuppan, 1967, p. 219.
10 Mikami Sanji 'Kokugo Mondai Sono Hoka ni Tsuite', in Yoshida Sumio, *Kinseigo to Kinsei Bungaku*, Tokyo: Tōyōkan, 1952, p. 378.

11 Tobiyama Junko 'Meiji Futsūbun no Kenkyū', *Nihon Bungaku* (Tōkyō Joshidai) 23, 1964, pp. 74–85. See also Okamoto Isao 'Meiji Futsūbun no Seijukuki to Shimbun', *Chūkyōdai Bungakubu Kiyō* 17, 3–4, 1984, pp. 36–54 for an analysis of *futsūbun* in the press from 1896 to 1903. Okamoto also examines *futsūbun* as used by Mori Ōgai in 'Ōgai no Futsūbun no Tōtatsuten', *Chūkyōdai Bungakubu Kiyō* 13, 3, 1980, pp. 1–40.
12 Kembō 'Meiji Jidai', p. 41.
13 Morita Shiken 'Nihon Bunshō no Shōrai' (1888), in *Meiji Bungaku Zenshū* 26, Chikuma Shobō, 1981, pp. 233–9.
14 ibid., p. 472.
15 Reproduced in *Meiji Bungaku Zenshū* 3, Tokyo: Chikuma Shobō, 1967, pp. 361–3.
16 Reproduced in Yamamoto *Kindai Buntai Keisei* pp. 505–6.
17 See Chapter 5.
18 Cited in Yamamoto Masahide *Kindai Buntai Hassei no Shiteki Kenkyū* (2nd edn), Tokyo: Iwanami Shoten, 1982 (1st edn 1965), p. 735.
19 See Chapter 9.
20 The text of Chamberlain's lecture, entitled 'Gembun'itchi', was later published in romanized form in the *Rōmaji Zasshi* 24, May 1887.
21 Yamada Bimyō 'Gembun'itchiron Gairyaku', *Gakkai no Shishin* 8 and 9 February–March 1889. Reproduced in Kindaigo Gakkai (eds) *Kindaigo Kenkyū* 4, Tokyo: Musashino Shoin, 1974, pp. 526–37. This quote occurs on p. 532.
22 Reproduced in Yamamoto, *Kindai Buntai Keisei*, pp. 522–4.
23 See Chapter 6.
24 Nishimura Shigeki 'Gembun'itchi o ronzu' *Tōyō Gakugei Zasshi* 18, 238, 1901, pp. 274–9.

8 THE STANDARDIZATION DEBATE

1 Hattori Shirō, *Gengogaku no Hōhō*, Tokyo: Iwanami Shoten, 1960, p. 733.
2 Kokugo Gakkai (eds) *Kokugogaku Daijiten* (2nd edn) Tokyo: Tōkyōdō Shuppan, 1982, pp. 254 and 776.
3 See Shibata Takeshi 'Hyōjungo, Kyōtsūgo, Hōgen', in Bunkachō (ed.) *Kotoba Shirīzu 6: Hyōjungo to Hōgen*, Tokyo; Ōkurashō Insatsukyoku, 1977, pp. 22–32. Also Suzuki Hideo 'Gendai Kyōtsūgo o tsukuridashita no wa dare ka', *Kokubungaku* 27, 16, 1982, pp. 52–6, and Uemura Yukio 'Hōgen, Kyōtsūgo, Hyōjungo', in *Kōza Gendaigo V. 1: Gendaigo no Gaisetsu*, Tokyo: Meiji Shoin, 1963, pp. 47–63.
4 Yamazaki Fumoto 'Edogo no Kōsei to Hensen', *Kokubungaku Kaishaku to Kanshō* 4, 7, 1939, p. 60.
5 San'yūtei Enshō *et al.* 'Edo no Kotoba, Meiji no Kotoba', *Gengo Seikatsu* 291, 1975, p. 7.
6 Matsumura Akira 'Edogo ga Kyōtsūgo ni naru made', *Kokubungaku Kaishaku to Kanshō* 27, 2, 1962, pp. 95–6.

7 Chamberlain, Basil Hall *A Handbook of Colloquial Japanese* 4th edn, London: Crosby Lockwood 1907, pp. 8–9.
8 *Tōyō Gakugei Zasshi* 7 and 8, April–May 1882.
9 Hikami Kakutarō 'Gembun'itchi', *Rōmaji Zasshi* 37 and 38, June–July 1888.
10 *Kana no Shirube* 2, 3 and 6, August, September, December 1884.
11 *Kana no Shirube* 7, January 1885.
12 *Kana no Shimbun* 20, 15 April 1886.
13 Published Tokyo: Jūichidō, 1886. May be found in *Meiji Bunka Zenshū* 20 (2nd edn), Tokyo: Nihon Hyōronsha, 1967, pp. 129–39.
14 This was *Jinjō Shōgaku Tokuhon*.
15 Jespersen, Otto *Mankind, Nation, and Individual*, London: Allen & Unwin, 1946, p. 51.
16 Garvin, Paul 'Some Comments on Language Planning', in Fishman, Joshua (ed), *Advances in Language Planning*, The Hague: Mouton, 1974, p. 71.
17 *Teikoku Bungaku* 1, 1, 1895.
18 Published later in *Kokumin no Tomo*, April 1895.
19 Suzuki 'Gendai Kyōtsūgo', p. 52.
20 Fujioka Katsuji 'Gembun'itchi', *Gengogaku Zasshi* 2, 5, 1901, pp. 427–39.
21 Among them Satomi Yoshi's *Gazoku Bumpō* (1887), Matsushita Daizaburō's *Nihon Zokugo Bunten* (1901), and Yoshioka Gōho's *Nihon Kōgohō* (1906).
22 Garvin, Paul and Mathiot, Madeline 'The Urbanization of the Guarani Language: A Problem in Language and Culture', in Fishman, Joshua (ed), *Readings in the Sociology of Language*, The Hague: Mouton, 1972, pp. 369–70.

9 THE PROBLEM OF ORTHOGRAPHY

1 Arai Hakuseki 'Seiyō Kibun', in *Arai Hakuseki Zenshū* 4, Tokyo: Kokusho Kankōkai Sōsho, 1906, p. 763. He makes a similar observation in *Sairan Igen*, ibid., p. 814.
2 Both books are cited in Sugimoto Tsutomu, *Kindai Nihongo no Seiritsu* (2nd edn), Tokyo: Ōfūsha, 1961, pp. 155 and 163.
3 'Kanji Gohaishi no Gi', in *Maejima Hisoka Jijoden*, Hayama: Maejima Hisoka Denki Kankōkai, 1956, p. 153.
4 ibid., pp. 155–6.
5 The petitions may all be found in *Maejima Hisoka Jijoden*.
6 A private academy founded in 1868 by Fukuzawa Yukichi, which later became Keiō University.
7 Yamamoto Masahide *Kindai Buntai Hassei no Shiteki Kenkyū* (2nd edn), Tokyo: Iwanami Shoten, 1982 (1st edn 1965), p. 261.
8 'Kana no Kai no Mondō' (Oct.–Dec. 1883), in *Meiji Bunka Zenshū* 20, Tokyo: Nihon Hyōronsha, 1967, pp. 59–96.
9 A government office teaching history, law and arithmetic, and handling all matters relating to those subjects.
10 Yamamoto *Kindai Buntai Hassei*, p. 313–14.

302 *Language and the Modern State*

11 Inoue Tetsujirō 'Shinkokuji Kakutei no Jiki', *Tōkyō Gakushi Kaiin Zasshi* 20, 1898, pp. 368–9.
12 In Shiratori's system, for example, the right-hand side of the difficult character 鯵 for *aji* (mackerel) would be replaced with *aji* in katakana, while retaining the fish radical.
13 For an extensive discussion of twentieth-century reforms, see Seeley, Chris 'The Japanese Script Since 1900', *Visible Language* 18, 3, Summer 1984, pp. 267–301.
14 For example, those found in the *Dai Nihon Komonjo* and *Meiji Bunka Zenshū* collections.
15 My example is taken from the third volume; the two forewords to this volume offer an interesting example of the range of punctuation practices then extant. One is unannotated pure Chinese, totally without punctuation; the other is a variety of *hentai kambun* in which full stops have been used not only to indicate clause and sentence boundaries but also subjects, topics, objects, and so on, as well as replacing commas in lists.
16 Futabatei Shimei 'Yo ga Honyaku no Hyōjun', (1906) in *Meiji Bungaku Zenshū* 17, Tokyo: Chikuma Shobō, 1971, p. 108.

Selected bibliography

This section presents a not exhaustive but nonetheless reasonably comprehensive guide to source materials for those working in the field of Japanese language history of the Meiji and Taishō Periods. It is divided into two sections: works in English and works in Japanese. The latter begins with a special subsection devoted to the works of Yamamoto Masahide, whose prolific and wide-ranging work on the *gembun'itchi* movement leaves few avenues unexplored and offers a wealth of empirical detail. The remainder of the Japanese language references, after a section of general references on the topic, are presented in the form of groups of references dealing with the same general theme.

All Japanese-language books and periodicals are held in the National Diet Library, Tokyo, unless otherwise stated. Japanese names are given surname first for Japanese materials.

WORKS IN ENGLISH

Altman, Albert A 'The Press', in Jansen, Marius B, and Rozman, Gilbert (eds) *Japan in Transition: From Tokugawa to Meiji* Princeton: Princeton University Press, 1986, pp. 231–47.

Anderson, C. Arnold 'The Modernization of Education', in Weiner, Myron (ed.) *Modernization: The Dynamics of Growth*, New York: Basic Books, 1966, pp. 68–80.

Beckmann, George M. *The Modernization of China and Japan*, New York: Harper and Row, 1962.

Black, Cyril Edwin 'Change as a Condition of Modern Life', in Weiner, Myron (ed.) *Modernization: The Dynamics of Growth*, New York: Basic Books, 1966, pp. 17–27.

Blacker, Carmen *The Japanese Enlightenment: A Study of the Writings of Fukuzawa Yukichi*, Cambridge: Cambridge University Press, 1964.

Bowen, Roger W. *Rebellion and Democracy in Meiji Japan: A Study of Commoners in the Popular Rights Movement*, Berkeley: University of California Press, 1980.

Braisted, William (tr.) *Meiroku Zasshi: Journal of the Japanese Enlightenment*, Cambridge, Mass: Harvard University Press, 1976.

Chamberlain, Basil Hall *A Handbook of Colloquial Japanese* (4th edn) London: Crosby Lockwood & Son, 1907.

Crawcour, Sydney *An Introduction to Kambun*, Ann Arbor: Center for Japanese Studies, University of Michigan, 1965.

Deutsch, Karl *Nationalism and Social Communication: An Inquiry into the Foundations of Nationality*, Cambridge, Mass: MIT Press and Wiley, 1953.

—— *The Nerves of Government: Models of Political Communication and Control*, New York: The Free Press, 1966.

Dilworth, David and Hirano Umeyo (tr.) *Fukuzawa Yukichi's An Encouragement of Learning*, Tokyo: Sophia University Press, 1969.

Dore, R. P. *Education in Tokugawa Japan* Berkeley: University of California Press, 1965.

Emery, Edwin, Ault, Phillip H. and Agee, Warren K. *Introduction to Mass Communications* (2nd edn), New York: Dodd, Mead and Company, 1966.

Fagen, Richard R. *Politics and Communication: An Analytic Study*, Boston: Little, Brown and Company, 1966.

Ferguson, Charles 'Language Development', in Fishman, Joshua A. *et al.* (eds) *Language Problems of Developing Nations*, New York: John Wiley & Sons, 1968, pp. 27–35.

—— 'The Language Factor in National Development', *Anthropological Linguistics* 4, 1, 1962, pp. 23–7.

Fishman, Joshua A. *Language and Nationalism: Two Integrative Essays*, Rowley, Mass.: Newbury House, 1972.

—— 'Language Problems and Types of Political and Sociocultural Integration: A Conceptual Postscript', in Fishman, Joshua *et al.* (eds) *Language Problems of Developing Nations*, New York: John Wiley & Sons, 1968, pp. 491–8.

—— 'The Impact of Nationalism and Language Planning', in Rubin, Joan and Jernudd, Björn H. (eds) *Can Language Be Planned?*, Honolulu: East-West Center Press, 1971, pp. 3–20.

Garvin, Paul 'Some Comments on Language Planning', in Fishman, Joshua (ed.) *Advances in Language Planning*, The Hague: Mouton, 1974, pp. 69–78.

Garvin, Paul and Mathiot, Madeleine 'The Urbanization of the Guarani Language: A Problem in Language and Culture', in Fishman, Joshua (ed.) *Readings in the Sociology of Language*, The Hague: Mouton, 1972, pp. 365–75.

Guxman, M. M. 'Some General Regularities in the Formation and Development of National Languages', in Fishman, Joshua (ed.) *Readings in the Sociology of Language*, The Hague: Mouton 1972, pp. 766–79.

Habein, Yaeko Sato *The History of the Japanese Written Language*, Tokyo: University of Tokyo Press, 1984.

Hackett, Roger F. 'Nishi Amane – A Tokugawa-Meiji Bureaucrat', in Harrison, John A. (ed.) *Japan* Tucson: University of Arizona Press, 1972, pp. 11–23.

Hall, Ivan Parker *Mori Arinori*, Cambridge, Mass.: Harvard University Press, 1973.

Hall, John Whitney 'Changing Conceptions of the Modernization of

Japan', in Jansen, Marius B. (ed.) *Changing Japanese Attitudes Towards Modernization*, Princeton: Princeton University Press, 1965, pp. 7–41.

Hane Mikiso 'The Movement for Liberty and Popular Rights', in Wray, Harry and Conroy, Hilary (eds) *Japan Examined: Perspectives on Modern Japanese History*, Honolulu: University of Hawaii Press, 1983, pp. 90–7.

Haugen, Einar 'Dialect, Language, Nation' *American Anthropologist* 68, 1966, pp. 922–35.

—— 'Linguistics and Language Planning', in Bright, William (ed.) *Sociolinguistics: Proceedings of the UCLA Sociolinguistics Conference 1964*, The Hague: Mouton, 1966, pp. 50–71.

Havens, Thomas R. H. *Nishi Amane and Modern Japanese Thought*, Princeton: Princeton University Press, 1970.

Huffman, James L. 'Managing the News: Fukuchi Gen'ichirō Attempts to Balance Two Worlds', in Conroy, Hilary *et al.* (eds) *Japan in Transition: Thought and Action in the Meiji Era, 1868–1912*, 1984, pp. 50–72.

—— *Politics of the Meiji Press: The Life of Fukuchi Gen'ichirō* Honolulu: University of Hawaii Press, 1980.

—— 'The Popular Rights Debate: Political or Ideological?', in Wray, Harry and Conroy, Hilary (eds) *Japan Examined: Perspectives on Modern Japanese History*, Honolulu: University of Hawaii Press, 1983, pp. 98–103.

Hunter, Janet 'Language Reform in Meiji Japan: the views of Maejima Hisoka', in Henny, Sue and Lehmann, Jean-Pierre (eds) *Themes and Theories in Modern Japanese History*, London: Athlone Press, 1988.

Jensen, Hans *Sign, Symbol and Script*, London: Allen and Unwin, 1970.

Jespersen, Otto *Mankind, Nation and Individual*, London: Allen & Unwin, 1946.

Keene, Donald *Appreciations of Japanese Culture*, Tokyo: Kodansha International, 1981.

—— *Dawn to the West: Japanese Literature of the Modern Era* 1, New York: Holt, Rinehart and Winston, 1984.

—— *The Japanese Discovery of Europe, 1720–1830* (2nd edn), Stanford: Stanford University Press, 1969.

—— *World Within Walls: Japanese Literature of the Pre-Modern Era, 1600–1867*, London: Secker and Warburg, 1976.

Kelman, Herbert C. 'Language as an Aid and Barrier to Involvement in the National System', in Rubin, Joan and Jernudd, Björn H. (eds) *Can Language Be Planned?* Honolulu: East-West Center Press, 1971, pp. 21–51.

Kinmonth, Earl H. *The Self-Made Man in Meiji Japanese Thought: From Samurai to Salary Man*, Berkeley: University of California Press, 1981.

Kiyooka, Eiichi (tr.) *The Autobiography of Fukuzawa Yukichi*, New York: Columbia University Press, 1966.

Kornicki, Peter *The Reform of Fiction in Meiji Japan*, London: Ithaca Press, 1982.

Lensen, George Alexander *Russia's Japan Expedition 1852–1855*, Gainesville: University of Florida Press, 1955.

Lent, John A (ed.) *The Asian Newspapers' Reluctant Revolution*, Ames, Iowa: Iowa State University Press 1971.

Lerner, Daniel 'Toward a Communication Theory of Modernization: A Set of Considerations', in Pye, Lucian W. (ed.) *Communications and Political Development*, Princeton: Princeton University Press, 1963, pp. 327–50.

Miller, Roy Andrew 'Chinese Script in Korea and Japan', *Asian and Pacific Quarterly of Cultural and Social Affairs* 19, 2, 1987, pp. 1–18.

—— *The Japanese Language*, Chicago: University of Chicago Press, 1967.

—— *The Japanese Language in Contemporary Japan*, Washington D.C.: American Enterprise Institute for Public Policy Research, 1977.

Miyoshi, Masao *Accomplices of Silence: The Modern Japanese Novel*, Berkeley: University of California Press, 1974.

Najita Tetsuo *Japan: The Intellectual Foundation of Modern Japanese Politics*, Chicago: University of Chicago Press, 1974.

Nakamura Mitsuo *Modern Japanese Fiction 1868–1926*(2nd edn), Tokyo: Kokusai Bunka Shinkokai, 1968.

Neustupný J.V. 'Basic Types of Treatment of Language Problems', in Fishman, Joshua A. (ed.) *Advances in Language Planning*, The Hague: Mouton, 1974, pp. 37–48.

Nitobe Inazo et al. *Western Influences in Japan* Chicago: University of Chicago Press, 1931.

Passin, Herbert *Society and Education in Japan*, New York: Teachers College Press, Columbia University, 1965.

—— 'Writer and Journalist in the Transitional Society', in Pye, Lucian W. (ed.) *Communications and Political Development*, Princeton: Princeton University Press, 1963, pp. 87–93.

Pool, Ithiel de Sola 'Communications and Development', in Weiner, Myron (ed.) *Modernization: The Dynamics of Growth*, New York: Basic Books, 1966, pp. 98–109.

Ray, Punya Sloka 'Language Standardization', in Fishman, Joshua (ed.) *Readings in the Sociology of Language*, The Hague: Mouton, 1972, pp. 754–65.

Rejai, Mostafa and Enloe, Cynthia 'Nation-States and State-Nations', in Smith, Michael, Little, Richard and Shackleton, Michael (eds.) *Perspectives on World Politics*, London: Croom Helm and the Open University Press, 1981, pp. 37–46.

Rose-Innes, Arthur *Japanese Reading for Beginners*, Yokohama: Yoshikawa Co., n.d.

Rubin, Joan and Jernudd, Björn H (eds.) *Can Language Be Planned?*, Honolulu: East-West Center Press, 1971.

Ryan, Marleigh Grayer *Japan's First Modern Novel: Ukigumo of Futabatei Shimei*, New York: Columbia University Press, 1967.

—— *The Development of Realism in the Fiction of Tsubouchi Shōyō*, Seattle: University of Washington, 1975.

Samson, Geoffrey *Writing Systems: A Linguistic Introduction*, London: Hutchinson, 1985.

Sansom, George *An Historical Grammar of Japanese*, Oxford: Clarendon Press, 1928.

Schramm, Wilbur *Mass Media and National Development: The Role of Information in the Developing Countries* Stanford: Stanford University Press, 1964.

Seeley, Chris 'Aspects of Writing in Edo Period Japan', in Miyaji Yutaka

(ed) *Ronshū Nihongo Kenkyū* v. 2: *Rekishi-hen* Tokyo, Meiji Shoin, 1986, pp. 470–97.
— 'The Japanese Script Since 1900', *Visible Language* 18, 3, 1984, pp. 267–301.
Shafer, Boyd C. *Faces of Nationalism: New Realities and Old Myths*, New York: Harcourt, Brace, Jovanovich, 1972.
Shibuzawa Keizō (ed.) *Japanese Life and Culture in the Meiji Era* tr. Charles S. Terry, Tokyo: Ōbunsha, 1958.
Smith, Wilfrid Cantwell *Modernisation of a Traditional Society*, London: Asian Publishing House, 1965.
Takagi Akimitsu *Honeymoon to Nowhere*, Brisbane: Anthos Press, 1972. This is an English translation of *Zero no Mitsugetsu*, Tokyo: Kobunsha, 1965.
Twine, Nanette (tr.) *The Essence of the Novel*, Department of Japanese, University of Queensland, Occasional papers No 11, 1981. (A translation of Tsubouchi Shōyō's *Shōsetsu Shinzui*).
Yanaga Chitoshi *Japan Since Perry*, Connecticut: Archon Books 1966.

WORKS IN JAPANESE

All books are published in Tokyo unless otherwise stated.

Yamamoto Masahide

The following is a list, not exhaustive, of Yamamoto's books on the *gembun'itchi* movement and those of his articles I have been able to locate. Monographs are listed first, followed by articles in chronological order.

Yamamoto Masahide *Kindai Buntai Hassei no Shiteki Kenkyū* (2nd edn), Iwanami Shoten, 1982 (1st edn 1965).
— *Gembun'itchi no Rekishi Ronkō*, Ōfūsha, 1971.
— (ed.) *Kindai Buntai Keisei Shiryō Shūsei: Hasseihen*, Ōfūsha, 1978.
— (ed.) *Kindai Buntai Keisei Shiryō Shūsei: Seiritsuhen*, Ōfūsha, 1979.
— *Gembun'itchi no Rekishi Ronkō: Zokuhen*, Ōfūsha, 1981.

The two edited collections above contain reproductions of many of the original documents found elsewhere in this bibliography, and are an invaluable aid to the scholar of this period of Japanese language history.

— 'Gembun'itchitai Shōsetsu no Sōshisha ni tsuite', *Kokugo to Kokubungaku* 10, 9, 1933, pp. 1150–77.
— 'Gembun'itchi to Ozaki Kōyō', *Kikan Meiji Bungaku* 3, 1934, pp. 77–96.
— 'Tsubouchi Shōyō to Gembun'itchi', *Kokugo to Kokubungaku* 13, 5, 1936, pp. 66–80.
— 'Natsume Sōseki no Bunshō', *Kokugo to Kokubungaku* 14, 11, 1937 pp. 51–69.

— 'Gembun'itchi Undō no Igi oyobi Shiteki Kubun', *Kokugo to Kokubungaku* 26, 1, 1949, pp. 42–9.
— 'Kokugoshi yori mita Gendai Nihon Bungaku no Seiritsu', *Kokugo to Kokubungaku* 27, 4, 1950, pp. 64–75.
— 'Gembun'itchishijō no Saganoya Omuro', *Nihon Bungaku Kenkyū* 14, 1950.
— 'Taguchi Ukichi no Kindai Buntai Sōken to Jisseki', *Kokugo to Kokubungaku* 29, 12, 1952, pp. 30–42.
— 'Gembun'itchishijō no Mittsu no Shinshiryō ni tsuite', *Ibaraki Daigaku Bunrigakubu Kiyō (Jimbun Kagaku)* 3, 1953 pp. 108–220.
— 'Gembun'itchi no Hensen', *Meiji Taishō Bungaku Kenkyū* 11, 1953.
— 'Gembun'itchi no Rekishi to Tokushoku', in *Nihon Bumpō Kōza* 3, Meiji Shoin, 1958, pp. 255–79.
— 'Kindai Bungaku no Buntai no Hensen', *Kokubungaku* 4, 12, 1959 pp. 8–16.
— 'Koshimbun Danwatai Bunshō no Jitta', *Ibaraki Daigaku Bunrigakubu Kiyō (Jimbun Kagaku)* 10, 1959, pp. 27–40.
— ' "Kana No Kuwai" Kikanshijō no Gembun'itchi Genshō', *Ibaraki Daigaku Bunrigakubu Kiyō (Jimbun Kagaku)* 11, 1960, pp. 53–71.
— 'Bungaku Kairyō Undō to Gembun'itchi', *Kokubungaku* 6, 11, 1961, pp. 44–9.
— 'San'yūtei Enchō no Ninjōbanashi Sokkibon to Sono Eikyō', *Gengo Seikatsu* 132, 1962, pp. 49–57.
— 'Jiyū Minken Shisōka to Gembun'itchi Undō', *Kokugo to Kokubungaku* 39, 11, 1962, pp. 1–15.
— 'Kōtoku Shūsui no Gembun'itchi Katsudō', *Ibaraki Daigaku Bunrigakubu Kiyō (Jimbun Kagaku)* 14, 1963, pp. 53–66.
— 'Kaikaki no Buntai o megutte', in Tokieda Motoki, Endō Yoshimoto et al. (eds) *Kōza Gendaigo* 2, Meiji Shoin, 1964, pp. 102–30.
— 'Sakai Karekawa no Gembun'itchi Katsudō', *Ibaraki Daigaku Bunrigakubu Kiyō (Jimbun Kagaku)* 15, 1964.
— 'Meiji no Gembun'itchi Undō', *Kokubungaku* 10, 5, 1965.
— 'Mori Ōgai no Shoki Gembun'itchitai', *Nihon Buntairon Kyōkai Kaihō* 2, 1963, pp. 21–5.
— 'Shimamura Hōgetsu no Gembun'itchi Katsudō', *Kokugo to Kokubungaku* 43, 6, 1966, pp. 1–12.
— 'Gembun'itchitai no Seiritsu', *Ibaraki Daigaku Bunrigakubu Kiyō (Jimbun Kagaku)* 17, 1966.
— ' "Gengogaku Zasshi" to Gembun'itchi', *Kokugo to Kokubungaku* 44, 5, 1967, pp. 47–66.
— 'Meiji Sanjūnendai no "Yomiuri Shimbun" no Gembun'itchi Katsudō', in *Kindaigo Kenkyū Dainishū*, Musashino Shoin, 1968, pp. 124–50.
— 'Nishi Amane no Kokugo Kaikaku Katsudō', *Gengo Seikatsu* 196, 1968, pp. 86–94.
— ' "Shōnen Gembun'itchikai" no Katsudō', *Ibaraki Daigaku Bunrigakubu Kiyō (Bungakubu Ronshū)* 1, 1968.
— ' "Degozaru'tai kara" de aru'tai e', *Buntairon Kenkyū* 12, 1968, pp. 18–27.

— 'Maejima Hisoka no Kanji Haishi Kenkoku to Gembun'itchi Katsudō', *Gengo Seikatsu* 198, 1968, pp. 86-94.
— 'Mori Ōgai no Buntai', *Bungaku* 40, 11, 1972, pp. 148-56.
— 'Yamada Bimyō no Gembun'itchiron Jūhen', in Kindaigo Gakkai (eds) *Kindaigo Kenkyū: Daiyonshū*, Musashino Shoin, 1974, pp. 485-586.
— 'Meiji no Buntai Kakumei', *Buntairon Kenkyū* 21, 1974, pp. 1-17.
— 'Ueda Kazutoshi Hakushi to Gembun'itchi', in *Kindaigo Kenkyū: Daigoshū*, Musashino Shoin, 1977, pp. 625-48.
— 'Gembun'itchitai', in *Iwanami Kōza: Nihongo 10: Buntai*, Iwanami Shoten, 1977, pp. 309-48.
— ' "Kaidan Botan Dōrō" Shoki Kampon to Shōyō no Jobun', *Kokugo to Kokubungaku* 56, 4, 1979, pp. 48-57.
— 'Gembun'itchibun no Bumpō', in *Kōza Kaishaku to Bumpō 7: Gendaibun*, Meiji Shoin, 1960.
— 'Yamada Bimyō no Meiji Nijūsannen Igo no Gembun'itchi Katsudō', *Senshū Kokubun* 17, 1976, pp. 45-85.
— 'Watashi no Gembun'itchi Kenkyūshi', *Senshū Kokubun* 22, 1979, pp. 41-61.

Language and modernization: The Japanese experience

Andō Masatsugu 'Gengo Seisaku Ronkō', *Andō Masatsugu Chosakushū* 6, Yūzankaku, 1950.
— 'Kōgobun no Kifuku' (1925) in *Kokugogaku Ronkō* 1, Yūzankaku, 1974, pp. 264-404.
Aragaki Hideo, Morioka Kenji and Yamamoto Masahide 'Gembun'itchi no Kako to Shōrai', *Gengo Seikatsu* 123, pp. 2-14.
Ekoyama Tsuneaki 'Kindai no Gengo Seikatsu to Buntai', *Kokubungaku* 5, 6, 1960, pp. 8-13.
— *Nihon Bunshōshi*, Kawade Shobō, 1956.
Endō Yoshihide 'Tegamibun ni okeru Kindai Buntai no Seiritsu', *Bungei Kenkyū* 92, 1979. p. 68.
Fukuda Tsuneari, *Kokugo Mondai Ronsōshi*, Shinchōsha, 1962.
Fukushima Kunimichi, 'Kindaigo Kenkyū Bunken Mokuroku (Edo Jidai)', in Kindaigo Gakkai (eds) *Kindaigo Kenkyū Daiisshū*, Musashino Shoin, 1965, pp. 471-96.
Furuta Tōsō, 'Kindaigo Kenkyū Bunken Mokuroku (Meiji Igo)', in Kindaigo Gakkai (eds) *Kindaigo Kenkyū Daiisshū* Musashino Shoin, 1965, pp. 505-26.
— 'Kōgo Bumpō no Seiritsu', in *Kōgo Bumpō Kōza 1: Kōgo Bumpō no Tembō* Meiji Shoin 1965, pp. 40-62.
Hara Shirō and Inoue Hisashi 'Meiji no Nihongo o kataru', *Kokubungaku* 25, 10, 1981 pp. 14-35.
Hashimoto Shinkichi *Kokugogaku Gairon*, Iwanami Shoten, 1946.
— *Kokugogakushi, Kokugo Tokushitsuron*, Iwanami Shoten, 1983.
Hata Shoko 'Meiji Bunshō Hensenshi', *Chūgaku Sekai* 9, 15, 1906, pp. 2-25.
Hatano Kanji 'Kindai Buntai no Tenkai', *Kotoba* 2, 8, 1949, pp. 2-16.

Hida Yoshifumi 'Meiji Jidai no Gengo', *Gengo Seikatsu* 266, 1973, pp. 81-96.
—— 'Nihon no Kokugo Mondai wa dōshite okotta ka', *Gengo Seikatsu* 200, 1968 pp. 44-51.
Hirota Eitarō et al. (eds) *Bunshō Hyōgen Jiten* (7th edn) Tōkyōdō Shuppan, 1966.
Homma Hisao 'Gembun'itchi no Hattatsu', in *Nihon Bungaku Kōza 12: Meiji Taishō-hen* Kaizōsha, 1934, pp. 279-90.
Ichikawa Hiroshi 'Gembun'itchi no Hensei to sono Hattatsu', *Kokugo Kokubun no Kenkyū* 6, 1927, pp. 114-19; 7, pp. 119-23; 8 pp. 123-8; 10 pp. 121-6; 12, pp. 128-36.
Iide Takehito (ed.) 'Kokugo Kokuji Mondai Kenkyū Bunken Sōran', *Kokubungaku* 6,7, 1961, pp. 173-88.
Inagaki Tatsujirō 'Meiji no Gembun'itchi wa doko made Jikō sareta ka', *Gengo Seikatsu* 1, 1955, pp. 15-21.
Isogai Hideo 'Bunshōgo toshite no 'Gembun'itchi', *Kokubungaku* 25, 10, 1980, pp. 50-6.
Isota Kōichi 'Gembun'itchiyaku no Kōzai', *Honyaku no Sekai* 3, 12, 1979, pp. 33-7.
Kamei Hideo 'Gembun'itchitai no Tanjō', *Kokugo Kokubun Kenkyū* 56, 1976, pp. 53-9.
Kamei Takashi, Ōfuji Tokihiko and Yamada Toshio (eds) *Nihongo no Rekishi V 6: Atarashii Kokugo e no Ayumi*, Heibonsha, 1965.
Kanzaki Kiyoshi 'Gembun'itchi no Sōshutsu Katei', *Kokubungaku Kaishaku to Kanshō* 4,7, 1939, pp. 95-9.
Kataoka Yoshikazu 'Gendai no Bunshō', *Kokugo to Kokubungaku* 7, 4, 1929, pp. 603-53.
Kindaichi Haruhiko *Shinnihongoron* Chikuma Shobō, 1971.
Kisaka Motoi 'Kindai Bunshō no Seiritsu ni Ōbummyaku wa donna Yakuwari o hatashita ka', *Kokubungaku* 27, 16, 1982, pp. 118-23.
—— 'Kindai Bunshōshi ni okeru Ōbummyaku no Mondai', *Hyōgen Kenkyū* 32, 1981, pp. 1-9.
Kobayashi Yoshiharu 'Kotoba no Junka', *Kokubungaku Kaishaku to Kanshō* 4,7, 1939 pp. 7-15.
Kokugo Gakkai (eds) *Kokugogaku Daijiten* (2nd edn), Tōkyōdō Shuppan, 1982.
Kubo Yumi, 'Ukiyozōshi no Gohō to Buntai', *Kyōto Daigaku Jimbun Gakuhō* 54, 1983, pp. 21-70.
Matsumura Akira 'Gendai Kokugo no Seiritsu', *Kokubungaku* 8, 2 1963, pp. 8-16.
—— 'Meiji Shoki no Kōgo: Gendaigo no Genryū toshite no', *Kokubungaku Kaishaku to Kanshō* 18, 6, 1953, pp. 4-9.
Morioka Kenji (ed.) 'Gembun'itchitai Seiritsu Shiron', *Kokugo to Kokubungaku* 62, 5, 1985, pp. 78-92.
Nakajima Kenzō 'Buntai Kakumeiron: Gembun'itchi Undō to Kindai Buntai', *Bungaku* 20, 12, 1952, pp. 27-33.
Nakamura Mitsuo 'Kōgobun to Gaikoku Bungaku', *Bungaku* 12, 20, 1952, pp. 34-8.
Nakamura Shin'ichirō *Bunshō Tokuhon*, Bunka Shuppankyoku, 1975.
Nishio Mitsuo *Kindai Bunshōron Kenkyū*, Tōkyō Shoin, 1951.

Ogata Tomio, Kuno Osamu, Morioka Kenji and Yano Kentarō, 'Kotoba no Kindaika to Nihongo', *Gengo Seikatsu* 200, 1968, pp. 4-19.
Okamoto Isao 'Bunshō, Buntai', *Kokugogaku* 137, 1984, pp. 79-85.
Ōno S. and Shibata T. (eds) *Iwanami Kōza Nihongo 10: Buntai*, Iwanami Shoten, 1978.
Ōta Saburō 'Kōgo Buntai no Seiritsu to Honyaku Bungaku', *Gengo Seikatsu* 74, 1957, pp. 22-31.
Satō Kiyoji *Kokugogaku Kenkyū Jiten*, Meiji Shoin, 1977.
Seko Katashi *Kindai Nihon Bunshōshi* (2nd edn), Hakuteisha, 1968.
Shimonaka Kunihiko (ed.) *Nihongo no Rekishi 5: Kindaigo no Nagare*, Heibonsha, 1964.
Shindō Sakiko *Meiji Jidaigo no Kenkyū: Goi to Bunshō*, Meiji Shoin, 1981.
Shioda Ryōhei *Kokugo Zuihitsu*, Sekkasha, 1965.
Shiozawa Kazuko 'Gembun'itchitai no Seiritsu', *Kokubungaku Ronshū (Jochidai)* 12, 1980 pp. 91-124.
Sugimoto Tsutomu 'Kindai Nihongo no Seiritsu', *Kokugogaku* 46, 1961.
— 'Kindai Nihongo no Seiritsu Katei', *Nihon Bungaku* 7, 1958, pp. 1-20.
— 'Kindai Nihongo no Seiritsu: Yōgaku to no Kanren ni oite', *Kokugogaku* 46, 1961, pp. 52-68.
— *Kindai Nihongo no Shinkenkyū*, Ōfūsha, 1967.
— *Kotoba no Bunkashi*, Ōfūsha, 1977.
— 'Tenkanki no Nihongo: Edo kara Tōkyō e', in Kindaigo Gakkai (eds) *Kindaigo Kenkyū Daiisshū*, Musashino Shoin, 1965, pp. 305-24.
Takamatsu Kayamura *Meiji Bungaku Gembun'itchi*, Taiheiyō Bungakusha, 1899.
Tanji Yoshio 'Kōgobun no Seiritsu Jiki', *Chūō Daigaku Kokubun* 24, 1982, pp. 25-32.
Todani Mitoe 'Kokugo Kokuji Mondai Kankei Bunken Tenji Mokuroku', *Gakuen* 259, 1960, pp. 72-85.
Tokieda Motoki 'Kōgobun no Honshitsu', *Kokugo to Kokubungaku* 4, 4, 1927, pp. 377-86.
Tokieda Motoki, Endō Yoshimoto et al. (eds) *Kōza Gendaigo 5: Bunshō to Buntai*, Meiji Shoin, 1963.
— *Kōza Gendaigo 2: Gendaigo no Seiritsu*, Meiji Shoin, 1964.
Tokuda Shūsei *Nihon Bunshōshi*, Matsuyōdō, 1925.
Usui Yoshimi, Itō Sei, Jinzai Kiyoshi, Kinoshita Junji and Umesaki Haruo 'Gendai Bunshō o kataru', *Bungakkai* 6,6, 1952.
Yagyū Shirō ' "Kindai Bungaku to Kotoba" Kankei Bunken Mokuroku', *Bungaku* 16, 7, 1958 pp. 72-90.
Yamada Yūsaku 'Buntai "Kairyō" no Imi', *Kokubungaku Kaishaku to Kanshō* 45, 3, 1981, pp. 98-107.
Yanagida Izumi 'Gembun'itchi no Rekishi', *Nihongo* 3, 12, 1943, pp. 14-20.
Yoshitake Yoshinori 'Kōgobuntai no Hattatsu', *Kokubungaku Kaishaku to Kanshō* 5, 2, 1940, pp. 60-8.
— 'Meiji Bunshōshi ni oyoboshita Gaikoku Bungaku no Eikyō: Gembun'itchi Undō to Gaikoku Bungaku', *Kotoba* 3, 8, 1941, pp. 50-5.
— 'Meiji Bunshōshi ni oyoboshita Gaikoku Bungaku no Eikyō: Yamada Bimyō to Ōbummyaku', *Kotoba* 3, 4, 1941, pp. 17-30.

Yuchi Takashi 'Meiji no Kotoba', *Kokubungaku Kaishaku to Kanshō* 4, 7, 1939, pp. 69–78.
Yuzawa Kōkichirō 'Kōgo, Bungo no Seishitsu', *Kokubungaku Kaishaku to Kanshō* 3, 12, 1938, pp. 44–56.

Pre-modern styles

Asami Kazuhiko 'Hōjōki no Buntai', *Bungaku* 52, 5, 1984, pp. 22–4.
Ekoyama Tsuneaki *Nihon Bunshōshi*, Kawade Shobō, 1956.
Hasegawa Kanehira ' "Keikoku Bidan" no Buntai ni tsuite', *Bungaku* 8, 1940, pp. 324–6.
Hirata Tomoko 'Gohōjō yori mita Meiji Shobuntai no Seikaku', *Bungaku* 18, 1962, pp. 40–58.
Hirohama Fumio 'Meiji Shoki no Tegami to Sakubun', *Gengo Seikatsu* 99, 1959, pp. 57–66.
Ichikawa Takashi 'Bunshō wa dono yō ni Bunrui sarete kita ka', *Kokugo to Kokubungaku* 31, 11, 1954, pp. 43–53.
Ikenoue Teizō 'Meiji Shoki no Bunshō', *Gengo Seikatsu* 6, 1952, pp. 28–33.
Imaizumi Nakayoshi ' "De gozaimasu" to "de arimasu" to', *Kokugo Bunka* 4, 3, 1944, pp. 52–6.
Inoue Seinosuke 'Motoori Morinaga no Kokugo Kenkyū to sono Kokugokan', *Kokubungaku Kaishaku to Kanshō* 7, 12, 1942, pp. 54–69.
Itasaka Gen 'Saikaku no Gohō', *Kokubungaku Kaishaku to Kanshō* 18, 1, 1953, pp. 40–3.
Kameshima Yoshiko 'Bakin no Bungo: Gohōmen kara no Kōsatsu', *Kokubun* 55, 1982 pp. 54–64.
Kembō Gōki 'Meiji Jidai no Bungobun' *Gengo Seikatsu* 74, 1957, pp. 32–41.
—— ' "Wakankonkōbun" to iu Meishō no Kigen', in Kokuritsu Kokugo Kenkyūjo (eds) *Kotoba no Kenkyū*, Shūei Shuppan, 1959, pp. 303–14.
Kirin Fujihiko 'Santo Kyōden no Kōgobun to Bungobun to no Kakawari' in Kindaigo Gakkai (eds) *Kindaigo Kenkyū Dairokushū*, Musashino Shoin, 1980, pp. 305–24.
Kojima Toshio 'Goki Edogo ni okeru "desu", "de arimasu", "masen deshita" ', *Kokugogaku* 39, 1959, pp. 75–84.
Komatsu Hisao 'Goki Edogo no Buke no Kotoba', *Kokugo to Kokubungaku* 62, 5, 1985, pp. 33–45.
Kono Shigeo 'Kambun Kundokutai no Gohō', *Kokubungaku Ronshū (Jochidai)* 7, 1975, pp. 172–94.
Maeda Isamu 'Keihan no "desu" Hyōjungo Inyūsetsu', *Kokugo Kokubun* 29, 4, 1959 pp. 35–45.
Murayama Yoshihiro 'Kambummyaku no Mondai', *Kokubungaku* 25, 10, 1980, pp. 40–5.
Nagazumi Yasuaki 'Wakankonkōbun no Keisei', *Bungaku* 12, 12, 1952, pp. 11–21.
Nakamura Michio ' "De arimasu" Kotoba', *Kokugo Kenkyū* 9, 4, 1941, pp. 1–18.
—— ' "De aru" Saikō', *Chūō Daigaku Bungakubu Kiyō* 45, 1967, pp. 19–48.

— ' "De aru" Shokō', *Chūō Daigaku Bungakubu Kiyō: Bungakuka* 11, 26, 1962, pp. 119–60.
— ' "Desu" no Goshi ni tsuite', *Kokugo to Kokubungaku* 13, 3, 1935 pp. 70–96.
Negishi Masayoshi 'Gembun'itchi Zengo', *Kotoba to Bungaku* 1, 1962, pp. 1–11.
Nishio Mitsuo 'Meiji Jidai Shoki no Bunshō', *Kokugo to Kokubungaku* 40, 2, 1963, pp. 1–12.
Noguchi Takehiko 'Saikaku to Shōsetsu Gengo', *Kokubungaku* 24, 7, 1979, pp. 106–13.
Okamoto Isao 'Meiji Shoki Gesakusha no Bunshō', *Kokugo to Kokubungaku* 62, 9, 1985, pp. 62–75.
Okamura Kazue 'Gunki Monogatari no Buntai', *Kokubungaku Kaishaku to Kanshō* 28, 1, 1963 pp. 68–73.
Ōta Saburō 'Kōgo Buntai no Seiritsu to Honyaku Buntai', *Gengo Seikatsu* 74, 1957, pp. 22–31.
Saeki Kōsuke 'Nihongo Hyōki no Keifu o tadoru: Meiji Ishin no Kanji Haishiron', Chapter 4 in Takefu Tatsuo and Watanabe Takeshi (eds) *Gendai Nihongo no Kensetsu ni Kurō shita Hitobito*, Sekibunsha, 1976, pp. 43–64.
Saeki Umetomo *Kokugo Gaisetsu* (3rd edn) Shūei Shuppan, 1967.
— ' "Ni ari" kara "de aru" e', *Kokugogaku* 26, 1951, pp. 1–6.
Seki Ryōichi 'Kotenbun no Hensen', *Kokubungaku Kaishaku to Kanshō*, special spring issue, 1960, pp. 36–40.
Sugimoto Tsutomu *Kindai Nihongo no Seiritsu* (2nd edn), Ōfūsha, 1961.
— 'Nihongo no Rekishi', in *Iwanami Kōza Nihongo 2: Gengo Seikatsu*, Iwanami Shoten, 1977, pp. 249–372.
Suzuki Hideo 'Meiji Zenki Bungobun no Gohō', *Kokugo to Kokubungaku* 53, 2, 1976, pp. 57–72.
Takenouchi Satoko 'Kanamoji no Seiritsu to Buntai', *Gengo Seikatsu* 296, 1976, pp. 36–43.
Teruoka Yasutaka 'Edo Jidai Shōsetsu ni okeru Zokugo no Yakuwari', *Kokubungaku Kaishaku to Kanshō* 4, 7, 1939, pp. 90–4.
Tōdō Akiyasu *Chatō Shiki Shirīzu: Kambun Kaishaku*, Sūken Shuppan, 1969.
Tsuchiya Shin'ichi 'Edogo Tōkyōgo no Dantei Hyōgen', in Kokuritsu Kokugo Kenkyūjo (eds) *Kotoba no kenkyū* 5, 1974, pp. 45–64.
Tsujimura Toshiki ' "Desu" no Gohō: Kinseigo kara Gendaigo e", in Kindaigo Gakkai (eds) *Kindaigo Kenkyū Daiisshū*, Musashino Shoin, 1965, pp. 342–62.
— 'Meiji no Bungobun no Kaishaku to Bumpōjō no Mondaiten', in *Kōza Kaishaku to Bumpō 7: Gendaibun*, Meiji Shoin, 1960, pp. 190–218.
Watanabe Minoru 'Kanafumi no Seiritsu ni Kambun Kundokubun wa donna Yakuwari o hatashita ka', *Kokubungaku* 27, 16, 1982, pp. 114–17.
Yamazaki Fumoto 'Edo Jidai no Zokubun', *Kokugo to Kokubungaku* 7, 4, 1931, pp. 209–31.
Yanagida Kunio ' "De aru" to "desu" ', *Yanagida Kunio Shū* 31, Chikuma Shobō, 1964, pp. 292–302.
Yasuda Kiyomon ' "Masu" to "desu" ', in Kindaigo Gakkai (eds) *Kindaigo Kenkyū Daigoshū*, Musashino Shoin, 1977.

— ' "Masu" to "desu" no Zokuron', in Kindaigo Gakkai (eds) *Kindaigo Kenkyū Dairokushū*, Musashino Shoin, 1980, pp. 64-89.
Yoshida Sumio 'Kinsei Bungo no Shosō', *Kokugo to Kokubungaku* 36, 10, 1959, pp. 13-24.
Yoshikawa Yasuo ' "Desu" no Kigen ni tsuite', *Kokugakuin Zasshi* 63, 7-8, 1962, pp. 1-6.
Yoshizawa Yoshinori 'Kanamajiribun no Kigen: Meiji Shonen no Kanamajiribun ga umareru made', *Kokugo to Kokubungaku* 4, 4, 1927, pp. 25-37.
Yuchi Takashi 'Meiji Jidai no Bunshōsō', *Kokugo to Kokubungaku* 7, 4, 1929, pp. 231-59.

Early stirrings: education and the press

Fukuchi Gen'ichirō 'Gembun'itchi' (1901), in *Meiji Bungaku Zenshū* 11 Chikuma Shobō, 1965, pp. 394-7.
— 'Bunron' (1875), in *Meiji Bungaku Zenshū* 11 Chikuma Shobō, 1965, pp. 344-5.
— 'Bunshō Kairyō no Mokuteki' (1886), in *Meiji Bungaku Zenshū* 11 Chikuma Shobō, 1965, pp. 386-8.
— 'Bunshō no Shinka' (1885), in *Meiji Bungaku Zenshū* 11 Chikuma Shobō, 1965, pp. 376-9.
— 'Bunshōron' (1881), in *Meiji Bungaku Zenshū* 11 Chikuma Shobō, 1965, pp. 368-71.
Furuta Tōsō 'Fukuzawa Yukichi: Sono Kokugokan to Kokugo Kyōikukan', *Jissen Kokugo* 205, 1957, pp. 72-81.
Inatomi Eijirō 'Meiji Shoki no Kokugo Haishiron', *Kokugo Bunka* 3, 7, 1942, pp. 9-20 and 8, pp. 29-35.
Iwabuchi Etsutarō 'Meiji Shoki no Gengo Seikatsu', *Gengo Seikatsu* 291, 1975, pp. 18-23.
— 'Meiji Shoki no Kokugo Seisakuron', *Gengo Seikatsu* 86, 1958, pp. 15-22.
Kisaka Motoi 'Shingakusho no Bunshō', *Sagadai Kyōikugakubu Kenkyū Rombunshū* 28, 2, 1981, pp. 23-37.
Kokuritsu Kokugo Kenkyūjo (eds) *Meiji Shoki no Shimbun no Yōgo*, Shūei Shuppan, 1959.
Maejima Hisoka 'Kanji Gohaishi no Gi', in *Maejima Hisoka Jijoden*, Hayama (Kanagawa): Maejima Hisoka Denki Kankōkai, 1956, pp. 153-9.
Morioka Kenji 'Kōgoshi ni okeru Shingaku Dōwa no Ichi', *Kokugogaku* 123, 1981, pp. 21-34.
Mozume Takami 'Gembun'itchi' (1886), in *Meiji Bunka Zenshū* 20, Nihon Hyōronsha, 1967, pp. 129-39.
Nishio Mitsuo 'Meiji Keimōki no Buntai', *Kokubungaku* 4, 12, 1959, pp 17-21.
Okamoto Isao 'Bakumatsu Ishin no Shimbun no Bunshō, *Chukyōdai Bungakubu Kiyō*, 18, 1, 1984, pp. 28-52.
— 'Meiji Shoki Shimbun Shōsetsu no Bunshō', *Kokugogaku* 142, 1985, pp. 1-22.

Shindō Sakiko 'Kaikaki no Gengo no Yōsō', *Tōkyō Joshi Daigaku Hikaku Bunka Kenkyūjo Kiyō* 28, 1970, pp. 79–113.
—— 'Meiji Shoki no Koshimbun ni arawareta Danwatai no Bunshō', in Kokuritsu Kokugo Kenkyūjo (eds) *Kotoba no Kenkyū*, Shūei Shuppan, 1959, pp. 57–70.
—— ' "Seiyō Jijo" no Bunshō', *Tōkyō Jodai Hikaku Bunka Kenkyūjo Kiyō* 36, 1976, pp. 1–20.
—— 'Shimbun no Bunshō in Tokieda Motoki, Endō Yoshimoto et al. (eds) *Kōza Gendaigo 2: Gendaigo no Seirtsu*, Meiji Shoin, 1964 pp. 191–218.
Shiozawa Kazuko 'Gembun'itchitai no Seiritsu: Enzetsu Sokki no hatashita Yakuwari (2)', *Jochidai Kokubungaku Ronshū* 13, 1981, pp. 27–54.
Sugimoto Tsutomu 'Rangakusha no Gengo Shisō', *Gengo Seikatsu*, 309, 1977, pp. 42–54.
Suzuki Hideo 'Shimbun no Bunshō no Kindaika: Meiji Jūni – Nijūnen no Asahi Shimbun o Chūshin toshite', *Kokugo to Kokubungaku* 44, 4, 1967, pp. 67–77.
Taguchi Ukichi 'Nippon Kaika no Seishitsu Yōyaku Aratamezaru Bekarazu', *Tōkyō Keizai Zasshi* 239, 1884, pp. 608–10; 240, pp. 642–6; 241, pp. 675–8; 242, pp. 710–12; 243, pp. 746–9.
Yamada Yūsaku' Kōgo Buntai no Hassō to sono Riron: Enchō, Shōyō, Bimyō', *Bungakushi Kenkyū* 3, 1975–7 pp. 67–86.
Yoshida Tōsō *Kyōkasho kara mita Meiji Shoki no Gengo Moji no Kyōiku (Mombushō Kokugo Shirīzu* 36), Eifu Shuppan, 1958.
Yoshitake Yoshinori 'Meiji Bunshōshijō no Fukuzawa Yukichi', *Koten Kenkyū*, July 1940 pp. 95–100.

Language and politics

Fukuzawa Yukichi 'Fukuzawa Zenshū Shogen' (1897) in, *Fukuzawa Yukichi Zenshū* 1, Iwanami Shoten, 1958, pp. 3–65.
—— *Gakumon no Susume* (1872–6), in *Fukuzawa Yukichi Zenshū* 3, Iwanami Shoten, 1959, pp. 21–144.
—— *Tsūzoku Minkenron* (1878), *in Fukuzawa Yukichi Zenshū* 4, Iwanami Shoten 1959, pp. 571–97.
Itō Masao, 'Fukuzawa Yukichi to Kokugo no Mondai', *Gengo Seikatsu* 106, 1960, pp. 60–7, 107, pp. 64–73.
Katō Hiroyuki *Shinsei Tai-i* (1870), in Matsumoto Sannosuke (ed.) *Gendai Nihon Shisō Taikei* 1, Chikuma Shobō, 1963, pp. 364–81.
Kisaka Motoi 'Ronsetsuteki Gembun'itchi Bunshō no Yōgohō: "Shinsei Tai–i" to "Hyakuichi Shinron" no Fukushi', *Kinsei Bungaku Kō* 22, 1978, pp. 104–16.
Nakae Chōmin, *Min'yakuron Yaku* (1882), in *Meiji Bungaku Zenshū* 13, Chikuma Shobō, 1967, pp. 3–20.
Nishi Amane *Hyakuichi Shinron* (1874) in Matsumoto Sannosuke (ed) *Gendai Nihon Shisō Taikei* 1, Chikuma Shobō, 1963, pp. 382–422.
—— 'Yōji o mote Kokugo o shosuru no Ron' (1874), in *Meiji Bungaku Zenshū* 3, Chikuma Shobō, 1967, pp. 88–93.
Nishio Minoru, Maruyama Masao and Etō Jun 'Fukuzawa Yukichi no Buntai to Hassō', *Bungaku* 28, 12, 1958, pp. 1559–76.

Nishio Mitsuo 'Meiji Jidai Shoki no Bunshō', *Kokugo to Kokubungaku* 40, 2, 1963, pp. 1–12.
Shindō Sakiko 'Meiji Shoki no Gengo no Seitai', *Gengo Seikatsu* 90, 1959, pp. 51–61.
Tanabe Masao 'Hirata Atsutane to Kokugogaku', *Kokugakuin Zasshi* 74, 11, 1973, pp. 50–9.
Ueki Emori *Minken Jiyūron* (1879), in *Meiji Bungaku Zenshū* 12, Chikuma Shobō, 1973, pp. 119–27.
—— *Minken Jiyūron Nihen Kōgo* (1882), in *Meiji Bungaku Zenshū* 12, Chikuma Shobō, 1973, pp. 130–41.

The role of literature

Aihara Kazukuni 'Sōseki Sakuhin no Buntai o Bunseki suru', *Kokubungaku* 25, 10, 1980, pp. 128–39.
Aoki Toshihiro 'Tsubouchi Shōyō to Gembun'itchi Shōsetsu', *Kokugo Kokubun* 51, 12, 1982, pp. 15–32.
Ekoyama Tsuneaki 'Futabatei no Gembun'itchi', *Bungaku* 22, 10, 1954, pp. 11–22.
Endō Yoshihide 'Arishima Takeo no Tegamibun no Seiritsu', *Nihon Bungaku Nōto* 14, 1980 pp. 127–34.
—— 'Futabatei Shimei no Bungakuteki Shuppatsu: "Ukigumo" no Buntairon Josetsu', *Nihon Bungaku Nōto* 17, 1982, pp. 114–25.
Fukuda Kiyohito 'Iwaya Sazanami to Jidō Bungaku', in *Meiji Bungaku Zenshū* 39, Chikuma Shobō, 1968, pp. 386–9.
Futabatei Shimei 'Shaseibun ni tsuite no Kufū', *Bunshō Sekai* 2, 3, 1907, pp. 19–22.
—— 'Shōsetsu Buntai Iken', *Bungei Kurabu* 4, 3, 1877, pp. 261–2.
—— 'Yo ga Gembun'itchi no Yurai' (1906) in *Futabatei Shimei Zenshū* 5, Iwanami Shoten, 1965, pp. 170–2.
—— 'Yo ga Hon'yaku no Hyōjun' (1906), in *Meiji Bungaku Zenshū* 17, Chikuma Shobō, 1971, pp. 108–10.
Hara Shirō 'Futabatei Shimei, Naimen no Gengo e' *Kokubungaku* 25, 10, 1980, pp. 90–7.
Hasegawa Futabatei 'Bunshō Komon', *Bunshō Sekai* 1, 5, 1906, pp. 100–2.
Hata Yūzō 'Buntai no Sōzōshatachi: Futabatei Shimei', *Kokubungaku* 22, 14, 1977, pp. 80–4.
Hisamatsu Sen'ichi (ed.) *Nihon Bungakushi* 5, Tōbundō, 1960.
Homma Hisao *Meiji Bungakushi* 1, Tōkyōdō Shuppan, 1964 (Part 2, Chapter 3, 'Gembun'itchi').
—— *Nihon Bungakushi* 2, Tōkyōdō Shuppan, 1965.
Ikari Akira, *Ken'yūsha no Bungaku*, Hanawa Shobō, 1961.
Isogai Hideo 'Mori Ōgai no Buntai: Shoki Gembun'itchi o megutte', *Hirodai Bungakubu Kiyō* 33, 1975, pp. 194–214.
Izawa Masayoshi 'Shiga Naoya no Bungaku to Buntai', *Kokubungaku Kaishaku to Kanshō* 15, 3, 1950, pp. 7–12.
Izumi Kyoka and Oguri Fūyō 'Kōyō Sensei', *Myōjō* 11, 1903, pp. 1–31.
Kamei Masaji ' "Ukigumo" to sono Hyōgen', *Kokugo Kokubun* 31, 2, 1962, pp. 23–39.

Kanda Sumiko 'Gembun'itchishijō ni okeru Sokki Enzetsubun no Kenkyū', *Nihon Bungaku (Tōkyō Joshidai)* 19, 1952, pp. 43–57.
Katagami Tengen 'Shōsetsu no Bunshō no Shimmi', *Bunshō Sekai* 3, 1, 1908, pp. 98–105.
Kataoka Yoshikazu 'Bimyō no Ichi', *Ritsumeikan Bungaku* 1, 1934, pp. 826–34.
Kisaka Motoi 'Kindai Buntai to Shūji (1): 'Ukigumo no Hiyu', *Nīhama Kōkōsen Kiyō (Jimbun)* 11, 1976, pp. 1–8.
—— 'Meiji Bungo toshite no "Takekurabe" no Kotoba' pt. 1, *Kaishaku* 24, 7, 1979, pp. 4–8.
Kiyomizu Tsutomu 'Gyakusetsu no Setsuzokushi to Gembun'itchi Shoki Shōsetsu no Buntai: Bimyō, Shimei o Chūshin ni', *Nagoyadai Kokugo Kokubungaku* 34, May 1975, pp. 49–59.
Koizumi Kōichirō 'Mori Ōgai no Buntai to Buntai Ishiki', *Kokubungaku* 25, 10, 1981, pp. 116–20.
Kōjiro Sei 'Gembun'itchi Sōshisha Isetsusho', *Shomotsu Ōrai* 2, 1924, pp. 31–3. Held in Keiō University library.
Kumasaka Atsuko 'Sōseki no Shaseibun', *Kokugo to Kokubungaku* 54, 10, 1977, pp. 1–14.
Maeda Akira 'Gembun'itchi no Shōsetsu', *Bunshō Sekai* 7, 14, 1912, pp. 15–18.
Makibayashi Kōji 'Kitamura Tōkoku ni okeru Buntai no Imi', *Sagadai Kyōikugakubu Kenkyū Rombunshū* 23, 1975, pp. 1–16.
Masamune Hakuchō 'Sōseki to Futabatei', *Bunshō Sekai* 2, 1, 1907, pp. 123–8.
Masaoka Shiki 'Jojibun' (1900), in *Meiji Bungaku Zenshū* 53, Chikuma Shobō, 1975, pp 280–3.
Matsui Toshihiko 'Shasei Buntai no Sōshi', *Kokugo to Kokubungaku* 52, 8, 1975, pp. 58–71.
Matsushita Teizō 'Kindai Buntai no Sōshi (1): Shutoshite Futabatei ni okeru Mondai', *Nihon Bungaku* 4, 6, 1955, pp. 2–13.
—— 'Yamada Bimyō no Gembun'itchi Shisō', *Kokugo Kokubun* 29, 1, 1960, pp. 16–29.
Miyamoto Masayoshi ' "Ukigumo" no Sutairu Shoron', *Nihon Bungaku* 7, 5, 1958, pp. 349–59.
Muramatsu Sadataka 'Yamada Bimyō: Gembun'itchi Sōshisha toshite no Higekiteki Ummei', *Kokubungaku Kaishaku to Kanshō* 34, 1, 1969, pp. 55–61.
Murata Toshiko 'Gembun'itchitai Shōsetsu Sōshi ni tsuite no Bimyō no Kangaekata', *Kokubun* 6, 1956, pp. 32–9.
Nakagawa Kojūrō ' "Iratsume" to Gembun'itchi', *Ritsumeikan Bungaku* 1, 6, 1934, pp. 1–29; 1, 7, pp. 1–29.
Nakajima Kunihiko 'Gembun'itchi Shasei Byōsha', *Nihon Bungaku* 28, 4, 1980, pp. 1–7.
Ogata Osamu ' "Ukigumo" no Hyōgen', *Bengei to Hihyō* 5, 5, 1981, pp. 52–7.
Ōishi Hatsutarō 'Tayama Katai no Bunshō: 'No no Hana'kara 'Futon' made', *Senshū Jimbun Ronshū* 14, 1975, pp. 1–24.
—— 'Tayama Katai no Shoki Kōgotai Shōsetsu no Bunshō', *Senshū Kokubun* 15, 1975, pp. 59–83, 16, pp. 47–72.

Ōishi Shūhei 'Tajō Takon'ron', *Bungaku* 43, 11, 1975, pp. 16–27.
Okamoto Isao 'Mori Ōgai no Futsūbun', *Chūkyōdai Bungakubu Kiyō* 13, 1, 1978, pp. 62–105.
—— 'Tsubouchi Shōyō no Bungobun', *Kokugo Kokubun* 54, 2, 1985, pp. 1–18.
Ōnishi Hajime 'Bungakujō no Shinjigyō', *Ōnishi Hakushi Zenshū* 7, Keiseisha Shoten, 1904, pp. 573–85.
—— 'Mojiron oyobi Buntairon', *Rokugō Zasshi* 174, 1895, pp. 47–9.
Ōno Moto 'Hon'yaku Bunshō ni okeru Gembun'itchi ni tsuite: Futabatei Shoki Hon'yaku Bunshō no Bunseki', *Kokugo Kyōiku Kenkyū* 8, 1963, pp. 396–404.
Ōtsuki Fumihiko 'Kokugo Kairyō no Hanashi', *Kyōiku Jiron* 617, 1902, pp. 5–7.
Ōshima Mizuho 'Yamada Bimyō Kenkyū: Shōsetsu Buntai no Hensen', *Kokubun* 59, 1984, pp. 23–35.
Ozaki Akimitsu ' "Ninin Nyōbō" no Buntai to Kōyō no Gembun'itchi', *Nagoyadai Kokugo Kokubungaku* 34, 1975, pp. 61–74.
Ozaki Kōyō 'Gembun'itchiron', in Itō Sei *et al.* (eds) *Kanshō to Kenkyū: Gendai Nihon Bungaku Kōza*, 1, Sanseido, 1962, pp. 318–19.
Satō Kiyoji 'Kindaigo no Keisei: Futabatei no 'Ukigumo' o Chūshin ni', *Bungei Kenkyū* 81, 1977 pp. 1–9.
Satō Takashi 'Meijiki Bungaku no Bunshō: Gembun'itchitai no Hassei o Chūshin toshite', *Kindaigo Kenkyū Dainishū*, Musashino Shoin, 1968, pp. 151–74.
Seki Ryōichi 'Futabatei to Shōyō', *Kokubungaku Kaishaku to Kanshō* 28, 5, 1963, pp. 15–24.
—— 'Ōgai no Goi to Buntai', *Kokubungaku Kaishaku to Kanshō* 24, 8, 1959, pp. 22–30.
—— 'Ozaki Kōyō', *Kokubungaku Kaishaku to Kanshō* 34, 1, 1969, pp. 61–6.
—— 'San'yūtei Enchō', *Kokubungaku* 14, 2, 1969, pp. 74–82.
Shian Gaishi ' "Aibiki" o yonde', *Kokumin no Tomo* 30, 1888, pp. 304–5.
Shimazaki Tōson 'Gembun'itchi no Niryūha', *Bunshō Sekai* 1, 3, 1906, pp. 19–20.
Shioda Ryōhei 'Kindai Bungaku to Buntai', *Kokubungaku* 4, 12, 1959, pp. 2–7.
Shishido Gi'ichi 'Yamada Bimyō to Gembun'itchi Undō', *Gekkan Bunshō Zōkan* July 1938, pp. 92–5.
Sugimoto Tsutomu 'Kindai Bungaku Sakka to Buntai no Aida: Shōyō kara Tōson made', *Kokubungaku Kaishaku to Kanshō* 28, 9, 1963, pp. 81–5.
Sugiyama Yasuhiko 'Hasegawa Futabatei ni okeru Gembun'itchi', *Bungaku* 36, 9, 1968, pp. 34–51.
Takada Mizuho 'Wakamatsu Shizuko', *Kokubungaku Kaishaku to Kanshō* 13, 5, 1948, pp. 1–3.
Takahashi Hideo 'Shoki Sōseki no Buntai: Shaseibun to no Kanren de', *Kokubungaku* 24, 6, 1979, pp. 58–64.
Takebe Yoshiaki 'Kokugo Sokki no Shoki ni mirareta Kokugokan ni tsuite', *Kokugogaku* 52, 1963, pp. 47–55.
Takeshima Kiyoharu 'Gembun'itchi to Hirotsu Ryūrō', *Meiji Bungaku Kenkyū* 1, 8, 1934 pp. 65–6.

Tayama Katai 'Futabatei no Bunshō,' *Kindai no Shōsetsu* December 1921, pp. 38–44.
—— 'Rokotsunaru Byōsha' (1904), in *Gendai Nihon Bungaku Zenshū* 9, Chikuma Shobō, 1955, pp. 391–3.
Tokuda Shūsei, *Meiji Shōsetsu Bunshō Hensenshi*, in *Meiji Taishō Bungakushi Shūsei*, Nihon Tosho Sentā, 1982, pp. 1–181.
Tsubouchi Shōyō ' "Ukigumo" Jidai', *Shinshōsetsu* 14, 6, 1909, pp. 262–6.
Ueno Chikara ' "Ukigumo" to Samba: Kotoba o Chūshin toshite', *Tokoha Kokubun* 6, 1982, pp. 82–90.
Unsigned 'Shōsetsu Buntai to Shimpa Sakka', *Waseda Bungaku* 7, 5, 1898, pp. 96–8.
Wada Shigeki 'Shiki no Kōgoteki Hassō Hyōgen', *Bungaku* 52, 9, 1984, pp. 69–81.
Yamada Bimyō *Gembun'itchi no Gisei* (1907), in Itō Sei *et al.* (eds) *Kanshō to Kenkyū Gendai Nihon Bungaku Kōza V. 1, Shōsetsu: Kindai Bungaku no Akebono*, Sanseidō, 1962, pp. 312–15.
—— 'Meiji Bungaku no Yōran Jidai', *Chūgaku Sekai* 9, 15, 1906, pp. 132–40.
Yamada Yūsaku 'Gembun'itchi no Sakkatachi: Shōyō, Bimyō, Shimei-ra o megutte', Chapter 5 in Takefu Tatsuo and Watanabe Takeshi (eds) *Gendai Nihongo no Kensetsu ni Kurō shita Hitobito*, Sekibunsha, 1976, pp. 163–76.
Yanazida Izumi ' "Koko ya Kashiko" sono hoka', *Kokugo to Kokubungaku* 11, 8, 1934, pp. 70–80.
—— *Tayama Katai no Bungaku* 2, Shunshusha, 1957. N.B. Chapters 11 and 12, 'Katai no Shoki Bunshō', pp. 482–533.
Yonekawa Masao 'Futabatei no Hon'yaku', *Kokubun Kaishaku to Kanshō* 28, 5, 1963 pp. 88–96.

The final stages

Andō Masatsugu 'Kokugo Chōsa Shiken', *Taiyō*, August 1921, pp. 120–9.
Edwards Ernest 'Gengo Kairyō to Gembun'itchi', *Yomiuri Shimbun*, 30 July 1901–9 August 1901, p. 1 of each edition.
Fujimura Tsukuru 'Kokugo Mondai no Kako o Kaiko shite: Kokugo Shingikai no Kaizō o nozomu', *Kokugo to Kokubungaku* 17, 12, 1940, pp. 1–16.
Fujioka Katsuji 'Gembun'itchi', *Gengogaku Zasshi* 2, 5, 1901, pp. 427–39.
Gembun'itchikai (eds) *Gembun'itchikai no Kaishi* 1, Gembun'itchikai, 1902.
—— *Shimbun* 1, 1–2, 8, 1901.
Gotō Makita 'Gembun'itchi no Seiritsu ni tsuite', *Yomiuri Shimbun*, 25–28 June 1901, p. 1 of each edition.
Hayashi Shirō 'Nihon Kokkempō no Bunshō', *Gengo Seikatsu* 402, 1985, pp. 46–51.
Horie Hideo (ed.) *Gembun'itchi Bumpan, Tsūzoku Sakubun Zenshō* 15, 1907.
Inoue Tetsujirō 'Eisei to Kokutai yori Gembun'itchi no Hitsuyō', *Yomiuri Shimbun*, 18-24 June 1901, p. 1 of each edition.

—— 'Gembun'itchi ni tsuite', *Yomiuri Shimbun*, 30 June 1901, p. 1.
Kataoka Yoshikazu 'Gendai Kōgobun no Ketten', *Shisō* 92, 1929, pp. 88–97.
Katō Hiroyuki 'Gembun'itchi ni tsuite', *Yomiuri Shimbun*, 24–27 May 1901.
—— 'Kokugo Chōsa ni tsukite', *Kyōiku Jiron*, 622, 1902, pp. 4–6.
Kawano Shiun 'Gojin no Bunshōkan', *Shinsei*, July 1903, pp. 18–21.
Kikuchi Dairoku 'Gembun'itchi ni tsuite', *Yomiuri Shimbun*, 14–18 July 1901.
Maejima Hisoka 'Keizai yori Gembun'itchi o Kansatsu su', *Yomiuri Shimbun*, 14–17 June 1901, p. 1 of each edition.
Matsushita Teizō 'Meiji Sanjūnendai no Gembun'itchi Sakubunhō Shisō', in Kyōto Daigaku Kokubun Gakkai (eds) *Kokugogaku Ronshū, Tokushō Dai'ichi Daini Gōhon*, Kyoto: Chūō Tosho Shuppansha, 1966, pp. 425–37.
Mizuhonoya 'Kyōjusha yori mitaru Gendai no Bunshō', *Bunshō Sekai* 7, 1908, pp. 66–75.
Mukai Gunji 'Gembun'itchi no Buntai ni tsuki', *Yomiuri Shimbun*, 13 May 1901, p. 5, 20 May 1901, p. 5.
Nagano Masaru 'Gembun'itchi Undō to Kōgo Bumpō Kenkyū', in Kokugogaku (ed) *Kindaichi Haruhiko Hakushi Koki Kinen Rombunshū* 1, Sanseidō, 1984, pp. 345–74.
—— 'Ōtsuki Fumihiko', *Gengo Seikatsu* 205, 1968, pp. 87–95.
—— 'Yamamoto Yūzō Hyōden, Shinshiryō 38: Kokumin no Kokugo Undō Remmei to Nihon Kokkempō no Kōgoka', *Kokubungaku Kaishaku to Kanshō* 48, 15, 1983, pp. 187–95.
Nitobe Inazo 'Gembun'itchi no Sansei ni tsuite', *Yomiuri Shimbun*, 28–31 May 1901, p. 1 of each edition.
Okabe Seiichi, 'Hyakunen no Taikei', *Yomiuri Shimbun*, 19–29 July 1901, p. 1 of each edition.
Okada Masami 'Kanji Zempai o ronjite Kokubun Kokugo Kokuji no Shōrai ni oyobu', *Teikoku Bungaku* 1, 10, 1895, pp. 385–412.
Okamoto Isao, 'Meijiki no Kyōkasho no Buntai: Shōgakkō Chiri ni tsuite', *Chūkyōdai Bungakubu Kiyō* 15, 1, 1980, pp. 27–57.
Okazawa Shōjirō 'Gembun'itchi no Shusha', *Tōa no Hikari* 3, 2, 1908, pp. 54–61; 3, pp. 49–53; 4, pp. 68–73; 6, pp. 62–70; 7, pp. 47–58. Held in Keiō University Library.
S.K. Sei *'Gembun'itchi no Mihon'*, *Yomiuri Shimbun*, 26 August 1901, p. 5.
Sakai Karekawa *Gembun'itchi Futsūbun*, Naigai Shuppan Kyōkai, 1901.
Shiozawa Kazuko 'Meijiki no Kokutei Kokugo Kyōkasho: Gembun'itchitai no Kakutei ni hatashita Yakuwari', *Kokubungaku Ronshū (Jōchidai)* 11, 1979, pp. 117–60.
Shiraishi Daiji 'Hoshina Kōichi', *Gengo Seikatsu* 207, 1968, pp. 83–91.
—— 'Kanchō Yōgo no Hei'ika', *Kokugo to Kokubungaku* 24, 1, 1947, pp. 34–42.
Shiratori Kurakichi 'Gembun'itchi o Yōsuru Rekishiteki Gen'in', *Yomiuri Shimbun*, 1–13 June 1901, p. 1 of each edition.
Sonoda Jirō 'Shimbun Bunshō no Hei'ika o meguru Jakkan no Mondai', *Kokugogaku* 7, 1951, pp. 44–55.

Sugimoto Tsutomu 'Kindaigo no Hyōshō: "De aru"- tai no Hassei to Hatten', *Kokubungaku Kenkyū* 25, 1962, pp. 282-90.
Takatsu Kuwamira 'Kokugo Kokubun no Kairyō', *Taiyō* 6, 13, 1900, pp. 6-12.
Takefu Tatsuo 'Sengo Kaiso no Kokugo Shingikai to sono Kajitori o shita Toki Zenmaro-shi', Chapter 1 in Takefu Tatsuo and Watanabe Takeshi (eds) *Gendai Nihongo no Kensetsu ni Kurō shita Hitobito*, Sekibunsha, 1976, pp. 89-112.
Tanizaki Jun'ichirō 'Gendai Kōgobun no Ketten ni tsuite', *Kaizō* 11, 11, 1929, pp. 2-22.
Tokieda Motoki 'Kokugo Kokuji Mondai Kaiketsuan', *Ōsaka Asahi Shimbun* 22 February 1914, p. 1.
— 'Reimeiki no Kokugaku to Kokugo Seisakuron to no Kōsho', *Kokugo to Kokubungaku* 33, 1, 1956, p. 1-9.
Ueda Kazutoshi 'Kokugo Kaigi ni tsukite', *Kyōiku Jiron* 422, 1897, pp. 22-6.
— 'Kokugo Kenkyū ni tsuite' (1894), in *Meiji Bungaku Zenshū* 44, Chikuma Shobō 1968, pp. 114-18.
— 'Kokugo to Kokka to' (1894), in *Meiji Bungaku Zenshū* 44, Chikuma Shobō 1968, pp. 108-13.
Ume Kenjirō, 'Gembun'itchi no Hitsuyō ni tsuite', *Yomiuri Shimbun*, 19-23 May 1901, p. 1 of each edition.
Unsigned 'Gembun'itchi ni tsuite no Kibō', *Teikoku Bungaku* 7, 5, 1901, pp. 99-100.
Unsigned 'Gembun'itchi no Moji ni tsuite no Kibō', *Teikoku Bungaku* 7, 6, 1901, pp. 126-8.
Yamada Bimyō *Gembun'itchi Bunrei*, Naigai Shuppan Kyōkai, 1901.
Yoshida Sumio 'Kokugo Mondai no Kagenmatsu', *Gengo Seikatsu* 125, 1962, pp. 50-7.
Yoshida Tōsō 'Kōgo Buntai no Keisei: Shōgaku Tokuhon ni okeru', *Jissen Kokugo Kyōiku* 260-4, February-June 1962. (260, pp. 45-7; 261, pp. 53-7; 262, pp. 92-6; 263, pp. 71-5; 264, pp. 76-80).
Yoshitake Yoshinori, 'Yamada Bimyō-cho "Nihon Daijisho"', *Kotoba* 4, 10, 1941, pp. 35-42.

The opposition

Anezaki Shōji ' "Gembun'itchiron ni tsuite" ni tsuite', *Bun* 2, 12, 1889, pp. 740-1.
Aoki Yoshimasa 'Bimyō-shi no "Gembun'itchiron Aru Toi" o yomu', *Bun* 2, 12, 1889, pp. 741-3.
Aomi Rōjin 'Gembunron', *Bun* 2, 11, 1889, pp. 670-2.
Fujiyama Yutaka 'Bunshōron ni tsuite Kojima-kun oyobi Bimyō-shikun ni tsugu', *Bun* 2, 10, 1889, pp. 609-10.
Heigai Sei 'Meiji Bunshō no Gettan', *Nihon no Bunka* 1, 1, 1890, pp. 64-7.
— 'Shōsetsuka Buntaihyō', *Nihon no Bunka* 1, 8, pp. 24-36.
Hi-Gembun'itchikai (eds) *Dainippon to Bunshōteki Kokumin*, Bi-ikusha, 1902.
Hyōtan Sei 'Kojima-sensei e', *Bun* 2, 9, 1889, pp. 531-2.

— 'Kojima-sensei to Yoshimi-sensei e', *Bun* 2, 7, 1889, pp. 397-8.
Kamesoto Sei 'Meiji Bunshō no Gettan', *Nihon no Bunka* 1, 1, 1890, pp. 64-7.
Kanda Kōhei 'Bunshōron o yomu' (1885), in *Nishimura Shigeki* 2, Kyoto: Shibunkan 1976, pp. 122-8.
Kembō Gōki 'Meiji Jidai no Bungobun: Futsūbun ga dekira made', *Gengo Seikatsu* 11, 1957, pp. 32-41.
Kikuchi Dairoku 'Gembun'itchi ni tsuite', *Tōyō Gakugei Zasshi* 18, 237, pp. 243-9.
Kisaka Aikichi 'Shingen', *Bun* 2, 12, 1889, pp. 743-5.
Kishinoue Shikken 'Gembunron', *Nihon no Bunka* 1, 15, 1890, pp. 10-14.
Kojima Kenkichi 'Bunshōron', *Bun* 2, 6, 1889, pp. 346-51.
— 'Futatabi Bunshō o ronji Bimyōshi ni shimesu', *Bun* 2, 8, 1889, pp. 483-7.
— 'Futatabi Bunshō o ronzu', *Bun* 2, 9, 1889, pp. 538-40.
— 'Gembun'itchi o ronji Bimyō-sai Shujin no Kōgeki ni kotau', *Bun* 2, 11, 1889, pp. 600-5.
Komai Chikafusa 'Gembun'itchiron ni tsuite', *Bun* 2, 10, 1889, pp. 605-7.
— 'Zoku Gembun'itchiron Aru Toi', *Bun* 2, 11, 1889, pp. 668-70.
Komine Sei 'Bunshōron', *Nihon no Bunka* 1, 18, 1890, pp. 11-14.
Konakamura Kiyonori 'Bunshōron', *Nihon no Bunka* 1, 22, 1890, pp. 1-15.
— 'Yamatoda-shi no Buntai Itchiron o mite omoeru koto', *Kokkai*, 25 October 1891.
Matsui Hirokichi 'Bun', *Nihon no Bunka* 1, 21, 1890, pp. 1-2.
Matsushita Teizō 'Gembun'itchiron to sono Hantairon: Meiji Nijūninen made', *Kokugo Kokubun* 29, 11, 1960, pp. 39-56.
Miya Kasamatsu 'Meiji no Kokubun o ronzu', *Kokugaku* June-August 1895, pp. 5-14.
Miyake Yonekichi, 'Gembun'itchi no Ron', *Bun* 1, 10, 1888, p. 137.
Mori Ōgai 'Gembunron', *Shigarami Zōshi* 7, 1890, pp. 1-10. Also in *Ōgai Senshū* 9, Tōyōdō Shuppan, 1950, pp. 320-1.
Morita Shiken 'Nihon Bunshō no Shōrai' (1888), in *Meiji Bungaku Zenshū* 26, Chikuma Shobō 1981, pp. 233-9.
Mozume Takami 'Bunshō ni tsuite no Kōwa', *Nihon Bungaku* 1, 1888, pp. 28-9.
— 'Gembun'itchi no Fukanō', *Yomiuri Shimbun*, 17 December 1902, p. 2; 18 December 1902, p. 3; 19 December 1902, p. 2.
— 'Nihon Bunshōron', *Kōten Kokyūjō Kōen*, August 1889, pp. 21-31.
Nakamura Shukō 'Meiji Kyō no Bunshō', *Nihon no Bunka* 1, 5, 1890, pp. 323-6.
Nishi Moroi 'Gembun'itchiron', *Bun* 2, 12, 1889, pp. 736-40.
Nishimura Shigeki 'Bunshōron' (1884), in *Nishimura Shigeki* 2, Kyoto: Shibunkan, 1976, pp. 114-22.
— 'Gembun'itchi o ronzu', *Tōyō Gakugei Zasshi* 18, 238, 1901, pp. 274-9. Also in *Nishimura Shigeki* 2, Kyoto: Shibunkan, 1976, pp. 1272-9.
— *Nihon no Bungaku* (1889), in *Nishimura Shigeki* 2, Kyoto: Shibunkan, 1976, pp. 213-52.

Ochiai Naobumi, 'Bunshō no Gobyū', *Kōten Kokyūjō Kōen* 11, 1889, pp. 32–60 (Keiō University Library).
— 'Shōrai no Kokubun', *Kokumin no Tomo* 100 pp. 704–7, 101 pp. 755–8, 104 pp. 903–8, 1890. Also in *Meiji Bungaku Zenshū* 44, Chikuma Shobō, 1968, pp. 13–17.
Okamoto Isao, 'Meiji Futsūbun no Seijukuki to Shimbun', *Chūkyōdai Bungakubu Kiyō* 17, 3–4, 1984, pp. 36–54.
Ōmachi Keigetsu 'Bungei Jihyō: Tōdai Bunshō no Kuse', *Taiyō* 7, 1, 1901, pp. 38–40.
Satō Sadasuke, 'Bunwa', *Nihon no Bunka* 1, 5, 1890, pp. 6–8.
Suematsu Kenchō *Nihon Bunshōron* (1886) in *Meiji Bungaku Zenshū* 79, Chikuma Shobō, 1977 pp. 62–98.
Takamatsu Sei 'Sakai Karekawa Yamada Bimyō Nikun no Gembun'itchi Chosho o Hyō su', *Bunkō*, August 1901, pp. 47–9.
Tatsumi Kojirō 'Baku Gembun'itchiron', *Gakkai no Shishin* 2, 1887, pp. 17–21.
Tobiyama Junko 'Meiji Futsūbun no Kenkyū', *Nihon Bungaku* (Tōkyō Joshidai) 23, 1964, pp.74–85.
Tsubouchi Shōyō 'Bun no Sugata', *Nihon no Shōnen* 6,9, 1894, pp. 3–8.
— 'Buntai no Funran', *Waseda Bungaku*, October 1891, pp. 1–6.
— 'Buntai no Nariyuki', *Waseda Bungaku*, October 1891, pp. 6–10.
Unsigned, 'Bimyō-shi ni nozomu', *Teikoku Bungaku* 7, 6, 1901, pp. 128–30.
Unsigned 'Gembun'itchijō no Ōwasure', *Jogaku Zasshi* 104, 1888, pp. 82–5.
Unsigned 'Gembun'itchiron', *Bun* 1, 10, 1888, p. 137.
Yamada Bimyō 'Gembun'itchi Kogoto', *Bun* 2, 7, 1889, pp. 394–7.
— 'Gembunitchiron Aru Toi', *Bun* 2, 10, 1889, pp. 607–9.
— 'Gembun'itchiron Gairyaku', *Gakkai no Shishin* 8, 1888, pp. 24–8, 9, pp. 34–44.
— (Bimyō-shi) 'Gembun'itchiron ni tsuki Kojima Kenkichi-shi no Bakugeki ni kotaete', *Bun* 2, 9, 1889, pp. 532–8.
— 'Gembun'itchitai o manabu Kokoroe', *Iratsume* 56, 1890, pp. 5–6.
— 'Kojima Kenkichi-shi no 'Futatabi Bunshō o ronzu' o yonde', *Bun* 2, 10, 1889, pp. 599–600.
— 'Kojima Kenkichi-shi oyobi sono hoka no Higembun'itchi Ronsha Shoshi e', *Bun* 2, 11, 1889, pp. 663–7, 2, 12, pp. 732–6.
— 'Wareware no Gembun'itchitai', *Shigarami Zōshi* 18, 1890, pp. 10–14.
Yoshimi Keirin 'Bun ni tsuite', *Bun* 2, 6, 1889, pp. 351–3.

The standardization debate

Andō Masatsugu *Kokugogaku Ronkō 1: Andō Masatsugu Chosakushū* 1, Yūzankaku, 1974.
— 'Kokugoshi Josetsu', *Andō Masatsugu Chosakushū* 2, Yūzankaku, 1974, pp. 1–104.
Hashimoto Shinkichi, *Kokugogaku Gairon*, Iwanami Shoten, 1946.
Hattori Shirō *Gengogaku no Hōhō* Iwanami Shoten, 1960.

Hoshina Kōichi 'Kokugo Chōsa linkai Ketsugi Jikō ni tsuite', *Gengogaku Zasshi* 3, 2, 1903, pp. 70–86.
Iizumi Rokurō *Nihon no Kotoba Ima to Mukashi*, Shakai Shisō Kenkyūkai Shuppanbu, 1960.
Izui Hisanosuke, 'Hyōjungo no Gainen ni tsuite', *Gengo Seikatsu* 172, 1966, pp. 18–25.
Kamei Takashi, Ōfuji Tokihiko and Yamada Toshio (eds) *Nihongo no Rekishi V. 6: Atarashii Kokugo e no Ayumi*, Heibonsha, 1965. See Chapter 5 'Hōgen no Shōchō'.
Kembō Gōki 'Kyōtsūgo to Hōgen', *Kokubungaku Kaishaku to Kanshō* 18, 6, 1953, pp. 9–12.
Matsumura Akira 'Edogo ga Kyōtsūgo ni naru made', *Kokubungaku Kaishaku to Kanshō* 27, 2, 1962, pp. 93–7.
— *Edogo Tōkyōgo no Kenkyū*, Tōkyōdō Shuppan, 1957.
— *Kindai no Kokugo: Edo kara Gendai e*, Ōfūsha, 1978.
— 'Tōkyōgo no Seiritsu to Hatten: Gendai no Kokugo', *Kokubungaku Kaishaku to Kanshō* 19, 10, 1954, pp. 87–103.
Nakamura Michio 'Edogo ni tsuite', *Chūō Daigaku Bungakubu Kiyō* 29, 1963, pp. 79–90.
— 'Tōkyōgo no Keisei' *Kokugo Kyōikushi* 4, 5, 1941, pp. 60–7.
— 'Tōkyōgo no Mondai', *Nihongo* 1, 5, 1941, pp. 19–24; 1, 6, pp. 39–43; 1, 7, pp. 51–5.
— *Tōkyōgo no Seikaku* Kawade Shobō, 1948.
Okano Kyūin, 'Hyōjungo ni tsuite', *Gengogaku Zasshi* 3, 2, 1902, pp. 32–40.
San'yūtei Enshō et al. 'Edo no Kotoba, Meiji no Kotoba', *Gengo Seikatsu* 291, 1975, pp. 2–15.
Shibata Takeshi 'Hyōjungo, Kyōtsūgo, Hōgen', in Bunkachō (ed) *Kotoba Shirīzu 6: Hyōjungo to Hōgen*, Ōkurashō Insatsukyoku, 1977, pp. 22–32.
— *Nihon no Hōgen*, Iwanami Shoten, 1958.
Sugimoto Tsutomu *Kindai Nihongo*, Kinokuniya Shoten, 1966.
Suzuki Hideo 'Gendai Kyōtsūgo o tsukuridashita no wa Dare ka', *Kokubungaku* 27, 16, 1982, pp. 52–6.
— 'Meiji Tōkyōgo no Katoteki Seikaku', *Kokugo to Kokubungaku* 54, 9, 1977, pp. 35–45.
Tōjō Misao 'Hyōjungo to Hōgen', *Kokubungaku Kaishaku to Kanshō* 4, 7, 1937, pp. 100–8.
— *Kokugogaku Shinkō*, Chikuma Shobō, 1965.
Tsuchiya Shin'ichi 'Tōkyōgo no Seiritsu Katei ni okeru Ukemi no Hyōgen ni tsuite', *Kokugogaku* 51, 1962, pp. 25–43.
Tsukushima Hiroshi *Kokugogaku Yōsetsu*, Sōgensha, 1959.
Ueda Kazutoshi 'Hyōjungo ni tsukite', *Teikoku Bungaku* 1, 1, 1895, pp. 14–23.
Uemura Yukio 'Hōgen, Kyōtsūgo, Hyōjungo', in *Kōza Gendaigo V. 1: Gendaigo no Gaisetsu*, Meiji Shoin, 1963, pp. 47–63.
Unsigned 'Gembun'itchi no Jikkō', *Yomiuri Shimbun*, 10 August 1901, p. 2.
Yamazaki Fumoto 'Edogo no Kōsei to Hensen', *Kokubungaku Kaishaku to Kanshō* 4, 7, 1939, pp. 59–67.

Yanagida Kunio 'Hyōjungo no Hanashi', *Yanagida Kunio Shū* 18, Chikuma Shobō, 1963, pp. 509-22.

See also Works in English for articles on standardization

The problem of orthography

Amanuma Yasushi 'Kokugo Kokuji Mondai no Rekishi to Tembō', *Kokubungaku* 8, 2, 1963 pp. 153-60.
Chino Eiichi, Nomoto Kikuo *et al.* (eds) *Iwanami Kōza Nihongo 3: Kokugo Kokuji Mondai*, Iwanami Shoten, 1977, pp. 260-308.
Fukuda Ryōsuke 'Meiji Shoki no Kokuji Mondai ni tsuite', *Kokugo Kokubun* 7, 12, 1928 pp. 1-40.
Fukuzawa Yukichi *Moji no Oshie* (1873), in *Fukuzawa Yukichi Zenshū* 3, Iwanami Shoten, 1959 pp. 555-611.
Hida Yoshifumi 'Kutō Hyōshi no Seiritsu Katei', *Gengo Seikatsu* 277, 1975, pp 49-60.
Hirai Masao 'Tanakadate Aikitsu Hakushi to Tamaru Tatsuo Hakushi', *Gengo Seikatsu* 208, 1969, pp. 87-95.
Inoue Tetsujirō 'Shinkokuji Kakutei no Jiki', *Tōkyō Gakushi Kaiin Zasshi* 20, 8, 1898, pp. 335-56, 9, pp. 361-74.
Inoue Tetsujirō and Mikami Sanji 'Kokugo Kokuji Mondai no Kaiko', *Kokugo to Kokubungaku* 11, 8, 1934, pp. 11-22.
Kakei Itsumori 'Meiji Shoki Kokuji Mondai no Kaiko', *Kokugo to Kokubungaku* 5, 8, 1928, pp. 84-95.
Kasamatsu Yasuo 'Bimyō-sai no Kutōhō: Shimei e no Eikyō o Chūshin ni', *Gobun Kenkyū* 16, 1963, pp. 116-22.
Kawada Tetsuya 'Gengo no Hattatsu o ronjite Kokuji Kairyōron ni oyobu', *Shimbungei* 1, 3, 1901, pp. 10-18.
Morioka Kenji 'Meijiki ni okeru Kanji no Yakuwari', *Gengo Seikatsu* 378, 1983, pp. 44-51.
Murauchi Eiichi 'Meiji Jidai no Kanazukai Mondai', *Wakayama Daigaku Geigakubu Jimbun Kagaku Kiyō* 5, 1955, pp. 60-71.
Nishi Amane 'Yōji o mote Kokugo o shosuru no Ron' (1874), in *Nihon no Meichō* 34, Chūō Kōronsha, 1972, pp. 171-80.
Nishimura Shigeki 'Genkon Kyōikukai no Nimondai' (1900), in *Nishimura Shigeki* 2, Kyoto: Shibunkan, 1976, pp. 1193-212.
Ōno Saeko 'Gendai Kanji Kana Majiribun no Genryū', *Gengo Seikatsu* 6, 1952, pp. 34-9.
Ōrui Masatoshi 'Kutōten no Kōkatekina Tsukaikata', *Kaishaku to Kanshō* 39, 7, 1975, pp. 292-325.
Ōtsuki Fumihiko 'Kana no Kai no Mondō' (Oct.-Dec. 1883), in *Meiji Bunka Zenshū* 20, Nihon Hyōronsha, 1967, pp. 57-96.
Ozaki Kōyō 'Bunshō Tebikisō' (1889), in *Nihon Kindai Bungaku Taikei* 5, Kadokawa, 1971, pp. 488-97.
Shindō Sakiko 'Maejima Hisoka no Wakachigaki', *Gengo Seikatsu* 120, 1961, pp. 34-41.
Sugimoto Tsutomu 'Kutōhō no Shiteki Kōsatsu', *Musashino Joshi Daigaku Kiyō* 2, 1967, pp. 11-27.

—— 'Kutōten Kigō no Yōhō to Kindai Bungaku', *Kokubungaku Kenkyū* 35, 1967, pp. 1–13.

Tanakadate Aikitsu *Rōmaji Iken* (1885), in *Meiji Bunka Zenshū* 20, Nihon Hyōronsha, 1967 pp. 117–28.

Toki Zenmaro 'Rōmaji Nihongo no Bunken', *Nihon Bungaku Kōza* 15, Shinchōsha, 1935, pp. 293–322.

Uemura Masahisa 'Rōmajikai to Kana no Kai', *Uemura Masahisa to sono Jidai*, Kyōbunkan, 1955, pp. 838–53.

Unsigned 'Bunshō Fugō no Kaishaku', *Iratsume* 4, 34, 1889, pp. 15–16.

Yanagi Fushō 'Kutōhō: Hon'yaku de tsukurareta Kutōhō', *Geppan Kotoba* 2, 1, 1978, pp. 63–70.

Yanagida Izumi 'Meiji Nijūnen Zengo no Shinji Undō', *Kokkan*, November 1938, pp. 2–6, December 1938, pp. 2–10.

Yatabe Ryōkichi *Rōmaji Hayamanabi* (1885), in *Meiji Bunka Zenshū* 20, Nihon Hyōronsha, 1967 pp. 97–116.

Index

Andō Masatsugu 17, 179
Arishima Takeo 159, 161
ateji 49
attitudes to writing 8, 19–20, 32

bibun 56, 99, 154
bungotai 34, 97, 163

Chamberlain, B. H. 145, 164, 243–4
Chinese characters (*kanji*) 17, 19
  early use in Japan 35–6
  as men's characters 56
  reduction in numbers of 226–7, 249–50
civil rights movement (*jiyū minken undō*) 24, 74, 110, 120–4
classical Japanese (*wabun*) 17, 56–61, 64, 100, 102, 134–5, 150
colloquial style (*kōgotai*) 9, 11, 20, 32, 74–8, 105–7, 134–5, 257–60
  and constitution 179–81
  criticisms of 30, 69–70
  and government documents 181
  need for 23, 26, 33–4
  post-WW1 178
  terminations 70–2
  1889 controversy over 201–206
communications 22–4

da 30, 72, 96, 116, 148, 182–3
de arimasu 71, 103, 105, 182
de aru 72, 87, 103, 116, 154, 155, 156, 177, 183
de goza imasu 71, 99, 123, 182

de gozaru 30, 70, 85, 96, 114–23 *passim*, 181
desu 72, 148, 182
dialects 16
Dutch studies, influence of 27–8, 78–9, 224–5

education 21–2,
  and early language reform efforts 81–8, 104–7
  premodern 21, 29
engo (word associations) 60
Enlightenment press 87–8, 95–7, 115

foreign loanwords (*gairaigo*) 15
Fukuchi Gen'ichirō 89–91, 92–4, 110, 124–6, 132, 244
  The Aim of Style Reform (Bunshō Kairyō no Mokuteki) 101
  The Evolution of Writing (Bunshō no Shinka) 101
  'On Writing' ('Bunron') 89
  'On Writing' ('Bunshōror') 92–3, 124–5
  The Reform of Writing (Bunsh no Kairyō) 101
Fukuzawa Yukichi 19, 45, 82–5, 109, 111–15, 121
  The Encouragement of Learning (Gakumon no Susume) 84, 114
  The Teaching of Characters (Moji no Oshie) 53–4, 226–7

Futabatei Shimei 25, 48, 131,
  136, 137–42, 153–4, 254–5
  The Drifting Cloud (Ukigumo)
  138–9, 140, 141, 149, 217,
  255
futsūbun 162, 177, 184, 188–93,
  214

gabuntai 56, 134, 150
gazoku setchū 25, 64–8, 134, 135,
  142, 147, 151, 153, 159
gembun'itchi 73, 85, 98–110
  passim, 117, 136, 142, 143,
  149–51, 151–9 *passim*, 166, 177
  arguments against 184–206
  manuals of 173–7
Gembun'itchi Club 117–18, 165–6
  and 1902 petition 168–9
  splinter groups 171–3
Gengo Gakkai (Linguistics Society)
  165
gikobun 59–61, 64
goza imasu 71

hentai kambun 48–9, 55, 62
hiragana 38, 56–7
  see also Kana Club
Hirata Atsutane 70, 115, 117
Hoshina Kōichi 164–9, *passim*,
  220–1

Ihara Saikaku 64–5
Inoue Tetsujirō 247–9
intellectuals, role of 14, 25, 30–2

Jippensha Ikku 65–7
jun kambun 34–5

kakekotoba (pivot words) 58, 60
kambun, see Sino-Japanese
kambun chokuyakutai 35, 40
kambun kakikudashibun 35
kambun kundoku 35, 39–40, 46,
  47, 59–60, 61–2
kambun kuzushi 35, 41–3, 47, 91,
  99, 103, 116, 122, 177, 187
Kamo no Mabuchi 60
Kana Club 56, 214–16, 231–7
Kanda Kōhei 100
katakana 38

katakana-majiribun 61
Katō Hiroyuki 45, 85, 110, 115–18
Ken'yūsha 144, 147, 150, 151
Kikuchi Dairoku 167–8, 169
kōgotai, see colloquial style

language modernization 7–8,
  10–14, 218, 260
lexical change 7, 13
literacy, premodern 28–30
  early Meiji period 129–30
literature 14, 25–6, 33, 131–62
  and punctuation 254–6

Maejima Hisoka 23, 70, 165–9
  passim
  'Proposal for the Abolition of
  Chinese Characters' 50–2, 80,
  227–30
  other petitions 80–1, 228–9
makura kotoba 58, 60
man'yōgana 37–8, 49
Masaoka Shiki 155
Miyake Yonekichi 214–15, 216,
  234–5, 253
Mori Arinori 82, 104
Mori Ōgai 61, 151–2, 184
Motoori Norinaga 60
Mozume Takami 21, 101–3, 119,
  129, 145, 204–5, 236–7, 253
  Genbun'itchi 101–3
Mushakōji Saneatsu 159, 160

National Language Inquiry Board
  (*Kokugo Chōsakai*) 81
National Language Research
  Council (*Kokugo Chōsa Iinkai*)
  71, 118, 164, 169–71, 176, 191,
  212, 220–3
Natsume Sōseki 156, 255–6
Naturalism 156–9
newspapers 88–95, 98–104, 177–8
  political 126–9
  popular 47, 89, 94–5, 126
  serious 46–7, 89, 124–6
Nishi Amane 85, 109, 112,
  118–20, 238, 242
Nishimura Shigeki 87, 100, 104,
  110, 190, 195–6, 204

ōbun (European style) 34, 194
Ochiai Naobumi 150, 190–1, 193–4
okototen 36–7
okurigana 62
Ōnishi Hajime 154
Ōtsuki Fumihiko 56, 92, 166–9 passim, 185, 214, 236, 239
Ozaki Kōyō 151–4, 196–8

political education 24–5, 109–31
postal service 23–4
punctuation 17, 178, 250–5

risshin shusse 15
Rōmaji Club 214, 240–4

Saganoya Omuro 149
San'yūtei Enchō 136, 138
script reform 12–13, 224–56
shaseibun 155–6
Shiga Naoya 159, 161
Shimazaki Tōson 155–6, 158, 256
Shimizu Usaburō 85–6, 231, 251–2
Shimpo Iwatsugu 105, 145, 254
Shingaku 75
Shirakaba school 159–60
shorthand 136
Sino-Japanese (kambun) 17–18, 34–48, 64, 86, 88, 96, 100, 102, 108, 197
Sino-Japanese war (1894–5) 32, 164, 217–18
sōrōbun 17, 18, 48–56

standardization 10–11, 13, 28, 87–8, 166, 207–23
Suematsu Kenchō 245, 253

Taguchi Ukichi 61, 98–9, 130, 133, 241–2
Tayama Katai 158–9
Teikoku Kyôikukai (Imperial Society for Education) 165
  and petition 166–7
textbooks
  early 86–8, 105–7, 117
  and punctuation 253
  1903 and 1908 state series 170–1, 222
Tokuda Shūsei 158, 159
Tsubouchi Shōyō 25, 57, 67–8, 133–7, 142–3

Ueda Kazutoshi 163–5, 166, 167–8, 169, 218–19
Ueki Emori 85, 109, 120–4, 129

wabun, see classical Japanese
wakankonkōbun 18–19, 61–8, 132
Watanabe Shūjirō 91–2
  'Steps to Regulating Written Japanese' 91, 218, 230–1, 252–3
west, influence of 27–8, 31, 78, 224–5

Yamada Bimyō 136, 143–9, 152, 173–5, 200–2, 255
Yamamoto Yūzō 179–80
Yano Fumio 52, 126, 130, 188–9, 246–7

For Product Safety Concerns and Information please contact our EU
representative GPSR@taylorandfrancis.com
Taylor & Francis Verlag GmbH, Kaufingerstraße 24, 80331 München, Germany